Volker Hinnenthal 1978

THE
DAMNED
ART

THE DAMNED ART

ESSAYS IN THE LITERATURE OF WITCHCRAFT

Edited by
Sydney Anglo

Routledge & Kegan Paul
London, Henley and Boston

First published in 1977
by Routledge & Kegan Paul Ltd
39 Store Street,
London WC1E 7DD,
Broadway House,
Newtown Road,
Henley-on-Thames,
Oxon RG9 1EN and
9 Park Street,
Boston, Mass. 02108, USA
Set in Monotype Poliphilus
and printed in Great Britain by
Western Printing Services Ltd, Bristol
© Routledge & Kegan Paul Ltd 1977
No part of this book may be reproduced in
any form without permission from the
publisher, except for the quotation of brief
passages in criticism

British Library Cataloguing in Publication Data

The damned art.
1. Witchcraft—History—Sources
I. Anglo, Sydney
133.4'07   BF1566

ISBN 0-7100-8589-3

CONTENTS

Preface   vii

1   Evident authority and authoritative evidence: 1
The *Malleus Maleficarum*
SYDNEY ANGLO   *Reader in the History of Ideas, University College of Swansea*

2   Witchcraft and magic in Renaissance Italy: 32
Gianfrancesco Pico and his *Strix*
PETER BURKE   *Reader in Intellectual History, University of Sussex*

3   Johann Weyer's *De Praestigiis Daemonum*:   53
Unsystematic psychopathology
CHRISTOPHER BAXTER   *Lecturer in French, University of Sussex*

4   Jean Bodin's *De la Démonomanie des Sorciers*:   76
The logic of persecution
CHRISTOPHER BAXTER

5   Reginald Scot's *Discoverie of Witchcraft*:   106
Scepticism and Sadduceeism
SYDNEY ANGLO

6   A Tudor anthropologist: 140
George Gifford's *Discourse* and *Dialogue*
ALAN MACFARLANE   *Fellow of King's College, Cambridge*

CONTENTS

7   King James's *Daemonologie*:   156
Witchcraft and kingship
STUART CLARK   *Lecturer in History, University College of Swansea*

8   Pierre de Lancre's *Tableau de l'Inconstance des Mauvais Anges et Demons*:   182
The sabbat sensationalised
MARGARET M. MCGOWAN   *Professor of French, University of Sussex*

9   Cotton Mather's *Wonders of the Invisible World*:   202
Some metamorphoses of Salem witchcraft
M. WYNN THOMAS   *Lecturer in English, University College of Swansea*

10   Two late Scottish witchcraft tracts: 227
Witch-Craft Proven and *The Tryal of Witchcraft*
CHRISTINA LARNER   *Lecturer in Sociology, University of Glasgow*

Epilogue: 246
The desiderata of disbelief
SYDNEY ANGLO

Index   249

PREFACE

There is an academic convention, increasingly adhered to, whereby an author or editor devotes his preface to the shortcomings of his work, explaining its inadequacies, and attributing its scant virtues to the advice of those who did not write it. One cannot help wondering—if these books were really as bad as their authors claim—why they have been put into print. This kind of apology is surely an unnecessary affectation, as anybody who has thought about the difficulties of treating complex historical problems must recognise that, in a sense, all such efforts are doomed to imperfection; and that we are all simply trying to shed a little light into dark corners. This is certainly true of the present volume, which is directed toward one resolutely tenebrous recess—the literary remains of witchcraft.

The situation here is analogous to that prevailing some years ago in the study of court festivals. Jean Jacquot encouraged scholars to undertake a series of detailed analyses of individual occasions and specific problems; with the result that there has now been established a far more diverse, more subtle, and more accurate picture of the general problems than had hitherto been possible in that field. A similar approach should be of service in relation to the learned literature of witchcraft and demonology where, thus far, generalisations have preceded the detailed consideration of individual texts, with bizarre results.

I am aware, as is every one of the contributors here, that many more essays could be written on other texts, and that there are other scholars who might undertake similar tasks differently and with equal validity. But this corporate effort, like all others, is limited by practical factors. I have asked colleagues with whom I am personally acquainted, and whom I know to be interested in these areas, to write on any text they wished, and to do so in their own way. There has been no attempt to impose procedures upon anybody. Some of us are historians of ideas; others are more interested in literary considerations; others have sociological or anthropological inclinations. None of us is in total agreement with the others about how these things should be done. And certainly our views on individual texts vary considerably. Our principal agreement has been that the individual study of as wide a variety of primary literary sources as possible is a desideratum. Our only apology is that there are not many more essays in a massively augmented volume.

June 1976   Sydney Anglo

EVIDENT AUTHORITY AND AUTHORITATIVE EVIDENCE: THE *MALLEUS MALEFICARUM*

Sydney Anglo

It is astonishing that there should still be found today people who do not believe that there are witches. For my part I suspect that the truth is that such people really believe in their hearts, but will not admit it; for the Pagans have a lesson for them in this matter; they are refuted by the Canon and Civil Laws; Holy Scripture gives them the lie; the voluntary and repeated confessions of witches prove them wrong; and the sentences passed in various places against the accused must shut their mouths.[1]

It is thus that Henri Boguet introduces his *Examen of Witches* (1602): a manual based upon his own experiences as a judge concerned with the trial, torture, and burning of numerous victims of the witch scare in Burgundy towards the end of the sixteenth century. Boguet knows that witches exist because he can cite both learned authority and factual evidence to prove his case conclusively.

The study of witchcraft has recently enjoyed a boom at all levels, extending from the popular and merely sensational to the erudite and technical.[2] The majority of serious modern studies have concerned themselves with a number of difficult problems. They have considered the extent to which witchcraft practices at the folk level really existed in the Middle Ages and the Renaissance, and how these might be illuminated by comparison with the beliefs of modern primitive societies. They have pondered the relationship, or irrelation, between popular and learned magic. Or they have attempted to explore and to elucidate the popular mentality of past societies. Attention has accordingly been focused upon witch trial records rather than upon literary sources; and when such studies have attempted to explain the witch craze they talk about social tensions, economic pressures, and alienation; endeavour to psychoanalyse the past; and even seek to quantify the development of persecution. The temptation of such impossibilities is considerable; and their undertaking may be of value, though all attempts to reconstruct the inchoate prejudices of the illiterate multitude are hampered by the fact that they leave so few written records. However unfashionable, it is sometimes worthwhile to consider the beliefs of educated men who actually took the trouble to argue their case to posterity: and it is not unreasonable to address oneself to questions which admit of answers, and to study evidence which is clearly written on, rather than between, the lines.

It appears to be tacitly assumed by many scholars that discursive arguments by the learned have little relevance to the reality of witch persecution. It is usual to pass over long, and often elaborate, treatises with a few casual remarks; to summarise their intricacies within a single paragraph; or to cope with their obscurities by ignoring them. Many of these books are well known and frequently cited; yet there has been little analysis of their structure, arguments, language, and interrelation. For example, every student of witchcraft knows of the *Malleus Maleficarum*: but, in England, there is not a single study devoted to this text. Weyer and Scot were famous opponents of the witchcraft persecution in the late sixteenth century, and are constantly referred to; but significant work on the former is exclusively German and Dutch, while the substance of Scot's arguments has received no attention whatever. Perhaps the most distinguished name in the literature of witch persecution is that of Jean Bodin: but there has been only desultory study of his *Démonomanie* in relation to his other writings. The *Daemonologie* of King James I is a familiar text: yet it is only very recently that historians have troubled to read it in the light of James's political works. De Lancre's account of the sabbat is often plundered for lurid detail, but his work, as a whole, has scarcely been considered within its historical and literary context. From such indifference to some of the most notable texts in the witchcraft debate, it is not difficult to deduce the treatment accorded to less famous tracts. The fact that these works were published, and do not lie buried in archives; that they are discursive arguments, and not fragmentary records; that they are literary rather than *ad hoc* documentation, does not render further comment superfluous. The content of books is not absorbed by some process of historical osmosis. Books have to be read and pondered; and, just as their arguments demand closer analysis and elucidation than the endless sordidities of trial records and the trivia of folk beliefs, so do they offer considerably richer rewards to the historian of ideas.

The present volume, therefore, approaches witchcraft and demonology on the basis of their literary remains: treatises which deal, in various ways, with the theories underlying persecution. The majority of the following essays treat works specifically devoted to establishing the reality of a demonological system, to the elaboration of witchcraft beliefs, and to establishing the need for retribution. The others deal with authors who were trying to subvert such theories: but even their arguments illustrate both the limitations of sixteenth-century scepticism, and the compelling nature of the material ranged against them.

The principal purpose of this first essay is to comment upon the *Malleus Maleficarum*. But, by way of introduction, I wish to develop the ideas raised in the brief opening quotation from Boguet: for, though it is customary to treat witchcraft as a separate study, it does not constitute a self-sufficient body of doctrine. Quite the contrary, for it is firmly rooted in a complex of interrelated magical ideas which informs many aspects of medieval and Renaissance thought. How were these ideas treated by trained thinkers? Why were educated professional men such as Boguet so convinced about the reality and the horrors of witchcraft? In other words, what constituted a conclusive argument in the period between the fifteenth and late seventeenth centuries? Certainly, for the most part, it was something very different from what scholars now regard as valid argument: that is the deliberate attempt at objectivity; inductive reasoning; the evaluation of evidence rather than its mere accumulation; conscious scepticism of received authorities; and, above all else, the process of constantly testing hypotheses by controlled experiment.

The application of such critical techniques to the fabric of magical belief has tended to shred it asunder. But such techniques were scarcely known in the Middle Ages; only slowly developed in the Renaissance; and can hardly be deemed general in modern times. That magic, as an explanation for everything, has been largely set aside is due more to fashion than to a comprehension of any alternative theory of causation. Ernest Jones long ago suggested that the average modern man unhesitatingly rejects 'the same evidence of witchcraft that was so convincing to the man of three centuries ago, though he usually knows no more about the true explanation than the latter did'. And Keith Thomas, who cites this observation, himself goes on to remark that 'most of those millions of people who today would laugh at the idea of magic and miracles would have difficulty in explaining why'. They are, he says, 'victims of society's constant pressure towards intellectual conformity'.[3] To this one could add what are perhaps even more fundamental observations: the first being the limited capacity of the human intellect. Given the vast multiplicity of information increasingly available—and the paradox that the further knowledge is advanced, and the more avenues opened up for exploration, so the greater becomes the distance between actual and potential knowledge—the more assertions we are obliged to take on trust. In addition there remains the human need to reduce the infinite to finity; the divine to the anthropomorphic; the incalculable to the mensurable; and the unknowable to the comprehensible. Hence the creation of deterministic historical systems enabling man to foretell the future from his past. Hence the creation of number mysticisms empowering adepts to become prophets. Astrology may be rejected as untenable, and numerology dismissed as an arcane absurdity. Yet modern states do not hesitate to implement the recommendations of statistical prognosticators, despite the existence of the very factors which undermined earlier divinatory superstitions: the fact that the figures are susceptible to as many conflicting interpretations as there are experts; and that the predictions are frequently wrong. If we remain abject before our own seers, it is not difficult to comprehend the force of those beliefs with which this volume is concerned: beliefs which fashioned a world where magic was not merely possible but normal; and where witchcraft was simply its most lurid manifestation.

Scholarship has tended to separate the witch from the magician, and to treat, as discrete, low magic and higher magic. But witchcraft beliefs arose from the blurring of such distinctions and from a cosmic vision which saw witch and magus operating within a single system.[4] At its lowest level magic could be expected to operate through love potions, charms, secret cures and harms, as employed by 'cunning folk' and 'wise women'; but a problem arose when any attempt was made to explain how such cures and harms actually functioned, for such explanations could only be propounded by professional thinkers who provided a system of occult relationships which subsumed the witch. Few doubted that it was possible for someone to bring about transitive effects upon other people, beasts, or inanimate objects; and various methods of achieving these ends were recognised and commented upon. Macrocosmic and microcosmic imagery was commonplace, and it was generally accepted that the entire universe was composed of a vast system of correspondences and harmonies, so that anything carried out on one level must inevitably affect other levels of existence. Astral influences were postulated, where the spirits or essences of the planets held sway over lower levels of creation; and the cosmos was filled with demonic and angelic intelligences, all capable of affecting human affairs. Correspondences and harmonies, astral influences, demonic and angelic activity: all offered explanations as to the functioning of the universe. Given such explanations, it was also possible to suppose that knowledge of these functionings might, in turn, lead to their manipulation. Harmonies might be sympathetically exploited; the power of the stars might be attracted and harnessed; angels might be persuaded to lend their aid; and demons might be exhorted and even compelled. In short, the magician might be able to utilise superhuman powers for his own ends.[5]

Such a conviction was strengthened by another closely related magical mode which depended upon the innate properties of material things. Such properties might be easily comprehended as, for example, was the case with certain herbs and minerals possessing curative or harmful powers. On other occasions they might be less readily apparent as, for instance, the alleged efficacy of the emerald in restraining sexual passion, where the virtue was said to be occult.[6] Nevertheless, all such innate properties could be described as natural; and their exploitation was categorised as natural magic. As we shall see, natural magic could be a powerful intellectual weapon; and in the hands of Pomponazzi it became a distinct threat to all other magic, including religion. Pomponazzi explains every kind of magical effect and marvellous event by 'natural' causes, and thereby eliminates direct divine, demonic, or angelic agency.[7]

In the main, however, natural magic reinforced rather than undermined other magic. The efficacy of talismans provides an obvious example. Since stones were held to receive their innate qualities from the planetary influences, it was theoretically possible to attract the power of a particular celestial body by engraving the correct image at the correct time on the appropriate gem— a recondite skill which could only appertain to the learned magus. But what of the witch? She, too, was deemed to operate largely through the exploitation of natural magic and was commonly accused of employing drugs to procure effects such as love and the recovery of health, or, conversely, poisoning and death. How did she master knowledge which cost the magus a lifetime of arduous study? Such abilities could not be innate. Instead they were attributed to demonic pacts; and this arrangement, in effect, opened up all magical arts to the terrestrial partner since the devil and his demons know infinitely more than even the most learned mortal. Boguet, for instance, having established the authorities for the reality of witchcraft, goes on to say that, although the stories told of witches are very strange and seem supernatural and miraculous,

> Do we not know how great is the knowledge and experience of demons? It is certain that they have a deep knowledge of all things. For there is no Theologian who can interpret the Holy Scripture better than they; there is no Lawyer with a profounder knowledge of Testaments, Contracts and Actions; there is no physician or philosopher who better

understands the composition of the human body, and the virtue of the Heavens, the Stars, Birds, and Fishes, of trees and herbs and metals and stones. Furthermore, since they are of the same nature as the Angels, all bodies must obey them in respect of local motion. Again, do we not know how great is the power which God in express words has given them upon earth. The Book of Job teaches us this so plainly that there is no need of other proofs; for God even says that there is no power upon earth which may be compared with that of Behemoth.[8]

Evident authority and authoritative evidence

Views such as those expressed by Boguet were typical of many erudite thinkers who were so certain about maleficent demonic activity that they were prepared to advocate the systematic torture and capital punishment of those accused and convicted of trafficking with the devil. These views were not vague apprehensions and superstitions. They were intellectual convictions arrived at on the basis of seemingly unassailable authorities and authenticated evidence. Throughout the Middle Ages and the Renaissance, arguments in virtually every field of human enquiry proceeded upon the basis of accumulated authority. The more authorities one could cite, the greater their names, and the more ancient they were deemed, the more cogent seemed one's argument. And the authorities supporting a system of magic in general, and the reality of witchcraft in particular, were overwhelming.

Within a Christian society both the first and the final authority in any debate must be the Holy Scriptures, despite the difficulty—when manipulating such mystical and allusive writings—of establishing precisely what words mean. Indeed, this difficulty became crucial in the case of Weyer and Scot, for their attempt to overthrow witchcraft beliefs, because it was possible so to reinterpret the Scriptures that the existence of witches in biblical times was eliminated. Nonetheless, the Bible seemed unequivocal on the general issue: it established conclusively (for those to whom scriptural evidence was *ipso facto* conclusive) that all the magical arts were real and that, without exception, they were to be condemned when practised by anybody other than an accredited prophet of God. The biblical universe teemed with spiritual intermediaries between God and man: angels, good and bad, were constantly appearing to, interfering with, and aiding mere mortals. The devil, too, as the principal of evil, though scarcely formed in the older Hebraic books, developed his powers throughout the biblical narrative;

assumed alarming menace in the pseudepigraphical Jewish literature; and became the direct adversary of Christ in the New Testament. His career, it was prophesied in the Apocalyptic vision of St John, would end in total defeat at the hands of the heavenly hosts. That battle is still eagerly awaited; and, in the meantime, the devil has apparently been more than holding his own.[9]

Human associates of the devil and of his minions were explicitly condemned in passages which themselves assumed almost magical potency in any argument. 'Thou shalt not suffer a witch to live' (Exodus, XXII. 18) was the most powerful text of all, though its validity depended upon an interpretation of the word *maleficos*, which came increasingly to be challenged. Were Exodus deemed insufficient, however, there was always Leviticus (XX. 27): 'A man also or woman that hath a familiar spirit, or that is a wizard, shall surely be put to death: they shall stone them with stones: their blood shall be upon them.' Most comprehensive was Deuteronomy (XVIII. 10–12):

> There shall not be found among you any one that maketh his son or his daughter to pass through the fire, or that useth divination, or an observer of times, or an enchanter, or a witch. Or a charmer, or a consulter with familiar spirits, or a wizard, or a necromancer. For all that do these things are an abomination unto the Lord: and because of these abominations the Lord thy God doth drive them out from before thee.

Such injunctions could not have been issued in vain. 'God has again and again forbidden us to sacrifice to devils or to idols which are of devils', wrote Noel Taillepied; 'now he would not have commanded this if there were no devils.'[10] Furthermore, the Bible provided historical examples as well as moral imperatives and prohibitions. Did not Pharaoh's magicians engage in a contest with Moses when, though undeniably inferior to their Hebrew adversary, they were able with the devil's aid, to work seeming miracles? Was not the conjuration of dead spirits—or, at the least, demonic simulation of the dead—attested by the woman of Endor, who apparently conjured up the two-year-dead Samuel to prophesy King Saul's impending doom?[11] Were not Balaam's curses against the Children of Israel deemed worthy of purchase by King Balak, and of intervention by an angel of the Lord? Did not Joseph practise hydromancy? Did not Jacob cause Laban's cattle to conceive spotted offspring by means of sympathetic magic? Did not Jesus himself cast out devils which had possessed people? Did he not himself accord this same power to his disciples? And did this not in turn indicate that evil spirits could and did take possession of human bodies? All this was clear from a purely literal reading of the Scriptures: but there were other passages which, in the light of a pre-existent belief in witchcraft, could be interpreted as further evidence of its reality. In short, to doubt the existence of demons and their activities, 'as do the epicurean Atheists', was to deny the very existence of God.[12]

Upon these foundations was erected a towering edifice of exegetical writings. The early Christian Fathers—many of whom, in desert solitariness, were able to add materials from their own hallucinatory experiences and from their knowledge of pagan sources—developed increasingly elaborate views concerning spirits and demons, witches and wizards. Endlessly they commented upon the key passages in the Scriptures. In the opinion of Justin Martyr and Origen, for instance, the woman of Endor really did conjure up dead Samuel before King Saul; Tertullian, Eustathius of Antioch, and Gregory of Nyssa, all argued that the vision was merely a demon impersonating the prophet; while Augustine, admitting that Samuel himself could have appeared only by divine dispensation, also inclines to the theory of diabolic impersonation.[13] Pharaoh's magicians, according to Tertullian, Origen and Eustathius, accomplished their miracles with direct demonic aid. Augustine pushes this belief even further by arguing the existence of a pact whereby demons give instruction in efficacious magical rites, so that magicians are subsequently able to work by themselves.[14] One thing, above all else, stood out in the patristic corpus. Evil spirits abounded and, under the malign leadership of Satan, they were constantly at work polluting man who was, in turn, always ready to deal with his tempters.[15]

Nor did such exposure of their wicked schemes deter the hosts of darkness, whose activities were documented in the work of every theologian from the days of the Christian Church's youth to those of its dotage. That dotage, according to the sceptical Pomponazzi, had already arrived in his lifetime: and certainly sixteenth-century religious writers were as obsessed by demons and by magic as their predecessors. The stock exemplars—Pharaoh's magicians, the woman of Endor, and all the rest—were as earnestly debated by the Reformers as by Catholic theologians. It is true that those to whom the word of God had been recently and exclusively revealed poured scorn on Catholic miracles, blasphemous rites, and magical relics: 'In the beginning and gathering of the Church, many things were necessary which now be needless. Miracles were used then, which outwardly be denied now.'[16] The truth had been established in apostolic times, and it was fruitless, the Reformers argued, to seek fresh signs and miracles which, 'in these latter days, have been ofter wrought by power of the devil than by Spirit of God'. Wicked spirits, wrote Calfhill,

> do lurk in shrines, in Roods, in Crosses, in Images: and first of all pervert the Priests, which are easiest to be caught with bait of a little gain. Then work they miracles. They appear to men in divers shapes; disquiet them when they are awake; trouble them in their sleeps; distort their members; take away their health; afflict them with diseases; only to bring them to some Idolatry.[17]

But this attribution to the devil of virtually all post-apostolic miracles increased, rather than diminished, the scope of diabolic interference in human affairs; and the Reformers' devil seemed even more immanent than in the works of their adversaries whom they were happy both to castigate and to plagiarise.[18] The devil was a very necessary fellow; and Luther, for one, would have been lost without his company.[19]

The anger of the Reformers against Catholicism is readily understandable. The Catholic Church itself practised magic: by producing effects on inanimate objects; inducing psychosomatic symptoms; and, above all, working miracles in the Mass with its music, words of consecration, incense, wine, and transubstantiation. It had long been recognised that grave difficulties confronted those who might attempt to show how such practices differed fundamentally from other magical activities—a problem illuminated by Jean Gerson's discussion of the authenticity of the visions of St Brigitta. He felt that too many people were being canonised, and was deeply concerned that there was no certain method of distinguishing between true and false visions, and no way of looking into people's inner experiences.[20] Subsequently, anti-Catholic theologians solved this problem by rejecting the greater part of modern miracles, and by simply attributing them to the devil. But a problem yet remained. Christianity was itself a religion founded upon, and authenticated by, miraculous occurrences; and intricate were the attempts to establish objective criteria whereby one might distinguish godly miracles from diabolic marvels. Three things, however, were generally agreed: true miracles had taken place; false marvels were still occurring; and it was impossible not to declare allegiance to one side or the other. As Henry Holland wrote, in his *Treatise against Witchcraft* (1590):

> There are two spirituall kingdomes in this world, which have continual hatred and bloody wars, without hope of truce for ever. The Lord and King of the one is our Lord Jesus, the tyrannical usurper of the other, is Sathan. Again, this also we are as clearly taught, that all men living,

without exception, are either true subjects of the one, or slaves unto
the other. For albeit, the Neuters of this worlde dreame that they may
indifferentlie view the scarres and woundes of other men, and never
approach neere those bloody skirmishes; yet the truth is they are fowlie
deceived: for the great Lord and King hath said with his own mouth,
Hee that is not with me, is against me.[21]

The theological authorities seemed conclusive; but Christian writers had
yet other sources to support their belief in magic and maleficence. Pagan
literature was full of the deeds of witches, magicians, and aerial spirits; and
the works of demonologists abound in references to Homer, Virgil, and
Ovid, despite the fact that much of this material had been rejected as
fantastic rubbish by many of those very Fathers whose views were otherwise
considered definitive. This abuse of poetry was one of many feeblenesses
discerned by Reginald Scot in Bodin's *Démonomanie*; but his withering
contempt did not prevent others from continuing to regard the poets as solid
evidence. Even in the seventeenth century such sources were still employed
as though they had historical validity. William Perkins, for example, in his
Discourse of the Damned Art of Witchcraft (1608), rejects any suggestion that
the witches of his own age were unknown in the days of Moses or Christ.
Ancient writings, he claimed, proved that, about 1,200 years before Christ's
birth, and shortly after the Trojan War (itself over a century prior to the
building of the temple of Solomon), there were 'the like witches that are
now, as the *Circes* and *Syrenes*, and such like, mentioned in the narration of
that warre, as is manifest to them that know the storie'. The *storie*, to which
Perkins so confidently refers, is that unimpeachable source, Homer's
Odyssey.[22]

There were other more significant traditions which added ancient authority
to the system of magic. Plato, especially as interpreted by the Neoplatonists,
was a tower of strength; while the way in which the anti-demonic Aristotle
was pressed into service by the demonologists represents one of the triumphs
of medieval ingenuity. But not even ingenuity was required to derive support
for the reality of magic from the *Prisci Theologi*. There abounded, in the
Roman Empire, a great variety of writings purporting to be either of divine
origin and authorship, or at least to be the work of ancient founders of
religion, men reputedly descended from the gods and themselves divinely
inspired. Such oracular and mystic writings pretend to immense antiquity,
often claiming origin in ancient Egypt and Chaldea. Texts such as these
claimed to disclose the secrets of the most ancient priesthoods, and were
replete with magic and mystic theologies expressed in inextricable ambi-

guities. The very existence of such material encouraged authors of astrological and alchemical works to pass off their own productions as part of the same venerable and cryptic tradition, so that there grew up a considerable body of mystical writings compelling attention by virtue of its antiquity and the unparalleled eminence of its originators: Orpheus the Theologian; Zoroaster the first magician; and Hermes Trismegistus whose fragmentary and spurious canon expounds the occult virtues of natural substances, magical procedures, and the intimate relationship between nature, stars, and spirits. 'Philosophy and magic', said Hermes, 'nourish the soul.'[23]

This farrago enjoyed a wide diffusion; and the acceptance of such texts as genuinely antique—in the case of Hermes, only a little less ancient than Moses and far more venerable than Plato—ensured their continuing authority throughout the Middle Ages and the Renaissance. Lactantius, as Frances Yates has pointed out, respected Hermes as a pagan prophet of the true God; whereas Augustine considered his work to have been demonically inspired.[24] Nonetheless, both Lactantius and Augustine, and the other Fathers of the Church, accepted that, for good or ill, this material was genuine; and thus a passage such as the following, from the *Asclepius*, was of importance for all who needed to establish the reality of demonic magic. The discussion concerned the way in which the ancient Egyptians invented the art of making gods on earth by creating idols with magical powers, and Asclepius demands to know the nature of these terrestrial gods. Hermes replies that it consists of

> herbs, stones, and aromas, which have in them a natural divine power. And it is for the following reason that people delight them with frequent sacrifices, with hymns and praises and sweet sounds concerted like the harmony of the heavens: that this heavenly thing, which has been attracted into the idol by repeated heavenly rites, may bear joyously with men and stay with them long.[25]

This passage had been cited by Augustine, and was always well known to demonologists; but it gained fresh significance when, in 1489, Ficino employed it to support his own theory of magically influencing the human spirit so that it might become receptive to celestial forces. It is a useful passage, too, for our enquiry: for it brings us back full circle to the fundamental authority of the Scriptures. Hermes tells us how the ancients invoked spirits, put them into images, and worshipped them. And does not David say—as all demonologists well knew—that the 'Gods of the Gentiles are devils'?[26]

For centuries all of this would have seemed irrefutable authority to a majority of thinking men; but it was not the only material available to silence scepticism. In recent years, distinctions between magic and experimental science have been increasingly blurred as historians have come to recognise the importance not only of intellectual traditions which continue to evolve, but also of those which proved ultimately to be dead-ends. There was in fact an enormous weight of medieval and Renaissance scientific writing which served to confirm magical correspondences, occult innate virtues, astral influences, talismanic magic, and the operation of aerial spirits both good and bad. Many writers condemned astrology for its impiety, and some attacked the exaggerated claims of its practitioners; but few disputed the reality of celestial influence over terrestrial affairs. The immense vogue of almanacs and prognostications, the scope and volume of serious astrological debate, the notice taken of astrologers by princes, and the number of serious panics caused by knowledge of unfavourable planetary circumstances, all testify to the grip in which the astrologers held both popular and erudite imagination. Much the same may be said of amulets, talismans, and images, the efficacy of which was maintained, explained, and elaborated by scientific writers from pagan antiquity to the Renaissance. It is impossible here even to summarise this complex of ideas: but one example may serve to illustrate the relation between magic and science within a demonological context. Albertus Magnus, discussing the differences between magical marvels and divine miracles, explains that, whereas the latter occur instantaneously, feats of magic are really normal natural processes enormously accelerated. Demons, harnessing astral influences, perform these lightning operations so that, to take the classic example, the rods which Pharaoh's magicians turned into serpents were merely undergoing, at immense speed, the process by which worms generate in decaying trees.[27] Here we have a perfect focus. Scriptural exemplar, demonic activity, astral influence, and natural process, combine to produce a feat of magic; and all this in the work of one of the greatest names in medieval intellectual history. Medieval erudition offered rich fare for the demonologist with an appetite for scientific corroboration.

All these varied authorities offer assertions that magic was done, together with explanations of how it was done. To illustrate precisely what was done, writers could draw upon an inexhaustible thesaurus of examples. This was partly provided by the literature devoted to prodigies, portents, and marvels (of which the *Dialogue on Miracles* by Caesarius of Heisterbach is an outstanding example), and partly by an army of chroniclers who set down extraordinary occurrences in the midst of their historical narratives.[28] Thus, since for most readers history was simply a storehouse of moral, immoral, and political exemplars, the miraculous episode had complete historical validity.

Finally, most dramatic and irrefutable of all, were the countless instances where evil-doers betrayed themselves. As Boguet pointed out, the demonologists could cite 'voluntary and repeated confessions of witches', and the 'sentences passed against them in various places'. Here was the factual evidence to destroy those sceptics who demanded more objective evidence than a battery of great names and authorities. A massive tradition of belief in the power of local witches to work harms and cures seemed to point to a continuity of witch activity from scriptural and classical times to the present. Various sorts of folk practices had long been identified with, and persecuted as, heresy; and there was thus a body of material deriving from trials all over Europe, which gave what seemed to be an empirical basis for witchcraft beliefs. As Bodin put it: the truth had been laid bare by thousand upon thousand 'presomptions violentes, accusations, tesmoignages, recollemens, confrontations, convictions, recognoissances, repentances, et confessions volontaires jusques á la mort'.[29] It was, above all, these voluntary confessions which seemed proof incontrovertible; and, although they came to be explained away as the result of social pressures, mental disease, or covert torment, there was still a substantial residue of cases where magic was knowingly employed to obtain some particular end.[30] And it is at this point that we return to the confusion between high and low magic. It was the flatulent claims of learned magicians such as Ficino which confirmed demonologists in their belief that diabolic magic was a present reality. Ficino might claim that he was dealing only with good spirits. His adversaries knew that there was no way in which he could be certain that this was so; that he was, indeed, deluded; and that such trafficking was almost certainly only possible with demons who delighted above all else in so deceiving mankind. How could there be any doubt when, in addition to all the scriptural, patristic, philosophical, and scientific authorities, they had not only the circumstantial confessions of vulgar low magicians, but also the eloquent and damnable testimony of divers books of ceremonial magic and pacts, the pretentious claims of astrologers, and the ambiguous ravings of alchemists, cabbalists, and a heterogeneous assortment of unlicensed visionaries and mystics. In due course, other savants added their incoherencies to the swelling volume of magical writings, and further horrified the demonologists. Henry Cornelius Agrippa, for whom religion and superstition were the two supports of ceremonial magic, defined magic itself as a very powerful faculty, full of the most elevated mysteries,

> and which comprises a very profound knowledge of the most secret matters, their nature, their power, their quality, their substance, their

effects, their difference, and their relation: whence it produces its marvellous effect by the union and application of the different virtues of the superior beings with those of the inferior. This is the true, the most elevated, and the most mysterious science—in a word the perfection and fulfilment of all the natural sciences.[31]

Agrippa doubtless deemed himself an erudite magus: but for the witch-hunters his writings merely confirmed the possibility of human dealings with the devil; and for Bodin he was 'le plus grand sorcier qui fut onques de son aage'.[32] Agrippa himself tells how he once intervened to save the life of a poor old woman accused of witchcraft; but his own magical proclivities and publications helped to justify the witchcraft persecution which swept Europe late in the sixteenth century.

Malleus Maleficarum

In the latter half of the fifteenth century there was a marked proliferation of treatises specifically devoted to witchcraft, employing the great corpus of authority to establish the reality of a perverted magical conspiracy.[33] The most important of these manuals, both in scope and practicality, was the *Malleus Maleficarum*, one of those rare works written—in the opinion of its most ardent modern admirer—'sub specie aeternitatis'.[34] This claim is, I believe, true: although not for any intrinsic merit the work possesses. The fact is that the *Malleus* affords a comprehensive summary of arguments for persecution, together with a persecution method, which has precisely that combination of unoriginality, popularity, and influence so valuable to the historian of ideas seeking to discover conventional, rather than atypical, modes of thought.

The book was written by two prominent Dominican inquisitors, Jakob Sprenger and Heinrich Kramer, and first published in 1486/87. This couple had been empowered by Pope Innocent VIII, in December 1484, to deal with those who 'unmindful of their own salvation and straying from the Catholic Faith, have abandoned themselves to devils, incubi and succubi', and who, by incantations, spells, conjurations, and other forms of magic have caused the death of unborn babies, destroyed crops, afflicted live-stock, caused dreadful sickness to both men and beasts, and hindered both the sexual act in men and conception in women.[35] Much of the *Malleus*'s early bibliographical history remains obscure; though its immediate success is attested by at least eight editions before the close of the fifteenth century.[36] The authors' purpose was clear. Witchcraft was a vast and vile conspiracy against the Faith; it was on the increase; witches were depopulating the whole of Christendom; and, through the impotence of the secular courts, these creatures remained unpunished. The *Malleus* was written to demonstrate precisely what witches were doing, and how they could be stopped. It first establishes the truth of the existence of witchcraft and its heretical nature; then elucidates the principal evils practised by witches and demons; and finally lays down formal rules for initiating legal action against witches, securing their conviction, and passing sentence upon them (pp. 20, 68, 104).

Underlying the entire structure of the *Malleus* are three beliefs: that witchcraft is real and that it is heresy to maintain the opposite; that demonic interference in human affairs is incessant; and that both witchcraft and demonic activity are permitted by God for his own purposes. The first two beliefs can be established by the authorities and by evidence: but the last can only be an inference from these—that is, since they are real, God must have permitted them. This is scarcely a satisfactory position, but its implications are alarming when one considers that, in the course of the *Malleus*, virtually every species of misery and misfortune is attributed to demonic agency. It seems that God, despite occasional assertions to the contrary, has given the devil *carte blanche* in terrestrial affairs. The *Malleus* admits the existence of natural disasters. Yet, overwhelmingly, the functioning of the universe is depicted as demonic and devilish. Even the stars play only a minor role in human affairs, and certainly cannot coerce demons to perform any actions against their will. Indeed, demons deliberately choose to appear when summoned by magicians at certain astrologically significant moments, because they thereby deceive men and lead them into idolatry. The stars, it is conceded, have a conditional influence upon human affairs, and it is thus possible for astrologers to have some success in their predictions. Nevertheless, anyone who argues more extensive celestial influence is undermining free will, and cannot be tolerated (pp. 11, 32–4). Kramer and Sprenger, however, never do satisfactorily explain why their own total commitment to demonic interference does not inhibit free will.

Catastrophes of the weather, failing crops, and diseases amongst livestock, are all generally regarded as demonic in origin; and, although both physical and mental ailments are possible within purely natural terms, these too are principally caused by demons. There are six ways in which witches, with the devil's aid, can injure humanity (p. 115). They can cause evil love; inspire hatred or jealousy; and interfere with the sexual act and childbirth. They can also cause disease 'in any of the human organs'; take away life; and deprive men of reason. There is nothing wonderful in demons' ability to cause delusions and frenzies, 'when even a natural defect is able to effect the same result', as is shown in the case of frantic men, melancholics, maniacs, and drunkards, all of whom see things which are not really there (p. 120). The *Malleus* gives a circumstantial account of the manner in which demons cause mental sickness: though it is noteworthy that—according to contemporary theories of the localisation of brain function—the authors place reason in the wrong ventricle.[37] Having entered our bodies, the demons 'make impressions on the inner faculties corresponding to the bodily organs', for the devil can

> draw out some image retained in a faculty corresponding to one of the senses; as he draws from the memory, which is in the back part of the head, an image of a horse, and locally moves that phantasm to the middle part of the head, where are the cells of imaginative power; and finally to the sense of reason, which is in the front of the head. And he causes such a sudden change and confusion, that such objects are necessarily thought to be actual things seen with the eyes. This can be clearly exemplified by the natural defect in frantic men and other maniacs (p. 125).

The *Malleus* thus employs natural disease to establish the reality of demonically induced sickness; and the authors' attempts to distinguish between the two afford infinitely greater scope to the latter.[38]

The entire range of these injuries is within the competence of the devil working by himself. He has no need of human agents to accomplish his designs. Nevertheless, he prefers to work through witches because

> he thus gives greater offence to God, by usurping to himself a creature dedicated to Him. Secondly, because when God is the more offended, He gives him the more power of injuring men. And thirdly, for his own gain, which he places in the perdition of souls (p. 122).

The majority of witches are women; and the monkish misogyny of the *Malleus* is blatant. Its explanations for female susceptibility are in themselves conventional and, like most such attacks, its arguments are confused. On the one hand, woman, having been formed from a bent rib, is an imperfect animal and is always a deceiver. Her very name, *Femina*, derives from *Fe* and *Minus*, 'since she is ever weaker to hold and preserve the faith': and this is the very root of witchcraft. Women are more given to carnal lust than men; more credulous and slippery tongued; 'intellectually like children'; feeble in memory; and easily provoked to hatred. On the other hand, there have been many examples of virtuous women; and above all in the New Testament we find the 'whole sin of Eve taken away by the benediction of MARY'—a pious reminder which is immediately followed by an affirmation that, in these times, the perfidy of witchcraft is more often found in women than in men 'since they are feebler both in mind and body' (pp. 41-7).

Women's insatiable lust is of crucial significance because witchcraft is spread, and its power augmented, through the venereal act. God allows the devil special powers to interfere in sexual intercourse, not only because of its 'natural nastiness', but also because it was this act 'that caused the corruption of our first parents and, by its contagion, brought the inheritance of original sin upon the whole human race' (pp. 93, 169). The devil has a thousand ways of doing harm, but his power is principally confined to the 'privy parts and the navel', because in men 'the source of wantonness lies in the privy parts, since it is from them that the semen falls, just as in women it falls from the navel' (pp. 23-4). So the devil spends his time gathering semen from concupiscent men by pretending to be a woman and then, masquerading as a man, he injects it into his witch partners during further acts of demonic intercourse. The semen is specially selected and is kept fresh and fertile because the devil is able to move it at lightning speed (p. 28). It is thus that demonic offspring are engendered; and this, together with his general encouragement to lechery, appears to be the main purpose of the devil's sexual machinations. Pleasure, we are told, cannot be the demons' aim, since they are not flesh and blood—a view contradicted within a few pages when the Scriptures are adduced to show how incubi and succubi lust after women (pp. 29-30).

The various ways in which the devil can render the penis totally useless are discussed in great and ingenious detail, as are the naughty tricks witches play with the same vulnerable member. Witches even collect the male organs, twenty or thirty at a time, and put them in a 'bird's nest, or shut them up in a box, where they move themselves like living members, and eat oats and corn, as has been seen by many and is a matter of common report' (p. 121). There is little that the forces of evil will not get up to when the sexual act is involved. Yet, anomalously, even demons draw the line at 'vices against nature', and refuse to engage in acts 'wrongfully performed outside the rightful channel' (p. 30).

None of this scholastic pornography is original; but it was of great importance to the witch-hunters because, in their view, not only did witches satisfy their own 'filthy lusts'; they also pandered to the desires of great men. And it was through such men, whom the witches protect from other harm, that 'there arises the great danger of the time, namely, the extermination of the Faith' (p. 48). Here we see the whole conspiracy laid bare. Men of the noblest birth, governors, the rich and the powerful, are all in thrall to their demonically dedicated lovers. Thus witches are themselves protected. Thus they increase in power.

No less unoriginal, and equally important, is the *Malleus*'s insistence on the reality of a pact between the devil and his human partners. This pact is no tacit or symbolic arrangement (pp. 81-2), but is 'exactly defined and expressed', blaspheming God and pledging harm to God's creatures (p. 20). The whole formal process is detailed in the text and concludes with an agreement for the witch to make unguents from the bones and limbs of children, especially those unbaptised, by which means she will be able to fulfil all her wishes. In return, the witch pledges to abjure the Christian Faith; to give herself to the devil, body and soul; to do her utmost to bring others into his power; and to leave behind her a survivor, carefully instructed, so that the number of witches may be increased (pp. 99-100, 144). This contract is designed to anger God more than either purely demonic evil or straightforward human malice can ever do. For witchcraft is no ordinary heresy. It is 'high treason against God's Majesty', and it must be treated accordingly (p. 6).

Anybody reading the *Malleus Maleficarum*—its authors confidently assert—will find therein 'nothing contrary to sound reason, nothing which differs from the words of Scripture and the tradition of the Fathers' (p. 21). Their arguments are constantly said to be 'proved by reason and authority'; and indeed the whole work is a perfect illustration of the appeal to established authority and time-honoured evidence. Reason is comprised simply in making that appeal, and—where authority and evidence are concordant—in drawing the inevitable conclusions. A considerable number of authorities are cited in the course of the work, and even include tags from Cicero, Seneca, Cato, Terence, Valerius Maximus, and Theophrastus. Dionysius the Pseudo-Areopagite, Jerome, Chrysostom, Lactantius, Gregorius Magnus, Origen, and Isidore, loom very large; and a host of historians, lawyers, and philosophers are drawn upon. Four principal authorities, however, dominate the *Malleus*: Aristotle, who provides both natural explanations and the logical structure of each proposition; the Scriptures, which form the basis for all theological, miraculous, and moral arguments; St Augustine, whose assertions concerning magic and demonology are scattered broadcast throughout the text; and St Thomas Aquinas, who furnishes a synthesis of the other three major sources. The handling of such writers is not over-scrupulous, and they are all employed selectively; so that single observations, sentences, and even mere phrases, are ripped out of context and used as if they have universal validity. This method enables its practitioners to prove anything they wish; though, Aristotle apart, the authorities valued by Kramer and Sprenger required little twisting to serve their turn.

Use and experience, says the *Malleus*, are of more value to judges in witchcraft cases 'than any art or text-book' (pp. 226, 244), and the authors certainly cite numerous examples in the course of their discussion. Some of their stories are taken from Nider, the principal specialist writer against witchcraft prior to their own work; but many are derived from their own experiences as inquisitors. Indeed, they claim to have collected enough evidence from the town of Innsbruck alone to make a book of them (p. 139). They constantly adduce 'examples that have been personally seen or heard, or are accepted at the word of credible witnesses' (p. 89); and they could turn the minds of their readers if they related all their experiences, were it not 'sordid and mean' to praise oneself (p. 90). There is truly no lack of evidence in the *Malleus*. The only problem is the attitude of its authors, epitomised in the chapters dealing with incubi and succubi. These extraordinary activities are denied by some but attested by many other witnesses: and, according to Aristotle, 'that which appears true to many cannot be altogether false' (pp. 25, 27). Thus, much that we would deem merely hearsay is admitted as proof; and, in this respect, the *Malleus* reads very much like earlier collections of miracles and prodigies.

It is, however, in its dialectical procedures that the *Malleus* is simultaneously at its most feeble and most devastating. Indeed, it is the very weakness of its logic that results in its terrifying conclusions: for, despite appearances to the contrary, this work is not an argument but rather a series of assertions masked by an accumulation of authorities and exemplars assembled in disputation form. Any methodology may be well or ill used, and—cumbrousness apart—there is little intrinsically amiss with the scholastic procedure of propositions, objections, and rejoinders. The method had achieved some notable triumphs of subtlety and ingenuity. But not in the hands of Kramer and Sprenger. They rarely succeed in overcoming the objections they themselves raise to their own propositions; sometimes an argument is left in mid-air; sometimes a proposition is assumed to have been proven when it patently has not; examples are frequently inadequate to support a conclusion advanced; and very often a position assumed at one point in the text is contradicted elsewhere as occasion demands.

Some of these weaknesses are inherent in the very process of arguing on the basis of authority. This technique operates rather like the law of diminishing fleas: each writer citing his predecessors and becoming, in turn, an authority worthy of citation. The *Malleus* is itself an example of this process; and its own pronouncements were cited as definitive throughout the following century and even beyond. Another problem arising when authority weighs so heavily is a tendency to incorporate conflicting ideas, a habit frequently deemed typically medieval, but just as typical of the Renaissance. And we find this inability to recognise or to resolve contradictions in historians, in writers on magic and science, and even in so practical a field as mechanics where one might imagine that necessity would eliminate totally discrepant theorems.[39]

The normal shape of the argument in the *Malleus* is circular. Everything is built upon the assumption that God permits the devil to perpetrate evil through human agents. In other words, the whole argument for persecution rests upon a monstrous paradox, since witches are merely serving God's mysterious purposes and might, on that account, be deemed more worthy of praise than of blame.[40] God, we are told, frequently allows devils to act as His ministers and servants (p. 8). Were the devil completely unrestricted he would destroy the works of God. But he cannot destroy the works of God (p. 11). Therefore whatever he does can only be with divine permission. Should one attempt to break this circle by demanding why God goes to such trouble, Kramer and Sprenger have an abundance of authorised arguments, if not to convince, at least to stupefy any critic. Not only does God punish by the power of evil angels, but He also allows the devil to work willy-nilly entirely for His own glory, for the commendation of the Faith, for the purgation of the elect, and for the acquisition of merit (pp. 16, 23, 85). So we see the devil tormented very greatly, for

> it is certain that nothing can be more galling to the pride of the devil, which he always rears up against God . . . than that God should convert his evil machinations to His own glory. Therefore God justly permits all these things.

God allows evil so that He can draw good therefrom; and he will not prevent all evil because otherwise 'the universe should lack the cause of much good' (pp. 29, 69). Evil exists to perfect the universe, and God is 'glorified in sin, when He pardons in mercy and when He punishes in justice; therefore it behoves Him not to hinder sin'. It is, nonetheless, difficult for us to see how God is 'glorified in sin' when he permits the innocent to suffer with the guilty; allows child-eating witches to accomplish almost everything they wish; and tolerates diabolical changelings (pp. 77, 99, 128, 192). Nor does it seem either merciful or just when—although the devil can do nothing without divine permission—God is still so offended when witches use image magic that He allows plagues to fall upon the earth 'in punishment of their misdeeds' (p. 20). Similarly it is strange that God takes special offence when witches pay homage to the devil (p. 101); and that, because demons do most of their evil on holy days, He is so angry that He 'allows them greater power of injuring even innocent men by punishing them either in their affairs or their bodies' (p. 113). It thus appears that because the devil employs the power allowed him by God, God is increasingly vexed and, as a result, grants further powers to His enemy—a truly 'incomprehensible judgment' (p. 129).

Even stranger is the contradictory behaviour of the devil. We are told at one point that he assails good people more bitterly than he does the wicked because, whereas he already possesses the latter, he is eager to draw the just into his power by tribulation (pp. 86, 97). Yet we are subsequently assured not only that God allows demons more power against the wicked than against the just, and that when God does permit injury to the good it is only to increase their merit, but also that demons know this full well and are therefore 'the less eager to injure them' (p. 136). All of this makes one wonder why demons arrange for the murder of unbaptised children and dedicate them to the devil. The theory is that, since such children are debarred from the Kingdom of Heaven, 'by this means the Last Judgment is delayed, when the devils will be condemned to eternal torture; since the number of the elect is more slowly completed, on the fulfilment of which the world will be consumed' (p. 141). But the fulfilment of the number of the elect, the Day of Judgment, and the end of the world, must all be for God's decision alone. It is impossible to see either how demons can delay such matters even for a fraction of a second, or (since their maleficence depends solely upon divine permission) why they bother.

The phrase, 'with the permission of God', recurs throughout the *Malleus*, and every similar witch-hunting manual, like an involuntary mental spasm afflicting authors whenever inconsistent, nonsensical, or impossible assertions are made. It is employed like some invincible chess piece empowered, in moments of emergency, to remove all the opposing pieces from the board. It is an argument favoured by Catholic theologians and Reformers alike; and it reveals a colossal arrogance on the part of those who believe that their vapid subtleties really do elucidate the most intimate divine purposes which they alone fully comprehend. It is impossible to argue rationally against those who have been taken entirely into God's confidence.

Privileged though they are, Kramer and Sprenger encounter difficulties over the knotty problem of free will, which they are unable to resolve. Man has the choice between good and ill: but the devil's will is 'made up for evil', and he causes evil will in men, and especially in witches (p. 32). The latter 'do enjoy absolute liberty' when they make their compact with the devil

(p. 16), despite the fact that divine providence and knowledge extend to all created things, 'not in the mass generally, but also in the individual particularly' (p. 69). Thus evil—as we have seen—must be part of God's purpose; and He does indeed extract good from evil. On the other hand, we are told that God will not bestow the quality of impeccability, not because of any imperfection in His power 'but because of the imperfection of the creature: and this imperfection lies chiefly in the fact that no creature, man or angel, is capable of receiving this quality' (p. 70). This is as strange as it is unfortunate, since all creatures including witches were made by God in the first place.

Divine permission and free will had troubled and perplexed Christians long before the *Malleus Maleficarum*, and it is scarcely surprising that its authors remain confused on these issues. But their work is full of other feeblenesses, too. Circular arguments are rolled out ceaselessly; *non sequiturs* follow hard upon each other; and questions are begged without embarrassment. Incomprehensibilities are sometimes almost inspired as, for example, the assertion that it is not the least surprising that an innocent man should be demonically possessed for the slight fault of another person, 'when men are possessed by devils for their own light fault, or for another's heavy sin, or for their own heavy sin, and some also at the instance of witches' (p. 130)—or, the authors might have added in the same vein, for any reason (or no reason) whatsoever. Kramer and Sprenger are able to combine fallacies within a single argument. They affirm that even virtuous people can be deceived by the devil, and their imagination perverted by his fiendish wiles. Yet they also maintain with equal certainty that the devil can in no way enter the mind or body of any person, nor has the power 'to penetrate into the thoughts of anybody, unless such a person has first become destitute of all holy thoughts, and is quite bereft and denuded of spiritual contemplation' (p. 120). It follows, *ipso facto*, that all who are so deluded must be lacking in the gift of divine grace, and that the virtuous can never be taken in by the devil.

An interesting minor instance of the authors' major failure to pursue the logic of their own argument may be seen in their approval of a story concerning a certain holy man who once found the devil, in the form of a devout priest, preaching in a church. The pseudo-priest was irreproachable in his attack on sin; so the holy man approached him after the sermon to demand the reason for this. And the devil answered, 'I preach the truth, knowing that because they are hearers of the word only, and not doers, God is the more offended and my gain is increased' (p. 128). The logical consequence of this must be that any preacher who inveighs against sin, and utters the truth, is offending God and aiding the devil. Kramer and Sprenger do not see this; and, even if they did, it would matter little since they are capable of contradicting themselves within the space of a short chapter or even on the same page. A particularly striking instance occurs in a discussion of a problem which constantly disturbed writers against witchcraft: how far should they go into details concerning the enemies' practices?[41] Some critics, says the *Malleus*, have argued that to preach and write about such matters is very dangerous, because people might thereby acquire evil knowledge. But this, claim the authors, is not possible. No matter how much folk might wish to do evil, and however much they invoke the devil in order to accomplish this, it can be of no avail unless they have paid homage to him and have abjured the Faith: 'it is impossible for anyone to learn from a preacher how to perform any of the things that have been mentioned' (p. 145). This seems decisive until we read, three short paragraphs later, that the very act of seeking the devil's help is apostasy: for 'if invocations, conjurations, fumigations and adorations are used, then an open pact is formed with the devil, even if there has been no surrender of body and soul together with an explicit abjuration of the Faith either wholly or in part. For by the mere invocation of the devil a man commits open verbal apostasy' (pp. 145–6).

Another contradiction which continued to baffle thinkers concerned the power of witches to harm those appointed as judges over them. Amongst the classes of men blessed by God, whom witches cannot harm, 'the first are those who administer public justice against them, or prosecute them in any public official capacity'. This is proved by 'actual experience' when witches have admitted that, 'merely because they have been taken by officials of public justice, they have immediately lost all their power of witchcraft' (pp. 89–90). Kramer and Sprenger forget this reassuring fact, and later they warn their readers against witches who can 'bewitch their judges by a mere look or glance from their eyes, and publicly boast that they cannot be punished' (p. 139); while others are able 'with the help of the devil to bewitch the Judge by the mere sound of the words which they utter'. Therefore judges must take every kind of precaution, including having the witch led in backwards so that he may see her before she can see him (p. 228). But if judges are immune from witchcraft, why take this trouble?

Such instances are typical of the *Malleus* and could be illustrated from every chapter throughout the text. However, by far the most serious logical flaws—because of their far-reaching practical consequences—relate to the accusation, torture, and punishment of witches. The authors seem, for much of the time, convinced that witch spells are extremely difficult, and frequently impossible, to cure; and they devote much space to discussing whether or not it is lawful to oppose witchcraft with witchcraft, or vanity with vanity. Their authorities are here in disagreement; and for once Kramer and

Sprenger recognise this fact explicitly and even promise to reconcile discrepancies. They never do so, but content themselves by quibbling that certain superstitious remedies may be safely employed—though their attempt to distinguish between lawful and unlawful cures results in total confusion (pp. 157, 268-9). They also produce a whole armoury of pious and religious magic which is sometimes effective against witchcraft: pilgrimages to holy shrines, true confession and contrition, 'the plentiful use of the sign of the Cross', devout prayer, and lawful exorcism by solemn words (p. 170). Judges, in particular, are advised to wear around the neck 'consecrated salt and other matters, with the Seven Words which Christ uttered on the Cross written in a schedule, and all bound together'. If possible this material should be made up 'into the length of Christ's stature', and worn against the naked flesh, 'for it is shown by experience that witches are greatly troubled by these things' (p. 231). Again one demands, why is all this necessary if judges are immune from witchcraft? But the fact is that ultimately, in Kramer's and Sprenger's view, nothing is really effective against witches. Much less conviction is carried by their lists of holy magical remedies than by their heartfelt exasperation at the way people persist in consulting witches for cures, and their exclamation:

> But alas! O Lord God ... who shall deliver the poor who are bewitched and cry out in their ceaseless pains? For our sins are so great, and the enemy is so strong; and where are they who can undo the works of the devil by lawful exorcisms? (p. 160)

The only effective remedy lies in the hands of the judges. Witches must be checked by relentless punishment; and there can be no doubt that, above all the criminals in the world, such creatures merit the most severe penalties. They are not merely heretics but apostates; and indeed in their apostasy they not only deny the Faith but pay homage to the devil, and afflict men and beasts with temporal injuries (p. 77). Counterfeiters of coin which is nothing more than a prop to the life of the body are sentenced to death by the secular courts; so how much heavier is the sin of the witch who corrupts the Faith which is the life of the soul (p. 153)? Exodus XXII is cited with approval (p. 193); and it is suggested that even where a witch is shown mercy by the spirituality on account of a last-minute confession (a proceeding not seriously envisaged), she is still liable to punishment by the civil authorities for the temporal crimes she has committed (p. 261).

Death is the only penalty for witches seriously considered in the *Malleus Maleficarum*. The authors are at pains to demonstrate precisely how convictions may be secured and, following the precedents established in heresy prosecutions, they produce the most one-sided judicial procedure it would be possible to devise. So great a crime, they say, cannot be proceeded against 'with no other warrant than a vague charge or a grave suspicion' (p. 164); and they maintain that no person ought to be condemned 'unless he has been convicted by his own confession, or by the evidence of three trustworthy witnesses'. The drawback here is that, within a single sentence, we slip from initiating a witchcraft accusation to the problem of condemning the accused. The procedure advocated by the *Malleus* is of the utmost simplicity: trustworthy witnesses comprehend all who are prepared to come forward, secretly and without fear of consequences, to make any wild accusation they choose; and confession may be extorted by duplicity or torture.

The single-minded one-sidedness of the argument is laid bare in a discussion of the three methods of beginning a witchcraft process (pp. 205-7). The first of these is when an accuser comes forward offering to 'submit himself to the penalty of talion if he fails to prove it'—that is to suffer the same penalty as would be inflicted on the accused if the charges could be substantiated. The second method is for someone to come forward 'not as an accuser but as an informer'; so that, should the accusation fail, he will not be liable to a penalty. The third method is where there is no accuser or informer, but simply 'a general report that there are witches in some town or place; and then the Judge must proceed, not at the instance of any party, but simply by virtue of his office'. Solemnly the *Malleus* assures us that the third method is the most usual, 'because it is secret'; and judges are enjoined to avoid the first method of direct accusation, for 'the deeds of witches in conjunction with devils are done in secret, and the accuser cannot in this case, as in others, have definite evidence by which he can make his statements good'. The accuser must therefore be advised to drop the formal method and to offer himself simply as an informer (p. 211). The argument is truly extraordinary. It is too dangerous to proceed on an accusation where the plaintiff is obliged to prove his case; and preferable to proceed on mere information or rumour. That it is easier, in the latter case, for both judges, informers, and witnesses, to be thoroughly irresponsible and malicious, is evident. But it can certainly be no easier to prove the accusations objectively since, presumably, gossip-mongers can have no more reliable access to facts than a genuine complainant. Indeed, as the *Malleus* points out, since witches never threaten their intended victims in the presence of a third party, there never can be witnesses to such matters (p. 213).

Personal enemies, especially mortal enemies, cannot—we are assured—be allowed as witnesses. But this caution is soon eroded by a reminder that the judge should not greatly heed such a plea on behalf of the accused: 'for in these cases it is very seldom that anyone bears witness without enmity, because witches are always hated by everybody' (p. 220). In effect, therefore, mortal enemies are allowed as witnesses in witch trials, along with everybody else. As in heresy proceedings, even people under sentence of excommunication, criminal associates and accomplices, notorious evil-doers and criminals, servants, family, and kindred—all are permitted to give evidence in these trials, although their identity must not be revealed unless perfect safety can be guaranteed. And such a guarantee is deemed virtually impossible (pp. 209, 216–17).

With this array of anonymous informers against her, the witch's chance of proving her innocence was already slender; but there were additional ways to prejudice her case. She was to be allowed an advocate only if she specifically requested one; and he was to be formally admonished not to incur the charge of defending heresy, which would render him liable to excommunication. Since the trial proceedings must be 'plain and summary', he must not introduce any complications or appeals; and if he 'unduly defends a person already suspect of heresy, he makes himself as it were a patron of that heresy' (p. 218). If, after such warnings, an advocate does accept the brief, then he finds himself going into battle with his hands firmly tied behind his back. He may see everything contained in the depositions against his client: but on no account may he have the names of the witnesses. It is thus extremely difficult for him to attempt the obvious defence of personal enmity on the part of the accusers; and even if he does try this, the judge is advised to ignore it. A second line of defence might be to suggest that there was no causal connection between a threat uttered by his client and some subsequent sickness. To this the judge must reply that 'if the illness is due to natural causes, then the excuse is good. But the evidence indicates the contrary' (p. 220). And what is that *evidence*? Simply if the disease cannot be cured by natural remedies; if the physicians themselves believe that it is due to witchcraft; if other witches are so convinced; or if the illness came on suddenly without warning. Since medieval medical science was likely to aggravate rather than to alleviate the symptoms of almost any ailment known to afflict mankind; since physicians were unlikely to admit that their ministrations had failed to cure a natural disease; since other witches would be convinced that most diseases were of demonic origin; and since many illnesses do manifest themselves without discernible warning—the implications of these criteria are obvious.

Supported by a reluctant and impotent advocate, and with her two most likely defences theoretically feasible but practically impossible, the witch was not likely to give a convincing answer to the charges against her. None the less 'common justice demands that a witch should not be condemned to death unless she is convicted by her own confession' (pp. 222–3), and this was to be obtained, where necessary, by deceit or by force. The deceit resides in using every kind of equivocation, false promise, spies and lies, to trap the accused into an admission of guilt: 'and finally let the Judge come in and promise that he will be merciful, with a mental reservation that he means he will be merciful to himself or the State; for whatever is done for the safety of the State is merciful' (p. 231). If, however, the traps fail, recourse must be had to less subtle means such as detaining the accused 'in case perhaps, being depressed after a year of the squalor of prison, she may confess her crimes' (p. 214). But, if 'after keeping the accused in suspense', with constant postponements and exhortations, she still denies the truth, then the judge should order his officers to proceed to the torture. 'Then let them obey at once', says the *Malleus*, 'but not joyfully' (p. 225). Thus the enthusiastic sadism of the tormenters is involuntarily betrayed. At first torture should be light, bearing in mind that such treatment is often 'fallacious and ineffective'. Some victims are so 'soft-hearted and feeble-minded' that, at the least pain, they will confess anything 'whether it be true or not'; whereas others are so stubborn that they will confess to nothing, however much they are tormented. Some, having suffered previously, are better able to endure the ordeal, 'since their arms have been accommodated to the stretchings and twistings involved'; while others, weakened by previous tribulations, confess too readily. Finally, there are some who, being bewitched, are able to support any pain and die rather than confess anything (p. 243).

This indictment of the inefficacy of torture is complete and convincing. What is the point of these cruelties, since those with nothing to confess are the likeliest to make confession; while the genuinely wicked have a good chance of confessing nothing whatever? The two Dominican authors' acquaintance with God enables them to resolve this difficulty. A witch may confess due to a 'divine impulse conveyed through a holy angel'; or she may confess when the devil withdraws his protection, thus fulfilling God's mysterious purposes (p. 102). So we are left with confessions elicited by torture, which condemn the accused out of her own mouth; and refusal to confess which is equally damning because it reveals demonic assistance. In the former case there is no problem; in the latter, after a suitable time has elapsed, the accused is to be declared an impenitent heretic and handed over to the secular powers for punishment (p. 214).

Even in those wholly hypothetical cases when, due to disagreement amongst witnesses, the accused is 'found to be entirely innocent', she is still not to be so declared. 'Let care be taken', admonish Kramer and Sprenger, 'not to put anywhere in the sentence that the accused is innocent or immune, but that it was not legally proved against him; for if after a little time he should again be brought to trial, and it should be legally proved, he can, notwithstanding the previous sentence of absolution, then be condemned' (p. 241). This is the treatment accorded to the entirely innocent. Others are to be shown commensurate consideration. Even if nothing but ill repute can be established, the accused must submit to a canonical purgation; and if she cannot find the requisite number of supporters she is held to be guilty, and duly convicted (p. 242). Anything worse than ill repute is granted no mercy whatever.

Cases concerning the Faith are to be conducted in a simple and summary fashion, and admit of no appeal. Inconsistently, however, the *Malleus* does envisage the possibility of an appeal to Rome. Should this happen, and should the judges be summoned to appear there, they must avoid fatigue, misery, labour, and expense, 'for by this means much damage is caused to the Church, and heretics are greatly encouraged'. Judges will be less respected and less feared; and other heretics, seeing the judges wearied and detained at Rome, 'will exalt their horns, and despise and malign them, and more boldly proclaim their heresies'. Worse still, when accused they will appeal in the same way, and judges will become less zealous through fear of being involved in similarly protracted proceedings. All this is most 'prejudicial to the Faith of the Holy Church of God; wherefore may the spouse of that Church in mercy preserve her from all such injuries' (p. 275). This awful prospect of endless litigation closes the *Malleus Maleficarum*. But the danger was not really imminent because the authors had already demonstrated how, in practice, appeals could be delayed, shelved, and ultimately denied.

The judicial process advocated in the *Malleus* is inexorable; its inquisitorial procedures were, theoretically, implacable; and technically there would appear to have been no escape once a witchcraft accusation had been initiated. Yet all was well. The devil simply could not defame innocent persons of witchcraft to the extent that they would be condemned to death. 'Here we are dealing with actual events; and it has never yet been known that an innocent person has been punished on suspicion of witchcraft, and there is no doubt that God will never permit such a thing to happen' (p. 136). And that was a comfort: not, perhaps, to the numberless multitudes accused, convicted, and executed for witchcraft; but certainly to the infallible authors, Heinrich Kramer and Jakob Sprenger. Their consciences—like those of Bodin, Rémy, Boguet, Del Rio, De Lancre, and all the other advocates of witch persecution, who followed in their footsteps—were clear. Who could doubt the truth of their case? Were not their authorities evident, and their evidence authoritative?

Notes

1 Henri Boguet, *An Examen of Witches*, trans. E. Allan Ashwin (London, 1929), p. xxxix.
2 The following books all differ in approach, are all open to challenge, but offer serious contributions to the general history of witchcraft. J. C. Baroja, *The World of Witches*, trans. N. Glendinning (London, 1964); R. Mandrou, *Magistrats et Sorciers en France au XVIIe siècle* (Paris, 1968); A. Macfarlane, *Witchcraft in Tudor and Stuart England* (London, 1970); K. V. Thomas, *Religion and the Decline of Magic* (London, 1971), repr. with corrections and additions (London, 1973); J. B. Russell, *Witchcraft in the Middle Ages* (Cornell University Press, 1972); H. C. Erik Midelfort, *Witch Hunting in Southwestern Germany 1562–1684: The Social and Intellectual Foundations* (Stanford University Press, 1972); N. Cohn, *Europe's Inner Demons* (London, 1975).
3 Thomas, *op. cit.* (1973), p. 774.
4 On this problem see Robert-Léon Wagner, *'Sorcier' et 'Magicien': Contribution à l'histoire du vocabulaire de la magie* (Paris, 1939).
5 For valuable general comments on the functioning of magic, see D. P. Walker, *Spiritual and Demonic Magic from Ficino to Campanella* (London, 1958); Frances A. Yates, *Giordano Bruno and the Hermetic Tradition* (London, 1964). On macrocosmology, see Rudolf Allers, 'Microcosmus: From Anaximandros to Paracelsus', *Traditio*, II (1944), pp. 319–407.
6 Lynn Thorndike, *A History of Magic and Experimental Science* (Columbia University Press, New York, 1923–58), II, p. 553.
7 Walker, *op. cit.*, pp. 107–11. See also below, pp. 132–4.
8 Boguet, *op. cit.*, pp. xli–xlii.
9 On demonology in general, see W. C. van Dam, *Dämonen und besessene. Die Dämonen in Geschichte und Gegenwart und ihre Austreibung* (Aschaffenburg, 1970). On aspects of scriptural demonology, see Johannes Smit, *De Daemoniacis in Historia Evangelica* (Rome, 1913); S. Eitrem, *Some Notes on the Demonology in the New Testament*, 2nd ed. (Oslo, 1966); R. S. Kluger, *Satan in the Old Testament* (Northwestern University Press, Evanston, 1967).
10 Noel Taillepied, *A Treatise of Ghosts*, trans. M. Summers (London, n.d.), p. 10.
11 M. Summers, *The History of Witchcraft and Demonology* (London, 1926), pp. 176–81, discusses this episode, and supports the view that it was, indeed, Samuel who appeared before Saul.
12 Jean Bodin, *De la Démonomanie des Sorciers* (Paris, 1580), fol. 1^v. Cf. Summers, *op. cit.*, pp. 191, 203–6. A good example of the extension of witchcraft ideas to passages in the Bible not specifically connected with them may be seen in the

treatment accorded to the First and Third Commandments in John Hooper, *Declaration of the Ten Commandments* in *The Early Writings of John Hooper*, ed. S. Carr (Parker Society, 1843), pp. 307–15, 326–34.
13 Thorndike, *op. cit.*, I, pp. 469–71, 509–10.
14 *Ibid.*, pp. 446, 464, 470, 506–9.
15 See F. X. Gokey, *The Terminology for the Devil and Evil Spirits in the Apostolic Fathers* (Catholic University of America Press, Washington DC, 1961). See also E. Schneweis, *Angels and Demons according to Lactantius* (Catholic University of America Press, Washington DC, 1944).
16 James Calfhill, *Answer to John Martiall's Treatise of the Cross*, ed. R. Gibbings (Parker Society, 1846), pp. 332–3.
17 *Ibid.*, pp. 316–18.
18 See, for example, Johann Bullinger, *The Decades*, trans. and ed. T. Harding (Parker Society, 1849–52), III, pp. 356–63.
19 See H. Obendiek, *Der Teufel bei Martin Luther: eine theologische Untersuchung* (Berlin, 1931).
20 Thorndike, *op. cit.*, IV, p. 129.
21 Henry Holland, *Treatise against Witchcraft* (Cambridge, 1590), sig. A2^r.
22 William Perkins, *Discourse of the Damned Art of Witchcraft* (Cambridge, 1608), p. 197.
23 Thorndike, *op. cit.*, I, pp. 287–97; Yates, *op. cit.*, pp. 1–61; D. P. Walker, 'Orpheus the Theologian and the Renaissance Platonists', *Journal of the Warburg and Courtauld Institutes*, XVI (1953), pp. 100–20.
24 Yates, *op. cit.*, pp. 6–12.
25 Walker, *Spiritual and Demonic Magic*, pp. 40–1.
26 'Dii gentium daemonia sunt' (Psalm 96, Vulgate version). See below, p. 128.
27 Thorndike, *op. cit.*, II, pp. 552–3.
28 *Die Wundergeschichte des Caesarius von Heisterbach*, ed. A. Hilka (Bonn, 1933–7); Caesarius of Heisterbach, *The Dialogue on Miracles*, trans. H. von E. Scott and C. C. Swinton Bland (London, 1929).
29 Bodin, *op. cit.*, fol. 251^{r-v}.
30 Bodin, *op. cit.*, fol. 1^r, opens his argument by defining *Sorcier* as 'celuy qui par moyens Diaboliques sciemment s'efforce de parvenir à quelque chose'.
31 Agrippa, *De occulta philosophia*, I, ii.
32 Bodin, *op. cit.*, fol. 219^v.
33 The most convenient, though too cursory, discussion of this material is in the two great works by Joseph Hansen: *Zauberwahn, Inquisition und Hexenprozesse im Mittelalter und die Entstehung der grossen Hexenverfolgung* (Munich, 1900); *Quellen und Untersuchungen zur Geschichte des Hexenwahns und der Hexenverfolgung im Mittelalter* (Bonn, 1901). H. C. Lea, *Materials Toward a History of Witchcraft*, ed. A. C. Howland (University of Pennsylvania Press, 1939; repr. New York, 1957), I, pp. 260–353, provides interesting though often inaccurate summaries and selection from a variety of fifteenth-century texts.

34 This was Montague Summers's characterisation in the Introduction to the 1946 reprint of his translation of the text. All my references in this chapter are to the first edition of Summers's translation, published by John Rodker (London, 1928).
35 Bull of Pope Innocent VIII, dated 9 December 1484, trans. M. Summers, *Malleus Maleficarum*, pp. xliii–xlv.
36 It now seems to be becoming fashionable to suggest that the *Malleus Maleficarum* has been accorded an exaggerated importance. This may well be true, for the influence of most books tends to be exaggerated by historians. On the other hand, it was reissued more frequently than any other major witch-hunting manual; it was long the most commonly cited; and it remained one of the works which the opponents of persecution sought especially to refute. But perhaps none of this matters.
37 For a concise account of theories concerning the brain, see E. Clarke and K. Dewhurst, *An Illustrated History of Brain Function* (Sandford Publications, Oxford, 1972). See also E. Ruth Harvey, *The Inward Wits: Psychological Theory in the Middle Ages and the Renaissance* (Warburg Institute Surveys, VI, London, 1975).
38 *Malleus Maleficarum*, pp. 87, 134–7, 178, 220.
39 A good example is given by Stillman Drake, 'Renaissance Music and Experimental Science', *Journal of the History of Ideas*, XXXI (1970), pp. 486–7.
40 Lea, *Materials*, I, pp. 264–5, has a brief but highly pertinent comment on the 'permission of God' theory.
41 It was this giving of details concerning infernal conjurations and the like, which so angered Bodin against Weyer. Scot went even further in spelling out such absurdities: and was subsequently used as a magical source book for his pains.

WITCHCRAFT AND MAGIC IN RENAISSANCE ITALY: GIANFRANCESCO PICO AND HIS *STRIX*

Peter Burke

I

Recent research on the intellectual history of Italy in the fifteenth and sixteenth centuries has been marked by a reaction against what might be called the 'whig interpretation' of the Renaissance. The 'whig interpretation of history' was defined by Sir Herbert Butterfield, who coined the phrase, as the tendency of historians to see the past as the story of the conflict between progressives and reactionaries, in which the progressives, or whigs, always win, and in so doing bring about the modern world.[1]

Jacob Burckhardt's famous book may reasonably be described as 'whig' in Butterfield's sense, for Burckhardt saw the Renaissance as the rise of modernity, the Italians of the time as 'the first-born among the sons of modern Europe'. Hence, when in his sixth chapter he came to discuss magic and witchcraft in Renaissance Italy, Burckhardt had a problem. The humanists, as he presents them, were enlightened progressives; magic and witchcraft, on the other hand, were old-fashioned and superstitious. Yet, as Burckhardt knows, humanists did not, for the most part, reject this 'popular superstition' (*populäre Aberglaube*); on the contrary, they took magic and witchcraft quite seriously. Burckhardt tries to resolve the contradiction by assuming that, had it not been for the French invasion and the Counter-Reformation, Italy would have overcome these 'fantastic fooleries' by her own powers.[2]

Burckhardt's solution to his problem has not satisfied his successors, from Aby Warburg onwards. Eugenio Garin, Perkin Walker and Frances Yates have all suggested that the interest in magic shown by Ficino, Giovanni Pico, Cardano, Porta, Bruno, and other Italian Renaissance intellectuals is less odd than Burckhardt thought. Magic was an important part of their world-views. Magic was praised by ancient writers they respected such as Iamblichus, Porphyry, and above all, Hermes Trismegistus, whom they thought an ancient Egyptian writer. The image of man the magus which emerges from the hermetic writings fitted in very well with humanist ideas about the dignity of man. Dr Yates suggests that there was a rise in the status of the magician in the fifteenth and sixteenth centuries, just as there was a rise in the status of the artist. Magic did not merely survive into this period; it was revived. In any case it is impossible to draw a sharp distinction between 'reactionary' magic and 'progressive' science.[3]

Burckhardt wrote about witchcraft and magic as if they were associated; Garin and Walker and Yates confine themselves to magic alone. However, in Italy the fifteenth and sixteenth centuries were not only the time of the revival of magic but also the time of the rise of the 'witch-craze', in the sense of the persecution of witches. Between 1460 and 1525, at least ten Italians published books denouncing witches.[4] Witches were taken very seriously by a number of Renaissance popes, patrons of humanism and the arts; Eugenius IV, Nicholas V, Innocent VIII, Julius II, and Leo X all issued decrees against witches, of which the most notorious is Innocent's bull of 1484, *Summis desiderantes affectibus,* associated with the witch-hunters' manual the *Malleus Maleficarum.*[5] Although reliable figures about executions and other punishments seem impossible to obtain, it appears that the period around the year 1520 marks a peak of witch-hunting in northern Italy.[6]

This coincidence in time between the rise of magic and the rise of the witch-craze in Italy suggests a number of questions. Should witches as well as magicians have a place in our picture of the Italian Renaissance? What was the relationship between humanists and witches? What was the relationship between witchcraft and magic?

A simple answer might run like this. The problem of Renaissance witches is a non-problem, the result of a linguistic confusion. 'Renaissance' is a term which commonly refers both to a movement and a period. Not everyone who lived in the period participated in the movement. On the contrary, there were at least two cultures in Renaissance Italy, that of the educated, who knew Latin and were interested in the revival of learning, and that of the rest, the 'people'. The educated believed in magic; the people believed in witchcraft. If the revival of magic and the rise of the witch-craze occurred together in Italy, that is pure coincidence, for witchcraft and magic in Italy—like witchcraft and magic among the Azande—were quite different activities.[7]

This answer is in fact too simple. Some educated Italians did believe in witchcraft; that is why they wrote treatises and issued decrees against it. In any case the distinction between magic and witchcraft was not a sharp one. There was a cluster of terms in Italian which might be translated 'magician': *mago, nigromante, incantatore* (feminine *incantatrice*), or *sortilego*. These terms referred to people whose use of rituals and spells gave them supernatural powers which they might use for good or evil. There was another cluster of terms which might be translated 'witch', notably *strega* or *stria* (masculine *strigone*), *lammia* and *fattucchiera*. These terms referred to people, mainly women, who did harm by supernatural means without ritual or spells and sometimes even without meaning to do so. A woman with the evil eye could harm children simply by looking at them.[8] However, as the use of the term *strigimago* suggests, the two clusters were not distinguished carefully or consistently. Magicians were often thought to be wicked, and witches to use spells and rituals. This blurring of the distinction between magic and witchcraft had a tradition behind it. In the twelfth century, Hugh of St Victor had divided magic into five parts, of which one was *maleficium,* which he defined as evil deeds done by the help of demons.[9] In the witch-trials of the fifteenth and sixteenth centuries, *maleficium* was one of the most common accusations.

Burckhardt's problem will not go away, however unhappy we may be with his attempts to solve it. The relationship between humanists, magicians and witches needs to be explored further.

II

Did humanists believe in witches? On what grounds? Did they distinguish between witchcraft and magic? For what reasons? To answer these questions it may be useful to begin by looking closely at a single text, although the enquiry obviously cannot end there, for the text may not express typical humanist attitudes, and there may not be any typical humanist attitudes to express. The text I have chosen was published in 1523 by Gianfrancesco Pico della Mirandola (1469–1533), the nephew of the still more famous Giovanni Pico. It is called *Strix*, 'the witch'. Unlike most sixteenth-century books on witchcraft, it is not voluminous and encyclopaedic; on the contrary, it is an elegant and lively little dialogue. It is not surprising that it was quickly published in Italian translation, and that it reached its fourth edition by 1556.[10]

In this dialogue there are four speakers: Apistius, Phronimus, Dicaste and Strix herself. There are three parts or scenes. Scene I begins with the people of Mirandola running to see a witch. This gives Apistius, whose name means 'unbeliever', occasion to express his scepticism about witchcraft. His arguments are answered by Phronimus, whose name means 'prudent'. Then they go and find the witch, and Dicaste, 'the judge', who is in charge of the case, tells her that nothing will happen to her if she answers all their questions.[11] Scene II, the next day, is an interrogation of the witch, and during this exchange Apistius begins to have doubts about his scepticism. Scene III, the same day, is a continuation of the discussion between Apistius and Phronimus, with frequent contributions from Dicaste, and it ends with the conversion of Apistius to the belief that witches really do exist.

Gianfrancesco Pico claims that 'when you listen to the witch speaking, you must believe that you are hearing an accurate account which I have in part seen with my own eyes and in part heard with my own ears, when the records of the trials were read to me.' He explains that his dialogue is a topical one; 'the evil-doing of the witches in our region a few months ago' has led him to write, and he has dashed the work off in ten days.[12]

What does the witch say? She confesses to various activities which she does not classify but which—employing the criteria of educated people of the time—it may be useful to divide into three groups.

In the first place, Strix declares that she goes to what she calls 'the game' (*ludus*) or 'the game of the Lady' (*Dominae ludus*): nocturnal festivities over which a lady presides and in which the participants eat, drink and make love. These festivities have several unnatural or supernatural features. Strix flies to the meeting-place on a linen-mallet—a local variation on the broom-stick—after drawing a circle and anointing herself with a special ointment. The food eaten at the game is not normal food; they kill and eat cattle, but after they have finished, they bring the animals back to life. Strix makes love to a being who is not quite like a normal man. He has goose-feet, a variation on the usual cloven hoof; he is a 'demon' or 'familiar spirit'.

So far the witch's activities (however odd) have sounded harmless enough, but she also confesses to *maleficium*. She causes thunder and hail by drawing a circle; she kills babies by pricking them with needles and sucking their blood; and she uses this blood in her magic ointment.

In the third place, the witch confesses to renouncing and mocking Christianity. She offers consecrated hosts to the 'Lady', who treads and pisses on them. Strix is allowed to continue going to Mass, but she is commanded to say under her breath 'you lie' when the Gospel is read, and at the elevation of the host she has to make a secret obscene gesture.[13]

The other three characters in the dialogue react to this confession as differently as their names imply. Apistius the sceptic begins by declaring that the witch is a bird he has searched for but never found (*strix* meant 'owl' in classical Latin), and that a witch is something which 'the ancients never saw'. In any case, he continues, it is a mistake to believe what the common people say, and it is laughable to think that old women can fly through the air. Apistius's interest in antiquity marks him out as a humanist, and so does the fact that he is presented as well-read in poetry and philosophy, subjects which he thinks closely related, holding that Homer and other poets are full of 'hidden philosophy'. By the middle of the dialogue, Apistius has changed his position on witches. He now declares that doubting should be done in moderation and that he is prepared to agree with the other two, provided that he is compelled by arguments and evidence. By the end of the dialogue his conversion is complete. He changes not only his opinion about witches but his whole way of thinking, and he becomes Pisticus, 'the believer'.

The remaining two characters do not change their minds as the dialogue proceeds, but argue throughout that witches really do exist. Phronimus the pious is presented to the reader as a man who is well-read in the classics and so able to meet Apistius on his own ground. He too assumes that the Greek and Roman poets are full of 'hidden philosophy', and so it is crucial to his argument to show that the ancients do in fact refer to witches. However, where Apistius stressed the need for rational argument and for evidence, Phronimus emphasises 'the authority of our elders, confirmed by public opinion'. Dicaste's role is the less important one of supporting Phronimus. He is not shown to be well-read in secular literature, and he relies on the Bible and the Fathers of the Church rather than the ancient poets and philosophers. Thus the common position held by Phronimus and Dicaste is based on two different kinds of argument, which may be worth considering one by one.

Dicaste's points are the more conventional and so they may be summarised briefly. Anyone who denies the existence of witches ought to be excommunicated, he says, because this is to deny the truth of the Scriptures. In the Old Testament, there are references to witches in Deuteronomy, Leviticus, Isaiah and Jeremiah. In the New Testament, St Matthew relates that the devil carried Christ to Jerusalem and set him on a pinnacle of the temple, and this shows that the devil has the power to make witches fly through the air. Dicaste also refers to the lives of the saints; the temptation of St Antony the hermit, and the attack on him by all sorts of ferocious beasts, is an illustration of the devil's power to create illusions. Is this remark a clue to the popularity of paintings of the temptation of St Antony in the early sixteenth century?[14]

The arguments of Phronimus are rather more unusual for the period, and their relevance to the humanists requires us to deal with them in rather more detail. Phronimus points out that the Greeks knew about witches. Circe was a witch, for Book X of the *Odyssey* describes how she turned the companions of Odysseus into swine by means of her drugs. Incidentally, the choice of this example suggests a possible topical meaning for Dosso Dossi's famous painting of Circe (about 1520); one might add that Gianfrancesco Pico was of the same generation as Dossi and, like him, had close associations with the court of Ferrara.[15] As for Medea, as described in Book III of Apollonius Rhodius's poem the *Argonautica*, she was a priestess of Hecate, a goddess often associated with witches. Medea helped Jason to win the Golden Fleece by giving him a magic ointment to make him invulnerable. She was also notorious for murdering her children. The parallel with witches' ointment and baby-killing is, if not close, obvious enough.

Again, when Apistius laughs at the idea that 'by drawing a circle ... and mumbling I don't know what words', the old women are able to take off on their sticks, Phronimus replies that Apistius really ought to take Homer more seriously: 'we must believe that all the necromancy practised by Odysseus had its origin in the circle'. The reference here is to the opening of Book XI of the *Odyssey,* where Odysseus sacrifices to the dead before he descends to the underworld. 'I drew my sharp sword from my thigh and dug a pit ... and about it, poured a drink-offering to the dead.'

As for Latin literature, two key witnesses called by Phronimus are Ovid and Apuleius. Ovid's *Metamorphoses* have a good deal to say about transformations, magical and otherwise, and in Book VI of his *Fasti* Ovid makes a reference to *striges*, who may be owls or women transformed into owls:

> They fly by night and look for children without nurses, snatch them from their cradles and defile their bodies. They are said to lacerate the entrails of infants with their beaks and they have their throats full of the blood they have drunk. They are called *striges*.

Ovid's treatment of the theme of the 'vampire', as we may call it, is close to the confession of Pico's Strix.

Another important piece of evidence comes from Apuleius, whose *Golden Ass* depends on the assumption that men and women can change their shapes as a result of rubbing themselves with ointment. This is how the hero, Lucius, came to be transformed into an ass, and his girl-friend's mistress, Pamphile, into an owl. Apistius does not make the objection that the *Golden Ass* is a work of fiction; perhaps novelists, like poets, offer hidden philosophy. Nor does he make the point that Strix has not actually confessed to changing her shape. Italian women accused of witchcraft not infrequently confessed to changing into cats, and perhaps Gianfrancesco, as he dashed off this dialogue in ten days, forgot to mention this detail. It should be added that the *Golden Ass* was a book which enjoyed considerable popularity in Italy, especially at the court of Ferrara, at about this time, another indication that we are dealing with a topical subject.[16]

Phronimus may be well-read in the classics, but he does not approve of classical antiquity. Like some medieval writers, he believes that the ancient gods and goddesses really existed, but that they were all 'demons', by which he means 'devils'.[17] In antiquity, the argument goes, the devil induced men to worship him 'under the veil of a false religion'. In the famous beauty contest, 'the devil deceived Paris in the form of three goddesses'. Proteus, so renowned for changes of shape, was a demon, and so was the goddess Diana, who was, he adds, not as chaste as she has been painted. It is Phronimus who identifies 'the game of the Lady' in which Strix had confessed to taking part, with 'the game of Diana', who went about at night with her nymphs. The game is at once a survival from classical antiquity and the work of the devil. It is tempting to juxtapose this account with the contemporary paintings of Diana and her nymphs by Correggio and Palma Vecchio. Were these paintings, like the ones by Bosch and Dossi, more topical than is usually thought?[18]

It should be emphasised that Phronimus does not believe in the power of magic without the devil's aid. 'I do not believe that anything can be transformed into something else by means of ointments or of incantations; . . . incantations . . . do no harm without the evil work of the demons'. The witches are not really transformed into animals, but to human onlookers they seem to be so transformed. It is all an enormous diabolical illusion. The subtitle of the dialogue, 'the deceits of the devil', underlines this theme.

The emphasis on the power of 'demons' is buttressed with references to Plato and his followers, without any allusion to the possibility that the word *daimon* as they used it did not mean 'evil spirit', but simply a being intermediate between the gods and men.[19] These demons, continues Phronimus, once 'had the world in their power', and could persuade 'kings, orators and philosophers' to worship them. However, since the Incarnation things have changed. Nowadays the demons 'can scarcely persuade evil old men and women' to worship them, and what used to be done openly and everywhere as something honourable 'is now done by a few, in secret, in remote and solitary places, as an evil and shameful thing'. Nevertheless devil-worship still goes on, as Apistius, after this prolonged battering with Christian and classical texts, is finally prepared to concede.

III

The beliefs of the four participants in the dialogue are presented vigorously and vividly. Did they also correspond to the positions held by Italians of the time? To answer this question will be our next concern. Only after an attempt has been made to relate the dialogue to the world around it and to see witchcraft through the eyes of contemporaries will it be safe to return to Burckhardt's more general problem of the relation of witchcraft to Renaissance humanism.

Did Dicaste, or someone with views like him, really exist? We are not told whether he is a lay or an ecclesiastical judge, but his arguments resemble those of a number of Dominican friars, 'the hounds of the Lord', some of whom were inquisitors and active in witch-trials. Obvious examples are the German friars Sprenger and Kramer, authors of the notorious *Malleus Maleficarum* (1486), a book cited by Pico. In Italy, denunciations of witches were published by a number of Dominicans, including Vincenzo Dodo (1506), the inquisitor Bernardo da Como (c. 1508), the inquisitor Silvestro de Prierio (1521), and his disciple Bartolomeo de Spina (c. 1523).[20] Like Dicaste, these writers took the confessions of witches seriously; like him, they believed in the physical reality of the game; like him, they cited the Bible and the lives of the saints in support of their arguments. A favourite text was I Kings, XXVIII, on the 'witch of Endor', a diviner who had a familiar (*mulier habens pithonem*), and was consulted by King Saul. These men tended to lump together magic and witchcraft, and the first use I know of the term *strigimagi* occurs in Prierio's book.

These clerical writers seem particularly interested in the sexual activities of witches and demons. The fear of women by the authors of the *Malleus* is apparent in their text and it is part of a medieval tradition of misogyny propagated by celibate clerics.[21] As one might have expected from theologians, these writers were more concerned with the witches' denial of the Faith than with the harm they may have done their neighbours. It is heresy which the inquisitors were most keen to sniff out. They saw the witches in terms of a traditional stereotype of the heretic or false believer. Witches were supposed to go to 'synagogues' or 'sabbaths' like the Jews, or to insult the cross, as the Albigensians were supposed to do. Witches like heretics were believed to have their own rituals, which were seen as an upside-down version of the true faith. Witches were believed to tread on the cross instead of worshipping it and to worship the devil instead of treading on him (as the Virgin does in many images). They were believed to do homage to the devil backwards, using their left hand and kissing his anus. Witches were, quite literally, 'perverse'. These beliefs seem to illustrate an intellectual principle of 'least effort', for it is easier to conceptualise alien beliefs as the exact opposite of our own than to enter into their structure.

The theologians also believed that witches and other heretics engaged in sex orgies, killed children and drank their blood, just like Pico's Strix. In fifteenth-century Italy, the heretic Franciscans, or Fraticelli, and their followers were supposed to have killed children, burned them and drunk their ashes mixed with wine from a cask or *barilotto*. Was this a way of suggesting that heretics were not human? Or did the devout project on to their enemies their own secret wishes?[22]

Did Apistius really exist? This question is rather more difficult to answer. One is tempted to identify him with Pietro Pomponazzi, a contemporary of Gianfrancesco Pico's whose philosophical views were at the opposite end of the spectrum. Where Gianfrancesco attacked Aristotle, Pomponazzi was proud to be an Aristotelian. Pomponazzi did not believe in miracles, in the sense of suspensions of the law of nature, and he did not believe in providence, in the sense of direct interventions by God in the course of history; Gianfrancesco believed in both. Pomponazzi argued that 'all prophecy ... has a natural cause', while Gianfrancesco passionately believed that true prophecy came from God. Pomponazzi argued that angels and demons did not exist, and that the common people simply attributed to demons whatever they were unable to explain, whereas Gianfrancesco saw the work of demons everywhere. Pomponazzi did not have much to say about witchcraft in his books, but it is clear that he could not believe in it because there was no place for it in his world-view. His basic assumption was that everything has natural causes, because 'Nature proceeds in an orderly manner' (*Natura ordinate procedat*). Pomponazzi might well have said that a witch was a bird he had never seen. However, his arguments are not those of Apistius.[23]

The same point may be made of three early-sixteenth-century Italians who wrote in defence of witches: Samuele da Cascini, Gianfrancesco Ponzinibio, and Andrea Alciato. They argue that most of the actions of which suspects are accused did not happen, and so they come out in favour of leniency.

The arguments for the defence, briefly summarised, are as follows. Cascini, a Franciscan friar, rests great weight on a theological argument. To be carried through the air to the game would involve a miracle, but 'no miracle can be involved in committing any sinful act'. The devil does not have the power to move people from one place to another for the purpose of *maleficium*. Consequently, continues Cascini, turning the tables on his opponents, inquisitors who believe that people are carried to the game 'in the body' are themselves heretics. It is true that the accused often confess to being carried in this way ('in body and soul' was Strix's phrase), but the accused are simple country folk who cannot distinguish dream from reality.[24]

Ponzinibio, a lawyer by profession, takes up this second point, which concerns the credibility of testimony. He argues that the misdeeds to which the accused confess are 'imaginary not real', and that one should not be surprised if they take dream for reality 'since they are women, or if they are men, they are rustics, and people who are easily deceived'. The witches do not really insult the host or suck the blood of babies. Ponzinibio also makes a great deal of a text from canon law, the so-called Canon Episcopi, which declares that 'certain wicked women', who are 'seduced by the illusions of devils', believe that they ride at night with the goddess Diana. In other words, witches are wicked and they do yield to the temptations of Satan, but the game is no more than a figment of their imaginations.[25]

If the witches are deceived, it is surely better to regard them as sick than as criminal. This step in the argument was taken by another lawyer, Alciato, who makes the dry comment that many of the supposed witches should have been 'purified' by hellebore (a standard purgative of the period) rather than by fire (*non paucae helleboro potius quam igne purgandae*). Some fifty years later, Montaigne's comment, after he had interviewed a supposed witch, was almost identical.[26]

Have we discovered an original for Apistius? Not exactly. Cascini was a Franciscan friar, and his arguments mainly theological. Ponzinibio and Alciato are more like Apistius because they are laymen and because they agree with him that the testimony of simple people should not be taken very seriously. Alciato quotes Ovid and Virgil in support of his arguments, which brings him still closer to Apistius. However, Ponzinibio and Alciato were professional lawyers, and their arguments often concern technical legal points, whereas the arguments of Apistius do not.

There is another argument in defence of witches which Apistius does not use, the medical, to the effect that witches suffer from melancholy which engenders illusions and makes the sufferers confess to actions which they have not committed. This point was made with force later in the sixteenth century by Girolamo Cardano and Johann Weyer, both professional physicians, but it was already known in Italy in the 1460s. One is left with the impression that Gianfrancesco has created an Apistius who would be more vulnerable to attack than the real defenders of witches were.[27]

What of Phronimus and Strix? Their cases are more complicated and will have to be considered in correspondingly greater detail.

IV

Some of the arguments of Phronimus had been put forward before. In a treatise written in the late 1460s, Ambrogio da Vignate had referred to the operations of Circe as an example of witchcraft.[28] Nevertheless, the emphasis on the argument from classical antiquity is remarkable, even in a dialogue in which other points of view are expressed. It is always dangerous to assume that one of the characters in a dialogue represents the author; the point of choosing the dialogue form is often to suggest to the reader that no one of the views expressed is right, or at any rate not the whole truth. In this instance, however, it seems reasonable to identify the views of Phronimus with those of Gianfrancesco Pico himself. Of the four characters in the dialogue, only three engage in argument. Of these one, Apistius, changes his mind, and another, Dicaste, intervenes mainly to support the third. In any case some of the points made by Phronimus had been made by Gianfrancesco in his own name in earlier writings. To these we must now turn.

In spite of an active political life, Gianfrancesco Pico found the time to write a great deal. A collected edition of his works, published in 1573, runs to 1,378 folio pages, and still leaves out a number of important books, *Strix* among them.[29] These books are dominated by a few recurrent themes; a suspicion of classical antiquity, an interest in the processes of illusion, and a fascination with the supernatural in all its forms.

One of his first books, dedicated in 1496, when he was twenty-seven, concerned *The Study of Divine and Human Philosophy*. Gianfrancesco argued that a Christian should be extremely cautious in reading pagan authors. 'Divine philosophy' is good in itself, but 'human philosophy', in other words secular learning, is good only if it is used for Christian purposes. Poetry is dangerous, for poets often mix obscenities into their verses. Learning is not really necessary for a Christian, for 'the apostles were simple men, for the most part fishermen', and 'God was not pleased to save His people by means of dialectic'. Gianfrancesco returned to this theme in his longest and most important work, the *Examination of the Vanity of Pagan Learning*, published in 1520, a critique of Aristotle in particular but one which calls into question the whole classical tradition.[30]

A second major theme in Gianfrancesco's work is his concern with illusion. In his little treatise *On the Imagination*, published in 1501, he suggests that what is wrong with the imagination is essentially its close connection with the body, so that a man's 'phantasms' or fantasies can vary with the changing balance of his four humours. He adds that bad angels (not, be it noted, melancholy) can 'produce deceitful phantasms in men and women called witches'. In his *Examination*, which I have just mentioned, Gianfrancesco goes further and undermines reason and sensation as well. For example, he points out that an imbalance of the humours can distort sense-perception; to a man with jaundice, the whole world seems yellow. Gianfrancesco has obviously learned from the Hellenistic writer Sextus Empiricus whose defence of scepticism, the *Pyrrhonian Hypotyposes*, was to be influential later in the sixteenth century.[31]

The third theme, the supernatural, dominates another of Gianfrancesco's major works, *On Foreknowledge*, published in 1506–7. Here he discusses a wide variety of ways of foretelling the future, such as: astrology; dream interpretation; prophecy; drawing lots; taking auguries; consulting oracles; chiromancy, geomancy, hydromancy, aeromancy, pyromancy (the 'reading' of hands, earth, water, air, and fire); and so on. He is opposed to all of these except true prophecy, which he thinks a gift direct from God; he thought Girolamo Savonarola, whom he knew personally, to be such a true prophet. Book IV of this treatise is particularly close to the arguments put forward in *Strix*. Gianfrancesco suggests that 'divining is always the result of a secret or open pact with the devil', and that the worship of the pagan gods was encouraged by 'the malice of demons'. The same examples occur here as Phronimus would cite some sixteen years later; the transformations of Proteus, Orpheus as a necromancer, Circe as a witch, and so on.[32]

Like Phronimus, Gianfrancesco Pico pressed new methods into the service of traditional aims, and found new arguments for traditional conclusions. For example, the method of textual criticism developed by Valla and Erasmus and other humanists in order to understand the classics better was taken over by Gianfrancesco to further his argument that the classics were not worth studying. In the *Examination*, he made an analysis of the writings attributed to Aristotle, looking for forgeries, interpolations and corruptions, but this was in order to undermine Aristotle's authority rather than to understand him better. He never seems to have asked the fundamental questions about the text of the Bible which Valla and Erasmus did ask and which he was himself prepared to ask about Aristotle.

Gianfrancesco's use of scepticism was like his use of textual criticism. He was radically sceptical about the possibility of deriving reliable knowledge from sense-data, but he was not prepared even to raise the same fundamental question about knowledge derived from Revelation. He finds it curiously easy to believe that old women could fly through the air and raise storms. One might suggest that he was so credulous (relative to others in his own time) because he was so sceptical; since he lacked the Aristotelian faith in sense-data, he could not dismiss old wives' tales on the grounds of inherent implausibility. Yet it is ironic, to say the least, that the preface to *Strix* stresses what he has seen with his own eyes and heard with his own ears, as if his own senses were less fallible than those of others. The point is surely that scepticism was for him not a way of life but a tool, a weapon; its purpose was 'to destroy philosophy to make more room for religion'.[33]

In short, throughout his life Gianfrancesco played the part of a Phronimus, meeting the humanists on their own ground in order to convert them. He might be described as a new Justin Martyr, for Justin was a second-century convert from paganism who spent the rest of his life trying to convert other educated pagans. Gianfrancesco translated a work he believed to have been written by Justin, the *Admonitorius*. Had he been born a generation later, Pico would have made an excellent Jesuit; like them he treated classical learning as the 'spoils of the Egyptians', something for Christians to pillage for their own ends.

V

The debate on witchcraft in early-sixteenth-century Italy suggests that the differences of opinion expressed in the dialogue corresponded to real disagreements between the educated men of the time, even if certain legal and medical points did not get a fair hearing. What of Strix herself? What did she think she was doing? Does her confession correspond to any reality? The attitudes and values of the uneducated in the sixteenth century are necessarily elusive, but if we do not attempt to recover them we risk misunderstanding the views of the educated as well.[34]

To begin with the obvious: Gianfrancesco did not make up the stories he puts into the witch's mouth. They correspond closely to stories current in earlier treatises, notably the *Malleus* and the books by Bernardo da Como and Bartolomeo de Spina. Gianfrancesco certainly read the *Malleus* and he probably read the other two as well.[35]

Do the confessions of Strix represent anything more than a literary tradition? Similar confessions were in fact made by a number of Italians who had been accused of witchcraft in the years just before Gianfrancesco wrote, notably at Breno (north of Brescia) in 1518, and at Sondrio (north-west of Breno) in 1523. At Breno the accused declared that they went on horseback to a certain mountain, where they found a multitude of people singing and dancing and were given 'a certain ointment' which would carry them there in future mounted on sticks. This festivity they called the *zuogo*, a dialect form of *giuoco*, 'game'. They also confessed to denying the faith; 'making a cross on the ground they trampled upon it and spat upon it'. Finally, they confessed to taking an oath to do 'all kinds of evil', and they were given 'a certain powder', which could kill people or raise tempests. The proceedings were supervised by a Lord, not a Lady, but the parallel between these confessions and Strix's account remains close.[36]

The Sondrio trials follow the same pattern. For example, a certain Bartolomeo Scarpategio confessed to going to 'the game of the cask' (*il zogo del bariloto*), a term reminiscent of the trials of the fifteenth-century Fraticelli. There he saw 'a large fire . . . a great multitude of people who danced around it . . . a great lord who sat in a chair, dressed in red, who had horns on his head, and claws on his hands and feet, who was the devil'. There Bartolomeo 'denied God and the faith' (*renega la sancta fede e Messer Domenedio*), and promised to be faithful to the devil, touching his left hand. He also trod, spat and pissed on a wooden cross and 'made figs at it' (*ge fece le fiche*), precisely Strix's gesture at Mass. He carried the host there and insulted it. In return he was given a demon mistress.[37]

In neither of these trials was any reference made to Diana, or indeed to any 'Lady', but this gap is filled by two trials at Modena, which is south of Mirandola, in the 1530s. Domenica Barbarelli declared in 1532 that she went 'on the journey of Diana' (*ad cursum Diane*) and that she profaned the cross and danced with demons by order of 'the Lady of the game'. Orsolina la Rossa, seven years later, confessed to going to the 'Sabbath' over which 'a certain woman' presided, and renouncing the Christian faith.[38]

Thus we have no reason to doubt Gianfrancesco's word when he says that Strix's confession is an accurate account derived from the records of the trials at Mirandola.[39] However, our problems do not end here; they only begin. If we try to use the confessions as a source for popular beliefs of the time, we find that they are not pure but contaminated. The confessions are the product of a situation in which an interrogator, usually a friar, is face to face with the accused, who more often than not has no formal education, while a clerk takes down what is being said. The historian has access to the clerk's record, often in Latin, of an interrogation in which the interrogator, who was often a stranger to the region, probably spoke literary Italian while the accused replied in dialect. The possibilities for misunderstanding are considerable. The interrogator has been through it all many times before and knows, all too well, what he is trying to find. The accused is new to the business and may be searching frantically for cues and clues as to what is wanted. The interrogator had power over the accused, including the power to torture, and the accused knew this. As Girolamo Cardano pointed out in the 1550s, confessions by witches are not to be trusted because 'these things are said under torture, when they know that a confession of this type will bring the torture to an end'.[40] In other words, the accused will tell the interrogators what they expect to hear, and what they expect to hear is what they have read about in treatises like the *Malleus*. The treatises describe what is confessed in the trials, but then the confessions follow the model of the treatises. It is a vicious circle.

Have we any more chance of escaping from this circle than the accused and their interrogators? Yes, on two conditions. The first is that we allow for alternative hypotheses at almost every stage of the investigation. The second condition is that we put the question, 'Was X guilty of witchcraft?', on one side and ask a series of more open questions instead. What kinds of people were accused of being witches? What was the social context of these accusations? We can then put the crucial question of what (if anything) the accused thought they were doing, of what their actions meant to them.[41]

What kinds of people were accused of witchcraft in Italy? Members of all the main groups in society might be accused of witchcraft on occasion, but not with the same frequency. Until more quantitative studies are made, we shall have to rely on impressions, and my impression is that in Italy, as elsewhere, women were accused of witchcraft more frequently than men, and also that the clergy were accused more frequently than the laity, relative to their proportion in the total population. It was not just any woman or priest who would be accused of witchcraft. Most vulnerable to the accusation were those who regularly foretold the future, discovered thieves, sold love-philtres, worked abortions, delivered babies and cured the sick by means of herbs, prayers and rituals. In Italy these people were known as *herbarie*, *girovaghi*, *guaritori*, *sortilegi*, and so on, terms which might best be translated into the sixteenth-century English 'cunning men' and 'wise women'.

Thus Guglielmo Campana, a parish priest of Modena, tried in 1517, detected thefts and prepared philtres; Benvegnuda, a woman accused at Breno in 1518, was said to have cured many people, especially from *maleficium*, and to possess 'an incantation to make a man love a woman or a woman a man'; Giuliano Verdena, a weaver of Mantua, tried in 1489, was said to fill a vessel with water and discover the images of thieves in it—an example of the 'hydromancy' attacked by Gianfrancesco Pico.[42]

It is not difficult to see how people like this should have been identified as witches by inquisitors like Dicaste. They were sometimes accused by members of their local community, and this too should occasion no surprise. Since they were in close touch with the supernatural, the 'witch-doctors' were liable to be treated as witches themselves. As a witness in a trial in

Modena put it in 1499, 'Knowing how to heal means knowing how to harm' (*Qui scit sanare scit destruere*).⁴³ If misfortune struck, if a man were taken ill, if he found himself impotent on his wedding night, if his crops were destroyed by hail, then the wise women were the obvious scapegoat, though not the only one. We do not have the evidence to reconstruct the victim's point of view in depth and detail. We can only link the fragments of evidence by speculation, but we must do this (however briefly or reluctantly) in order to understand what was going on. Perhaps the victim felt guilty for some offence done to the accused; perhaps he felt envied. In any case it is not too difficult to see why private accusations of witchcraft were made, or why laymen appealed to the inquisitors. Thus in Lombardy in the mid-fifteenth century, the inhabitants of two communities, Bellano and Porlezza, petitioned the duke of Milan to call in the Inquisition against the local witches.⁴⁴

But what did the accused think they were doing? This is the most elusive of all the questions. 'Nothing at all' might be the answer in some cases, because the accuser had imagined everything. More complicated are the cases involving folk-healers. The accused tried to cure their clients by means of rituals and formulae, including prayers like the Our Father and the Hail Mary. Under interrogation they might claim to cure by the power of God and the saints; Benvegnuda, accused at Breno in 1518, declared that she cured people in the name of the Virgin Mary and St Julian. What is one to make of a man who practised love-magic using texts of the Psalms?⁴⁵ It is virtually impossible to decide whether he thought he was acting like a good Christian or whether he was consciously playing with fire. He seems to have thought of the Psalms as possessing supernatural power by themselves; and this suggests the hypothesis that if the accused really did take away consecrated hosts from church, as they sometimes confessed to doing, like Strix in Pico's dialogue, this was to make use of its powers, not, as the inquisitors thought, to insult it. Where the healers must have known they were on trickier ground was where they worked *maleficium* against their clients' enemies, sticking pins into images and so on; and from the victim's point of view, even love-magic was a form of *maleficium*.

However, *maleficium* was not what the inquisitors were really looking for. What about the orgies, the flights through the air, the homage to the devil and all the rest of it? One possibility is (as Cardano suggested) that the accused simply admitted to whatever their interrogators seemed to want in order for the torture to end. This explanation seems plausible enough, yet it does not always work; one writer against witches, the layman Paolo de Grillandi, tells us that he was convinced of the reality of witchcraft after hearing confessions where torture was not applied. There are records of such trials still surviving, and they deserve to be taken seriously as evidence, all the more because the confessions sometimes surprised the interrogators; in other words did not conform to their stereotype of the witch. A series of cases which took the inquisitors by surprise occurred in the 1570s in the north-east corner of Italy, in Friuli; they have recently been the subject of a brilliant monograph. The accused called themselves 'go-gooders' (*benandanti*). They met at night four times a year. They denied being witches on the grounds that they fought the witches on these expeditions; they fought with sticks of fennel and the witches with sticks of maize; 'And if we win, that year is an abundant one, and if we lose there is famine that year'. They went on to explain that they did not go in the body but in the spirit; it was important that their body was lying face upwards while the spirit was away, so that it could re-enter.[46]

This point supports another suggestion of Cardano's, that confessions of attendance at the 'sabbath' were merely descriptions of dreams. He raises the objection that it is odd for many different people to dream the same dream, but this point can be answered on the basis of twentieth-century research. There is evidence that culturally stereotyped dreams often occur in some societies. The Ojibwa Indians are a case in point, and so are the Nyakyusa of Tanzania, among whom 'defenders' (*abamanga*) regularly fight witches in their dreams, just like the *benandanti*.[47] People may dream in a stereotyped way if they expect to do so, and they often dream the folklore of their culture. The story of Diana and her ladies going about at night and entering people's houses was part of Italian folklore, the local equivalent of the English tales of Robin Goodfellow. It would not be too surprising if people dreamed of Diana, or if lonely old women had wish-fulfilment dreams of feasting and sexual intercourse and of doing their enemies harm.

It seems reasonable to conclude that the idea of witchcraft is a composite one, including popular elements, such as destructive magic and flight through the air, as well as learned or clerical elements, such as devil-worship.[48]

VI

In the last few pages we have looked at witch-trials as a form of drama in which the fantasies of the victim, the accused, and the inquisitor all had their part. It is necessary, in conclusion, to explain why the plot of this drama changed over time, and so to return to the Burckhardtian problem with which we began. In England in Tudor and Stuart times there is evidence of increased demand at the village level for witches to be tried and condemned.

No evidence of this kind has been found for Italy, at least so far. What changed was the clerical view of the witch.

The clerical stereotype of the witch as a human servant of Satan seems to have been formed in the fourteenth and fifteenth centuries. If we ask, Where did this stereotype come from? the answer is fairly simple: heretics had long been believed to engage in sex orgies, worship the devil, kill children and drink their blood. All that was new was the tendency to attribute these crimes to people accused of the equally traditional offence of *maleficium*.[49]

But why should the stereotype of the heretic have been extended to include the witch? Why should inquisitors have become more concerned with witches in the fourteenth and fifteenth centuries? One possibility is that they were worried by the rise of heresy (the Lollards in the fourteenth century, the Hussites in the fifteenth) and so began to find heretics everywhere. In the case of Italy, we find inquisitors acutely concerned with both heresy and witchcraft in the 1520s, the decade of Pico's dialogue, the treatises of Prierio and Spina, but also of the penetration of Lutheran ideas into Italy.[50]

Yet why should witches in particular come to be seen as dangerous? I believe that the arguments which Gianfrancesco Pico puts into the mouth of Phronimus give us a valuable clue and that, in Italy at least, the rise of the witch-hunts and the rise of the Renaissance are connected. In Florence, it has recently been noted, 'the advent of humanism coincided with a revival of sorcery persecution', in the late fourteenth and early fifteenth centuries.[51] What could the connection between witches and the Renaissance be? That complex movement we call the Renaissance involved, among other things, the revival of interest in antiquity, including the ancient gods and goddesses. For some of the clergy, as for Phronimus, these gods were 'demons', so they believed that they were witnessing a revival of the demonic. In this context the confessions of certain women that they had attended 'the game of Diana' must have confirmed clerical suspicions.[52]

The Renaissance also involved a revival of interest in magic among the learned, in Italy and elsewhere. Humanists were careful to distinguish 'spiritual' from 'demonic' magic, let alone from witchcraft. The clergy, as we have seen, did not make these distinctions. For them a rise of magic was a rise of witchcraft, which had to be fought; an interest in demons was an interest in devils. When one reads in *Pimander* (one of the hermetic writings taken most seriously by the humanists) that the soul leaves the sleeping body and consorts with demons in order to obtain magical powers, and when one turns to the confessions of the *benandanti* about their adventures out of the body, it is not difficult to see how the inquisitors might have thought that they were dealing with a unified movement.[53]

Perhaps it is not so surprising to find cultivated Italians like Nicholas V, Innocent VIII, Leo X and Gianfrancesco Pico taking witches as seriously as they did. If men could gain control of supernatural forces for good purposes, why not also for evil? Given this possibility, the traditional rituals and fantasies of cunning men and wise women now appeared in a new and sinister light, as a conspiracy of the servants of Satan. Inquisitors were dispatched to bring the conspirators to justice, and the witch-craze got under way.

Notes

1. H. Butterfield, *The Whig Interpretation of History*, London, 1931.
2. J. Burckhardt, *Kultur der Renaissance in Italien* (1860), ch. 6; cf. H. R. Trevor-Roper, *The European Witch-Craze*, Harmondsworth, 1969, p. 116.
3. E. Garin, 'Magia ed astrologia nella cultura del Rinascimento', and 'Considerazioni sulla magia', both repr. in his *Medioevo e Rinascimento*, second ed., Bari, 1961; D. P. Walker, *Spiritual and Demonic Magic from Ficino to Campanella*, London, 1958; Frances A. Yates, *Giordano Bruno and the Hermetic Tradition*, London, 1964.
4. Giordano de Bergamo, Bernardo da Como, Vincenzo Dodo, Paolo de Grillandi, G. F. Pico, Silvestro de Prierio, Bartolomeo de Spina, Gianbattista Theatino, Tommaso de Vio, Girolamo Visconti.
5. J. Hansen, *Zauberwahn, Inquisition und Hexenprozesse im Mittelalter*, Munich, 1900, pp. 500f.
6. W. G. Soldan, *Geschichte der Hexenprozesse*, ed. M. Bauer, 1911, I, pp. 554f.
7. E. E. Evans-Pritchard, *Witchcraft, Oracles and Magic among the Azande*, Oxford, 1937.
8. On the evil eye in Italy, compare L. Vair, *De fascino* (1583; I used the Venice, 1599 ed.), with E. de Martino, *Sud e magia*, Milan, 1959.
9. Quoted in Lynn Thorndike, *A History of Magic and Experimental Science*, Columbia University Press, New York, 1923–58, II, p. 14.
10. G. F. Pico, *Strix*, Bologna, 1523 (I have not seen this edition, but worked from that of Strasbourg, 1612). Italian versions were published in 1524, 1555 and 1556.
11. Leandro Alberti, who made the 1524 translation, pointed out what the names of the protagonists meant.
12. G. F. Pico, preface.
13. 'Flexis post tergum manibus sub veste digitos . . . complicarem'. The 1555 translation renders this as 'facere la fica', itself defined in Hoare's *Short Italian Dictionary*, Cambridge, 1923, as 'a gesture of insolent contempt made by extending the hands with the thumbs clasped between the first and second fingers'.
14. Examples include the paintings by Bosch in Berlin, Madrid and Lisbon.

15 The Circe is discussed by F. Gibbons, *Dosso and Battista Dossi*, Princeton, 1968, pp. 215f.
16 At the court of Ferrara, Matteo Boiardo translated the *Golden Ass* and Duke Ercole d'Este read it with enthusiasm; E. H. Gombrich, *Symbolic Images*, London, 1972, p. 209, n. 58.
17 J. Seznec, *The Survival of the Pagan Gods*, Eng. trans., New York, 1961 ed., p. 48.
18 E. Battisti, *L'Antirinascimento*, Milan, 1962, p. 143.
19 The classic account of demons as good spirits is Apuleius, *On the God of Socrates*; the classic attack on this view is Augustine's *City of God*, VIII, 14.
20 These writers are most accessible in J. Hansen, *Quellen und Untersuchungen*, Bonn, 1901, pp. 281f. See also G. Bonomo, *Caccia alle streghe*, Palermo, 1959, pp. 253f (Bernardo) and pp. 331f (Prierio and Spina); and H. C. Lea, *Materials Toward a History of Witchcraft*, New York, 1957, pp. 354f.
21 On the misogynist tradition, see Bonomo, pp. 201f.
22 N. Cohn, *Europe's Inner Demons*, London, 1975, pp. 44f (the Fraticelli), and pp. 259f (projection).
23 P. Pomponazzi, *De naturalium effectuum causis sive de incantationibus* (written 1520; posthumously published, Basle, 1556).
24 S. da Cascini, *Question de le strie* (1505), repr. in Hansen, *Quellen*, pp. 263f. On Italian defenders of witches, see Bonomo, pp. 359f.
25 G. F. Ponzinibio, *De lamiis* (written c. 1520), Frankfurt, 1592.
26 A. Alciato, *Parergon* (written c. 1515), in Hansen, *Quellen*, pp. 310f. Cf. Montaigne, *Essais*, III, 11, 'Je leur eusse plustost adonné de l'ellebore que de la cicue'.
27 G. Cardano, *De rerum varietate*, Basle, 1557, especially ch. 8; J. Weyer, *De Praestigiis Daemonum* (1563), Basle, 1566 ed., especially Book 3, ch. 23. On Cardano, see Bonomo, pp. 379f; and Lea, pp. 435f.
28 Ambrogio's remarks on Circe can be found in Hansen, *Quellen*, pp. 215f. Cf. Augustine, *City of God*, XVIII, 17; and the *Malleus*, Part 2, Question 1, ch. 8.
29 On him see C. B. Schmitt, *Gianfrancesco Pico della Mirandola and his critique of Aristotle*, The Hague, 1967; bibliographical details in appendix A.
30 G. F. Pico, *Opera*, Basle, 1573.
31 G. F. Pico, *De imaginatione*, ed. H. Caplan, New Haven, 1930, p. 56. On Sextus in the sixteenth century, see R. H. Popkin, *The History of Scepticism from Erasmus to Descartes*, Assen, 1964, ch. 1.
32 G. F. Pico, *Opera*, Basle, 1573, pp. 481f.
33 E. Garin, *Italian Humanism*, Eng. trans. Oxford, 1965, p. 133.
34 On this elusiveness, P. Burke, 'Oblique approaches to the study of popular culture', in C. Bigsby, ed., *Approaches to Popular Culture*, London, 1976.
35 Spina takes some of his evidence from the Ferrara region and says that the plain of Mirandola is an important meeting-place for witches. He and Pico both mention the unusual detail of the witches calling their meeting-place the 'Jordan'.

36 For the Breno trials, the evidence is a letter written to the Venetian government by the local castellan, which summarises the confessions and was copied by Sanudo into his diary; M. Sanudo, *I Diarii*, 58 vols, Venice, 1879–1901, vol. 25, pp. 545f, 632f.
37 F. Odorici, *Le Streghe di Valtellina*, Milan, 1862, pp. 92f, prints the confessions. On the *barilotto*, see Cohn, pp. 46f.
38 C. Ginzburg, *I Benandanti*, Turin, 1966, pp. 35f; cf. Bonomo, pp. 65f, on Diana in one of the earliest Italian witch-trials, at Milan in 1385.
39 These records do not appear to have survived.
40 'Haec in tormentis fatentur, cum sciant huiuscemodi confessionem exitio illis futuram.' G. Cardano, *De rerum varietate*, Basle, 1557, p. 567.
41 Cf. recent approaches to the study of English witches: A. Macfarlane, *Witchcraft in Tudor and Stuart England*, London, 1970; and K. V. Thomas, *Religion and the Decline of Magic*, London, 1971.
42 On Campana, see Bonomo, p. 234; on Benvegnuda, see Sanudo (as note 36); on Verdena, see Ginzburg, pp. 56f.
43 Ginzburg, p. 88. The first use of the term 'witch-doctor' (in 1718) cited by the *O.E.D.* comes from an English context of folk-healing.
44 L. Fumi, 'L'inquisizione romana e lo stato di Milano' in *Archivio Storico Lombardo*, XIII–XIV, 1910, pp. 105f.
45 A certain Jacopo of S. Miniato, whose case is described in G. Brucker, 'Sorcery in early Renaissance Florence', in *Studies in the Renaissance*, X, 1963.
46 Ginzburg, *op. cit.*
47 Cardano, *op. cit.* On culturally stereotyped dreams in the sixteenth and seventeenth centuries, see P. Burke, 'L'histoire sociale des rêves', in *Annales, E.S.C.*, March–April 1973, pp. 329f. On the Nyakyusa 'defenders', see M. H. Wilson, 'Witch-beliefs and social structure', in M. Marwick, ed., *Witchcraft and Sorcery*, Harmondsworth, 1970, p. 254. E. Jones, *The Nightmare*, second ed., London, 1949, pp. 203f, discusses the relation between dreams and the witches' sabbath.
48 On Diana in medieval folklore, see Cohn, *op. cit.*, pp. 212f; on witch-beliefs as an 'amalgam', pp. 147f.
49 Cohn, chapters 2 and 3, correcting Hansen's dating of the stereotype to the late fifteenth century.
50 On heresy in Italy in the 1520s, D. Cantimori, *Eretici italiani del '500*, second ed., Florence, 1967, ch. 4.
51 Brucker, *op. cit.*, p. 8.
52 See notes 17 and 38.
53 Walker (note 3) is concerned with the distinction between spiritual and demonic magic; the passage from *Pimander* is discussed by Yates, p. 280.

JOHANN WEYER'S *DE PRAESTIGIIS DAEMONUM*: UNSYSTEMATIC PSYCHOPATHOLOGY

Christopher Baxter

Johann Weyer (1515/16–1588) was a Lutheran physician, doctor to Duke William III of Berg, Julich and Cleves, territories on the lower Rhine.[1] He gained notoriety for his bold stand against the burning of witches in the *De Praestigiis Daemonum* (On the Wiles of Devils), the first edition of which appeared in 1563 at Basle, and was quickly followed by many genuinely revised and enlarged editions, and several translations.[2] It was largely discredited by Jean Bodin's scathing refutation in the *Démonomanie* (1580).

Weyer has become a symbol, as he is for example to Trevor-Roper, of courage and lucidity in the face of intolerance and ignorance.[3] This interpretation derives largely from the writings of the great rationalist historians of witchcraft, and to a much lesser extent from a reading of the *De Praestigiis* taken as a whole. For whilst Weyer wants greater tolerance towards alleged witches, he also, and in the first instance, even in the notorious sixth book, wants greater severity towards magicians. In the preface he describes the sixth book as 'un accessoire aux precedens' in which '[il] donne avis touchant la punition des magiciens infames, lesquels avec Simon et Elymas divertissent l'estat public lors qu'il est en paix'. He felt impelled to add it because the 'magiciens et sacrileges, qui estoient grievement punis sous la loy de Moyse, conversoyent aujourd'hui impunément, voire avec louange, entre plusieurs'. In a real sense the work is a protest against policies of toleration.

We should bear in mind that Weyer constantly advocates the persecution of the sorcerer as defined by Bodin in the *Démonomanie*. He has simply reversed back on the figure of the magician the late medieval transference of the image of the learned, demon-worshipping magician onto the popular image of the witch.⁴ And this image of the demon-worshipping magician is then applied to the Catholic priest. Far from demolishing the stereotype of the evil sorcerer, he gives it immediate and dangerous application.

The fifth book is largely devoted to an attack on Catholic magic as it is used to cure the possessed; and against this magic Weyer advocates a simple non-ceremonial piety, and the use of the 'sacrez remedes de la médecine', an advocacy which constitutes 'le principal but de toute la peine que j'ay entreprise en cest oeuvre'.⁵ In other words the work is—in its very conception —an ideological attack on Catholic idolatry and superstition, and cannot be seen as an innocent work of Erasmian non-sectarian tolerance.⁶

Weyer is nothing if not honest, and the preface begins with an open declaration of incompetence. The task of outwitting the devil in his craftiness is 'une chose malaisee et dificile, laquelle surmonte mes forces'. Demonic guile is such that 'l'on se void manifestement trompé et deceu, nonobstant tous les moyens par lesquels on les pense assaillir'. Weyer says he has found in the Gospel the thread, the clue, to escape from the 'labyrinthe des enchante-ments'. It is the main theme of this present essay that Weyer's evangelical escape route is more like a blind alley, and that the scriptural thread leads him into inextricable tangles.

Referring, like subsequent critics, mainly to the sixth book, Weyer's translator writes that the work should be judged 'en regardant au but, qui est de se destourner de Satan pour adherer à Jesus Christ'. The translator himself cautiously refrains from judgment on Weyer's arguments about witches and adds Erastus's attacks on Weyer, and advocacy of witch burning, so that we may make up our own mind. He does, however, give the last word to Erastus, who concludes firmly but compassionately that just as Weyer has excused witches on the grounds that they are deluded by melancholy, so Weyer himself is to be excused on the grounds that he is deceived by misplaced, sentimental humanitarianism.⁷ Erastus's balanced conclusion is all the more striking because he shares Weyer's religious view-point, and is thus attacking from a quarter from which Weyer had not expected to be challenged; and because he fully admits that many witch prosecutions involve cases of mistaken identity.

Book One: The Devil

Book One begins with a history of the devil, from the original revolt of Satan to the recent revolt of Luther, against Rome. The main stress lies on the terrifying quasi-universality of his powers. After seducing Eve, he so successfully gained people's worship that God angrily wiped out the entire human race with the exception of Noah's family.

Even then the devil was soon back in business, and taught Misraim, son of Ham, son of Noah, the impious blasphemy of black magic, 'la magie infame'. It was not long before he had skilfully recaptured the worship of the whole world by engineering seductive but diabolical ceremonies. And this is the world we live in. After affirming that Catholic saints are worshipped in just the same way that Turks worship their devils, Weyer defends the enormous length of his catalogue of gentile gods—who are quite literally devils—as a necessary warning to those still in thrall to pagan deities: 'a celle fin que ceux qui pour le iourd'huy s'en aident encores, se puissent souvenir que les diables se cachent souventesfois en leurs barboteries et exorcismes, sous le manteau des paroles barbares et inconues' (ch. 6, p. 18). All this comes close to equating Catholic saints themselves with devils.

Not that such a degree of effrontery and cunning is beyond Weyer's devil, who to enhance his credibility, enabled the Sibyls to prophesy the coming of Christ (ch. 8). More immediately alarming is Weyer's view that the superstitious ceremonies prevalent in the Catholic world are directly inspired by the devil:

> En fin, et non sans grande astuce, le diable a machiné . . . que non seulement une mesme façon de luy servir fust observee es parties de tout le monde, les plus esloignees les unes des autres . . . mais aussi (ce qui est plus esmerveillable, et plus à douloir) que l'honneur lui fust rendu par une mesme ceremonie en nostre Chrestienne Europe, sous des idoles de diverse matière, et de divers noms (ch. 9, p. 25).

The devil has, then, turned the Roman Church into a front organisation. For instance, the baptism and exorcism of bells, ceremonies overtly designed to prevent the devil getting hold of them, are in fact devilish deceits to fill the organisation's coffers. We should however note that Weyer does think that exorcism of people *is* legitimate if carried out by those who 'ont puissance et don particulier de chasser les diables hors de leur siege',[8] that there is, in other words, a good (Protestant) Christian magic as well as a bad (Catholic) pseudo-Christian magic. Weyer ends these first nine chapters on the powers of the enemy with an extraordinary lamentation on the powers of the enemy drawn from Lactantius, Tertullian and St Augustine (ch. 9, pp. 27-9).

The rest of the first book is largely concerned with the various *modi operandi* of devils. These powers are said to derive, as in the Augustinian view, from their 'tenureté, subtilité, vitesse incroyable'. It is these physiological qualities, combined with the fact that they have been accumulating experience ever since the Creation, that enables them to prophesy successfully—as via the Sibyls—on the basis of their knowledge of the Scriptures (ch. 10, p. 30).[9]

In these circumstances one would think it difficult to be sure whether any prophecy is true and divine, true and diabolical, or false and diabolical. Of the longstanding Scholastic debate on the possibility of *divine* deception Weyer seems unaware.[10] Weyer's tone is sanguine, his confidence complete. Yet chapter ten gives several examples of partly truthful but diabolical prophecies, whose deceptiveness is by no means immediately apparent (ch. 10, pp. 30ff). Later Weyer will refer to the witch of Endor and Samuel's ghost which, whilst it prophesied truthfully, was yet inspired by the devil (Bk II, ch. 10). Similarly, the devil recognised Christ as son of God before the apostles did, and foresaw Christ's power to overthrow him. In this case Weyer does admit to some embarrassment, and concludes that the devil, in his hatred, will stop at nothing (Bk II, ch. 11, p. 36).

Weyer seems almost literally fascinated, spell-bound, by the cunning of the devil, and spends five chapters recounting with leisured glee the crafty tricks he gets up to, in order to obtain worship and so occasion eternal torment to those he deceives. A hint of the reason for the blissfully sanguine mood in which these hair-raising stories are told appears when Weyer recounts his successful treatment of a young girl tossed around by the devil, who had filled her ears with insects (earwigs?). Weyer, the evangelical doctor, tackles the case with confidence, for as he says, 'pourquoy Dieu ne m'auroit il autant fait de graces pour subvenir à telles afflictions comme il a permis au Diable de poursuyvre ses practiques en mal faisant?' (ch. 12, p. 42).

Weyer's staunchly anti-Catholic faith enables him coolly to treat as absolutely parallel exorcisms by holy water and by some magic root. He is almost aggressively simple-minded, treating the tale of the Pied Piper of Hamelin as obvious fact; assuming that a story about a mouse running in and out of a soldier's mouth is a devilish trick to encourage belief in a corporeal soul; solemnly recounting a choice cock-and-bull story told him by a friend, who claimed to have met the devil, as evidence that all the rest of his stories are *not* 'controuvees comme folies'.[11] As Weyer enters into the spirit of the thing, the 'tromperies des diables' become quite blatantly frauds perpetrated by Catholic priests, and are nothing to do with diabolic delusions. The stories are told because they are good stories from the stock of a simple-minded Lutheran believer.

The function of the devils in all this is clear. Without the struggle against them man could not earn eternal salvation. Since, without them, there would presumably be no eternal damnation either, we may legitimately muse on the disturbing theological implications. Weyer concentrates only on the saving message of the Gospels, and of Christ's power over devils (Luke VIII): 'Il y avoit encore des impostures du diable il n'y a pas long temps: assavoir un peu devant que la doctrine de l'Evangile eust reconnue et repurgee des tenebres de superstition'. These fairy dances have stopped since the 'pure et fervente predication de l'Evangile a commencé à sonner aux oreilles des hommes' (ch. 22, p. 97).

Weyer now attempts to give criteria for distinguishing diabolical from divine activity. The first criterion is this: miracles produced by good spirits are beneficial—like those of Christ; wonders produced by evil spirits are useless—like those of Simon Magus. But no reason is given for supposing that Christ's healing miracles are not another diabolical blind; or, on the other hand, for supposing that cures effected by witches are not beneficial. And whilst Simon Magus did 'useless' things like flying, and mountainshifting, it is also the case that such activities were hardly condemned by Christ, who proved the faith that can move mountains, and who walked on water.

The second criterion advanced by Weyer is that good spirits create a mood of reassurance and confidence, and that evil spirits instil terror. Yet here again, how does one distinguish between the genuine activities of an angel of light and those of a transformed devil? How does one account for the lack of fear in the Hermetic magi of the sixteenth century, or for that matter of the Catholic worshippers of saints? It may be some such thoughts of the scope afforded to the activities of the devil by any of his criteria, that leads Weyer to discuss next the limitations set on the devil's power.

According to Weyer, devils can imitate miracles, but not effect them in reality. Thus Pharaoh's wizards only apparently changed their rods into serpents, turned the rivers to blood and brought up frogs upon the land of Egypt. But other miracles of Moses they could not even imitate. The sense in which we should regard the plagues that smote the land of Egypt as beneficial is not explored. Furthermore, just as devils can imitate miracles, arbitrarily limited to those acts which are testified by Scripture, witches cannot be enabled by devils to perform any supernatural acts at all. Indeed their minds are literally so thick, that the subtle powers of the devil would be blunted if he were to try to operate through them (ch. 24, p. 108).[12]

Book Two: Magicians

We are left to assume in the preceding discussion that magicians who attempt to collaborate with a devil do not labour under the same difficulty.

But even though clear differentia between witches and magicians are crucial to the success of Weyer's arguments against the burning of witches, his imprecision about the exact dividing line is again obvious when he analyses the different meanings of the German word 'Zauberer'. He insists on his originality in wishing clearly to distinguish the three different types of operator—magician, poisoner and witch—referred to by the one word, but immediately adds: 'encore que ie ne vueille nier que les magiciens et les sorcieres n'ayent quelque chose de commun en leurs arts et impostures' (ch. 1, p. 120).

Then again, we might expect, if Weyer is the tolerant Erasmian that he is painted by Trevor-Roper, that he would try, in making these distinctions, to restrict the class of potential victims of persecution. One could expect him to make magicians a small class of dangerous criminals, and witches a large body of innocent, deluded victims. In fact Weyer makes magician the larger concept: 'Le nom donques de Magicien sera plus general, et ne sera enfermé en si estroites bornes, comme celuy des sorcieres.' He goes on to elaborate the concept of magician in various indefinitely extensible ways:

> J'apele Magicien celuy qui contre le cours et loy de nature, estant apris par le diable, *ou par autres*, ou sciemment par les livres, s'eforce d'atirer illicitement les esprits malins, afin de s'en aider en quelque ministere d'imposture falacieuse, ou d'importance, ou *pour faire quelqu'autre oeuvre* . . . et ce par le recit et application de quelques mots barbares . . . à celle fin . . . qu'ils respondent . . . par voix . . . par notes, *ou par quelque autre maniere que ce soit. Je comprens aussi* sous ce mesme mot, tous ceux qui . . . devinoyent les choses futures superstitieusement. . . . *Je comprens encor* . . . tous ceux qui . . . ont recours aux maistres de ce mestier (ch. 2, pp. 120, 121).

According to Weyer, all magical operations are a species of *fascinatio,* of diabolical illusion. The magical arts were taught by Hermes Trismegistus in Egypt, where they were learned by Plato, and on these arts were founded the religious ceremonies of Egypt, Greece and Rome. The tradition of Hermetic magic thus formed, and which is based on the operations of devils, is a continuing danger, since it has received written formulation, and will not therefore of itself conveniently decline. Hence a conscious and systematic counter-action is required:

> Il faut que les Theologiens et medecins taschent et essayent par tous moyens que cest artifice diabolique et pernicieux soit chassé bien loin des ceremonies de nostre religion: et du tout banni hors du camp de la

sacree medecine, atendu qu'il a souillé et gasté l'une et l'autre, par les exorcismes fardez, par les barboteries de mots barbares, par le recit de paroles inconues. . . . Ainsi nous lisons que par le moyen de cest art, la plus secrette interpretation de la loy divine, nommee Cabale, a esté depravee et gastee entre les juifs: tellement que ces infideles n'ont point d'horreur de dire, qu'au moyen de ceste Magie Cabalistique Iesus Christ a fait des miracles esmerveillables et incomparables (ch. 3, p. 127).[13]

To the tradition of demonic Hermeticism, Weyer opposes the non-demonic magic of Christ, who cast out devils and carried out his magical healing works without the use of diabolically operated charms.

In his eagerness to show the miserable fate attendant on those who practise the demonic arts, Weyer makes only too plain his underlying intolerance. It is indeed hard to see, in some of the instances, by what criterion Weyer had decided that he is dealing with criminal magic, rather than with innocent witchcraft—except by the simple criterion of sex. And even here Weyer inconsistently approves the harshness of divine justice in a case involving the burning alive of a magician whose 'crime' reads like a perfectly standard example of witchcraft (ch. 4, p. 132).

One magician Weyer does defend; his old master, Agrippa von Nettesheim. Weyer's technique—of untypical subtlety—is to quote from the spurious fourth book of Agrippa's *De Occulta Philosophia*, which is indeed full of magic spells (ch. 5). Weyer denies, correctly, that it is by Agrippa, and dismisses it as simple rubbish. What is odd in this, is that Weyer, who certainly knew that the genuine third book of the *Occulta Philosophia* is full of openly demonic magic, does not refer to it, nor to Agrippa's recantation of this magic in his book on the *Vanity of Sciences*, possibly because he is fully aware of the insincerity of this recantation. More fundamental is the fact that Agrippa analyses all religions as forms of magic, something that is implicit in Weyer's work too. (In particular, Agrippa, like Weyer, considered Catholicism to be a form of 'Egyptian' idolatry.)[14] What is more, Agrippa was a famous defender of alleged witches, whom he saved from the clutches of the law, an activity in which Weyer was very skilled and successful.[15]

Operative magic is for Weyer a hoax perpetrated by the devil. Certainly magical spells are attended by apparent or real effects. But the effects are not caused by any magical properties in the objects or spells used, only by the 'natural' powers of the devil to fool slow-witted, credulous observers. Pharaoh's wizards, on this account, did not really transform their rods into serpents, as is shown, rather bizarrely, by the fact that they were eaten up by the real serpents produced by Moses (ch. 8, p. 152). They did not turn water into real blood, or produce genuine frogs, as is shown, even more strangely, by the fact that the wizards could not reverse their spells and remove the spurious blood and the fake frogs. The muddle Weyer has got himself into is compounded when he says that because of the speed with which devils operate they could anyway remove objects and replace them (by, for instance, real snakes) without observers seeing what was going on (ch. 8, p. 153). This is, of course, another explanation altogether of the mechanics by which Pharaoh's magicians turned rods into serpents. Weyer's explanation of the turning of the rivers into blood is similarly confused: he asserts both that the devil acted on the visual spirits of the observers, and that he acted on the river directly (ch. 8, pp. 154, 155).

In explaining the *purpose* of the wizard's pseudo-miracles, Weyer takes the rigorous line that God could not have punished the Egyptians so justly if they had not connived at the devil's impostures (ch. 8, p. 156). It is hard to see how they could have done otherwise whatever interpretation of the mechanics we adopt, or, since the Egyptians in general were not magicians, why they should be punished. It is an example of the way that diabolical illusions are supervised and ultimately engineered by Weyer's God.

Weyer is particularly fierce against those who, unlike himself, blame the illness of patients they cannot cure on a malevolent third party:

> Il y a plusieurs prestres et moynes ... qui doyvent à bon droit estre escrits au papier de Magiciens, et pour quelque occasion que ce soit n'en doyvent estre rayez. ... Mesme ils en donnent le plus souvent le blasme à quelque honeste, innocente, et bonne matrone, dont jamais elle ne pourra, ni mesme sa posterité estre du tout purgée (ch. 17, p. 186).

Whilst we should admire Weyer's commonsense on such points, we should nevertheless be disturbed by the conclusion he draws about such practitioners: that, unless they repent, 'il y a danger que ce qu'a escrit Isaie ne se raporte à eux: Nous avons traité alliance avec la mort, et avons fait apointement avec l'enfer' (ch. 17, p. 188).

Book Three: Witches

The opening chapter of this book describes at length the humanist sources of the witch stereotype, and the leisurely ironic exposition is justified on the assumption that their manifest absurdity will impose itself upon the reader: a strangely unimaginative assumption in the second half of the sixteenth century.[16] Reginald Scot and Cyrano de Bergerac saw the necessity of making much more open and robust fun of what they found ridiculous in the witch image.

The second chapter likewise stresses the variety and inconsistency to be found in the witchcraft practices reported in the *Malleus Maleficarum*, and suggests that such inconsistency shows their obvious unreliability. In fact observers then and now are much more impressed by their extraordinary homogeneity, and see this as a problem to be explained. Amongst these practices, Weyer holds up to particular ridicule the pact with the devil. It is not binding, on the oddly legalistic grounds that one party, the devil, has no intention of keeping it; that devils cannot shake hands to confirm it; that there are no witnesses or guarantors to validate it, as there are at baptism; and that in any case the prior baptismal contract is of greater power. Here Weyer discusses the pact as if it physically occurs. At the same time he asserts that it is a delusion.

A fundamental reason for Weyer's shakiness is presumably that the alleged practices of witches are not odder than, or different in principle from, the ceremonies of either Protestant or Catholic Christianity. Thus he argues that, even if the witches' initiation ceremony involves scraping away the baptismal chrism, no serious harm can be done by such an action, since the efficacy of baptism does not lie in the chrism anyway (ch. 3, pp. 209–12). An argument like this shows the close similarity for Weyer between the sacraments and diabolical rites, where not the substances used, but the divine or diabolical agents are efficacious, in conjunction with the proper mental disposition of the patient. Weyer moves on especially dangerous ground here. He argues that many of the apparently anti-religious actions involved in the pact, such as fasting on Sunday or eating meat on Friday, have positive spiritual value as expressions of Gospel freedom.

A Catholic could equally well argue that Lutheran practices are here plainly shown by Weyer to be probable diabolical double-crosses. This is the sort of argument that Weyer uses himself, claiming that some at least of the Catholic practices thus flouted by the devil are thereby given a spurious validity. As he puts it, such infringements are 'folies de vieilles, lesquelles ont esté mises en avant par les diables, afin d'establir une superstition et impieté sous pretexte de religion' (ch. 4, p. 216).

Now Weyer's case for distinguishing between witches, who are female and *used by* the devil, and magicians who are male and *use* the devil, is that women are subject to melancholy vapours, on which the devil imprints fantasies, thereby persuading them of entirely imaginary phenomena. Weyer certainly does not lack authorities by which to establish the naturally weak physical constitution of women (ch. 7, pp. 222–6). But it is surely quite extraordinary that in a chapter intended to prove the depraved imagination of melancholics, and including a dozen interesting cases of melancholia, not one of them concerns a woman. We are forced to conclude that Weyer is determined to find a theory by which to inculpate magicians, far more than he is concerned to construct a theory by which to exculpate women. In short, the Lutheran practitioner, incensed by Catholic idolatry, and no doubt the 'unfair' practices of his medical rivals, is often more important than the humanitarian physician, concerned with the objective nature of melancholia.[17]

In one area, Weyer takes a notably rational stand: the only physically dangerous form of witchcraft, in his view, is based not on spells, but on poison (chs 37–41). We should note too that Weyer's descriptions of cases of melancholy which he has himself observed are marked by careful clinical detail.[18] And he gives quite ingenious and plausible explanations of cases of alleged lycanthropy.

But why are people led to conceive of themselves as witches or as werewolves? To answer this question, Weyer uses St Augustine, who refers to:

> hommes cupides de mauvaises choses, lesquels par un oculte iugement de Dieu sont livrez pour estre trompez et deceus selon le merite de leurs volontez, par les anges prevaricateurs, qui les trompent et decoyvent: et esquels par la loy de la divine providence, et selon l'ordre des choses, la partie la plus basse du monde est assuiettie (ch. 11, p. 237).

Weyer thus takes care to safeguard the appearances of divine justice by insisting that witches' intentions are being punished. But this is hardly consistent with his basic wish to exculpate alleged witches and werewolves by insisting that they are used and abused by the devil, and hence not responsible for their delusion. This inconsistency is rooted in the difficulty of getting rid of the burning of witches without also getting rid of the burning in Hell. We are back at the disturbing heart of Weyer's outlook: that ultimately witch trials are arranged by God, that the processes of human judgment echo an 'oculte iugement de Dieu'.

As a staunch and unsophisticated Evangelical, Weyer has a similarly pressing dilemma in denying the possibility of witch flights to the Sabbat.

> Nous lisons qu'Abacuc le Prophete fut veritablement transporté en peu de temps, par les cheveux, depuis Judee iusques en Babylone . . . [et]

il est plus que certain qu'il [*sc.* le Diable] porta nostre Seigneur Iesus Christ sur le pinacle du temple. . . . St. Thomas d'Aquin argumente fort bien qu'une possibilité posee en une chose, par consequent se peut faire en toutes autres, qui sont de mesme grandeur et pesanteur (ch. 12, pp. 240, 241).

Weyer's conclusion again does nothing to help to exculpate the witch:

> Dieu tout iuste et tout bon ne permet toutes choses, et n'endure que Satan face tout ce qu'il voudroit bien et pourroit faire par la subtilité de sa nature: ains seulement les choses qu'il a deliberees, non pour establir une superstition, mais pour rappeler au bon chemin, ou pour punir les meschans.

Destructive storms are caused not by diabolical magic but by divine magic, and in no way involve the intervention of witches. Weyer begs those who do not see the hand of the Lord in destructive storms to 'reprendre le droict chemin; car si l'esprit de ces obstinez s'endurcit à cest miene priere, ie prevoy qu'ils s'enlasseront en un si difficile labyrinthe du diable, qu'il n'y aura moyen de les en pouvoir retirer si le fils de Dieu misericordieux n'y met la main' (ch. 16, p. 272).

It is Weyer himself, one might say, who in this discussion remains trapped in the labyrinth of his evangelical beliefs, for he continues to suppose that the devil, however limited his powers, can yet perform those operations he is said to perform in the Scriptures (ch. 35, p. 332).[19] And we may call to mind the basic vision of history with which Weyer confronted us at the beginning of the work, a vision in which Satan's powers are quasi-universal.

Book Four: Demoniacs

Weyer's curious mixture of tolerance and intolerance, perceptiveness and credulity, is nowhere more apparent than in Book Four, which is concerned with demoniacs. He wishes to show that the possessed are *merely* possessed, and have not been rendered so by the intervention of witches. Again, one of the criteria used is scriptural: the Scriptures give no instance of diabolic possession being caused with the help of human agencies. Consequently, witches who think they bewitch should themselves be called bewitched (ch. 1, p. 360).

According to Weyer, the vomiting of strange objects by the possessed is deceit. Such objects have been skilfully placed in the mouth of the sick person by the devil and have never actually been swallowed. The quickness of the devil's hand deceives the eye. Such illusions are permitted by God, who permits the belief in witchcraft, and the belief in Catholic antidotes to it (ch. 3, p. 370). The cessation of the symptoms of possession is arranged to coincide with the application of totally inefficacious Catholic remedies, so as to create the illusion that the witch is guilty of causing the possession. Her death at the hands of the magistrate renders him, too, guilty of mortal sin (ch. 4). Weyer does not see the need to tackle the unanswerable question as to how, in this version of events, the pain suffered by the innocent old women, and which he so movingly describes, is reconcilable with his image of a 'Dieu tout juste et tout bon'.

The whole book is full of extraordinary cases of diabolical guile behind cases of possession. In one typical case of mass hysteria in a convent, a cat appears in a basket left in the convent, and Weyer claims that 'mesmes si le chat estoit naturel, il ne faut point douter que le diable ne l'eust mis en la corbeille: et certes ie penserois plustost que ce fust le diable mesme sous la figure d'un chat' (ch. 10, p. 387). The baffling element in Weyer's handling of these phenomena is that time and again he is conscious of the sexual frustration involved in the artificial life of the convent, aware of the way it has triggered off the attacks of hysteria, and aware of the therapy immediately available in the form of normal sexual outlet in marriage.

The most extraordinary case of all concerns a young girl who for a year seems to have had a knife lodged subcutaneously in her side (chs 13, 14). Weyer argues with the most incredibly dogged and perverse ingenuity that the devil engineered a fantastic sequence of double-crosses falsely to convince observers that a simple natural phenomenon was involved. Weyer, claiming greater perspicacity than the great majority who have studied and written about the case, thinks he can go beyond all the facts, which appear to suggest that only natural causes were involved, to the underlying diabolic reality. In doing so, he greatly enhances his own thesis that he would indeed require superhuman help to outwit the wiles of so crafty a devil.

Book Five: Counter-magic

Prevention is better than cure, and all it involves is a basic evangelical trust in the Lord. But where cure of the possessed is necessary, it should be 'aucunement commune, tirée des sainctes Escritures, non pas magique ny superstitieuse, telles que plusieurs la desirent et l'ont exercée' (ch. 1, p. 458). For Weyer, the practices of Catholic exorcists are nothing more than a revival of Hermetic diabolic magic. Such ecclesiastical magicians are in fact largely using ceremonies prescribed for the exorcism of the possessed by the Catholic authors of the *Malleus Maleficarum*. Thus it is claimed that 'l'eau beniste, outre la premiere benisson que Dieu luy donna, aspergée ou donnée à boire, à grande efficace en ceci: aussi a le sel exorcisé, une partie du cierge de Pasques . . .' (ch. 3, p. 472). Catholic magic appears to be seen as an attempt to superimpose another layer of magical power on the original sacramental power, or to transfer it illegitimately to other objects.

Weyer is particularly upset by the use of gibberish, of 'paroles inconues par lesquelles on ne sait si lon prie en bien ou en mal,' formulae which 'se sont peu à peu escoulez parmi nostre saincte et sacree medecine' (ch. 8, p. 491).[20] Weyer seems equally upset by the related mechanical nature of many cures, the fact that they must be said a fixed number of times. Such criticisms are of course to be expected from a Protestant whose conception of religion stresses inward faith more than outward ritual.

Weyer ridicules the use of amulets and talismans on the orthodox Thomist grounds that no human artefact can carry magical astrological properties, and he will have no truck with the defence of talismans by Albertus Magnus and Ficino, 'grand philosophe au demeurant' (ch. 9, p. 499). But he hardly bothers to argue the case out, and dismisses the conception by his normal vulgar humour, suggesting for instance that a spell to reduce a woman's infatuation, which involves putting dung into her lover's shoe, required no recondite explanation of its efficacy (ch. 9, p. 500). And in arguing the inefficiency of the drugs by which witches are said to resist torture, Weyer forgets—with his usual logical myopia—to make any mention of the unpermissibility of extracting any confessions by torture. It might be said that the myopia is general to the whole work rather than local to this passage, since it is a grave weakness of the case he later argues against the torture of witches that he never argues a case against torture as such.[21]

Magic, then, requires credulity, in just the way that religion requires faith:

> Les exemples, comme dit Agrippa, monstrent assez comment la superstition ensuit et contrefait la vraye religion: à scavoir lors que lon excommunie les vers et les sauterelles, afin qu'elles ne facent mal aux bleds: lors que lon baptize les cloches et les images, et que lon fait plusieurs choses semblables (ch. 17, p. 529).[22]

But by admitting that the spells of witches do result in cures and in claiming here that the spells of Roman Catholics do result in at least apparent magical effects, Weyer is again left with the problem, of which he seems unaware, of showing by what criteria one could possibly prove that the miracles of

Christ were not produced by diabolical magic.[23] However, he insists that the only permissible exorcism is that based on Gospel magic, by which 'les apostres et les disciples ont commandé en son nom [sc. de Christ] et en peu de paroles que les diables sortissent: car ils portoyent en leurs bouches la puissance, de toute la nature et le commandement de toute la vertu cachee tant au ciel qu'en la terre' (ch. 27, p. 573).[24]

When at last Weyer comes to discuss the types of remedy of which he is in favour, his proposals are quite sane, even if applicable only in Lutheran territories.[25] First of all, the doctor should treat for natural illness, and only if he is convinced of the presence of supernatural causes should he hand over the apparently bewitched patient to the priest. It is his evangelical magic alone which can possibly be effective. And, Weyer concludes in an emotional and highly lyrical vein:

> Voila la coniuration, voila le grand et fort exorcisme, voila la certaine maniere de chasser le diable, voila le moyen sommaire, voila les characteres par lesquels la puissance infinie est apelee pour faire les choses par dessus la commune force de la vie: voila la vraye doctrine, le ferme fondement, et la pierre des philosophes (ch. 37, pp. 601–2).

Belief in Christ enables one to do what Christ did: 'He that believeth on me, the works that I do he shall do'. Weyer's magic is both a *participatio* and an *imitatio Christi*, a re-enactment of the magical works of Christ, the great and only good magician.[26]

Book Six: Punishment

Weyer presents his views on making the punishment fit the crimes of black magicians, white witches and poisoners as the views of a doctor, as a supplement to the preceding books, and as a paradox—an 'opinion contraire à la vulgaire desia par plusieurs annees inveteree et receue' (ch. 1, p. 613). In fact it is mostly a compendium of views expressed by others. Thus while the division in Chapter 1 of magicians into three classes has an authentically Weyerian ring to it, his major principle throughout that magicians should be distinguished from witches as learned professionals from untutored amateurs has a history stretching back ultimately to Plato.[27]

The least dangerous magicians are those who conjure up spirits. These magicians are quite harmless and should at most be fined to make them give up 'l'accointance qu'ils ont avec le diable [et] afin que cy apres ils n'attrapent plus les deniers du simple peuple' (ch. 1, p. 615). The second class are

(Catholic) exorcists, 'magiciens qui sont religieux de profession', who attribute possession and misfortune to 'une pauvre femme souvent [sic] toutesfois innocente' (ch. 1, p. 616). These should be prosecuted for defamation. As for punishment, Weyer cautiously suggests destitution or exile, but not death. The most dangerous, most criminal class are what he calls 'medecins magiciens, tous ceux qui contre la ... parole de Dieu, et au mepris insupportable de la medecine sacree et tres utile entre toutes sciences, donnent ... du sel exorcisé [et] ... de l'eau exorcisée', and who, generally, misuse the Word of God, or employ gibberish (ch. 1, p. 617). But again there is a curious reluctance clearly to spell out the nature of the punishment necessary:

> Il n'y a point de doute, et faut confesser que toutes telles gens surpassent les bornes de superstition: et pour ceste cause ils doivent estre repris aigrement et refrenez de peur que tant ceux qui font ces choses, que ceux qui les permettent, ne trebuschent en meschanceté et sacrilege d'idolatrie (ch. 1, p. 617).

The second chapter presents a similar puzzle. As with the last two categories of magician, Weyer is discussing people who claim to be able to detect witches, in this case by divination. He very firmly counsels exile for such 'perturbateurs de la République et des faussaires', yet continues without explanation: 'Je ne leur souhaite pas la punition qui leur a esté ordonnée par Moyse en la loy selon la volonté de Dieu', which he follows with a whole page of uncommented Pentateuchal legislation enjoining the death penalty (ch. 2, pp. 618–19). Weyer also advocates the burning of the books and equipment of those diviners who evoke spirits, and supports it by likewise uncommented reference to decisions which in some cases actually involved burning the magician too. Weyer has fewer scruples about poisoners, and quotes at some length in his muddled third chapter the severe canon and civil law texts against magicians, whilst insisting that they do not pertain to witches.

Chapter 4 rises to impressively eloquent heights. A return to the safeguards of German law would largely prevent the horrors of witch prosecutions, which have come to be initiated on simple rumour and lead inevitably to barbarities:

> Bon gré maugré, tant innocentes puissent elles estre, on ne les oste point de la torture qu'elles n'ayent confessé le forfait dont on les acuse. Par ainsi il avient qu'elles aiment mieux estre bruslees et mourir innocentes en peu d'heures, à l'apetit de ces sanguinaires, que d'estre continuelle-

ment tirees sur les gehennes et tortures de ces cruels bourreaux . . . Mais quand celuy qui sonde les reins et les coeurs, cest enquesteur et iuge de la verité plus cachee, aparoistra, vos procedures seront mani﹣ festes, ô iuges sanguinaires, ô hommes cruels, inhumains, et devestus de compassion (ch. 4, p. 628).

Weyer powerfully argues the case for leniency to the repentant (ch. 3, pp. 5, 6) and eloquently rejects the assimilation of witchcraft to heresy: 'l'erreur en l'esprit ne fait pas l'heretique, mais bien l'opiniastreté de la volonté' (ch. 8, p. 638). Those who err should be brought gently home, not incarcerated with punitive ferocity. In a particularly skilful Chapter 10, Weyer insists that professional medical opinion should be consulted as to the possible efficacy of the charms alleged to be used by the witch, for 'il faut que les preuves soient plus claires que le jour', and he counsels: 'ne jugeons nullement des choses incertaines'.

These concerns are further pursued over the next four chapters, which attempt to demolish various witch confessions. In spite of his medical knowledge, Weyer does not get much further than a blanket use of Cardano's diagnosis of melancholia. Whilst Weyer is probably right to insist on the relevance of medical diagnosis in many cases of witchcraft, medicine was then too primitive to suggest convincing explanations. For instance, the epidemics of uncontrollable muscular spasms described in Chapters 11 and 12 seem to be cases of ergotic poisoning, and the lycanthropy cases described may well be cases of autistic behaviour. But ergotic poisoning was not dis﹣ covered for another two hundred years, and the possibility of lycanthropy involving abandoned autistic children has only recently been proposed.[28] Weyer's most important contribution in the field of medical diagnosis may well be the understanding that undernourishment was the cause of much witchcraft melancholia (ch. 12).[29]

The following chapter constitutes a sad chronicle of cruelty on the part of false accusers, cruel judges, ignorant rabble, and a stern establishment. It attempts to put such events into the reassuring perspective of a good inter﹣ ventionist deity, who redresses the balance by himself punishing such cruelty. But it is mainly interesting as a faint harbinger of recent attempts to explore the entire social nexus in which witchcraft accusations arise, and generally for its awareness of the social realities of witchcraft persecution: 'Il avient de la que Dieu juste juge punit quelquesfois les sentences iniques des magistrats, la folle croyance du peuple, et la trop grande rigueur des grands' (ch. 15, p. 668).[30]

Chapters 16 to 23 rehearse a series of very different authorities in favour of leniency, and realistically begin with the ruling classes who could—and in lower Germany at this period frequently did—intervene to prevent prosecutions. Weyer begins Chapter 16 by citing the shining example of William of Cleves himself, and concludes it with the salutary moral: 'il vaut beaucoup mieux pardonner à coulpables que de faire mourir un innocent'.

In the following chapter Weyer uses the Church Fathers to excellent effect, especially Augustine, who advocates killing the error, not the man, and who is aware

> avec combien de labeur et de peine on trouve la verité, par combien de dificultez on se garde des erreurs, et par combien de souspirs et gemissemens on fait tant que Dieu soit ouy et entendu de toutes parts (ch. 17, p. 675).

It is an interesting argument, for the analogy between heresy and witchcraft, often seen as a reason for sixteenth-century intolerance, is here successfully used as an argument in favour of liberalism.

In Chapter 18 the patristic arguments for toleration used by Erasmus are employed with a keen sense of their contemporary relevance.[31] 'Au reste lon void dequoy ont servi envers le menu peuple les seditieux sermons et la rage de quelques prescheurs' (ch. 18, p. 681). Whilst Erasmus denies any intention of commenting on secular justice, he does insist that 'le devoir des moines est de s'estudier plutost à guérir qu'à faire perir' and that princes should 'accommoder et fleschir la rigueur de leurs loix à la douceur d'une modération Chrestienne' (ch. 18, p. 682). Erasmus is only too well aware that repression might mean that 'au lieu d'heretiques on n'eut des Chrestiens hypocrites' (ch. 18, p. 680)—a development which was indeed one result of the religious strife of the sixteenth and seventeenth centuries, and the subsequent establishment of state churches.

In the following two chapters, Weyer uses the arguments of Ponzinibio, Grillando and Alciati in favour of scepticism and tolerance, including Alciati's notable pronouncement on the butchered Piedmontese witches: 'elles devoyent estre plustost purgees par hellebore que par le feu' (ch. 20, p. 688).[32] He concludes the section by arguments from civil law in favour of milder treatment for women, conveniently forgetting that Moses had singled out the female witch for especially severe treatment, and then concludes in favour of 'la douceur chrestienne' which brings back the lamb to the fold, and might involve fining and perhaps temporary exile; for after all, as he says, witches have consented to the devil's blandishments, whatever the mitigating circumstances.

The rest of the work consists basically of redefinitions, recapitulations and refutations. In Chapter 24 he maintains that modern witches are accused of actions 'tout autres que ceux dont Moyse et l'Escriture saincte font mention'. Whilst there are difficulties in this view, this is a promising line, much developed by Reginald Scot. Unfortunately Weyer does not stick to it. He even writes that magicians *should* be burned 'et je l'ay suffisament prouvé en mes livres' (ch. 24, p. 699), even though, as we have seen, he has tried consistently to avoid spelling out this requirement which is plainly enjoined by Mosaic law. And he then inconsistently argues that the death penalty has been abandoned in other areas where it was called for by Moses, such as the crime of perjury (*ibid.*).

One of Weyer's most interesting arguments against witch-hunting is a strong and empirical one, largely verified by subsequent events:

> Il n'y a endroit au monde, auquel on vive plus asseuré de toutes ces choses que là où ces victimes et sacrifices n'ont plus de lieu, là où on ne les brusle plus, là où les ruses, les finesses et impostures des diables sont descouvertes (ch. 25, p. 714).

Perhaps the strongest theoretical argument used by Weyer is his argument in Chapter 27 that operative magic is impossible. The argument is not well developed, if only because it could be used to exculpate black magicians as well as white witches, urban intellectuals as well as country peasants.

He moves on from rejecting this possibility of non-demonic spiritual magic to maintaining that the only other alternative, diabolical magic, does not in fact involve the agency, and therefore the culpability, of witches. And even if the devil *could* perform the destructive magic falsely ascribed to the power of witches, in fact, 'il fait ce que le grand Dieu veut, et lorsqu'il luy semble bon'. This leaves it open that diabolical magic—seen here again as ultimately divine magic—could precisely be a temptation which witches could still rightly be punished for succumbing to.

Weyer concludes the chapter by trying to close this loophole by a new argument. Judges can punish only deeds, not intentions. And since God in this world punishes even the righteous, 'aussi ne doit-on presumer quand quelqu'un est affligé de la verge de Dieu que ce soit pour un mefait, lequel doit estre puni par les hommes' (ch. 27, p. 734). Whilst it may be true that 'il est premièrement beaucoup plus grief d'offencer la Maiesté eternelle que l'humaine et temporelle' (ch. 27, p. 738), as advocates of witch persecution maintain, it is equally true that all sin is of this nature, and if anything more excusable in the case of old, deluded women than of men.

Weyer seems to be only one step away from asserting that *no* sin should be punished by secular or religious authority, by whomsoever committed. It is a step which would genuinely take him outside the realm of witch persecution. But here, as throughout the sixth book, his simplistic theological commitment prevents him from pushing through to a logical and systematic re-interpretation of traditional attitudes an unprecedentedly diverse, though individually unoriginal, range of arguments for tolerance.

Conclusion

Weyer, as we have seen, ends up in these concluding pages with some of his central tenets. There are diabolic magicians who try to bring magic under *their* control. We are commanded by Holy Writ to prevent them. So why did Erastus and Bodin, who shared these views, both 'refute' Weyer's views on the persecution of witches?

In part, it is because the very bulk of Weyer's work seems to promise a more substantial case than the rather thin argument that witches—who do carry out most of the acts they are traditionally said to—are merely deluded. The simple astonishment of Erastus and Bodin that Weyer should actually repeat in his *De Lamiis* (1577) the arguments of the *De Praestigiis* is indicative of a genuine shock.[33] Until an implicitly or explicitly non-Christian stance would be taken up to combat witch burning, the only effective liberal course—apart from practical intervention—was silence.[34]

The apparent naiveté of Weyer's book is perhaps to be explained in part by the untypically ordered, tolerant government of the small, static society he knew under Duke William III; a society which tolerated even Weyer; a society temporarily removed from the increasingly disordered and divided European world outside. However that may be, Weyer's writings badly misfired as a defence of witches: first, by raising the issue at all in the first full-scale work since the *Malleus*; secondly and disastrously, by utilising witchcraft beliefs in the pursuit of religious polemic; thirdly and most immediately, by evoking the counterblast of two intellectually outstanding writers, not only his fellow Lutheran Erastus, but also Jean Bodin, a man who had just acquired a European reputation for his political masterpiece, the *République* (1576). Indeed, Bodin's *Démonomanie* largely adopts Weyer's theory of magic.

Weyer's disastrous mistake, then, is to discuss magic and witchcraft in the context of religious polemic. Conversely, his most significant achievement is perhaps his incautious discussion of religion in terms of magic and witchcraft: Christianity and diabolic magic are comparable, complementary forces. For this insight Weyer is indebted to the poetic, mysterious and liberal-minded Agrippa, whose influence on him far outweighs that of the rather prosaic, rational and liberal-minded Erasmus.[35]

This insight remains of value to the historian charting the intellectuals' later disenchantment with magic and witchcraft and, in so far as the intellectuals controlled the apparatus of repression, it contributed to the decline of witch persecution, which was paralleled by a decline in religious persecution. This evolution in attitudes is, however, hard to trace in detail, since it consists in a partly unconscious and unarticulated adoption of the doctrine of 'double truth', according to which religious language is meaningful at a different level from other types of discourse. But we are, I think, forced to conclude that by advocating an evangelical and divine remedy for Catholic and diabolical evils, Weyer, the famed defender of witches, exacerbated, far more than he relieved, the tensions which contributed to the European witch craze.

Notes

1 Duke William reigned from 1539 to 1592. Weyer was his doctor from 1550 to his death. On Weyer's life see C. Binz, *Doctor Johann Weyer, ein rheinischer Arzt* (Bonn, 1885): J. J. Cobben, *De opvattingen van J. Wier over bezetenheit, hekserij en magie* (Assen, 1960); L. Dooren, *Doktor Johannes Wier, Leven en Werken*, Academisch Proefschrift, N.V. (Aalten, 1940).

2 See the bibliographies in Binz, *op. cit.*, pp. 25ff, and in U. Schneider, 'Das Werk "De praestigiis daemonum" von Weyer und seine Auswirkungen auf die Bekampfung des Hexenwahns', unpublished dissertation (Bonn, 1951), p. 4. Page references in this essay are to an anonymous translation, *Histoires, disputes et discours, des illusions et impostures des diables, des magiciens infames, sorcières et empoisonneurs: des ensorcelez et démoniaques et de la guerison d'iceux: item de la punition que méritent les magicians, les empoisonneurs et les sorcières* (Geneva, 1579). This version was reprinted in Paris, 1885, with different pagination. The translator adds two dialogues derived from the writings of Erastus, and a partial reproduction of Weyer's *De Lamiis* (1577) in the form of a *Reponse aux arguments du premier dialogue*. There had been a French translation of an earlier five-book version of the *De Praestigiis* by Jacques Grevin, 1567.

3 H. R. Trevor-Roper, *The European Witch-Craze* (Harmondsworth, 1969).

4 See N. Cohn, *Europe's Inner Demons* (London, 1975), chs 9, 10.

5 Whilst Weyer never completely openly refers to *all* forms of Christianity as magic, the analogy is plainly there: see notes 22 and 24.

6 Bodin is far ahead of his time in analysing witchcraft from a systematically non-Christian viewpoint, outside confessional dispute. It is not new to see Weyer as an eirenic Erasmian rather than as an aggressive Lutheran. In his edition of

Weyer's *Opera Omnia* (Amsterdam, 1660), the publisher Peter van den Berge, congratulating himself for re-issuing Weyer's neglected works, describes himself in the dedication as 'one of those whom Erasmus called liberators of man (saeculorum sospitores)'.

7 In the *judicium* by Martin Schook in *Joannis Wieri Opera Omnia* (1660) an identical dissenting opinion is expressed.
8 See Mark XVI. 17, 18.
9 See also, e.g., *Preface*; and Bk III, ch. 9, p. 315.
10 See T. Gregory, 'Dio Ingannatore e Genio Maligno, Nota in margine alle "Meditations" di Descartes' in *Giornale Critico della Filosofia Italiana*, 1974, which shows Descartes's acquaintance with the tradition. The really crucial steps needed to eliminate witch beliefs are taken by Descartes when he constructs a system of knowledge without a Christian reference and immune from divine or diabolic fraud. It is Pascal's peculiar strength as an apologist for Christianity that he faces up to the facts of deception: 'On n'entend rien aux ouvrages de Dieu, si on ne prend pour principe qu'il a voulu aveugler les uns, et éclairer les autres', *Pensées*, ed. Lafuma, 232; ed. Brunschvicg, 566.
11 For these incidents see Bk 1, ch. 12, p. 43; Bk 1, ch. 16, p. 62; Bk 1, ch. 14, p. 50 ('une histoire assez gentille'); Bk 1, ch. 15, p. 59.
12 H. C. Lea's judgment on the first book that Weyer has largely dethroned the devil is rather surprising. See *Materials toward a History of Witchcraft* (Philadelphia, 1939; repr. New York, 1957), p. 494.
13 For the reference to the Cabbala here, see Frances A. Yates, *Giordano Bruno and the Hermetic Tradition* (London, 1964), ch. 5, especially p. 97.
14 Agrippa's *De Vanitate*, ch. 56; and *De Occulta Philosophia*, Bk III, ch. 63. For all religion as magic see the whole of *De Occulta Philosophia*, Bk III.
15 Weyer gives several instances, e.g. in Bk VI, ch. 4, p. 629; ch. 15, p. 668; ch. 24, p. 700. Weyer lived with Agrippa at Bonn in 1533.
16 On the vogue of prodigy literature in this period see R. Schenda, *Die französische Prodigienliteratur* (Munich, 1961). The translator of the *De Praestigiis* has done well to translate it as *Histoires, disputes et discours*. He says in his *Epistre* that he has felt it necessary to tone down the vulgarity of the original. Like Agrippa's *De Vanitate* the work is often close to the *genre* of the *declamatio*. No analytical résumé, as this essay, can adequately convey its Rabelaisian flavour. Weyer's constant quotation of his adversaries, especially his savouring of the picturesque, is very attractive: interestingly, he does not use this technique in the *De Lamiis* (1577).
17 Melancholia is traditionally associated with intellectuals and contemplatives. It barely serves the purpose Weyer puts it to, of exculpating irrational and stupid old women. Bodin reserves some of his most scathing remarks for Weyer's ascription of melancholia to women: see his *Réfutation*. In any case, many witch suspects were neither female nor old; on the other hand, all Catholic priests are male, and this may be the real reason why Weyer sticks to his mechanical and unconvincing distinction between white female witches and black male

magicians. Agrippa, as well as Cardano, imputes melancholy to witches; see *De Occulta Philosophia*, Bk III, ch. 43.

18 This is the aspect of Weyer mainly discussed in the preface and introduction by Bourneville and Axenfeld to the 1885 reprint of Weyer. Both were doctors influenced by the work of Charcot on hysteria.

19 Copulation is not one of these operations, in spite of the abnormal conception of Christ. Weyer spends fifteen chapters on the subject (chs 19–33), which constitutes a particularly tiresome problem for him. He must reserve the virgin birth as the only non-natural event of its kind, since 'le principal fondement de nostrè foy se ruineroit avecques le mystère caché de l'incarnation du Christ' (Bk III, ch. 24, p. 305).

20 The works of Weyer and Bodin could be used to support Dr Yates's suggestion (*op. cit.*, p. 143) that anti-magical literature is indicative of an increase of magical ceremonies in Christianity (though I think they convey, rather, an increased *awareness* of such magic). The same remarks apply to the development of medicine. Weyer hotly attacks Paracelsans. See Bk V, ch. 4, p. 48; and Bk II, ch. 18, p. 191.

21 Erastus points out this weakness in the *Second Dialogue*, p. 857. See also E. T. Withington, 'Dr John Weyer and the Witch Mania', in Charles Singer, *Studies in the History and Method of Science*, 1917, pp. 189–224. His comments on the evils of torture (p. 200) do not take into account normal criminal procedures at the time.

22 The source of this is Agrippa, as Weyer says. Surprisingly he even quotes approvingly, and without acknowledgment, Agrippa's extraordinary statement that 'chascun en sa religion, ores qu'elle soit fausse, pourveue qu'il l'estime vraye, esleve son esprit, a raison de cette incrédulité, jusques à ce qu'il soit semblable aux esprits' (Bk V, ch. 17, p. 528). (*De Occulta Philosophia*, Bk III, ch. 4.)

23 Yet another difficulty for Weyer (it is one for Bodin too), is that Tobias did not rely simply on credulity or faith to expel the devil, but used perfumes (Bk V, ch. 21, p. 541.) Both Weyer and Bodin rather lamely treat this as an exception.

24 The vocabulary here (cf. Acts XVI. 18) is exactly that of magic, as it is in the next passage quoted in the text. See D. P. Walker, *Spiritual and Demonic Magic from Ficino to Campanella* (London, 1958), pp. 75–84, on the 'General theory of natural magic'. Weyer's outright rejection of all Hermetic magic, whether spiritual or demonic, derives from his awareness that such mysteries are a rival to his own Christian ones. Consequently he will only allow devils to operate, unlike Christ, with 'natural' forces (see Bk II, ch. 36, *passim*). Walker points out (*op. cit.*, p. 162) that Erastus uses the same arguments as Weyer to maintain that Pharaoh's magicians only had access to a spurious, 'natural' imitation of supernatural power: cf. the analysis of Bks I and II above. Weyer's theory of magic, like his definition of the magician, is virtually identical to that of Bodin. The major difference is that Bodin thinks that magicians and Christians—as

well as witches—are deluded. To most Christians he does not attribute criminal responsibility; to witches and magicians he does.

25 See Schneider, *op. cit.*, pp. 67–72.
26 John, XIV. 12. See Mircea Eliade, *Le Mythe de l'éternel retour* (Paris, 1969).
27 Plato, *Laws*, XI, 932, frequently quoted by Weyer.
28 Bruno Bettelheim, 'Feral Children and Autistic Children', in *American Journal of Sociology*, vol. 64, no. 5, 1959; reprinted in *Understanding Society* (The Open University Press, 1970).
29 Weyer was interested in the subject of undernourishment and of fasting, on which he wrote a separate work, *De commentitiis jejunis*. He implies that his father fostered his interest (*De Praestigiis*, Bk VI, ch. 12, p. 653), which may also have derived from Agrippa; see *De Occulta Philosophia*, Bk I, ch. 58.
30 Weyer's insistence that conviction must be justified by proof of actual harm inflicted by the witch (Bk VI, ch. 14, pp. 664, 665) may come from Agrippa, *De Vanitate*, ch. 96. In Bk VI, ch. 19, p. 687, Weyer quotes Ponzinibio to the same effect.
31 The whole chapter is taken from Erasmus's *Apologia adversus articulos aliquot per monachos quosdam in Hispaniis exhibitos* (Basle, 1529).
32 This *mot* was used by Montaigne of the imprisoned witches he confronted on his journey to Italy (*Essais*, Bk III, ch. 11). The whole essay derives from Weyer.
33 See Erastus, *Second Dialogue*, pp. 787, 801; Bodin's *Réfutation*, appended to the *Démonomanie*, begins by explaining that the appearance of the work was delayed by the need to rebut Weyer's recidivist *De Lamiis*. Bodin makes no bones about treating Weyer as a diabolical double-agent. Erastus on the other hand refers to *De Lamiis* as if ignorant of its authorship!
34 Contemporary chroniclers of a liberal and sceptical cast, like Etienne Pasquier and Montaigne, remain virtually silent about the witch trials, with the exception of Montaigne's one essay. For the same attitude in England, see R. Trevor Davies, *Four Centuries of Witch Beliefs* (London, 1947), ch. 3.
35 Weyer calls Agrippa his 'précepteur' (Bk III, ch. 35, p. 332; Bk II, ch. 5, p. 135) and constantly refers to him. From Erasmus he just lifts one chapter. This is particularly striking in view of the Erasmian atmosphere at the court of Clèves. See J. C. Margolin, 'La politique culturelle de Guillaume, duc de Clèves', in F. Simone, *Culture et Politique à l'Epoque de l'Humanisme et de la Renaissance* (Turin, 1974).

4

JEAN BODIN'S *DE LA DÉMONOMANIE DES SORCIERS*: THE LOGIC OF PERSECUTION

Christopher Baxter

Background

> Le jugement qui a esté conclud contre une Sorcière auquel je fus appellé le dernier jour d'Avril, mil cinq cens septante et huict, m'a donné occasion de mettre la main à la plume, pour esclarcir le subiect des Sorciers qui semble à toutes personnes estrange à merveilles, et à plusieurs incroyable.

The sober directness with which Bodin thus introduces, and goes on to describe, the trial of Jeanne Harvillier, at the start of his preface to the *Démonomanie*, is not the least impressive characteristic of a work which immediately attained European recognition.[1] However sensational the 'facts' in the case of Jeanne Harvillier might be—and they possess an archetypal quality which makes Bodin refer to it more than any other case of witchcraft reported in the *Démonomanie*—these 'facts' are reported with the restraint and economy of a stenographic summary (which is what they probably are). This sobriety characterises Bodin's references to the dozen or so other cases of witchcraft occurring in the last twenty years: several of them around Laon (where Bodin lived), and all of them reported to Bodin by 'reliable sources', in the main, minor officials, whom Bodin knew and trusted. The bare telling of them only increases their poignant, ridiculous, and tragic pathos. Bodin seems to move in a world as raw, as exposed, and as honestly reported as the world of *King Lear*. Thus, in the case of Jeanne Harvillier:

> Elle persista en la confession qu'elle avoit faicte du dernier homicide, ayant jetté quelques poudres, que le diable luy avoit preparées, que elle mist au lieu où celuy qui avoit battu sa fille devoit passer. Un autre y passa, auquel elle ne vouloit point de mal, et aussi tost il sentit une douleur poignante en tout son corps. . . . Elle promist de le guarir . . . et confessa que le Mercredy devant que d'estre prisonniere, qu'elle avoit prié le diable de guerir son malade, qui avoit faict responce qu'il estoit impossible: Et qu'elle dist alors au Diable qu'il l'abusoit tousiours, et qu'il ne vint plus la voir. Et lors qu'il dist qu'il n'y viendroit plus, et que deux jours après l'homme mourut. Et aussi tost elle s'alla cacher en une grange, où elle fut trouvée.[2]

Or again:

> Pendant que j'escrivois ceste histoire, on m'advertit qu'une femme enfanta d'un crapaut, pres de la ville de Laon: De quoy la sage femme estonnee, & celles qui assisterent à l'enfantement, deposerent, et fut apporté le crapaut au logis du Prevost, que plusieurs ont veu different des autres.[3]

The immediate background, then, to the *Démonomanie* is dramatic and alarming. It has not been created out of Bodin's fantasies, but out of the minds of local officials and peasants. In the case of Jeanne Harvillier, Bodin seems to have played only an unofficial and advisory role at the trial. The elaboration of the witch image is a centuries-long process antedating the sixteenth century, and Bodin added little to it. Nor does he seem to have initiated the prosecution of witches: the widely held view of Bodin as a witch-hunter has no foundation in fact.[4]

The specific issue for Bodin, in the trial of Jeanne Harvillier, was not her guilt, but the form of her punishment. Should she be hanged or burned? And the more general purpose, arising out of this issue, is to attack judicial leniency, and to 'faire cognoistre au doigt et à l'oeil qu'il n'y a crimes qui soyent à beaucoup près si execrables que cestuy-cy, ou qui meritent peines plus griefves'.[5] Bodin tackled this task with enormous intellectual confidence, and the *Démonomanie* was, as a result, completed with impressive dispatch. The dedication is dated 20 December 1579, and Bodin then appended the brilliant refutation of Johann Weyer at breakneck speed.

The measured firmness of the main body of the *Démonomanie*, which is based on the elaboration of a coherent and individual religious system, stands in some contrast to the wrathful vehemence of the refutation of Weyer. This is written out of the same sense of astonished outrage, at Weyer's sheer nerve in repeating in his *De Lamiis* the logically flimsy attack he made on witch-burning in his *De Praestigiis*, as is displayed by Erastus in his refutation of Weyer.⁶ But it is worth stating here that Monter's description of the 'devastating skill' of Bodin's refutation is far nearer the mark than Trevor-Roper's slighting dismissal of both *Démonomanie* and refutation.⁷

It is often supposed that the witch craze was the responsibility of magistrates like Bodin, who foisted their own fevered imaginations on to innocent old women by intimidation and torture. There is little hard evidence for this interpretation. On the contrary, it would seem that the pressure for witchcraft persecution arose from below, except perhaps in some very exceptional and notorious cases.⁸ Thus in the case of Jeanne Harvillier 'il fust presque impossible de garder les paysans de la ravir des mains de Justice pour la brusler, craignans qu'elle ne reschapast'. Or again: 'M. d'Aventon Conseiller en Parlement ... fist brusler quatre Sorciers tous vifs à Poictiers, l'an M.D.L.XIIII ... se plaignant de ce qu'on avoit envoyé absoubz auparavant d'autres Sorciers appellans, qui depuis avoient infecté tout le pays, et tout le peuple se mutinoit'.⁹ The lynching mentality of the peasants is even more dramatically illustrated in another recent instance:

> C'est doncques chose bien fort salutaire de punir sévèrement les Sorciers: autrement il y a danger que le peuple ne lapide et magistrats et sorciers: comme il est advenu depuis un an à Haguenone pres ceste ville de Laon, que deux Sorcières qui avoyent merité justement la mort, furent condamnees, l'une au fouet, l'autre à y assister: mais le peuple les print, et les lapida et chassa les officiers.¹⁰

The *Démonomanie* derived its success in part from its obvious value as a handbook for the secular courts, whose job it was in France to handle witchcraft cases. Apart from its intrinsic merits for this purpose, it was the first in the field to respond to an urgent contemporary demand. In this respect it is the late-sixteenth-century equivalent to the *Malleus Maleficarum* which was the standard textbook for the prosecutions in the ecclesiastical courts of Germany, and which remained the major authority on witchcraft until displaced to a large extent by the *Démonomanie*. It is significant that, apart from the examples of the lynching mentality given above, and which are taken from the recent French past, Bodin gives only two other instances, and these from the *Malleus*.¹¹ In the second of the two cases a witch is seized by peasants who 'le démembrent en pièces, sans forme ne figure de procès'. Now the remarks of the authors of the *Malleus* in their preface would suggest that witchcraft accusations had become widespread in areas of acute economic distress, areas of exceptionally high infant mortality, disease and hunger. The *Démonomanie* suggests a very similar picture. Most of the accusations of witchcraft it refers to seem to arise from deaths or illnesses, particularly of children.

Of course, this is no more than anecdotal evidence of a situation of high infant mortality and economic crisis, but it is strengthened by Bodin's remarks on countermaleficia, where he writes that 'les sorcières confessent que celuy qui est aumosnier, ne peut estre offensé des sortilèges, encores que d'ailleurs il soit vicieux. . . . Voilà peut estre l'un des plus grands et des plus beaux secrets qu'on puisse remarquer pour oster à Satan, et à tous les Sorciers la puissance de nuire'.[12] Charity, then, will reduce the incidence of witchcraft.

It has recently been suggested by Macfarlane that the refusal of charity is to be seen as the crucial trigger in the initiation of witchcraft proceedings: 'an accusation of witchcraft was a clever way of reversing the guilt, of transferring it from the person who had failed in his social obligation . . . to the person who had made him fail'.[13] Bodin may well be the first writer to have seen a link between the inability or unwillingness to give charity and the spread of witchcraft. His capacity to make this sort of link is not altogether surprising, for he had already demonstrated in the *République* (1576) and even more strikingly in the *Réponse aux Paradoxes de M. De Malestroit* (1568) a quite exceptional awareness of the significance and the causes of the economic crisis which overtook France in the form of runaway inflation in the late sixteenth century.

Although it has received little, if any, attention, there is probably no greater contrast in Bodin's work than between his first major work, the *Methodus ad facilem historiarum cognitionem* (1566) and the *Réponse*, which followed it only two years later. The *Methodus*—an ambitious, lengthy work, arising out of long-standing interests in the methodology of law and of history—is a landmark in both these fields. It maps out a scheme for an encyclopaedic programme of study covering all areas of knowledge— divine, natural, and human history—and includes the plans of three major works to be devoted to these topics. It moves towards, but does not in fact define, the concept of sovereignty, nor does it concern itself with contemporary problems. The few passages concerned with the contemporary French situation were added to the 1572 edition. Its mood is positivistic, optimistic, and above all scholarly and detached. Its concerns are intellectual and cultural, not practical and political.

The *Réponse* stands in total contrast. First of all, it is in French. Like the *République* and *Démonomanie*, it is designed to have an immediate impact on public opinion. Like them, it addresses itself to the immediate problems facing Bodin's contemporaries. All three works should, in fact, be seen as *oeuvres de circonstance*, analysing, in turn, the economic, political, and social problems of the day. Just as the *Démonomanie* was Bodin's immediate response to the Jeanne Harvillier case, where some of the judges would not draw what to Bodin seemed the obvious conclusions from the evidence, and recognise its real gravity, so the *Réponse* was his immediate reaction to Malestroit's 'petit livret de paradoxes, où il soustient contre l'opinion de tout le monde que rien n'est enrichi depuis trois cens ans ... ce qu'il a fait croyre à plusieurs, et par ce moyen appaisé les plaintes de beaucoup d'hommes'.[14]

Bodin's discussion of the remedies to the economic crisis is interesting in two ways. Firstly, because he bases them in large part on the Pentateuch. He is not in favour of out-and-out mercantilism, because of a general duty to foster international trade and friendship: 'Platon et Lycurgue ont défendu la trafique avec l'estranger. ... Toutesfois l'un et l'autre eust mieux fait ... de permettre la trafique, comme sagement a fait Moyse'.[15] Foreign residents, apart from those undesirables 'qui hument le sang, rongent les os et sucent la mouelle du prince et du peuple', are to be protected: 'je desire qu'on les traite en douceur et amitié, ains aussi qu'on venge l'injure à eux faite à toute rigueur, comme la loy de Dieu commande'.[16] Bodin's lengthy defence of encouraging increased fish consumption, as an alternative to expensive meat, is also supported by the 'loy de Dieu'; gluts of fish are provided by 'ce grand proviseur du monde [qui] les a créés pour nos nécessités'.[17]

Secondly, Bodin's discussion is dominated by the needs of the 'menu peuple'. Time after time he describes their plight. It is this aspect of his analysis which he develops most interestingly in the *République*. Already in the *Réponse* Bodin criticises the Elizabethan monetary reforms as causing

> un grand dommage au pauvre peuple. ... Car la moindre monnoye, qui est un Pené bien fort petit, vaut huit deniers obole: tellement que le pauvre peuple est contraint d'user de mailles de plomb, et ne peut achepter en menues denrées sans perte: et quant à l'indigent, il ne peut trouver aisément qui luy face une charité; qui est couper la gorge aux pauvres.[18]

In the *République* Bodin advocates a programme of public works to alleviate poverty, financed by taxation. This he justifies by reference to Hebraic authority—ultimately Deuteronomy XVII:

> In old time the first article set downe in the expences of the treasure, was for almes deeds; the second for the Kings house; and the third for reparations: but the order is quite changed. As for almes-deeds, the wise and antient princes of the Hebrews, have left this discipline to posteritie, the which they received from the Holy Prophets, who sayd,

That the surest preservation and defence of treasure, were Almes deeds, and liberalitie to the needie: the which they restrained to the tenth part of everie mans good, which should be employed upon the ministers of the church and the poor.[19]

In the *République*, though not in the *Methodus*, the sovereign is said to be bound by the law of God. If he infringes this law he is subject to divine sanctions. It is Bodin's submission that the cause of the growth of witchcraft is the failure to observe the injunction in divine law to punish severely crimes like murder and witchcraft (which involves murder). This thesis he develops most fully in the *Démonomanie*. In the preface he writes that: 'M. Barthélemy Faye President aux enquestes de la Cour, s'est plaint en ses oeuvres, que la souffrance de quelques Juges de ne faire brusler les Sorciers comme le Parlement a faict de toute ancienneté, et tous les autres peuples, a esté cause des grandes afflictions que Dieu nous a envoyées.' Bodin takes as a prime example the failure to punish the notorious magician Trois Echelles

> dequoy Dieu irrité a envoyé de terribles persecutions, comme il a menacé par sa loy d'exterminer les peuples qui souffriront vivre les Sorciers . . . Or les secrets des Sorciers ne sont pas si couverts, que depuis trois mil ans on ne les ayt descouverts par tout le monde. Premierement la loy de Dieu, qui ne peut mentir, les a declarez, et specifiez par le menu, et menassé d'exterminer les peuples qui ne feroyent punition des Sorciers.[20]

An emphasis on the paramount authority of the Pentateuch; on the miraculous intervention of daemons, good and bad, in the natural world; and on the state of crisis in contemporary political affairs: these three emphases characterise Bodin's preface. Only the first emphasis, on the Pentateuch, is apparent in the *Methodus* of 1566, and there it conflicts with the predominantly positivistic, secular, and optimistic tone. How the three emphases are related, and how they come to have such importance in Bodin's subsequent thinking, is explained in the first book of the *Démonomanie*.

Book I: Divinatio

The cultural background to the European witch craze is no doubt to be found in the reaction of the medieval church to spiritual dissidence. The crusades against Saracens, Waldensians, Templars, and Jews all went to create the attitudes behind the witch craze. There is probably not much to distinguish the crusading combativity of the Catholic evangelical preaching orders who crushed the allegedly fornicating, witchcraft-practising heretics of Upper Germany and the Rhine Valley, from those of the Catholic evangelical preaching orders who expelled the allegedly fornicating, witch-craft-practising Jews and Moors from Spain. The spiritual empire of Rome had to be preserved from subversion in each case.

Apostasy from Rome is, indeed, the central theme of the introduction to the *Malleus Maleficarum*, which interprets the muddled beliefs and practices of half-christianised peasants in terms of a coherent doctrine of witchcraft. In the sixteenth century, after the Reformation break with Rome, witchcraft treatises are, in the main, to be seen as a part of the ensuing confessional struggle. The *Démonomanie* is, therefore, exceptional in avoiding discussion of matters internal to this debate.

Even in his *Oratio* of 1559, Bodin had declared his neutrality in the confessional battlefield.[21] By the *Methodus* of 1566, this stance has changed into one of a 'positive neutrality', committed to the search for the true religion, and, one suspects, already liberated from the competing Christian ideologies. In the writing of that work Bodin seems to have gone a long way towards seeing in Judaism the criteria by which all other religions should be assessed. What is not entirely clear is whether Bodin thought that Rabbinical Judaism gave a true interpretation of the Mosaic revelation, and, if so, whether Christianity had any claim to truth. At all events, Bodin says of the Jews, towards the end of the *Methodus*, that 'from these people flow as from a fountain the religions which are accepted by the whole world'.[22]

The incipient Judaic colouring of the *Methodus* is far more apparent in the *République*, where the law of God, the Torah of the Jews, is made a criterion at all the most crucial points of the argument. Even ideas such as harmonic justice, already well elaborated in the *Methodus* turn out in the *République* to have a specifically Jewish source: and Bodin's actual prescriptions for tackling the political situation are derived directly from the Pentateuch.[23] It is likely that the whole concept of sovereignty with its monistic, authoritarian overtones is to be seen as being Hebraic in flavour and origin. And the whole conception of the book seems to derive from Bodin's conception of himself as no longer a mere scholar, but as a prophet, with a duty to preach an Hebraic message.[24]

The basic categories used by Bodin in his investigation of witchcraft in the *Démonomanie* are 'lawful' and 'unlawful': in conformity, or not in conformity, with the Jewish Torah, the law of God. Book I contains an exposition of a very basic Hebraic religious system, and includes within this exposition a long and circumstantial account, reported anonymously, of the emotional crisis during which Bodin consciously adopted it. The system is perhaps best described as daemonic Judaism, since in it the rewarding and punishing functions of a strictly monotheistic and rigidly transcendent deity are carried out through a complex bureaucracy of good and evil daemons.[25] The central Christian mysteries—the fall of Satan, original sin, the incarnation, eternal bliss and damnation—are replaced by a simple moral theology which has no need of the mediation of Christ.

Chapter 1 opens with a very embracing definition of the sorcerer: 'sorcier est celuy qui par moyens Diaboliques sciemment s'efforce de parvenir à quelque chose'. The word sorcerer here covers the lofty Neoplatonic magus of the Renaissance Hermetic tradition; the lowly medieval necromancer; and the old crone of the European witch craze. In Bodin's eyes it would almost certainly also refer to Christ, who is treated as a rather inferior magician in Bodin's *Heptaplomeres*.[26]

However, the *Démonomanie*, unlike the *Heptaplomeres*, is a public work, and this explains why the demolition of Christianity has to assume an oblique and condensed form. Thus Bodin frequently refers to the Christian view on the matters he is discussing; and the incautious reader would certainly assume mistakenly that when Bodin makes remarks about the 'opinion receue des Chrestiens', or says of a Christian viewpoint: 'comme nous tenons', he is not merely referring to a cultural fact, but espousing the view himself.[27] When Bodin prints in full, at the end of his preface, the *Determinatio* of the Sorbonne on witchcraft, and refers to it constantly, this is no more than a token of orthodoxy—for the *Determinatio* does not involve the central Christian mysteries. The same is true of Bodin's vehement rejection of the Neoplatonic usage of the word 'daemon' to cover both good and evil spirits, in favour of Christian usage. In this instance Bodin does not even conform to his overt position, but uses words like *daemon*, *esprit*, *ange* and even *diable* interchangeably.

Bodin's constant reference to Christian authorities might be compared with the discussion of religious matters in the *Heptaplomeres*, a debate between seven speakers of different religious persuasions. The discussion is conducted according to Jewish principles derived by the Jewish speaker from Rabbinical tradition. The deist is in philosophical agreement, and the Moslem in practical agreement, with the Jew. Only the eclectic pagan speaker does not accept the principles of daemonic Judaism, whilst yet being pious towards all religious systems. The three Christian speakers on the other hand share an unacceptable deviation from the norm of Judaism; i.e., their assumption of the divinity of Christ.

Now at several points the Jew and one or other of the Christians are in agreement, and this is sometimes taken as a basis for arguing that Bodin is himself some sort of Christian. In fact, the agreement is merely based on the compatibility of certain points in Christianity with the law of God. Thus the Zwinglian, like the Jew, rejects the worship of saints, which offends the Mosaic prohibition of idolatry. Similarly the Catholic argues the necessity of colourful ritual, and this is in accordance with the motivation behind the ceremonial legislation of the Pentateuch. And so on.

Bodin takes good care in the *Démonomanie* to render the extreme unorthodoxy of his views as inconspicuous and inoffensive as possible by the studiously detached and academic tone of the book. Only in places where Bodin is launching fierce attacks on 'atheistic' targets, which would be targets for Christians too, does he allow himself to argue *ad hominem*. The two most obvious examples are the attack on Aristotle in the preface, and the attack on Weyer in the *Refutation*, neither in the main body of the work, where as often as not Weyer is actually used to support Bodin's arguments, with effortless ease.

The sorcerer, then, for Bodin, intentionally used diabolical agencies. Christians, who only do so unintentionally, are not the subject of attack. Having pointed out the importance of the criterion of intentionality on the first page, Bodin leaves it on one side, to use it later in order to exculpate many kinds of magical operator. He then goes on to the second element in his definition—diabolical agencies—but immediately puts this on one side too, and spends the rest of the first book discussing either the divinatory use and nature of non-diabolical agencies (divine, natural and human) or else their unwitting, and therefore innocent, use. In other words the first book is not concerned with demonomania, but with an exploration of all forms of behaviour except the intentional use of diabolical agencies.

Chapter 1 concerns the retributive functions of evil daemons; Chapter 2 the rewarding functions of good daemons, in particular their role in *divinatio divina*, or prophecy. After a chapter in which good and evil daemons are distinguished according to the criterion of rigid monotheism, comes a chapter distinguishing divine from diabolical *divinatio*. Chapter 5 is a defence of non-magical divinatory astrology, and an attack on Cabbalistic and Hermetic magical astrology. The unlawful magic discussed in Chapter 6 does briefly describe witchcraft, but is mainly concerned with its unwitting use in divination by lot. The final chapter discusses the legitimate use of divinatory interpretation of prodigies.

Bodin supposes that the function of Satan and his minions is to 'ruiner en perdition le genre humain'. This uncontroversial view is immediately represented as being Hebraic: 'pour ceste cause les Hébrieux l'ont appellé Sathan, c'est à dire l'ennemy, comme dit Salomon'; and as involving belief in the creation of the devil *ab aeterno tempore*: 'en quoy il presuppose qu'il a esté créé dès le commencement, comme il est dict en Job'.[28] Whilst Bodin spends half a page asserting the intellectual respectability of the doctrine of the fall of Satan and the evil spirits from an original state of grace, this doctrine is not even seen as a specifically Christian one, but as a far older opinion, 'laquelle opinion pour son antiquité et pour l'auctorité de ceux qui l'ont tenue, est receue des Chrestiens'.[29] In fact, throughout the work, Bodin writes as if there were no such thing as a specifically Christian revelation.

Whilst the Christian doctrine on the fall of Satan receives an incidental reference only, and that within a mere half-page of discussion, the Judaic tradition is discussed with a wealth of Rabbinical support over the next three and a half pages. The fate of good men, according to this tradition, is to end up as good daemons, whilst the wicked 'serviront comme Diables, et bourreaux de la justice de Dieu'. This curious eschatology is made even more wildly unorthodox by the assertion that whereas the angels and the elect 'auront la vie eternelle', bad daemons and the reproved 'mourront eternellement, apres avoir souffert les tourmens condignes à leurs meschancetés'. These purgatorial sufferings, then, are unlike orthodox conceptions of purgatory, in that they are for the damned not the elect, and that they precede annihilation, not eternal torment.

The second chapter is the most extraordinary that Bodin wrote, and crucial to an understanding of his intellectual development. The first four pages are characterised by a peculiarly insistent logical articulation, which expresses clearly the weight Bodin attaches to his eschatology: 'Mais . . . car . . . et tout ainsi . . . or . . . c'est pourquoy . . . puis doncques . . . et pour montrer . . . et par ainsi,' etc. Men are good, bad, and indifferent. The fate of the latter, described vividly as those who 'ne levent jamais l'esprit plus haut que leur gueule', is to die body and soul together. The bad man's soul 'dégénère en nature diabolique'. The good man may, even in this life, enjoy: 'telle societé avec l'Ange de Dieu qu'il ne sera pas seulement gardé par iceluy, ains il sentira sa presence, et cognoistra les choses, qu'il commande, et qu'il luy defend. Mais cela advient à peu d'hommes, et d'une grace, et bonté spéciale de Dieu.'[30] We have already learnt in these pages that the function of angels is the exact converse of that of demons: man was created as the link between brute creation and the intelligible world, a link perpetuated between 'les Anges, et les saincts personnages, par la prière et moyen desquels le genre humain est conservé'. In other words there has been no original sin requiring the redeeming action of Christ.

In a second section, beginning and ending with the daemon of Socrates, Bodin shows that the Hebrews were particularly favoured with this angelic guidance; that, as shown in psalm 91, this guidance is a gift from God; and that the highest form of guidance is the revelation by the daemon of prophetic knowledge. The crux of this chapter, and in a sense of the whole work, is the description of the appearance to an unnamed contemporary—in fact, Bodin—of just such an inspiring angel. The experiences described must have come to Bodin soon after he finished the *Methodus*—probably in 1567, during or after a trip to Poitiers. The occurrence is central to the *Démonomanie* in two ways, which are discussed at the end of the daemonic narrative. First, if men can have intercourse with good daemons, it is not surprising that they should communicate with bad daemons too: the existence of prophecy proves the existence of sorcery. *Divinatio divina* means there is also *divinatio diabolica*. Secondly, the daemon gave Bodin a sense of security, a revelation of religious truth, which was confirmed by the similarity between it and the illumination of the Hebrew prophets.[31] No wonder that he ends the chapter by criticising the Christian notion of a guardian angel for every man, since this would torpedo the whole conception elaborated in this chapter of prophecy as a reward given only to the few. And no wonder that he preserves the anonymity of his informant, in a chapter which leaves no room for a doctrine of original sin or of redemption.

At the beginning of the next chapter, 'sorcier' is contrasted with 'enfant de Dieu', the wicked with the righteous. As the sorcerer aims to promote apostasy or idolatry, so the prophet calls to piety and monotheistic purity. Satan's aim is to secure belief in *his* oracles, instead of in God's. Thus West Indians are led to worship the sun, and make of it the God of prophecy, whilst the Greeks and Romans were led to worship Apollo.[32] And no wonder if even Plato was taken in, for so often what the devil recommends appears to be pious, even to the extent of encouraging imitation of the behaviour of the prophets.

How then can true and false piety be distinguished? 'La vraye marque et pierre de touche est la loy de Dieu, qui faict cognoistre au doigt et à l'oeil le Sorcier, et la difference des bons et mauvais esprits'.[33] Deuteronomy simply forbids *all* forms of witchcraft and idolatry. Thus nothing is more erroneous, in the first instance, than to suppose any tradition of Judaic magic, such as the works traditionally ascribed to Solomon. Exorcism—the driving out of evil daemons—is a trap engineered by Satan, and was certainly never practised by Solomon. Now those who would defend exorcism do so on the grounds that the evil daemon can be driven out only by a *good* daemon, since no evil spirit could be brought to chase away another. On the contrary, says Bodin, 'le royaume de Sathan en ce cas n'est pas tant divisé, qu'il est estably et assuré'.[34] It can hardly escape attention that Christ's justification for exorcism, his proof that he was operating with the Spirit of God, and not with the devils, is precisely that 'if Satan cast out Satan, he is divided against himself; how shall then his kingdom stand?'—a defence which is scornfully dismissed as trifling in the *Heptaplomeres*.[35]

According to Bodin, the origin of the confusion of good and evil spirits is in the Neoplatonic tradition: 'les nouveaux Academiques ont posé ceste maxime qu'il faut coupler et lier le ciel et la terre, les puissances celestes et terrestres, et conjoindre les uns avec les autres, pour attirer la puissance divine . . . sur laquelle hypothese on peut dire que le maistre en l'art Diabolique . . . a fondé toutes les sorceleries et invocations de Diables'. This is expressly forbidden by the law of God: 'Dieu semble avoir defendu bien expressement, qu'on ne feist point de degrez, pour monter à son autel, ains qu'on vint droict à luy.' In so far as the Neoplatonists were ignorant of the prohibition their conscience is clear. But this excuse is not open to Agrippa, the master sorcerer in question, or to Pico, whose Orphic hymns, says Bodin, were addressed to the devil. 'Celuy qui a cognoisance de la loy de Dieu, et qui sçait, que toutes ses divinations diaboliques sont defendues, et qui en use pour parvenir à quelque chose, cestuy-là est Sorcier.'[36] It is remarkable that in the list of 'Anges, et petits Dieux' who are to be attracted by the ceremonies of *divinatio diabolica,* there appear, in the *Heptaplomeres,* the names of Mary and Jesus and the saints, and that the prohibition of building steps to the altar is specifically levelled against Christianity.[37]

Chapter 3 had confirmed that Bodin's daemon was good, since it meets the criterion of recommending a strictly monotheistic piety. Chapter 4 continues the demonstration at greater length by developing the theories of Moses Maimonides on prophecy. *Divinatio divina* is distinguished from *divinatio diabolica,* the former being marked by repose and truth, the latter by rage and untruth. It is important to make the distinction since the word for prophet in Hebrew, and in Latin, also applies to the magician. And, although the Mosaic revelation is complete and entire, 'Dieu ne laisse pas d'envoyer aux hommes, songes, visions et ses bons Anges, par lesquels il leur faict cognoistre sa volonté pour se guider et instruire les autres'.[38]

In discussing *divinatio naturalis* in Chapter 5, Bodin opposed to the magical universe of the Hermetics and Cabbalists his own Judaic picture of a world which, after the creation *ab nihilo,* is operated by a daemonic machinery. 'Depuis la premiere creation de toutes choses, Dieu a distribué ses Anges, par le moyen desquels il renouvelle et entretient ses creatures . . . non pas que Dieu ne puisse de son vouloir, sans autre moyen, conduire toutes choses: mais il est plus seant à la Maiesté divine d'user de ses creatures.' Bodin refers to Scriptural passages 'que tous les Hébrieux interpretent du ministere des creatures, desquelles il se sert en toutes choses'. This insistence on the consensus of Rabbinical tradition—'tous les Hébrieux'—is typical. Thus, immediately afterwards, Bodin is referring to the seven-armed candlestick in Zechariah IV, 'que tous les Hébrieux interpretent les sept planettes'.[39]

Astrological divination is, within limits, quite legitimate, so long as it is realised that 'il ne faut rien craindre à celuy qui se fie en Dieu'. Uses of astrology which foster the notion of the power of God are to be applauded; indeed, 'cette puissance, et vertu si admirable des corps celestes' is an occasion for praising the Lord, in the manner of the psalmist. There follows a curiously ecstatic description of the powers of the moon. The powers of the heavenly bodies are indicated by their Hebraic names. What is wrong with Neoplatonic magic is the assumption that, in some way, astrological influences which act on the material world might be made to attract or control the intellectual world.

The distinction being made by Bodin is one between the active operative magic of, say, Pico, and a merely passive contemplative magic. This operative magic is in any case merely illusory, when it tries to manipulate words and characters, since, although Adam did indeed name all things 'selon leur propriété naturelle', this is not to say that the nature of the universe is in any way verbal, as assumed in the magical Cabbala. Therefore Pico's magic is 'une vraye magie pernicieuse et qui destruit entierement les fondements de la loy de Dieu . . . Car la Caballe n'est rien autre chose, que la droite interpretation de la loy de Dieu.'[40]

The rest of the chapter is concerned with the innocent *divinatio humana,* the social sciences seen as bodies of predictive knowledge. The remaining two chapters clear the ground for Book II by considering briefly various forms of illegitimate divination, *other* than that of the modern witch, and insist on the innocence of all illegitimate divination undertaken in good faith.

Book II: Magia

Book I follows the paths of righteousness and of innocence. Book II tracks down the unrighteous, and in its first chapter expands those remarks at the end of Chapters 3 and 5 of Book I where Renaissance magic was condemned as being not merely daemonic (using spirits) but demonic or diabolic (using *evil* spirits). However, magic as such is innocent: 'Le mot de Magie est Persique, et signifie, Science des choses divines et naturelles: et Mage, ou Magicien, n'estoit rien autre chose, que Philosophe.'[41] In other words the *prisca magia* was the passive contemplation of the truth. It will be the purpose of the *Theatrum Naturae* to show the Old Testament as the repository of knowledge of 'choses naturelles', and the *Heptaplomeres* will show it as the repository of 'choses divines': the *République* had already shown the authoritativeness of the Old Testament in 'choses humaines'. In the development of Bodin's work the *Démonomanie* forms a transition concerned with the link between human affairs (especially political change) and divine matters, a link effected by daemonic agencies, who, being corporeal, belong to the world of 'choses naturelles'. It would be illuminating to look at all Bodin's work after the *Methodus* as an attempt to renew the study of man, the universe, and God, in the light of the law of God, which itself renews the *prisca magia* of Adam and the patriarchs.[42]

In the case of the passive, divinatory magic discussed in Book I, 'les moyens . . . sont tirez du sort, et semble qu'il n'y a rien que le hazard'. In the types of active, operative magic discussed in Book II, the mediation of evil spirits is, for Bodin, obvious, because Bodin has no theory of magical forces by which magical operations might otherwise be effected. Consequently all magic involves a pact with the devil, and the intention of the operators is of prime importance.

Bodin structures his discussion of magic in the first three chapters according to whether it involves no invocation of spirits (Chapter 1), tacit invocation (Chapter 2), or express invocation (Chapter 3). In his discussion of tacit invocation Bodin dismisses the possibility of operative Cabbalistic magic. Cabbala is either natural philosophy—knowledge of the physical world— or else knowledge of the providential activities of daemons, both of which are to be found in the Bible. But Cabbalistic number magic is blasphemy: even the Hebrew form of the Lord's name, the tetragrammaton, has no magical efficacy. Whilst it is true that demons flee before the name of the Lord, 'l'effect des merveilles ne gist pas [aux] figures, aux caracteres, aux syllabes, aux paroles, mais en la crainte de Dieu'.[43] The emphasis, again, is on the operator's state of mind.

The Cabbala, then, for Bodin, is the 'secrete intelligence des merveilles de Dieu, couverte d'allegories par toute la Saincte escripture'. As an example of the allegorical method, Bodin takes the commandment of Leviticus on the treatment of lepers.[44] It fits neatly into the context of a discussion of apparently pious magic, since Philo's elucidation of the moral sense of the commandment refers it to the man who 'soubs le voile de religion . . . entremesle la poison d'impieté, comme font les Sorciers avec les noms de Dieu'. The 'natural' sense refers to the increased dangers of infection when the leprosy is active. It is a sense 'que pas un n'a escript' and the fact that Bodin gives it shows how firmly he considers himself to be in the authentic Hebraic tradition himself, carrying on the line of Philo, Leo Ebreo, Maimonides. His genuine indifference to, and ignorance of, the magical Cabbalistic tradition is apparent in his extraordinary statement that the *Zohar* is not yet translated from the Hebrew.[45] After giving many examples of Rabbinical exegesis, which all recur in the *Heptaplomeres*,[46] Bodin declares that on no account must scriptural passages be used as spells: it is not even legitimate to 'prononcer un certain verset des Psalmes pour s'esveiller à telle heure qu'on voudra, pour prier Dieu'.

Bodin then rejects the use of verbal and talismanic magic: first, because the words or characters are not made by God, but by men or evil daemons and are therefore in themselves inefficacious; but second (and contradictorily), because they are only rendered efficacious by credulity in the operator. So when Bodin rejects the Cabbalistic use of the 'parolles de Dieu' he does not do so because they are inefficacious, but because their efficacy consists in procuring eternal life—surely the highest form of magic—and not in the raising of storms.

Bodin introduces his discussion of express invocation in Chapter 3 by a history of the growth of bad magic out of idolatry. His source is Moses Maimonides. The crucial step towards the development of overtly demonic magic consisted in the deification of the Roman Emperors, since this involved the making of 'un nombre infini de Dieux'. Now although consultation with spirits is prohibited by divine law, Lactantius used the Sibylline Oracles to help establish the truth of Christianity, in the eyes of pagans. Bodin states firmly that 'la loy de Dieu defend de s'enquerir à autre qu'à luy des choses futures'.[47] The person who accepts demonic help deserves to die, but this does not apply to demoniacs, those possessed involuntarily by an evil spirit—a phenomenon denied by doctors like Weyer who thereby 'dementent la Loy de Dieu'. Bodin ends the chapter by referring at some length to cases within his own knowledge of people so molested after trying to break their compact with the devil.

The first three chapters concerning demonic magic have dealt essentially with differing degrees of intention and therefore culpability, and are strongly marked by Bodin's personal experience and his private religious practices. The last four deal with the stereotype of the witch who has renounced her faith: they are much more like the normal pattern of witchcraft treatises, from which their material is mainly drawn. There are chapters on the pact and the Sabbat (4); on flying (5); on lycanthropy (6); and on copulation (7). The material is from standard sources, such as Daneau, Sprenger, and Grillandus: but, whilst unoriginal, it is fairly well organised. There is a lot of it, simply in order to establish the weightiness of the case evidence against the sceptics: 'Je mets beaucoup d'authoritez de plusieurs peuples et nations, à fin que la verité soit mieux esclarcie, et par tant d'exemples si souvent experimentez, non par songes, ny resveries. . . .'[48]

All the same, a specifically Bodinian flavour can be felt in these pages: the stress on the concurrence of the most recent cases reported to him personally by legal officials with the experience of the Hebrews and antiquity; the assertion that witch behaviour is a deliberately sacrilegious parody of Hebraic (and not Christian) ceremonial; and the persistent organisation of the argument to block the two major escape routes for sceptics: the tolerant Canon Episcopi, and the assimilation of witchcraft to melancholy. In addition to the standard witchcraft writers, Bodin adduces the prodigy writers, notably Fincelius and Torquemada.[49] And these chapters read rather like prodigy literature, and like pages of the *Apologie de Raimon Sebond*; they impress on us the simple strangeness and sheer inexplicability of the phenomenal world, its literal wonderfulness.

Trevor-Roper has argued the irrelevance of the Renaissance revival of Neoplatonic magic (Hermetic or Cabbalistic) to the late-sixteenth-century witch craze.[50] The second book of the *Démonomanie*, dealing in one continuous argument with Neoplatonic magic and with witchcraft, both seen as diabolical sorcery, is some indication of the fragility of his thesis. Trevor-Roper has also argued that Aristotelean writers rather than Christian Platonists were responsible for the witch craze.[51] This is true to the extent that it is in the Christianised Aristoteleanism of St Thomas Aquinas that the main shapers of the witchcraft tradition in the fifteenth century find their authority. Now Bodin may be the Aristotle of the sixteenth century. But it is against the mechanistically determined, amoral, Aristotelean world that Bodin argues at length in the *Préface*, in the last chapter of Book I, and throughout the four chapters describing the witch stereotype. Indeed, it is a constant criticism of Aristotle in the sixteenth century that his conception of the Deity excludes His providential intervention in the world.

Bodin developed his rejection of this aspect of Aristotelean physics as early as the *Methodus*.[52] What was lacking there was an explanation of just how God's providential purposes operate. This the *Démonomanie* gives us. And the last chapter of Book II situates the activities of witches within the theological framework described in the first two chapters of the *Démonomanie*. All operative magic is not merely diabolical, it is, necessarily, destructive. The devil can promise creative magic, but 'il n'y a rien que des impostures en tout ce qu'il promet'. Demons carry out the retributive functions of divine justice, and *only* the retributive functions. They only operate when God allows it, or indeed, as the *Theatrum* puts it, when he so commands.[53] In other words, Bodin accepts what is obviously the case: that the mechanism of divine miracle and that of diabolic prodigy is essentially the same. The magic of Pharaoh's magicians is weaker than the magic of Moses because God so decided. The power of both magics came from God; but Moses knew this, whereas the wizards thought the power came from the rod, not God.

The emphasis on the intention of the operator, and the irrelevance of his techniques, explains the inconsistency to be observed in magical practices. For example, 'tels Sorciers (qu'on appelloit Archers) ne se trouvent plus en Alemaigne, depuis que ceux qui les tirent, ne croyent pas que le crucifix soit Dieu, ou qu'il ayt quelque divinité en luy: comme ils faisoyent au paravant que la religion eust changé'. It is surprising that Lange sees this as an anticipation of Margaret Murray's thesis of a continuing, underground witchcraft movement. On the contrary it is an explanation of the lack of any such continuous tradition.[54]

Secondly, and paradoxically, Bodin's theory of magic denies the possibility of magic as a set of techniques. There is no body of magical forces with which the sorcerer may operate, and the effectiveness of 'magical' operations depends on the attitude of the sorcerer. This is not so very different from Pomponazzi's views on magic, in spite of the fact that Pomponazzi has virtually done away with daemons. It is certainly an odd fact that Bodin does not attack Pomponazzi, in spite of his Aristotelean mechanistic philosophy, and the reason may perhaps be found here. For ultimately, like Pomponazzi, Bodin does away with natural, diabolical, and angelic magic. Magic is miracle. The study of magic is, as Bodin said at the beginning of this book, the 'science des choses divines et naturelles'. There is *no* science of *operative* magic, merely knowledge, embodied in the Old Testament, of how *God* operates.

Book III: Witchcraft in Perspective

The alarming subject matter in Book II had been dealt with in a remarkably sober and unprovocative spirit. The discussion of the Sabbat, for instance, is almost prudishly reserved and dry. Bodin's aim seemed to be genuinely to establish the facts of the case, in a manner equally removed from the attitude of a defender of witches like Weyer—who conveys an innocent glee at the very incredibility of what he relates; or of a persecutor of witches like De Lancre—who communicates an aesthetic relishing of the orgiastic frenzy of the Sabbat.

In Book III Bodin gives an even more extended treatment of contemporary magical practices, based on more personal documentation than in the previous book. Again he defuses the issues by putting the practices of witches into a number of perspectives which suggest that they constitute a problem both limited and controllable.

At the end of the *Préface* Bodin had written: 'Au troisième livre j'ay parlé des moyens licites et illicites pour prévenir ou chasser les sortilèges'. The structure of the book is only slightly more complicated than this summary suggests. Licit counter-maleficia, as one would expect, are those in conformity with the law of God. Such licit counter-maleficia, both effective and simple, are described in the second half of Chapter 1. This is preceded by an exposé of the history of witchcraft, which argues that thanks to these counter-maleficia, this history is one of containment and catastrophic decline. The discussion in Chapter 5 of unlawful, contemporary counter-maleficia is likewise preceded by a discussion in three chapters of the narrow limitations within which witches can operate. The final chapter is not, strictly speaking, about witchcraft, which is intentional, but about possession by evil spirits, which is not. Bodin, however, sees in the practices of contemporary exorcists just the same dangers as in contemporary counter-maleficia.

In spite of the severely critical tone of most of Book III, Bodin avoids any sense of vindictive or personal polemic. Sprenger the Catholic and Weyer the Protestant are constantly referred to as sources of information about magical practices: that their views on these practices are being vigorously and systematically refuted would be obvious only to the person who had read them. This aspect of the *Démonomanie* has received little acknowledgment. The indignant, overheated brilliance of the refutation of Weyer has led critics to overlook the restraint of the main part of the *Démonomanie*. What characterises the *Démonomanie* itself is a precisely focused passion, certainty of conviction, sureness of intellectual grasp, qualities it shares with the *Réponse* and the *République*. All three define their subject, and assert their originality, with boldness and clarity.[55] The poise and definitiveness of these three works stands in some contrast to the invigorating sense of intellectually pioneering incompleteness in the earlier *Methodus* on the one hand, and the relatively enervated, catechising dogmatism of the *Naturae Theatrum* and the *Paradoxon* on the other. On these general grounds one would be inclined to date the conception of the *Heptaplomeres* from the seventies. Its concerns are very like those of the *Démonomanie*, only transferring to a mood of lively and open debate the Judaism merely sketched and implied here.

Bodin's daemon advised him to sing the ninety-first psalm, a psalm which represents and expresses Bodin's total sense of joyful security in the one and only God of Judaic monotheism. Interestingly, the ecstatic conclusion to

Bodin's listing of counter-maleficia at the end of Book III, Chapter 1 echoes the same mood and repeats the imagery of the psalm: 'le plus asseuré moyen [i.e. countermaleficium] et qui passe tous les autres, c'est de se fier en Dieu, et s'asseurer de luy comme d'une forteresse tres-haute et inexpugnable: c'est dit Philon, le plus grand et le plus agreable sacrifice qu'on sauroit faire à Dieu.'[56] Even more strikingly climactic is the conclusion to the discussion of the limitations on the powers of witches which follows in the next three chapters: 'les sorciers ne tuent pas la dixieme partie de ceux qu'ilz voudroyent... ainsi voit on que les sorciers n'ont pas la puissance d'offencer les meschans si Dieu ne le permet. Comment doncques pourroient ils offencer celuy

> Qui en la garde du haut Dieu
> Pour jamais se retire?'

Here virtually the whole psalm is printed, including the reference to the protective daemon:

> Car il a faict commandement,
> A ses Anges tresdignes,
> De te garder soigneusement
> Quelquepart que chemines.[57]

Now, this sense of existential security is undoubtedly responsible for the control of mood in the *Démonomanie*. When challenged as basically as it was by Weyer's assertion of our insecurity, the reaction was bound to be violent, as it is in the *Refutation*.

Unlike most writers of witchcraft treatises, Bodin does not feel that civilisation faces a crisis of infinite proportions. In this he is unlike even Weyer, for example, who, although he criticises the persecution of witches, believes firmly in eternal damnation and the incredibly resourceful cunning of the devil in his struggle to plunge witches and devils alike into Hell. For Weyer, as for all Christian writers on witchcraft, the Pauline notion of the powers of darkness engaged in a remorseless struggle against the powers of light lies at the back of this conception. But in Bodin's Judaic system, the God of Justice is the God of Mercy—and the retributive functions of the evil spirits are carried out on behalf of, and not in spite of, divine will. Demons punish and angels reward because reward and retribution are complementary aspects of divine providence. What is more, God rewards more than he punishes.

Chapter 1, then, describes how the implementation of the rigid prohibition of sorcery in the law of God has reduced its incidence one hundredfold. Satan's counter-tactics are described according to Hebraic exegesis of the description, in Job XLI, of Behemoth and Leviathan. In particular (and the transition to the present situation is neatly done),

> Satan cherche les Princes superbes et hommes hautains, celà s'est veu, et voit encores.... Et si le Prince est Sorcier, les mignons et courtisans, puis le peuple y est attiré.... Il faut donc pour eviter ces malheurs prescher la Loy de Dieu souvent et imprimer sa crainte aux grands, aux moyens, aux petits, engraver au coeur sa fiance sur tout.[58]

The specific means by which witchcraft is to be combated are little more than the religious counsels given to Bodin by his daemon, as described in Book I, Chapter 2. First: 'chacun doit instruire sa famille à prier Dieu matin et soir, benir, rendre graces à Dieu devant et apres les repas: et donner pour le moins une ou deux heures en un jour de la sepmaine [sic], à faire lire la Bible par le chef de famille, en la presence de toute la famille'. Here the example should be set by the king. Second: 'ne craindre aucunement Satan, ny les Sorcieres.... Et pour ceste cause plusieurs fois en la Loy de Dieu, il est expressément defendu de ne craindre aucunement le Dieu des Payens.' Third: 'celuy qui est ausmonier ne peut estre offensé des sortileges.' This prescription, closely tied up with events in Poitiers in 1567, is so important that 'toute l'Escriture saincte n'est pleine d'autre chose'. Fourth: 'le plus asseuré moyen, c'est de se fier en Dieu.' This advice, discussed above, is followed by an interesting anecdote in which Bodin describes an incident when he impressed this advice on the bishop of Langres, Charles des Cars! In a separate concluding section Bodin upholds the duty to observe the Sabbath and castigates those who sully it with 'toutes les desbauches et folies dont on se peut aviser au grand deshonneur de Dieu, qui n'a rien comandé plus estroittement que chommer le jour du repos: et sur peine de la vie'.[59]

Whilst the third book contains some forty references to recent cases of demonic activity in France, Bodin's account of them shows, on the whole, a not particularly credulous cast of mind. The credulity seems to be that of his contemporaries. After all, the whole culture was surrounded by the supernatural, in a manner conveyed hectically in Weyer, Ronsard, D'Aubigné, Du Bartas, and Boaistuau, to name but a few. Prophets, court astrologers, magicians were many. Christian mysticism, Hermetic magic, and the belief in witchcraft, seem to have been quickened into their most intense life in the last part of the century.

Against this background, Bodin is intent to show the error in the widespread delusion that witches can call on the devil to give protective magic against illness. The fact is, he says, that even apparently beneficial magic is in fact retributory, for 'Satan est si maling, qu'il ne souffre point qu'on face bien, si on ne fait un plus grand mal'.[60]

If witches cannot help others, the theme of Chapter 3 is that they cannot even help themselves: they are ugly, evil-smelling; even their intercourse with the devil is unpleasant; they do not make friends, or influence people. Bodin will not even accept the view of Protestant polemicists that Popes have come to their position by diabolic means. As always, the theme is developed as a specifically Hebraic one, and involves the notion that any rewards or blessings the witch does acquire are acquired only in this world. The anecdotes with which Bodin illustrates his case are told with considerable freshness and economy.

Bodin repeats his rejection of all counter-maleficia apart from trust in the one and only God, and naturally excludes all charms and talismans. Interestingly, he is led to make an exception for the use of incense, fish liver, and salt, since these substances are sanctioned by the Old Testament. He insists that these are inoperative without monotheistic piety, yet the concession does seem extremely awkward, and would seem logically to require greater theoretical justification, since it would not be hard to re-construct a case for the magical properties of other substances, so long as the pious trust in the Lord was also present.[61] However, Bodin is firm about this. Any other substances or any other ritual practices than those expressly sanctioned in the Old Testament are merely a device of the devil to encourage idolatry and a belief in the non-existent magical properties of substances (such as holy water) to expel devils. In fact, according to Bodin 'il n'y a puissance sur terre qui puisse resister à la puissance de Sathan'. Whilst the practices condemned are in fact recommended by the Catholic Sprenger, Bodin largely avoids polemic against him.

The concluding chapter of this book extends the rejection of superstitious counter-maleficia to embrace exorcism. (Catholic exorcism is condemned as both ineffective and dangerous to the operator.) The devil's apparent flight before the exorcist's power is a simple blind. Bodin is especially worried about those cases of exorcism in which the spirit's advice is followed: advice which, in the examples freely given, involves the practice of superstitious Catholic ritual.

A permissible form of exorcism would involve the use of music, as it was used to calm the possessed Saul. This concession is not what it might appear to be, for the efficacy of the music in question, which is enjoined by the 'anciens Hébrieux', derives from its being music in praise of the Lord and not from a theory of magical musical properties. Exorcism, as currently practised, bears no such relationship to the practice of the prophets.

It must be admitted that Bodin's discussion of exorcism is highly relevant to the question of witchcraft. His attack on it is justified and perceptive. He believes that many cases of alleged possession in convents in fact involve no more than straightforward cases of bestiality, which is forbidden in the law of God. And he believes that the unhealthy atmosphere of many convents is a result of the compulsory entry into them of unwilling novices. He removes the most serious aspect of many such cases by insisting that it is not possible for cases of possession to be caused by a third party bringing about the possession.

The course of the witch craze could well have been altered, or indeed prevented, had exorcism not acted as a powerful irritant on the popular imagination. Not only was the witchcraft epidemic in the Laon area triggered off by a notorious case of exorcism, but the European witch craze was probably rather artificially kept alive in seventeenth-century France—and in Northern America—by some highly publicised cases of exorcism, which involved the denunciation by the possessed of sorcerers or witches who were allegedly responsible for causing the possession.[62]

It would be tempting to divide the *Démonomanie* into three books of theory, concerned with the definition of witchcraft, and a final book on practice, concerned with the handling of witchcraft cases. In fact, the thematic link in the first three books is the classification and description of witchcraft phenomena, in order to give practical guidance to judges; and the most interesting section of Book IV, on the other hand, is concerned with an important theoretical point, the justification of punishment.

Book III has suggested that witchcraft is, when all is said and done, a limited threat. The witch, as we saw, is poor, ugly and ill, a social outcast whose wretchedness lies in isolation from both God and the community. But as God has rejected the witch, so he will reject those who do not persecute her. The fierce intolerance which Bodin preaches in this respect should perhaps be seen as the obverse of his rationalistic optimism. His insistence on man's responsibility for his own acts, his conviction that irrationality is a manifestation of intentional sin, places a tremendous burden of potential guilt on man. Thus all violent storms are ultimately to be explained by moral and not meteorological forces, as retribution for evil conduct.

This theory of punishment had already been argued out in the *République*. The king, being bound by the law of God, is necessarily bound to punish infringements of it. He cannot, in particular, exercise the prerogative of mercy in the case of crimes against the law of God:

The wilful murderer, 'you shall take him (saith the Law) from my sacred altar neither shalt thou have pitie on him, but cause him to dye the death: and afterwards I will stretch forth my great mercies upon you. . . .' Now pardons graunted to such villaines drawe after them plagues, famine, warres, and ruines of Commonweales; and that is it for which the law of God saith, That in punishing them that have deserved to dye, they shall take away the cause from among the people.[63]

The simple preaching of the law of God should of itself suffice to 'retenir les meschans en la crainte de Dieu [et] destourner les Sorciers de leur vie detestable'. If not, 'il faut appliquer les cauteres et fers chaux, et couper les parties putrifiees'. In those cases where the king himself is a sorcerer, the retribution will be carried out by God.

Book IV: Retributio

The ruler's duty is to tighten up the legal machinery by which the persecution of witches is carried out. Chapter 1 of Book IV suggests means for expediting the process for obtaining confessions. Any scruples about the methods used should bear in mind that witches suffer already by the mere fact of being witches, so much so that even slow death by burning should not be seen as contributing significantly to their suffering. The judge should obtain evidence by secret accusations against witches, by feigned kindness towards suspects, by threatened or actual torture, by lies about the evidence given by stool-pigeons—'alors pour se venger [le sorcier] rendra peut-être la pareille'. Bodin's dismissal of the traditional case against mendacity is cavalier: 'Tout cela est licite de droit Divin et humain, quoy que Sainct Augustin au livre *De Mendacio*, et Thomas d'Aquin soyent d'advis qu'il ne faut jamais mentir de huict sortes de mensonges, qu'ils mettent bien au long: mais les Juges ne suyvent pas ces resolutions.'[64] He is able to support this from the Old Testament. Abraham, Isaac and Sarah all lied, as did Rahab and the Israelite midwives in Egypt, and the attempt by the Canonists to deny this is merely frivolous.

This Old Testament authority is used very interestingly in the *Heptaplomeres* to justify mere apparent and mendacious conformity to the State religion, so long as the aim is to avoid religious observance in general being brought into disrepute. It is an argument which Bodin undoubtedly adopted for his own conduct, and it helps to explain the efforts Bodin makes in the *Démonomanie* and his other published works, not to offend unnecessarily the Christian reader. All religions contain sanctions for evil conduct, and to this extent, any established religion is legitimated—including inherently idolatrous Christianity.

In the discussion over the next three chapters of the types of proof sufficient to establish the guilt of an alleged witch, Bodin constantly has recourse to the law of God. Thus in Chapter 2 he clinches the discussion of the first type of evidence, 'verité de fait notoire et permanent', by reference to Exodus XXII. 'La loy de Dieu a determiné ceste preuve comme trescertaine et suffisante pour convaincre le Sorcier d'avoir paction expresse avec Sathan, etc.' In the discussion of the second type of evidence, that of 'tesmoins sans reproche', Bodin goes so far as to allow the evidence of accomplices and close relatives. This he justifies by the somewhat alarming precedent of Moses, who commanded the Levites to

> prendre les armes, et tuer chacun son frere et son prochain qui avoyent idolatré apres le veau d'or. . . . Il ne faut donc pas s'arrester aux voyes ordinaires qui deffendent d'ouyr en tesmoignage le fils contre le pere ny le pere contre le filz, car ce crime passe tous les autres . . . ains au contraire c'est droictement proceder selon le droict de laisser l'ordre de droict.[65]

The third form of conclusive evidence is obtained in confession, the subject of Chapter 3. In it, Bodin counters the argument that no confession of supernatural activities is admissible in a court of law, by the simple device of reiterating the evidence of 'autorités divines et humaines' for the actual occurrence of supernatural actions: 'Car les grandes oeuvres et merveilles de Dieu sont impossibles par nature, et toutesfois veritables.'

In dealing with presumptive as opposed to conclusive evidence in Chapter 4, Bodin argues from the start that 'il faut presumer que le sorcier est parricide, attendu la presomption du droict Divin'. This opens the door to supposing that evidence of guilt concerning one act of witchcraft is indicative of guilt concerning all other acts of witchcraft. Moreover, although a cure obtained by exorcism of an evil spirit is not considered a capital offence by civil law, 'si est-ce que la loy de Dieu veut que le Sorcier soit puny à mort. Car il est certain qu'il a traicté avec Sathan'. And in spite of the weight of legal opinion rejecting the testimony of a condemned person who implicates other persons: 'Il se peut faire qu'elle sera veritable, comme nous avons monstré cy dessus, que les Sorciers font souvent mourir les sorciers: et que Dieu ruine ses ennemis par ses ennemis, comme dit Jeremie.'

So far, Bodin has argued on the basis of Roman law, using divine law to interpret it in the direction of severity. In the final chapter Bodin rests his case for judicial rigour squarely on divine law. It is the longest chapter of the whole work, and encompasses a discussion of the judicial attitude towards every kind and degree of sorcery which has been described therein. After an assertion of the seven main purposes of punishment—the first of which is to 'apaiser l'ire de Dieu, et sa vengeance sur tout un peuple', the second to 'obtenir la benediction de Dieu sur tout un pays', and the third to 'donner frayeur et terreur aux autres' (all with exclusively Hebraic support)—Bodin discusses the difference between witchcraft and heresy. He first distinguishes nine criteria by which the pact-maker directly offends against God. All but two, infanticide and incest, are specifically described as being prohibited by divine law, and all without exception are 'directement contre Dieu et son honneur, que les Juges doivent venger à toute rigueur, et faire cesser l'ire de Dieu sur nous'. Witches are further guilty of six crimes against man.

What is to happen in the absence of conclusive proof? Only in the case of 'presomptions faibles' should an accused person be released without punishment. Otherwise the accused must be punished, and the presumptive evidence treated as a form of proof: 'la preuve n'est pas seulement celle qui est necessaire, ains aussi celle qui approche de la preuve indubitable, mesmement [especially] des choses qu'on a de coustume d'executer en secret.' Thus punishment by 'fustigations, sections, marques, emprisonnemens perpetuels, amendes pecuniaires, confiscations, et autres semblables peines' must be infligée. Of course the severity which Bodin goes on to enjoin has to be defended, and this he does: on the grounds that 'il ne faut pas pour un inconvenient, qu'il n'adviendra pas souvent, que on laisse à faire une bonne loy'. A judge who is lenient towards witches is himself guilty of the crime— he should be killed himself for calling in question the law of God.

As for the cases of witchcraft which do not involve a pact with the devil, and which were discussed in Book II, Bodin argues that much of it infringes divine law. In any case, 'en toutes choses où l'esprit humain est effrayé de crainte superstitieuse, ou retiré de la fiance d'un seul Dieu, pour adherer aux vanitéz quelle qu'elle soit, Dieu y est offencé et est vraye idolatrie'. Whilst many peasant superstitions cannot properly be punished but only corrected by the 'parole de Dieu', the magistrate must still punish those who encourage superstitious practices, such as the wearing of relics and allegedly sacred objects.

Bodin is predictably fierce against those in authority who condone superstition: the priest, the magistrate, and the ruler. On the other hand, 'L'obeissance d'une jeune fille envers sa mere, d'un jeune enfant envers son pere, et d'un jeune serviteur envers son maistre, merite que la peine soit adoucie, si on apperçoit la confession, et repentance devant la conviction.' Ignorance can be an argument for clemency in the case of witchcraft which does not involve a pact. But no one who makes a pact with the devil can possibly plead innocence, 'car il n'y a personne qui puisse dire par erreur qu'il ait renié Dieu son Createur, pour se donner au diable'. And the man of letters has no excuse for any crime of sorcery. Almost never, says Bodin, should a person accused of witchcraft escape entirely free of punishment; the exception is to be only those cases where the accusation is shown without any shadow of doubt to be unfounded. And it is hard to see how this would ever arise.

To encourage the magistrate in his severity, Bodin ends the *Démonomanie* with five instances of the death of witches being followed by the cessation of the sickness or mortality which they had allegedly provoked: 'Qui est bien pour monstrer que la cause principalle cessant, les effects cessent, encores que Dieu face tomber les afflictions sur ceux qu'il luy plaist.'[66]

Conclusion

These final words of the *Démonomanie* remind us that its purpose is like that of Bodin's pioneering works on economics (the *Réponse*) and on political theory (the *République*): the attempt to cope with a situation of serious social, economic and ideological disturbance.

Posterity has perhaps been too harsh on the *Démonomanie*, especially with respect to Book IV. We do well to remember that even here Bodin includes in theory nearly all the safeguards which the 'defender of witches', Weyer, had advocated, and that the judicial procedures he recommends were not unusual. Indeed, Mesnard suggests that Bodin's recommendations are untypically lenient for the period.[67] But if in this respect Bodin is only doubtfully in advance of his contemporaries, the general framework of his discussion of witchcraft is far more original. Even Weyer thought that witches carried out all the activities that they were alleged to. He merely denied that they were in control of the forces they sought to use, and saw them as helpless victims. Above all, Weyer wrote within a Christian frame of reference; but since sarcastic common sense would reject the beliefs and practices of Christians as well as those of witches, the pioneering efforts of Weyer and Scot along the lines of ridicule were bound to fail to convince.

Bodin's non-Christian standpoint led him to see the witch as the social deviant, the person who rejects the religion of the tribe (any tribe), and who deliberately stands accepted values on their head. As he puts it in the opening sentence: 'Sorcier est celuy qui par moyens diaboliques sciemment s'efforce de parvenir à quelque chose.' No doubt Bodin here projects on to the figure of the apostasising witch the terrible fears of social and ideological chaos caused by his own rejection of Christianity.[68] But we should remember that the positive achievements of the *République* and the *Démonomanie* were conceived as answers to these fears.

I believe that when the *Démonomanie* is given its proper place as a key text for the understanding of Bodin, we may be less inclined to dismiss out of hand the actual existence of witchcraft practices.[69] We shall also see in his works a passionate search for lasting social and cultural norms in a period of profound cultural shock. In political and religious theory alike, Bodin sought for a synthesising principle above the conflicts which had torn his country apart. He found it, in the *République*, in the concept of sovereignty. He found it, in the *Démonomanie* and in the *Heptaplomeres*, in the strict monotheism of his system of daemonic Judaism.[70]

Notes

1 R. Chauviré, *Jean Bodin* (Paris, 1914), pp. 518-19. This is the standard, but dated, work on Bodin. For recent research and bibliography, see *Verhandlungen der internationalen Bodin Tagung*, ed. H. Denzer (Munich, 1973). For a good, recent study of the *Démonomanie*, Ursula Lange, *Untersuchungen zu Bodins Démonomanie* (Frankfurt, 1970).
2 *Préface*, sig. ã iiij. All my references to the *Démonomanie* are to the first edition (Paris, 1580).
3 *Dém.*, Bk II, ch. 8, fol. 114.
4 Thus, Françoise Mallet-Joris, *Trois Ages de la Nuit* (Paris, 1968; translated as: *The Witches*, London, 1970).
5 *Préface*, sig. ã iiij^v.
6 It is significant that these two immediate attacks on Weyer both concentrate on Weyer's clumsy attempts to get round the authority of the Old Testament.
7 E. W. Monter, 'Inflation and Witchcraft. The Case of Jean Bodin', in K. T. Rabb and J. E. Seigel, *Action and Conviction in Early Modern Europe* (Princeton, 1969), pp. 371-89; H. R. Trevor-Roper, *The European Witch-Craze of the 16th and 17th centuries* (Harmondsworth, 1969), p. 74.
8 E.g. De Lancre, Nicolas Rémy, and Matthew Hopkins.
9 *Préface*, sig. ã iiij, ẽ.
10 *Dém.*, Bk IV, ch. 1, fol. 166.
11 *Dém.*, Bk II, ch. 8, fols III^v, 117^v.
12 *Ibid.*, Bk III, ch. 1, fols 124, 125.
13 Alan Macfarlane, *Witchcraft in Tudor and Stuart England* (London, 1970), p. 302.
14 *Réponse aux Paradoxes de M. De Malestroit* (Paris, 1568). Cf. Hauser's edition (Paris, 1932), p. 3.

15 *Réponse*, p. 33.
16 *Ibid.*, p. 35.
17 *Ibid.*, p. 39.
18 *Ibid.*, p. 45. Repeated in the *République*, Bk VI, ch. 3, p. 691. Page references are to Knolles's translation, *The Six Books of a Commonweale*, ed. K. D. McRae (Harvard, 1962).
19 *Rép.*, Bk VI, ch. 2, p. 676.
20 *Préface*, sig. ẽ iij.
21 *Oratio*, p. 25B, in *Oeuvres Philosophiques de Jean Bodin*, ed. P. Mesnard (Paris, 1951).
22 *Methodus*, p. 362, Beatrice Reynolds trans. (New York, 1945; repr. 1966).
23 That, at least, is Bodin's view. He is, of course, highly eccentric and unreliable in his ideas about intellectual history. His persistent attempts to isolate and reconstruct a Judaic tradition need much further study; see final note.
24 For Bodin as a prophet, see my article, 'Jean Bodin's Daemon', in the *Verhandlungen, op. cit.*
25 In this chapter, 'demon' means retributory spirit, 'angel' means rewarding spirit, and 'daemon' includes both.
26 *Colloquium Heptaplomeres*, ed. L. Noack (Schwerin, 1857; reprinted Hildesheim, 1970), Bk VI, p. 260 (p. 498 of the French manuscript translation, partially published by R. Chauviré, *Colloque de Jean Bodin*, 1914). There is a new English translation by M. L. Daniels Kuntz (Princeton, 1975).
27 *Dém.*, Bk I, ch. 1, fols 2, 4.
28 *Ibid.*, fol. 1^v.
29 *Ibid.*, fol. 2.
30 *Ibid.*, Bk I., ch. 2, fol. 9.
31 *Ibid.*, Bk I, ch. 2, fol. 13. Since the daemonic experience, he has always known what to believe and has been assured of his salvation; *ibid.*, fol. 11.
32 Sun worship is said to be actually rewarded, not merely excused, in *Heptaplomeres*, Bk II, p. 123 (Noack); *Colloque*, Chauviré, p. 228.
33 *Dém.*, Bk I, ch. 3, fol. 18^v.
34 *Ibid.*, fol. 19.
35 *Heptaplomeres*, p. 260; *Colloque*, p. 499. See Matthew XII, 25, 26.
36 *Dém.*, Bk I, ch. 3, fols 19^v, 20.
37 *Heptaplomeres*, pp. 153, 333; *Colloque*, pp. 328, 628.
38 *Dém.*, Bk I, ch. 4, fol. 27. The *Démonomanie* is, of course, part of Bodin's attempt to 'instruire les autres'.
39 All these quotations from *Dém.*, Bk I, ch. 5, fols 30, 30^v.
40 *Ibid.*, fol. 38.
41 *Ibid.*, Bk II, ch. 1, fol. 51.
42 Properly understood, then, magia, philosophia, and cabbala, are the same for Bodin. All are contained in the Old Testament.
43 *Dém.*, Bk II, ch. 2, fol. 63.
44 *Ibid.*, fol. 63^v; and Leviticus, XIII, XIV.

45 On the Zohar in Christian Cabbala see J. Blau, *Christian Interpretation of the Cabala in the Renaissance* (New York, 1944), and on Postel's translations, F. Secret, *Les Kabbalistes Chrétiens de la Renaissance* (Paris, 1964).
46 See *Heptaplomeres*, Bks II, III, *passim*.
47 *Dém.*, Bk II, ch. 3, fols 70, 75. Bodin's discussion of the origin of magic closely follows Maimonides, and is unlike that to be found in the liberals of the Hermetic tradition. He seems not to be referring at all to the Hermetic god-making ceremonies of the *Asclepius*, and his rejection of the Sibylline Oracles here is exceptionally categorical. See Frances A. Yates, *Giordano Bruno and the Hermetic Tradition* (London, 1964); and D. P. Walker, *Spiritual and Demonic Magic from Ficino to Campanella* (London, 1958).
48 *Dém.*, Bk II, ch. 4, fol. 86.
49 *Ibid.*, fol. 84. Antonio de Torquemada, *Jardin de flores curiosas*, 1570. Bodin thinks Torquemada deserves to be translated: he was, only two years later (*Hexameron, ou six journees*, trans. Gabriel Chappuys, 1582). This is a neat illustration of how close Bodin is in these four chapters to contemporary intellectual fashion. Compare, too, the following remarks from the dedicatory epistle of Boaistuau's *Histoires Prodigieuses*, 1559, which is one of the genre: 'nous y descouvrons [sc. dans les prodiges] le plus souvent ung secret jugement et fléau de l'ire de Dieu . . . nous sommes contrains d'entrer en nous mesmes, frapper au marteau de nostre conscience'. This is a mood which Bodin had gone out of his way to attack in the *Methodus*. On the genre, see R. Schenda, *Die französische Prodigienliteratur* (Munich, 1961).
50 Trevor-Roper, *op. cit.*, pp. 59–62.
51 *Ibid.*, p. 114.
52 Especially in ch. VIII, 'A system of universal time'.
53 *Universae Naturae Theatrum* (Lyons, 1596), p. 178.
54 *Dém.*, Bk II, ch. 8, fol. 118; and Lange, *op. cit.*, p. 141.
55 Compare the opening sentences of all three works.
56 *Dém.*, Bk III, ch. 1, fol. 125.
57 *Ibid.*, ch. 4, fols 142, 143.
58 *Ibid.*, ch. 1, fols 120^v, 121^v.
59 These *countermaleficia* in *Dém.*, Bk III, ch. 1, fols 123, 124, 125, 127.
60 *Ibid.*, ch. 2, fol. 131^v.
61 *Ibid.*, fol. 145. Bodin had introduced the chapter by writing that 'ceste question est des plus difficiles qu'on peut former en ce traicté'. He is fully aware that his assumption of the exclusive authority of the Old Testament is the crux of the matter. The *Heptaplomeres* can be seen as an extended justification of the assumption.
62 For instance, the notorious cases at Salem, and at Loudun. See R. Mandrou, *Magistrats et Sorciers en France au XVIIe siècle* (Paris, 1968). Mandrou sees the refutation of Weyer by Bodin as the *fons et origo* of the witchcraft debate. It is worth noting that Bodin is at one with Weyer in recommending the dispersal of nuns when a religious community has become infected with hysteria.

63 *République*, Bk I, ch. 10, p. 174, with marginal reference to Deuteronomy XIX and XXI; see also Bk III, ch. 5, p. 341; Bk IV, ch. 6, p. 509.
64 *Dém.*, Bk IV, ch. 1, fol. 171^v.
65 *Ibid.*, ch. 2, fol. 179.
66 *Ibid.*, ch. 5, fol. 217^v.
67 P. Mesnard, 'La Démonomanie de Jean Bodin', in *L'opera e il pensiero de G. P. della Mirandola* II (Florence, 1965), pp. 333–56.
68 A somewhat similar psychological explanation of the witch craze has been suggested in the postscript to N. Cohn, *Europe's Inner Demons* (London, 1975). But in Bodin's case there is no question of unconscious resentment against Christianity as too strict a religion. On the contrary he deliberately rejects the Christian ethics of forgiveness as socially dangerous.
69 The evidence in support of widespread peasant belief in the reality of witchcraft practices is hard to refute, and the soundness of Bodin's use of such evidence is properly acknowledged in *Les Sorcières* (Paris, 1973), p. 25. In this catalogue of the Bibliothèque Nationale exhibition on the iconography of witchcraft Bodin is the most utilised primary source.
70 In addition to Lange's work, and the Munich symposium (see note 1), consult in particular F. von Bezold, *Jean Bodin als Okkultist und seine Démonamanie*, in *Historische Zeitschrift*, vol. 105 (1910); J. Guttmann, *Jean Bodin in seinen Beziehungen zu dem Judentum* (Breslau, 1906), also in *Monatsschrift für Geschichte des Judentums*, vol. 49 (1905); G. Roellenbleck, *Offenbarung, Natur and Jüdische Uberlieferung bei Jean Bodin* (Kassel, 1964).

REGINALD SCOT'S *DISCOVERIE OF WITCHCRAFT*: SCEPTICISM AND SADDUCEEISM

Sydney Anglo

Reginald Scot is among the best-known figures in the history of the witch-craft controversy: though, as is so often the case with those who write very thick books on outmoded disputes, he is more often cited than read, and references to his *Discoverie of Witchcraft* generally reveal only a superficial knowledge of the text. These passing allusions tend to suggest that Scot—however laudably inspired by a humanitarian concern for wrongly accused old women—was merely an amateur dabbler, and that his book is a rambling collection of miscellaneous and often irrelevant information, designed merely to discredit belief in witchcraft. In fact, Scot presented a serious and sustained argument, and was able to construct not only a coherent and solidly planned book, but also a personal cosmology providing radical answers to a host of contemporary intellectual problems: the nature of spirits, demons, and angels; the nature of the devil; spiritual, demonic, and natural magic; and the possibility of purging Christianity of magical practices.

The man who grappled so daringly with these fundamental issues was, on the face of it, a very unlikely candidate for intellectual honours. We know very little about his life; and what we do know seems uneventful. Scot was born about the year 1538 of a highly respected Kentish family; and his cousin, Sir Thomas Scot—one of the dedicatees of the *Discoverie*—was destined to become a man of considerable significance in the county. But Reginald, having studied at Hart Hall, Oxford, without completing a degree, settled down to life in Kent, where he was active, though not especially prominent, in public affairs and private business till his death on 9 October 1599.[1]

His only other published work, antedating the *Discoverie* by a decade, is

SCEPTICISM AND SADDUCEEISM

A Perfite Platforme of a Hoppe Garden, which, while scarcely impinging upon the great intellectual battles of the Renaissance, nevertheless demonstrates certain qualities of mind fitting the author for his greater task.[2] The *Hoppe Garden* has an honoured place in the history of horticultural writing. It is, perhaps, the first English treatise devoted to one particular form of husbandry; and it was a subject for which there existed no native guide. Scot had to discover techniques by his own endeavours, and his accuracy and clarity are such that it is still possible to use his book as a practical manual. The illustrations, too, devised by Scot to supplement the text, remain useful, and anticipate the plates later employed in the *Discoverie* to elucidate various complicated conjuring tricks. But there is, at the very end of the *Hoppe Garden,* an even clearer hint of things to come. Scot surmises that his little book will be attacked by 'Momus, and hys companyons': that is by unlearned and idle scoffers.

> For some will take uppon them to be Judges, that (for their integritie) are not meete to be impanelled in a true Jurie, nor for theyr credite scant worthy to be hangmen to false theeves, their iudgementes being corrupt, and alwayes tending to the condemnation of the unguiltie, their wisdome servynge them to no other ende, but to quarrell with other mens simplicities, the sharpenesse of their wits to nothing but to the maintenaunce of contencion. Some will be Controllers that neither have authoritie in their persons, nor wit in their heades, reprooving that which neyther they (being fooles) knowe, nor other (beeing wyse) myslyke. Finally, some are so possessed with the spirite of Scurrillitye, that they cannot gape, but Tauntes appeare in their mouthes, confounding iest and sobrietie in suche sorte, as though all things were but mockerie. I saye therefore, that from the hyest to the lowest, from the Iudge to the Hangman, from the top of the Gallowes, to the nethermost steale of the Ladder, and from Scoggin to Will Summer, there remayneth not one of these scoffers more favoured of himselfe, than abhored of others.

Ten years later, this brief challenge to established authority, ignorance, and lack of understanding, was to be developed, by Scot himself, into a major assault upon the accepted cosmology of his time. The horticulturalist was metamorphosed into an intellectual iconoclast: and the minions of Momus, who had not, in fact, descended upon his *Hoppe Garden,* wreaked their wrath upon his *Discoverie of Witchcraft.*[3]

It seems likely that the increasing pace of witchcraft prosecutions in England during the decade following the publication of the *Hoppe Garden*—

and especially the St Osyth case to which Scot may well have been witness—must have weighed heavily upon him and led him to a systematic study of the evidence presented at such trials.[4] Moreover, in these same years, the campaign against witches, and the debate concerning spiritual and demonic magic, was increasing in fervour on the Continent: the works of Bodin, Daneau, Hemmingius, Anania, and Vair, were all published at this time, as were the later editions of Weyer's *De Praestigiis Daemonum* with Erastus's dialogues, and Weyer's briefer treatise, *De Lamiis*.[5] Several factors appear to have inspired Scot's work: horror at the prejudice of the judges in witch trials; the fatuity of the charges brought against helpless and often senile women; the way in which, to his mind, the evidence adduced in trials was totally inadequate and unsubstantiated; the violation of accepted legal practice; and the fact that his own religious convictions—reinforced, paradoxically, by an extremely sceptical temperament—seemed to invalidate even the possibility of magical activity. Furthermore, Scot appreciated, as few contemporaries did, the inconsistency and gross credulity of the apologists for witch-hunting, and the distance between their intellectual structures and the sordid trivialities of the persecution itself.

The principal purposes of the *Discoverie* are briefly set out in an *Epistle to the Readers* (sig. B. iv).

> First, that the glorie and power of God be not so abridged and abased, as to be thrust into the hand or lip of a lewd old woman; whereby the worke of the Creator should be attributed to the power of a creature. Secondlie, that the religion of the gospell may be seene to stand without such peevish trumperie. Thirdlie, that lawfull favour and christian compassion be rather used towardes these poore soules, than rigor and extremitie. Bicause they, which are commonlie accused of witchcraft, are the least sufficient of all other persons to speake for themselves; as having the most base and simple education of all others; the extremitie of their age giving them leave to dote, their povertie to beg, their wrongs to chide and threaten (as being void of anie other waie of revenge) their humor melancholicall to be full of imaginations, from whence cheefelie proceedeth the vanitie of their confessions.

Stated thus, Scot's aims sound modest enough: but their achievement proved beyond the capacity of every writer, apart from Scot, in the entire history of the witchcraft controversy.

In the preparation of his *Discoverie,* Scot followed the empirical and experimental bent already demonstrated in his study of hop cultivation. As with the earlier work, there was no native English study which might be employed as a guide; and, in any case, Scot liked to test things for himself. He interviewed people whom he had heard were involved in witchcraft cases, and discovered that even voluntary confessions to diabolic practices should be taken with large doses of salt (pp. 48, 55-7). He experimented with feats which had baffled ignorant onlookers (pp. 309, 352, 478). And he even attempted demonic conjurations to see whether they really worked (p. 443). Moreover, he studied all the major demonological and magical writings of his time; and the fact that he makes use of Leonard Vair's *De Fascino* and of Henry Howard's *Defensative against the poyson of supposed prophesies*—both of which were published in 1583—suggests that he was collecting and sifting material for his book till shortly before going to press, and accounts for the slips, inaccuracies, and other evidence of rapid composition discernible in the *Discoverie*.[6]

For Scot the study of demonology meant much more than merely haggling over the verities of witchcraft: over whether witches could work wonders, charm people, fly through the air, attend sabbats, or copulate with devils. The whole problem of magic was involved. Was it possible for anybody to bring to pass things totally outside the normal field of human experience, and totally alien to generally recognised natural phenomena? Demonologists invariably buttressed their arguments concerning the possibility of miracles and wonders by referring to the authority of the Holy Scriptures. How could the numerous allusions to demonic activity contained therein be gainsaid? And this, in turn, involved the entire question of scriptural interpretation: patristic accretion *versus* biblical fundamentalism; allegory *versus* literality; myth *versus* historicity; orthodox Catholicism *versus* Protestantism. Moreover, the Catholic Church still had its own magic; and it maintained the possibility of miraculous occurrences. But what were these miracles, and how did they differ from the wonders attributed to witchcraft against which the Church had itself instituted an Inquisition? And, finally, there was the fundamental problem posed by all miracles: were they still possible, or had they ceased for ever?[7]

All these issues were inevitably raised by Scot's modest statement of purpose: and his answers may, for the sake of clarity, be summarised before his work is analysed in detail. He appreciates the scope of 'natural magic' which, being but the skilful operation and exploitation of natural causes and effects, is not—in the modern sense—magic at all; but denies the possibility either of spiritual or demonic magic. He denies the operation of spirits or demons in human affairs; and, indeed, goes so far as to eliminate even the possibility that extra-terrestrial beings have anything other than a metaphorical significance. He is a biblical fundamentalist in that he denies validity to the accretions of the Fathers; but his interpretation of the Scriptures is neither literal nor entirely allegorical, and depends far more upon a purely common-sense response to context. For Scot, the Scriptures are an historic document. They chronicle the events leading up to the coming of Christ, and the events of Christ's life. The miraculous occurrences contained therein were worked by God in order to establish the truth of Christianity. This being so, the age of miracles ceased in apostolic times, and to seek further evidence for the faith is to imply that Christ's own deeds had been inadequate. It follows from this that any other seemingly miraculous deeds described in the Scriptures (when not performed by accredited prophets of God or by Christ himself) could not possibly have been miraculous at all, and it becomes necessary to seek non-magical explanations for stories such as the necromancy of the witch of Endor, or the performances of Pharaoh's magicians. Scot's view of Catholicism is consistent with these beliefs: both the deeds attributed to saints, and the magical enactments of the Mass, are false; and the rites of the Roman Church are comparable in character and efficacy to the diabolical rites of the demonic magician, being blasphemous, sacrilegious, but totally devoid of practical results. Thus we are left with a final question: what then is witchcraft? And Scot defines it simply as a cozening art

> wherin the name of God is abused, prophaned and blasphemed, and his power attributed to a vile creature. In estimation of the vulgar people, it is a supernaturall worke, contrived betweene a corporall old woman, and a spirtuall divell. The maner thereof is so secret, mysticall, and strange, that to this daie there hath never beene any credible witnes therof. It is incomprehensible to the wise, learned or faithfull; a probable matter to children, fooles, melancholike persons and papists.

It will be seen from this brief summary that Scot's position is a highly defensible one—far less assailable, for example, than that assumed by his immediate predecessor as a writer against witch persecution, Johann Weyer. It has been generally assumed that Scot 'accepted the arguments of Weyer'[8] who was bitterly hostile to the ritual of the Roman Church, spent much energy attacking priests, and attempted to construct a Christianity purged of magic. But Weyer was working upon an impossible foundation: for he accepted the reality of the devil and of his operations amongst men; he accepted the reality of demons, attributing to them many of the apparent and alleged operations of witches not merely during his own time but also in the Scriptures; and he did not face up to the question of the continuance or cessation of miracles. Weyer defends those accused of witchcraft on the

SCEPTICISM AND SADDUCEEISM

grounds that they are generally 'melancholic'; silly, senile, folk deluded sometimes by themselves and sometimes by the devil himself. But, by conceding the actuality of the devil's dealings with men, Weyer had destroyed his own case. If the devil and his host of demons could wreak physical effects, could work corporeally, and could traffic with men, there remained no logical objection to the idea that men might equally traffic with demons. Scot thoroughly understood this, and concentrated upon destroying belief in demons and in the devil himself, knowing full well that when that diabolical edifice was demolished witchcraft would collapse with it. One has only to compare Weyer and Scot on two of the *loci classici* of the witchcraft debate—the witch of Endor; and the contest between Moses, Aaron, and Pharaoh's magicians—to measure the distance, or rather the gulf, between them.

The vision of Samuel was frequently adduced to support the possibility of necromancy. Weyer had cudgelled his brain over this riddle, and had argued laboriously that Samuel had been dead for two years and that therefore 'si son corps n'estoit du tout pourry, pour le moins il est certain qu'il estoit tellement deffiguré, que ceste belle face vive ne se pouvoit monstrer, en laquelle devant que mourir il paroissoit, & en laquelle derechef ce feinct Samuel estoit aparu'. So, says Weyer, since it was not Samuel, it must have been an illusion created by the devil himself who already knew what Samuel had previously foretold concerning Saul and 'il peut encore coniecturer assez bien ce qui pouvoit avenir à Saul de ceste bataille'. Weyer notes that, amongst the rabbinical authorities, the majority share this view that the vision of Samuel was 'un ouvrage Pythonique', with a demon personating the prophet. There are others, he notes in passing, who think that all these things 'ont esté feintes par l'art de la femme, laquelle par certaines coniectures trompa ainsi Saul'. But his own view is clearly stated at the outset of his discussion: the vision was a 'fantosme diabolique sous la figure de Samuel'.[9]

For Scot, however, Weyer's solution is no solution at all. If the devil were able to deceive Saul by simulating the figure of a dead prophet in response to the wishes of an old woman, then, of course, he could deceive anybody by simulating anything. Weyer's argument was tantamount to accepting the reality of witchcraft; so Scot axes the whole story, root and branch. There was no dead body conjured up; no ghost; nor even a demon in the guise of the dead man. It was all a 'meere cousenage', for, says Scot, this is the most obvious explanation of the text and therefore the most likely; 'for it is ridiculous (as Pompanacius saith) to leave manifest things, and such as by naturall reason may be prooved, to seeke unknowne things, which by no likeliehood can be conceived, nor tried by anie rule of reason' (p. 142).

On the power of Pharaoh's magicians, Weyer was more equivocal.[10] Possibly, he suggests, the magicians 'ont mis au devant des yeux du Roy la feinte figure d'un serpent fait par la folie Magique'; or, if the serpents were real, they had been brought by the devil who was able to travel at prodigious speeds.[11] Scot does not consider it worth while even to mention the theory of a devil running errands on behalf of the magicians; for this is one explanation which his system totally excludes. He does, however, concede that Pharaoh's magicians might well have performed real miracles if God had compelled them 'in their ridiculous wickednes to be instruments of his will and vengeance, upon their maister Pharao' (pp. 318-19). Nevertheless, he thinks it more likely that they were skilled jugglers, or even that they had a considerable knowledge of the natural properties of things, far beyond the ignorant multitude who thus regarded their tricks as truly miraculous. 'And (as *Pompanacius* saith) it is most true, that some for these feats have beene accounted saints, some other witches' (p. 317).

It cannot be denied that Scot was greatly impressed by Weyer. The *De Praestigiis Daemonum* is a treasure-house of witchcraft delusion, anti-Catholic anecdotes, and demonological lore. It attacks magic from many directions, all of them interesting and potentially effective. In Weyer's hands, however, they lose their force. His most characteristic mode of argument displays a laborious ingenuity whereby he seeks to explain away self-evident absurdities, employing notions frequently more far-fetched than those he is refuting. Scot, conversely, is uncompromisingly empirical, always eschewing a laborious and inconsistent explanation for any phenomenon when, as Pomponazzi said, there is a more straightforward one. Weyer's inconsistencies make witchcraft not only feasible but decidedly the most likely explanation for the situations he describes. Scot's system renders witchcraft impossible.

Nevertheless, in one respect Weyer was of crucial significance to Scot. He was, perhaps, the first to perceive how biblical evidence might be subverted by challenging the interpretation of the actual words employed in the Greek, Hebrew, and Latin texts of the Scriptures. We read, he says, 'le nom de Magicien, ou de sorcier, ou d'enchanteur, ou d'empoisonneur, ou d'imposteur, (comme aucuns l'interpretent) par lesquels on afferme sans distinction les sorcieres estre entendues, & remarquees'.[12] But, in fact, the words so translated were very different both from each other and from language to language. Accordingly, he had consulted Andreas Masius—one of the most celebrated Hebrew scholars of the time—and had received an explication of eight key words employed in the Scriptures in connection with magical practices.[13] Weyer argues that a good deal of the confusion concerning witchcraft derives from a misunderstanding of these words, and, in particular, he chastises German writers who translate everything by the word *Zauberer,* thus concealing the essential meanings of the Word of God. Scot recognises that a similar ambiguity exists in English, and argues that there are various kinds of magician mentioned in the Scriptures 'whereof our witchmongers old women which danse with the fairies, &c. are none'. All of them are, in one way or another, cheats or abusers of the people: but because 'they are all termed of our translators by the name of witches in the Bible: therefore the lies of *M. Mal* and *Bodin,* and all our old wives tales are applied unto these names, and easilie beleeved of the common people, who have never hitherto beene instructed in the understanding of these words' (p. 109). And Scot, acknowledging his debt in this matter to Weyer, and referring from Weyer to Masius, uses the eight key words to provide a framework for the greater part of his work.

The *Discoverie of Witchcraft* is a carefully organised treatise with a solid structure sometimes obscured, not by irrelevancies or digressions, but rather by an excess of detail; and Scot rarely loses the thread of his argument. He begins by introducing the main lines of enquiry to be pursued and developed throughout his long work, and he states his position at the very outset: the fable of witchcraft has so possessed men's minds that they cannot endure God's correction. Every adversity is attributed to witches, as though there were no God 'that ordereth all things according to his will; punishing both just and unjust with greefs, plagues, and afflictions in maner and forme as he thinketh good: but that certaine old women heere on earth, called witches, must needs be the contrivers of all mens calamities, and as though they themselves were innocents, and had deserved no such punishments' (p. 1). As soon as anything goes amiss, people cry out against witches and conjurors, though it is obvious that terrible things happen just as frequently when alleged witches are absent as when they are present, 'yea and continue when witches are hanged and burnt: whie then should we attribute such effect to that cause, which being taken awaie, happeneth neverthelesse?' (p. 14). Furthermore, Scot asks, if witches could indeed accomplish such deeds, why should Christ's miracles have seemed at all remarkable? Extraordinary powers are attributed to witches by 'witchmongers, papists, and poets': yet when we look into the matter we find that such as are said to be witches are commonly 'old, lame, bleare-eied, pale, fowle, and full of wrinkles; poore, sullen, superstitious, and papists; or such as knowe no religion'; and despite the bargain they are thought to have made with the devil, they never receive 'beautie, monie, promotion, welth, worship, pleasure, honor, knowledge, learning, or anie other benefit whatsoever'.

It is easy to see how an old woman might earn a reputation for maleficence. She is usually poor and reduced to beggary; she is refused charity; she curses first one neighbour, then another, till at length everybody has at some time incurred her displeasure and imprecation. Eventually somebody falls sick, or dies, whereupon the ignorant suspect witchcraft, and are confirmed in this opinion by unskilful physicians who use superstition as a convenient cloak for their own ineptitude. Other misfortunes are similarly laid at the woman's door, while she in turn, seeing her curses taking effect, believes that she has indeed wrought magic. Thus, for Scot, this kind of witch is simply the innocent victim of a chain of circumstances and superstition.[14] But there are other people with a reputation for witchery; and these are 'absolutelie cooseners', deliberate frauds who take upon themselves, 'either for glorie, fame, or gaine, to doo anie thing, which God or the divell can doo: either for foretelling of things to come, bewraieng of secrets, curing of maladies, or working of miracles'. Scot's book is concerned with both kinds of witch: to expose the stupidity involved in persecuting the one; to expose the false claims of the other; and to show how the deceits of the latter have provided fuel for the persecution of the former.

In Scot's view, the basic crime of witchmongering lies in the very belief that such nonsense is possible, and thereby in attributing to witches powers proper to God alone. Whoever does this is a 'blasphemer, idolater, and full of grosse impietie' (p. 12). But he is further concerned at the way in which such attitudes are pressed to illogical conclusions on the basis of which an entire system of persecution has been erected; and his Second Book provides an account of the process whereby witchmongers secure convictions. Here Scot strikes at one of the foundations of the witchcraft argument: the evidence accumulated from trials and confessions, confidently alleged as irrefutable proof of the reality of witches' crimes. Elaborating upon Bodin's justification that, because it is an extraordinary matter, 'there must heerein be extraordinarie dealing' (p. 24), Scot demonstrates that, in witch trials, the judicial procedure is so distorted that the accused cannot possibly escape her inquisitors.[15] The only avenue to salvation is to produce, alive and well, somebody supposedly already slain: though, ironically, this is to be marvelled at since, according to the authorities, witches 'can bring the divell in any bodies likenesse and representation' (p. 27). The trials are 'parciall'—crudely weighted against the accused—and Scot, alluding to the test based on the allegation that witches cannot weep, points out that sometimes an honest woman cannot 'in the heavines of her heart shed teares; the which oftentimes are more readie and common with craftie queanes and strumpets than with sober women' (p. 28). As an instance of the terrible self-perpetuating nature of such illegal and biased proceedings, Scot cites the Marian persecutions in

England, arguing that the fear of death and the suffering of torture must inevitably extort confessions: the victim can scarcely bear the torment which will be continued for as long as she denies the charges against her; while, even if she were to hold out, the inquisitors would allege that she has charms for taciturnity. Either way she is trapped.

In his Third Book, Scot attacks the alleged diabolic pact. In the first place, he argues, such pacts violate our reason, since they are absurd in themselves and postulate an absurd situation in which the witch willingly consigns herself to eternal torment in return for absolutely nothing. It is obvious that, whatever promises he is said to make, the devil never helps his human partners, never rescues them from punishment, and never makes them rich or powerful; and it is a wonder that, from the dawn of time, nobody has ever thought to challenge him on these issues. Moreover, such pacts assume the possibility of a league between corporeal and spiritual beings, which is a self-evident impossibility. And finally, no credible witness has ever been forthcoming to testify to such goings-on, 'saving the confession of some person diseased both in bodie and mind, wilfullie made, or injuriouslie constrained' (p. 48). This is the fundamental flaw in his opponents' case. The evidence of confessions is worthless: either it has been extorted by torture; or, if apparently voluntary, it results from the mental illness of the accused persons.

Were the confessions of witches true, and were the writings of witchmongers to be credited, the world would be an impossible place. Butter, cattle, and corn, would all fail; and there would never be good weather or good health. 'What creature could live in securitie?' (p. 63). Not even princes would be safe, and witches could kill off every magistrate, if they so desired. Why should kings bother to raise armies, since one old witch could overthrow an 'armie roiall'? If it be naively objected that Christian rulers would never act thus, why then do not the Turks, who would 'make no conscience thereof', slit our throats with the help of their witches? The whole business is fatuous, and, further to discredit confessions, Scot cites that old thorn in the witchmongers' flesh, the Canon Episcopi, to the effect that all those who accept that witches can actually perform what is asserted of them are infidels and pagans. The illegality and inevitability of the proceedings in witch trials is manifest for, even when objections to confessions are upheld, the accusers fabricate other charges—such as idolatry, apostasy, seducing the people, or carnal copulation with the devil—all so frivolous as to be scarcely worthy of lengthy refutation.

Nevertheless, the belief in sexual intercourse between demons and human beings is so firmly held that Scot feels it necessary to discuss it in more detail, and accordingly devotes his Fourth Book to this topic: though not without entreating those readers whose 'chaste eares' cannot endure such abominable lecheries and 'beastlie and bawdie assertions' to pass over this material which has been thrust, as it were, into a 'stinking corner' covered 'as close as may be' in order to keep the rest of his writings 'sweet'. Scot here describes and ridicules current ideas on incubi and succubi. It is remarkable, he says, that according to the *Malleus Maleficarum*, Bodin, and other authorities, evil spirits are able to counterfeit every human action and 'especiallie excell in the use and art of venerie'. He wonders, though, why devils should bother with such acts since they must already have their alleged human partners' bodies and souls; and, having cited from the *Malleus* various stories about the loss, real or apparent, of men's genitals, he bitterly comments that 'these are no jestes, for they be written by them that were and are judges upon the lives and deaths of those persons' (p. 78). He has several down-to-earth comments concerning intercourse with demons. He points out, in the case of men supposedly so bewitched that they cannot copulate with their own wives but only with others, that such witchcraft is practised 'among manie bad husbands, for whom it were a good excuse' (p. 80). And he remarks, of a bawdy priest who persuaded a sick woman that she was bewitched and, as a cure, sang mass on her belly, that it was 'to the satisfieng of his lust; but not to the release of hir greefe' (p. 80). The myth of incubi is an excuse to maintain the lechery of priests and monks; and the only reality about these stories lies in the fact that some people are subject to natural disease or physiological disturbance arising in the stomach and affecting the mind of the sufferer during sleep. There are, says Scot, a number of silly verses and charms for the malady, which are but the 'common cloke for the ignorance of bad physicians' (p. 87); but he gives several practical remedies for sufferers and, in particular, refers to Leonardus Fuchsius for a sound medical cure.[16] Finally, to complete his case, he quotes the beginning of the Wife of Bath's Tale, for Chaucer, 'as he smelt out the absurdities of poperie, so found he the priests knaverie in this matter of *Incubus*, and (as the time would suffer him) he derided their follie and falshood' (p. 88).

A medical explanation of acts commonly ascribed to witchcraft similarly underlies much of the Fifth Book, which is concerned with transformations or transubstantiations of witches, and principally with lycanthropy. Scot ridicules the views of the great witch-hunting authorities, and especially of Bodin, on the possibility of metamorphosis. God made man, and everything else, including spirits, and assigned to each being its proper place. To accept that the devil, by means of witches, could turn one creature into another, would mean that 'Gods works should not onelie be defaced and disgraced, but his ordinance should be woonderfullie altered, and thereby confounded' (p. 101). Certainly, the witchmongers wielded both classical and scriptural texts to support their beliefs, but Scot pours scorn on such literal interpretations of the story of Circe, the fables of Ovid, and, more important, the fate of Nebuchadnezzar.[17] Who in his right mind could believe that the King of Babylon was, in verity, metamorphosed into an ox? In Scot's view, Nebuchadnezzar was transformed only in the sense that he was an exile from men, and lived among beasts 'in beastlie sort' (p. 102)—a psychological interpretation of metamorphosis strongly reminiscent both of Giovanni Pico della Mirandola and of Pietro Pomponazzi—and he concludes that lycanthropy is a mental disease, correctly diagnosed by Weyer, in which people imagine themselves to be wolves.[18]

There follows a discussion of the manner in which the devil is said to have set Christ on the pinnacle of the temple and on a mountain. This text was often regarded as evidence for the possibility of transportation: but, as Scot points out, even if literally interpreted, it could hardly be taken as proof that the devil would perform similar feats for witches. If, on the other hand, the action was wrought by the special providence of God, then the devil would not come into the picture other than as an agent of the divine will. Scot considers that the most likely reading of the text is that Christ was not transported, but rather that the whole episode was a vision, as is made clear by the devil displaying all the kingdoms of the world and the glory thereof. Calvin is cited in support of this view, and is again alluded to in the ensuing discussion of Job's afflictions, which were ordained by God, not by any devil.[19] But even more important for Scot is the fact that the name of *witch* is nowhere mentioned in the Book of Job: though 'what witchmonger now seeing one so afflicted as Job, would not saie he were bewitched, as *Job* never saith' (p. 105).

In the final chapter of this Fifth Book we come to the pivot of Scot's case: do the Scriptures prove the actuality of witches? Appealing to the authority of the 'most famous Hebrician in the world', Andreas Masius, who is cited via Weyer, Scot argues that the type of witch postulated by modern authorities—'our old women, that are said to hurt children with their eies, or lambs with their lookes, or that pull downe the moone out of heaven, or make so foolish a bargaine, or doo such homage to the divell'—are not once mentioned in the Bible (p. 110). The trouble arises from the fact that various types of malefactor, poisoners, cheats, false soothsayers, and lying pseudomagicians, are all indicated by the single word *witch* in modern translations of the Scriptures. It is Scot's purpose to expound the relevant Hebrew words; and to each of these he devotes a separate book. However, his argument by no means rests solely on biblical exegesis. He is not merely concerned to establish that witchmongers misinterpret the Word of God. The problem is more complex than this, and Scot's aim is largely practical. The witch, as postulated by modern authorities, had no existence either in scriptural times or now; but, says Scot, cheats and criminals, who use various skills to exploit human fear and credulity, have always existed. Thus, by exposing their frauds, two things might be accomplished: the ground could be cut from beneath the feet of those who mistakenly believe in demonic magic, diabolical pacts, and the whole paraphernalia of witchcraft; and, simultaneously, readers could be alerted against the fraudulent practices of those who pretend to supernatural powers. It is for this reason that the *Discoverie* incorporates so much material—as, for example, accounts of juggling tricks—which, superficially, appears irrelevant: and it is for the same reason that such material is not irrelevant at all.

Scot first considers the Hebrew word *chasaph,* which occurs in the text, 'Thou shalt not suffer a witch to live' (Exodus XXII), alleged by all witchmongers to justify their worst excesses. Following Weyer, Scot argues that the word *chasaph* means poisoning, and that to render it by *witchcraft* and *witches* in this context is misleading because it implies that the malefactors employed supernatural means to accomplish their crimes. Bodin had attempted to refute Weyer on the grounds of a mistranscription of the Greek *pharmakeis*: and Scot, too lightly, brushes aside the refutation on the grounds that Weyer's mistake was a printer's error, though Bodin had already anticipated and overcome this objection.[20] Scot is on slightly stronger ground when protesting that Bodin interprets *pharmakeis* as *magos* or *Praestigiatores*, whereas the more normal interpretation is '*veneficos*, poisoners by medicine'. Why, he asks, adopt an unusual reading in place of a normal one? 'Thus therefore he reasoneth and concludeth with his new found Logicke and old fond Greeke' (p. 125).

It is, however, in his examination of the word *ob,* that Scot starts to expound really radical views. *Ob*, he says, is translated *pytho* or *pythonicus spiritus*: but it most properly signifies a bottle and is used, for example in 2 Samuel XXIII, because the '*Pythonists* spake hollowe; as in the bottome of their bellies, whereby they are aptlie in Latine called *Ventriloqui*' (p. 126). As a modern parallel, Scot refers to an alleged demonic possession at Westwell in Kent, not six miles from his own home. The whole business had been exposed as a deceit wrought by ventriloquism, and Scot invites his reader to compare this with the story of the witch of Endor to see that 'both the cousenages may be done by one art' (p. 131). Indeed, from the assumption that all miracles of this kind were really trickery, Scot is able to launch a direct attack on writers such as Bodin who built their case upon such obvious charlatanism as maidens spewing pins.

Religious deception has a long history, and for Scot the Oracle of Apollo, with its 'amphibologicall' answers, was comparable to the Rood of Grace at Bexley in Kent which Catholics, even in his own day, refused to recognise as a fraud, though its mechanism had been exposed and burnt in the reign of Henry VIII.[21] 'Craftie knaves and priests' are at the root of these deceits: the latter with regard to oracles and miracle-working Catholic images; the former in a case such as the witch of Endor, which Scot subjects to a searching examination. His conclusion on this crucial issue—that the witch of Endor was a ventriloquist who deluded Saul, either alone or with the aid of confederates—is central to his thesis. The only miracles which have ever been brought to pass were those ordained by God. An extraordinary feat such as the conjuring up of the dead spirit of Samuel, or even of a devil in Samuel's likeness, would only have been possible for God himself. If it was not brought about by divine providence, then the woman must indeed have been a trickster: and this, in Scot's opinion, is the most feasible interpretation of the text. In any case, he is prepared to venture his life that witchmongers would not be able to adduce a single miracle 'such as Christ did trulie, or such as they suppose this witch did diabolicallie' which was not performed by trickery and confederacy.

Scot's challenge is that those who believe in witchcraft cannot produce, under controlled circumstances, even one verifiable instance of the operation of diabolic magic. He has already laid the foundation of his case by showing that his opponents' evidence was obtained either through torture and trickery, or from the mentally sick. 'Neither', he continues, warming to this theme, 'are there any such visions in these daies shewed' (p. 151). God did once send his visible angels to men; but to seek for modern miracles is a mark of infidelity, and Scot is quick to point out that Catholics, with their 'lieng legends', are at fault in this matter. All miraculous deeds and prophecies, subsequent to the Christian revelation, are impostures; and the Catholic Church is built upon a foundation of such pseudo-magic. It matters not a whit whether miracles are attributed to saintly relics or to a diabolical agency: both are empirically undemonstrable; and belief in either is a derogation of God's power. If we accept that the woman of Endor really conjured up the dead Samuel, then surely, demands Scot triumphantly, this would be a feat comparable to the raising of Lazarus (p. 154).

The following two books elaborate these views, and Scot points out that legends of saints have been as fully discredited as the old folk tales of Hobgoblin and Robin Goodfellow. Yet parallel absurdities, such as the deeds of modern witches, are credulously accepted because they have not been subjected to a similar scrutiny. The knaveries of the ancient oracles have long since ended, yet there is no end to the knaveries of priests; and those who consider popish pilgrimages will see both 'the oracles & their conclusions remaining, and as it were transferred from *Delphos* to *Rome*, where that adulterous generation continuallie seeketh a signe, though they have *Moses* & the prophets, yea even Christ & his apostles also' (p. 165). With regard to prophecy in general Scot, considering the word *kasam*, draws a clear distinction between the conjectures of astronomers, physicians, and philosophers, and the prognostications in the Scriptures. Both are legitimate: but the former are based upon the accumulation and weighing of evidence; the latter, in the Old Testament, relate to historical events and especially to the coming and the life of Christ; and in the New Testament are conditional upon repentance and salvation. Fresh signs from God would be superfluous.

Among those who falsely claim prophetic powers are the cozeners comprised under the word *onen*: the interpretation of dreams. And, in his Tenth Book, Scot examines the opinions of many learned writers, both ancient and modern, concerning the nature of dreams which, he maintains, cannot possibly provide revelations of future events. Dreams result from the 'inward actions of the mind', which dwell upon the great multitude of daily affairs, and so muddle them that any attempt to interpret the confusion would be a fruitless venture. So-called magical, or diabolical, dreams, in which horrible visions are seen, are due to an excess of black humours; and Scot refers to Porta, both for a naturalistic explanation of such phenomena; for recipes, herbs and potions to procure pleasant or fearful dreams; and for evidence that the ointments whereby witches are supposed to effect their wondrous transportations are purely hallucinatory in effect.[22]

The attack on prognostication is taken further in the Eleventh Book when *nahas*, comprising the whole art of augury, is expounded. Scot here deploys crushing arguments both against those who profess the art of augury, and against those who accept their pretensions. He believes that the origins of augury may be seen in pagan divination through sacrifices, and he delivers a brutal blow at the regular Roman Catholic sacrifices of Christ, declaring that, if such beliefs are really to be credited, they would be far more disgusting than anything perpetrated by heathens: for the celebrants would break up Christ's body, chew his flesh and bones, and finally 'in the end of their sacrifice (as they say) they eate him up rawe, and swallow downe into their guts everie member and parcell of him: and last of all, that they conveie him into the place where they bestowe the residue of all that which they have devoured that daie' (p. 191). Scot also ridicules ancient augury—observing the flying of birds, rummaging in the bowels of beasts, or lighting by chance upon some text of Virgil or Homer—acutely remarking that such practices depend upon a basic human failing: 'men in all ages have beene so desirous to know the effect of their purposes, the sequele of things to come, and to see the end of their feare and hope; that a seelie witch, which had learned anie thing in the art of cousenage, may make a great manie jollie fooles' (p. 197). The cabbalistic art of the Jews, with its mystical pretensions, also comes under scrutiny, only to be dismissed—in terms borrowed from Cornelius Agrippa —as mere 'allegorical games' to which the Hebrew tongue readily lends itself. Playing with words, signs, and the multiplicity of daily occurrences, is a simple matter; and it is all too easy to offer predictions of a comprehensive ambiguity.[23] Yet what reasonable man could really accept that God would commit his secret purposes to a bird, a pig, or a toad, or would hide them in the 'doong and bowels of beasts' (p. 207)?

Scot discerns two kinds of augury. The first, 'natural' augury, is based upon the experience and observation which enables a countryman to anticipate changes of weather, or a skilful physician to make a diagnosis. The second, 'casuall' augury, is accidental: when one occurrence, such as an encounter with a toad, has no causal relation to subsequent fortune, good or bad. The fatuity of the latter mode is demonstrated by the juxtaposition of two astrological beliefs. A noise in the house when the moon is in the sign of Aries is held to indicate good luck; whereas a beast entering a house when the moon is in the same sign indicates bad luck: 'and forsomuch as both may happen at once, the rule must needs be false and ridiculous' (pp. 209–210). There are an infinite number of variables in human affairs, and these, coupled with the limitations of human knowledge, make it impossible for man to predict the future.

From the impossibility of prognostication Scot moves on to the impossibility of enchantment, expounding the word *habar*—'to inchant or (if you had rather have it so) to bewitch'—when certain words, secretly uttered with careful attention to precise formulae, are supposed to have miraculous efficacy. Of course, Scot readily admits, words do have power, as is evident in persuasion and dissuasion; while in the Scriptures words had miraculous operations through God's providence. Nevertheless, the Scriptures also forbade the profanation of God's name and words in feigned fortune-telling and alleged miracle-working, 'as the papists at this daie by the like names, by crosses, by gospels hanged about their necks, by masses, by exorcismes, by holie water, and a thousand consecrated or rather execrated things, promise unto themselves and others, both health of bodie and soule' (p. 218). There is no evidence to suggest that either the magical incantations of the papists, or the words of witches and charmers, have any practical effect whatsoever; and Scot deals harshly with Bodin and the other major witchmongers for their use of 'poetical authorities', such as Ovid, Virgil, Horace and Lucan, to prove the miraculous powers of witches. Most readers, he feels, would admit that such poetic examples are fabulous; yet his adversaries, 'for lacke of scripture', are fain to produce 'these poetries for proofs'. They also adduce papal authority, which Scot counters by demonstrating the similarity between the 'charms, conjurations, blessings, cursings' of the Catholic Church and those said to be employed by witches. Many of these charms are derived from Weyer: and Scot, like Weyer, and like Pomponazzi before him, ascribes their efficacy to psychological causes. Where magic seems to have been efficacious, he points to the power of suggestion, citing, for example, the case of a sick woman who was cured by wearing a scroll which, unknown to her, contained a curse 'whereby partlie you may see what constant opinion can doo, according to the saieng of *Plato*; If a mans fansie or mind give him assurance that a hurtfull thing shall doo him good, it may doo so' (p. 246). Reflecting upon the curative power of the first chapter of St John's Gospel when, written in small letters, it is worn about the neck, he wonders at the devil's torment were one to wear the entire Bible (p. 271). And, when discussing the various hindrances to successful butter-making, commonly attributed to witchcraft, he advises that the best remedy is to 'looke well to your dairie maid or wife, that she neither eat up the creame, nor sell awaie your butter' (p. 281). The real answer to imaginary maleficence is to recognise and to despise the knavery both of priests and of so-called witches; to repair, if need be, to a good preacher or learned physician; and to put on the whole armour of God, as enjoined by St Paul. This last text is the 'charme of charmes', for its power lies not in the 'bare letter', nor in wearing it about one's neck, but rather in the reader's understanding of the inner meaning of Paul's epistle, and in living according to the Word of God.[24]

After his rejection of a magic wrought by words, Scot proceeds to other effects deemed miraculous by ignorant observers. *Hartumim*, the name applied to Pharaoh's magicians, were the stock exemplars for those seeking to prove the possibility of demonic magic: but, basing himself upon the authorities adduced by Weyer, Scot argues that *hartumim* were, first and foremost, men whose knowledge of nature enabled them to perform feats beyond common understanding. Not that there is anything evil in penetrating and using the secrets of nature. Sin only arises when such knowledge is employed to delude people, and when it forms the basis of pretensions to supernatural powers. Nature is full of mysteries; and stones, herbs and animals have an infinity of different properties which may be discovered by experiment, experience, and diligent study. However, there are flaws in the human temperament. When men habitually encounter even the most wonderful effects, they deem them less remarkable than an insignificant but unusual trick: 'the dailie use and practise of medicine taketh awaie all admiration of the wonderfull effects of the same. Manie other things of lesse weight, being more secret and rare, seeme more miraculous' (p. 291). Moreover, men tend to attribute everything beyond their comprehension to supernatural powers, so that when skill in natural magic is allied to deliberate fraud, prearranged tricks, and the use of confederates, then 'wit, faith', and 'constancie' are severely tested (p. 311).

It is to this combination of knowledge and trickery that Scot attributes the feats of Pharaoh's magicians, who could not have performed real miracles such as those accomplished, with the aid of God, by Moses and Aaron. If the magicians had really made frogs, asks Scot, why could they not drive them away again? Their ability lay simply in the skilful manipulation of natural phenomena, and in 'juggling knacks'; and it is because of this that the rest of the Thirteenth Book is devoted to legerdemain and illusion. It is not that tricks with balls, coins, cards, string, 'juggling boxes with false bottoms', and specially constructed books, constitute anything unlawful or sinful. Nor that 'desperate and dangerous' feats—such as thrusting nails or knives through one's head, tongue, and nose, or cutting off a boy's head and laying it on a platter—constitute witchcraft. Scot's point is simply that juggling tricks depend upon manual dexterity to deceive onlookers' eyes; verbal dexterity to confuse their minds; and the preparation of special effects to baffle their understanding; and that, if one did not know how such feats were accomplished, they might well seem miraculous. The best instance of this is the story of Brandon's pigeon, adduced as an example of 'private confederacie'; that is, a deceit prearranged by the juggler himself. Brandon astonished 'the king' by a wondrous trick. He painted a picture of a dove on a wall; and then, seeing a pigeon at the house-top, he uttered certain words, and pricked the picture with a knife. The pigeon promptly dropped dead, and the king immediately prohibited such magical experiments lest murder might result: 'as though he, whose picture so ever he had pricked, must needs have died, and so the life of all men in the hands of a juggler: as is now supposed to be in the hands and willes of witches'. In fact, all that Brandon had done was to give the pigeon a dram of nux vomica or some similar poison, before releasing it. He knew that the bird habitually resorted to the top of the next house, and that it could not live beyond half an hour. In the meantime, he drew his picture, said his words, and deluded the onlookers.

Scot knows that the trick works because he has himself tried it on 'crows and pies'; and he laconically observes that 'if this or the like feate should be done by an old woman, everie bodie would crie out for fier and faggot to burn the witch' (pp. 308-9).[25]

Natural magicians are learned men; and jugglers are skilled in manual dexterity. But another kind of magical pretension, the art of 'alcumystrie'— in the 'bowels' whereof both 'witchcraft and conjuration lie hidden'— achieves its effect in a different manner. Alchemy, however overladen with hermetic obscurities, spiritual pretensions, and arcane intricacies, is yet another cozening art whereby ordinary people are deluded with a battery of technical jargon. What plain man would not believe that they are

> learned and jollie fellowes, that have in such readinesse so many mysticall termes of art: as (for a tast) their subliming, amalgaming, engluting, imbibing, incorporating, cementing, ritrination, terminations, mollifications, and indurations of bodies, matters combust and coagulat, ingots, tests, &c. Or who is able to conceive (by reason of the abrupt confusion, contrarietie, and multitude of drugs, simples, and confections) the operation and mysterie of their stuffe and workemanship (p. 354).

Nobody can even begin to understand the involuted nonsense written by these people; yet it is no marvel that their art can 'allure men so sweetlie, and intangle them in snares of follie, sith the baits which it useth is the hope of gold' (p. 371). Even learned men have been deluded with the promise of transmuting base metal; and Scot concludes that alchemists are but 'ranke couseners and consuming cankers to the common wealth' (p. 375).

Iidoni, in the Fifteenth Book, are the most pretentious and sinful of all 'couseners', for, though similar to the soothsayers discussed under *Ob,* they are far more ambitious in the scope of their supposed activities. They deal with 'no inferiour causes', but claim to call up devils from hell and angels down from heaven; to raise up bodies 'though they were dead, buried, and rotten long before'; to fetch souls out of heaven or hell; to raise tempests and earthquakes; and, in sum, to do as much as God himself can do. These are 'no small fooles, they go not to worke with a baggage tode, or a cat, as witches doo; but with a kind of majestie, and with authoritie they call up by name, and have at their commandement seventie and nine principall and princelie divels, who have under them as their ministers, a great multitude of legions of pettie divels' (p. 377). The ensuing inventory of the names, shapes, powers, and government of devils and spirits, closely resembles Weyer's *Pseudomonarchia Daemonum* but was, apparently, drawn from an English manuscript translation made by 'one T.R.' in 1570—that is seven years before the first publication of the *Pseudomonarchia*.²⁶ The likelihood is both Weyer and 'T.R.' were working from different versions of that notorious gibberish *Clavicula Salomonis*, which is likewise drawn upon for the forms of conjuration and commanding devils, raising of dead spirits, locating of hidden treasure, and making of demonic pacts, all expounded in the *Discoverie* with the aid of sundry infernal diagrams.²⁷ The purpose of such detail is to make clear both the vanity and the blasphemy of these enterprises. The Scriptures, for example, are explicit that it is impossible for souls to leave Hell, yet we are expected to believe that magicians can not only call up souls but are also able to shut them up in a circle made of chalk which is so strongly 'beset and invironed with crosses and names, that they cannot for their lives get out; which is a verie probable matter' (p. 431). In any case, Scot sneers, he has himself experimented with these conjurations, and the only devil he has ever seen was in a play (p. 443). He can discern no essential difference between diabolical rites and 'popish conjurations', and finds it astonishing that Catholics have failed to realise the emptiness of demonic magic when, despite their own rituals—holy water, crosses, salt, candles, and words—'neither soule nor bodie anie thing recover, nor the candles last one minute the longer' (p. 450). Certainly, with such evidence at hand, Protestants, who are no longer beguiled by false Catholic magic, should likewise reject the parallel myths of witches and conjurers, especially as there is a gross discrepancy in the witchmongers' view of magic. The knowledge and skill required by the magus in order that he might communicate with, and command, demons is, apparently, both extensive and of a highly technical nature, necessitating a considerable outlay for books and equipment. If, therefore, the claims of magicians are to be credited—and witchmongers appear to credit them—how can it be possible for a poor, silly, and unlearned old woman to achieve similar results with no resources whatever? How can one accept the logic of a belief which ascribes extraordinary, supernatural powers alike to the erudite magus and the ignorant witch?

In his Sixteenth Book Scot provides a summary of his principal arguments together with the definition of witchcraft purposely deferred till this moment. It is, he says, 'a cousening art', which succeeds through ignorance, fear, and superstition. How can any thinking person accept these stories when scholars, such as Agrippa, after a lifetime of study, rejected them as void; when, if true, they would devalue the miracles of Christ; when the Scriptures, properly interpreted, give no support to the belief; when working of miracles and the gift of prophecy have ceased; when the books dealing with witchcraft are crammed with palpable lies, absurdities, and inconsistencies; and when their authors accept as miraculous the natural phenomena or trickery already exposed in the *Discoverie*? Were these stories true, the devil would be able to do whatever he liked with men. And surely one should ponder over the fact that these people, with all their alleged powers, never seem able to escape from prison or from retribution, and are never wealthy,

> when it were an easie matter for the divell, if he can doo as they affirme, to give them great store of monie, and make them rich, and dooth it not; being a thing which would procure him more disciples than any other thing in the world: the wise must needs condemne the divell of follie, and the witches of peevishnesse, that take such paines, and give their soules to the divell to be tormented in hell fier, and their bodies to the hangman to be trussed on the gallowes, for nichels in a bag (p. 483).

Scot's indictment of magical beliefs is an impressive one. But, though firmly based upon common sense, experience, and observation, it still leaves unresolved a question which any sixteenth-century reader would certainly have posed: is Scot denying all spiritual agency—good and bad—in human affairs? Modern scholars, certainly, have posed this question as though it exposes a great gap in Scot's case.[28] Yet, in the final section of his *Discoverie*, entitled *A Discourse upon divels and spirits*, Scot does provide an explicit refutation of the possibility of trafficking with the devil, of demonic magic, and of miracle-working, which completes his argument in the most radical manner possible. The two most recent 'editions' of the *Discoverie* blandly, and silently, omit the entire seventy-two pages of the *Discourse* as though they do not exist: but, in fact, this section comprises the *sine qua non* of Scot's work, for it makes clear both the extent to which the author was prepared to go in his denial of the supernatural, and the fact that he himself recognised the extreme nature of his views and sought to evade their logical consequences.[29]

The nature of spirits, he admits, constitutes the most difficult of all questions and, despite the theories advanced by different schools of thought, no-one has ever written adequately on the subject. He contrasts various extreme views: the 'ungodly' Sadducees who deny all existence to spirits and devils; the foolish superstitions of Plato, Proclus, Plotinus, and Porphyry; and the absurdities of Psellus and more recent witch-hunters such as Sprenger and Anania.[30] The whole notion of devils has, in Scot's opinion, largely come about through a misinterpretation of the figure Lucifer in Isaiah XIV. This purely metaphorical expression of the rise and fall of Nebuchadnezzar has been the basis for a vast intellectual battle involving such nonsense as debating the nature and number of the angels who fell with Lucifer, and whether or not these fallen angels became devils. The debate is, for Scot, an empty one, partly because devils and angels are not really implied in the text at all, and partly because he can find nothing in the Scriptures to support the view that either angels or devils have any corporeal existence. The fact that the Scriptures sometimes appear to discuss spiritual beings in corporeal terms is due simply to the necessity of accommodating divine truth to man's gross understanding by employing figurative language and parables. Confusion has arisen because some men are 'so carnallie minded, that a spirit is no sooner spoken of, but immediatlie they thinke of a blacke man with cloven feet, a paire of hornes, a taile, clawes, and eies as broad as a bason' (p. 507). It is, therefore, necessary always to take account of the context in which words such as *spirit* and *devil* occur in the Scriptures; and Scot advances a metaphorical interpretation which, in effect, approximates to a psychological theory, and which virtually reduces spirits to an operation of the human imagination.

> Also where it is said; If the spirit of gelosie come upon him: it is as much to saie as; If he be mooved with a gelous mind: and not that a corporall divell assaulteth him. It is said in the Gospell; There was a woman, which had a spirit of infirmitie 18 yeeres, who was bowed togither, &c: whome Christ, by laieng his hand upon hir, delivered of hir disease. Wherby it is to be seene, that although it be said, that sathan had bound hir &c: yet that it was a sicknes or disease of bodie that troubled hir; for Christs owne words expound it. Neither is there any word of witchcraft mentioned, which some saie was the cause thereof (pp. 510–11).

Provided that they are given sufficient time, even the preacher and physician have the power to cure man's soul or body. Christ's miracles consisted in his power to achieve such cures instantaneously, and Scot reiterates his argument that these were accomplished in order to establish the true faith.

The same naturalistic attitude prevails in Scot's discussion of devils. To say that somebody is possessed of a devil is as much as to say that the person is a lunatic. This madness is a disease which can be diagnosed and treated: but if everybody now deemed lunatic were in reality possessed of a devil 'then might it be thought, that divels are to be thrust out of men by medicines'. Similarly, the woman of Canaan's daughter who was said to be vexed by a devil was, in fact, troubled by some disease; and when we say of a wicked man that the devil is in him, we do not mean that a 'reall divell is gotten into his guts' (p. 513).

This metaphorical and psychological interpretation is completed by the argument that, since visions are always seen by the faint-hearted, weak, and diseased, and never by the strong and healthy, they must be 'onelie phantasticall and imaginarie' (p. 517). Weyer had suggested the same thing, but thought that mental debility rendered a person especially vulnerable to real attacks by the devil.[31] Similarly, Scot adopts, from Weyer, an argument that the devils mentioned in the Scriptures were, for the most part, idols of certain pagan nations; though Weyer characteristically believed that the heathens' idols represented devils who really existed.[32] Scot, equally characteristically, turns this notion upside-down. For him, though David did say that the 'gods of the Gentiles are divels', these devil-gods are nothing more than idols —projections of the human imagination, representations without objective reality, and, therefore, quite devoid of power. In this respect they are nothing different from the hated Catholic relics and images: 'what a divell was the rood of grace to be thought, but such a one as before is mentioned and described, who tooke his name of his courteous and gratious behaviour towards his worshippers, or rather those that offered unto him? The idolatrous knaverie wherof being now bewraied, it is among the godlie reputed a divell rather than a god: and so are diverse others of the same stampe' (p. 519). Roman Catholics seem even more idolatrous than the ancient pagans; and Scot makes a telling comparison between the numerous heathen gods and the host of saints—with their special relationships to countries and cities, to trades, to diseases, and to a multiplicity of separate significances—so that for 'everie heathen idoll I might produce twentie out of the popish church' (p. 527). This brings Scot back to witchcraft itself; for, as he points out, if one is to venerate a saint who has an aptitude to cure only one disease, how much more should one regard a mother Bungie, or any similar old witch, who is supposed to have power over so many ills? And again, as when paralleling demonic magic with the rites of the Roman Church, Scot is quick to denounce his co-religionists. Catholics are deluded. But Protestants are equally culpable for, while denying popish miracles and rejecting the whole paraphernalia of saintly relics, they are only too eager to swallow absurd stories relating to the demonic magic of witches.

Some modern commentators have observed that Scot does not explicitly deny the existence of extra-terrestrial creatures, and that he even describes spirits as beings created by God.[33] It is certainly true that he goes out of his way to attack both the Sadducees, who say that 'spirits and divels are onlie motions and affections, and that angels are but tokens of God's power' (p. 540), and the Pneumatomachi, who not only deny that the Holy Spirit is God but also 'with the *Sadduces* mainteine there is none such; but that under and by the name of holie spirit is ment a certeine divine force, wherewith our minds are mooved, and the grace and favour of God whereby we are his beloved' (pp. 548-9). But it is well nigh impossible to distinguish these views, which Scot carefully castigates, from his own definition of the word 'spirit' which for him

> dooth signifie a secret force and power, wherewith our minds are mooved and directed; if unto holie things, then it is the motion of the holie spirit, of the spirit of Christ and of God: if unto evil things, then it is the suggestion of the wicked spirit, of the divell, and of satan. Whereupon I inferre, by the waie of a question, with what spirit we are to suppose such to be mooved, as either practise anie of the vanities treated upon in this booke, or through credulitie addict themselves thereunto as unto divine oracles, or the voice of angels breakeing through the clouds? We cannot impute this motion unto the good spirit; for then they should be able to discerne betweene the nature of spirits, and not swarve in judgement: it followeth therefore, that the spirit of blindness and error dooth seduce them; so that it is no mervell if in the alienation of their minds they take falsehood for truth, shadowes for substances, fansies for verities, &c: for it is likelie that the good spirit of God hath forsaken them, or at leastwise absented it selfe from them: else would they detest these divelish devises of men, which consist of nothing but delusions and vaine practises, whereof (I suppose) this my booke to be a sufficient discoverie (pp. 547-8).

The truth of the matter is that Scot no more accepted the reality of spirits and demons than he accepted the reality of witches. To be sure he talks about *spirits* and *witches*. But the former have no physical being, can accomplish nothing, and can assume no body either of man or of beast. They cannot affect men; and are either purely metaphorical expressions of mysteries beyond human comprehension or, more usually, of psychological disorders and physical diseases perfectly susceptible to the ministrations of a skilled physician. As for witches, they are either tormented and deluded old simpletons, or cozening rogues; their magic is compounded of lies or trickery, is totally ineffectual, and cannot possibly be based upon infernal pacts because individual, corporeal devils have never existed. Thus Scot's spirits and witches are simply defined out of existence. And in this sense Scot was, indeed, the Sadducee his enemies have always considered him to be.[34]

Scot's conclusions are extreme, but they result from the fusion of several approaches to the problem of spiritual and demonic magic, which had been partially anticipated by earlier writers. Scot was certainly familiar with both Apuleius and Cicero: indeed he seems especially indebted to the latter's *De divinatione*, although, somewhat disingenuously, he specifically refers to that text at only one of several points where its influence is manifest.³⁵ Cicero had, for example, ridiculed prophecies which either do not come true or are contradictory; and had demanded to know how divine secrets could possibly be hidden in an animal's entrails. He had dismissed astrological prophecies as rubbish; criticised oracles as stupid and ambiguous; argued that dreams are random and therefore useless for purposes of prognostication; rejected the fictions of poets; and, above all, had scorned the argument based on mere assertions that all kings, peoples, and nations, used auspices—'as if there is anything so common as error is, or as if you yourself, in judging, were guided by the opinion of the multitude'. Only a few such attacks on magic have survived from classical antiquity; and Scot seems to have referred neither to Sextus Empiricus nor to Lucian. There was nothing parallel to this material in early Christian writing, apart from Hippolytus's *Refutation of all Heresies*, which attempted to destroy astrology by demonstrating its impracticability; and to undermine pagan magic by castigating it as merely trickery and deception.³⁶ However, Hippolytus's work was not rediscovered until the mid-nineteenth century; and the closest approach to Scot, prior to the Renaissance, is the work of that extraordinarily independent fourteenth-century thinker, Nicholas Oresme, who argued at length against demonic intervention in human affairs; that apparitions were, in general, the result of mental sickness; that magical effects were largely due to deceit, pretension, or the manipulation of natural properties; and that confessions wrung from accused people by torture had no validity as evidence of the reality of magic.³⁷

The *Discoverie of Witchcraft* does not, however, refer to Oresme; and it is more profitable to set Scot's own extreme beliefs firmly within the context of sixteenth-century traditions critical of magical activities. Obviously his view of the Scriptures as a chronicle of the only truly miraculous period in human history derives from Reformist doctrine; and his refusal to interpret the text with slavish literality is supported by reference to Calvin's pronouncements on the grossness of human understanding, and the corresponding need for myth. Similarly, the attack on relics and their magical effects had a long history. The iconoclastic movement represented the most extreme form of the Protestant Reformation, and a work such as the *Alcoranus Franciscanorum*, which is cited by Scot, was typical of many warning readers not to give credence to the 'blasphemous lies and Miracles' of the Roman church 'whiche are not possible to be true they are so directly againe the moost precious & holy word of god'. And the *Alcoranus* further enjoined everybody to give thanks for having been delivered from the bondage of those 'papistical Caterpillers', and for being able to laugh to scorn such 'folish and filthy doctrine, as in the time of ignorance we beleved and worshiped for truth'.[38] The saints, of course, were a regular butt of the Reformers, who argued that such holy folk were generally of recent invention and that, in any case, merely to read of their supposed miracles 'would make a horse to laugh'.[39] The comparison between Catholic rites and pagan magic, and the vanity of both, was another well-established tradition; and forty years before the *Discoverie*, Thomas Becon had demanded to know whether the old form of confirming children was anything 'but plain sorcery, devilry, witchcraft, juggling, legerdemain, and all that naught is?' and had derided the bishop who 'mumbleth a few Latin words over the child, charmeth him, crosseth him, smeareth him with stinking popish oil, and tieth a linen bond about the child's neck, and sendeth him home'.[40] The comparison between non-Christian magic and the practices of the Church had been made, on a more theoretical and less polemical level, many years before by Cornelius Agrippa in his influential *De Occulta Philosophia*; while the same author's very rhetorical *De Vanitate Scientiarum*, with its formal rejection of black magic, had included scathing chapters on the vanity of astrology, the fatuity of Cabbala, the falsity of alchemy; and had offered brief but pertinent observations on the tricks of jugglers which might easily delude ignorant onlookers.[41] Criticism of magic, more specifically concerned with witchcraft, had later been adumbrated by Weyer, who questioned both traditional interpretations of the Scriptures, the nature of evidence elicited from the weak or mentally sick by illegal methods, and the efficacy of Catholic rites. And similar attitudes are encountered in Ludwig Lavater's *De Spectris*, where a good deal of magic is attributed to mental and physical disorder, or to deliberate deception on the part of the Catholic clergy.[42]

Nevertheless, whatever Scot may have derived from these antecedent traditions, it is apparent that his conclusions are strikingly different. Reformers attacked Catholic images and rites: but they still considered that the universe was filled with angels and demons; they still thought of these—especially the latter—as being only too capable of trafficking with men; and they still tied their brains in knots trying to distinguish between miracles and wonders, in order to accommodate witches and devils into their system without derogating the performances of Christ and the true prophets. Calvin recognised the dangers of a literal interpretation of the Bible: but his own interpretation still preserved the devil as a potent force in human affairs; and he specifically denied what was central to Scot's thesis—that demons are merely evil impulses.[43] Calvin's demons have a very real existence, and, under his guidance, Geneva became a noted centre for witch persecution; while the credulity of the Calvinists, with regard to confessions of maleficence, was quite equal to that of their religious opponents.[44] Agrippa, even in his *De Vanitate Scientiarum*, does not totally deny occult practices; still postulates a universe filled with active spiritual intelligences; accepts demonic activity in such matters as the witch of Endor's necromancy, and the miracles of Pharaoh's magicians; and cites the case of Nebuchadnezzar as a true instance of metamorphosis. Weyer, too, for all his humanity, his horror of persecution, and his scepticism concerning so much that was accepted elsewhere as demonic magic, continued to ascribe extraordinary occurrences to the direct operations of the devil amongst men. And the same is true of Lavater, whose scepticism extended only to Catholic miracles, and whose arguments concerning the power of the devil, both to assume corporeal forms and to work wonders, ran completely counter to Scot's beliefs.

The only writer, prior to Scot, whose scepticism verged on the destruction of magical operations in general, was the great Paduan Aristotelian, Pietro Pomponazzi, whose *De naturalium effectuum causis sive de incantationibus*, in fact, provided the real muscle of Weyer's *De Praestigiis*, though it was atrophied by Weyer's credulity with regard to demons. Scot knew Pomponazzi at first hand, and even putting aside questions of direct influence, a comparison between the two writers makes it clear that they shared a considerable community of interest and outlook. There is a similar recognition on the part of both that their views challenge not merely current cosmology but also a massive body of traditional belief; and both feel it possible that they are right, and that everybody else has been wrong.[45] Both are decisive in excluding demons as intermediary agents between God and man, and both, therefore, seek to provide naturalistic explanations for all phenomena; although they frequently fail to test these explanations—and even the phenomena to which they relate—against observation and experience. Nevertheless, their empirical spirit is apparent in their attitude towards miracles and the part played therein by fraud and confederacy. Pomponazzi argues that many alleged miracles may be explained as fables meant to instruct the vulgar, or as deceits wrought by priests: though he is somewhat less willing than Scot to assign every extraordinary feat to these factors, and anticipates later criticism of the *Discoverie* itself by suggesting that merely to establish fraud in some instances does not necessarily mean that everything may be explained in this fashion.[46] However, with regard to the efficacy of saintly relics in working cures, Pomponazzi is as convinced as Scot was to become that the force of imagination might make something which is itself useless, or even harmful, achieve a good effect: and he scandalised his contemporaries by daring to suggest that, provided the patient has sufficient confidence in a cure, a dog-bone could be as efficacious as the most holy relic.[47] Again, although Scot refers to Calvin for the argument that the Scriptures are not to be interpreted too literally, the idea had also been stated—much more forcibly and with more relevance to Scot's rejection of demons—in the *De Incantationibus*. In Pomponazzi's opinion, religions themselves might be said to have their origins in the incapacity of the human mind to grasp fundamental truths about God and the universe. Accordingly it has been necessary to introduce angels and demons for the sake of the vulgar, although those responsible for introducing them know that they cannot possibly exist. Pomponazzi points out that there is much in the Old Testament intended for ordinary folk who cannot understand anything not presented in corporeal terms, and maintains that the language of religion, like that of poetry, employs fables which, however impossible, contain essential truths to help the ignorant multitude distinguish good from evil. Thus by corporeal things they are led to knowledge of the incorporeal: 'just as we lead children from liquid to solid food'.[48] This view of the Scriptures as being primarily metaphorical in conception also confirms Pomponazzi in his interpretation of metamorphosis as a psychological degeneration—that is, where the person affected becomes bestial in mind and manner—rather than as a truly corporeal change or as an hallucination affecting observers. On this point he specifically rejects St Augustine, and, among other examples, refers to the story of Nebuchadnezzar (later taken as a test case by Scot) as an instance of the folly of taking a scriptural text at face value.[49]

Even Pomponazzi's reputation and posthumous fate largely anticipated those endured by Scot. Both were accused of atheism, and both have had well-meaning defenders. Both professed the Christian faith: Pomponazzi by recourse to the double truth of philosophy and revelation; and Scot by his biblical fundamentalism, his attack on Sadduceeism, and his zeal for the divinity of the Holy Spirit. But both writers thought and said things difficult to reconcile with Christianity. Despite his double truth, Pomponazzi all too clearly rejected belief in an after-life; in the immortality of the soul; in the uniqueness of Christianity, which he regarded as but one of many religions claiming miraculous origins; and even in the eternal verities of Christianity, which he described as a religion in decay. He was also caught up in the same circularity of argument which afflicted Scot. Despite their substitution of psychological and physiological states for demons and angels, both professed to accept that the miracles related in the Scriptures were historically true. But the question was, how did they know that they were true? Their answer, that the Scriptures must be true because they are the revealed Word of God, simply begs the question. On what authority do they affirm that the Christian God is truth? Their answer seems to be that the authority of Christianity is vouched for by miraculous occurrences; but since these are testified to only in the Bible, we are no further on. As D. P. Walker has pointed out, 'the argument is circular and entirely destructive in its implications'.[50] It had, certainly, been employed by, amongst others, St Augustine himself to prove the validity of the word of God: but then, Augustine did not eliminate angels, demons, and the devil from his universe.[51] Pomponazzi and Scot did. As we have seen, it is impossible to distinguish Scot's position from the Sadduceean argument which he rejects; and posterity, on the whole, has refused to accept the special pleading either of Pomponazzi or of Scot; both have suffered vilification; and both may have shared the distinction of having their works publicly burned by irate opponents.[52]

Nevertheless, Scot differed from Pomponazzi, as he differed from everybody else, in one fundamental respect. This may best be exemplified by the way in which the Paduan considered the universe to function. For Pomponazzi, demons have been replaced, as God's intermediaries, by heavenly intelligences: so that, while excluding spiritual agency from all apparently miraculous occurrences, he subscribes to a kind of sidereal determinism. Scot, however, will have none of this. The influence of the heavens, in Scot's view, is another of those factors in human affairs which are so unsusceptible to study that they are simply a waste of time. And he is scathing on those who profess foreknowledge based upon so inexact a science as the motions of the heavenly bodies: where the rules of the experts are flatly contradictory; where there are an impossible number of variables; and where there may well be astral bodies 'which cannot be seene, either through their exceeding highnes, or that hitherto are not tried with anie observation of the art' (p. 211). The heavens, says Scot, 'doo not constraine but incline'; and so many ordinary, as well as extraordinary occasions interrupt even these inclinations that—like witchcraft, spirits, and every other supernatural belief—they are circumscribed to nothingness.[53]

This is really what distinguishes Scot not merely from Pomponazzi, but from every other writer on magic. He was neither a theologian, philosopher, nor magus. He was a learned, independent-minded country gentleman, used to making decisions on his own initiative, and in evaluating what he read against what he observed. And he waxed impatient with the manifest absurdities promulgated by erudite professionals who, it seemed from his position as a studious but pragmatic layman, advanced theories totally unwarranted by any evidence they had ever been able to adduce. Indeed, in his opinion, the matters upon which they discoursed could never, by their very nature, be productive of evidence. It is this very impatience with arcane subtleties of every sort which has caused Scot to be thought of, by some modern critics, as an unscholarly and unsophisticated amateur: as though there were some inherent virtue in accepting beliefs merely because they have been endorsed by the majority of contemporary professional thinkers.[54] Scot banished magic of every sort from his conception of human affairs; and were it not for his leap of faith in proclaiming an unshakeable acceptance of the Word of God on the very basis of the miracles contained therein, his philosophical position might aptly, if anachronistically, be described as thoroughly positivist. Certainly, those who came after him were unable to reconcile themselves to his version of the double truth, and few were willing to subscribe to his thorough-going rejection of magic.

Notes

1 Apart from directing his own, and his cousin's business affairs, Scot is known to have been collector of subsidies for the lathe of Shepway in 1586 and 1587, and to have been returned to the parliament of 1588–9 as member for New Romney. It is probable that he served as a captain at the county muster of 1588; and it has been conjectured that he was a justice of the peace. Practically all the exiguous information relating to Scot's life is collected in the introduction to Brinsley Nicholson's edition of the *Discoverie of Witchcraft* (London, 1886, repr. 1973). This is summarised and slightly augmented in the *Dictionary of National Biography*. All references in this chapter are to the first edition of the *Discoverie* (London, 1584).
2 *A Perfite Platforme of a Hoppe Garden, and necessarie instructions for the making and mayntenaunce thereof* (London, 1574). There were further editions in 1576, 1578, 1640, and 1654.
3 The bibliographical history of the *Discoverie* is fully set out in Nicholson's edition, pp. xxxvi–xliv, and is summarised in *DNB*. Montague Summers's edition of the *Discoverie* (London, 1930), pp. xxxiii–xxxvii, likewise provides a detailed bibliographical note. The editions are as follows: (*1*) London, 1584, by William Brome; (*2*) London, 1651, by R. Cotes (reissued in 1651 by R. Cotes, and in 1654 by E. Cotes); (*3*) London, 1665. The third edition is augmented by nine new chapters and a second book to the *Discourse* concerning devils and spirits, all by an unknown author and all completely contrary in spirit to Scot's own work. In addition to these editions, there was issued in 1609 a partial Dutch translation by the English printer, resident at Leiden, Thomas Basson. In 1637 Basson's son, Govert, printed a second edition at Leiden, and this was reissued in 1638. On Basson see J. A. van Dorsten, *Thomas Basson 1555–1613: English Printer at Leiden* (Sir Thomas Browne Institute, Leiden, 1961), especially pp. 49–51. Van Dorsten suggests that

Basson was encouraged to translate and publish Scot's work by Petrus Scriverius.

4 On the St Osyth affair, see Wallace Notestein, *A History of Witchcraft in England from 1558 to 1718* (Washington, 1911, repr. New York, 1965), pp. 41–5; C. L'Estrange Ewen, *Witchcraft and Demonianism* (London, 1933, repr. London, 1970), pp. 155–64; *Witchcraft*, ed. Barbara Rosen (London, 1969), pp. 103–57.

5 Jean Bodin, *De la Démonomanie des Sorciers* (Paris, 1580); second French ed. (Paris, 1581); first German ed. (Strasbourg, 1581). Lambert Daneau, *Les Sorciers, dialogue tres utile et necessaire pour ce temps* (Paris, 1574); English trans. by T. Twyne (London, 1575); Latin trans. (Geneva, 1574), (Cologne, 1575), (Geneva, 1581); German trans. (Cologne, 1576). Nicolaus Hemmingius, *Admonitio de superstitionibus magicis evitandis* (Copenhagen, 1575), Giovanni Lorenzo Anania, *De Natura Demonum* (Venice, 1585), Leonard Vair, *De Fascino* (Paris, 1583); French trans., *Trois livres des charmes, sorcelages ou enchantements* (Paris, 1583). For the various editions of Johann Weyer's *De Praestigiis Daemonum* and other works, see J. J. Cobben, *Johannes Wier* (Assen, 1960), pp. 182–7.

6 For some minor indications of hasty composition, see Nicholson's ed. of the *Discoverie*, pp. xxv–xxxvi. Vair is particularly referred to by Scot in the later chapters of his Twelfth Book; Henry Howard is cited at p. 166.

7 For some brief, but very pertinent, comments on the problem of miracles, see D. P. Walker, *Spiritual and Demonic Magic from Ficino to Campanella* (London, 1958), pp. 83–4.

8 H. R. Trevor-Roper, *The European Witch-Craze of the 16th and 17th Centuries* (Harmondsworth, 1969), p. 74, where it is pointed out that Weyer and Scot have traditionally been bracketed together, and where they are duly bracketed together again. E. T. Withington, 'Dr John Weyer and the Witch Mania', *Studies in the History and Method of Science*, ed. C. Singer (Oxford, 1917), pp. 189–224, likewise assumes that Scot and Weyer should be considered together.

9 Johann Weyer, *Histoires, disputes et discours, des illusions et impostures des diables, des magiciens infames, sorcières et empoisonneurs* (Geneva, 1579). I have used this version of the *De Praestigiis Daemonum* throughout the present chapter. Weyer reiterates this diabolic explanation of the witch of Endor in his *De Lamiis* (Basle, 1577), chapter II. For a discussion of various interpretations of the witch of Endor, excluding that of Scot, see J. G. Godelmann, *Tractatus de magis, veneficis et lamiis* (Frankfurt, 1591), pp. 33–6.

10 For a summary of various opinions, excluding that of Scot, concerning the serpents made by Pharaoh's magicians, see Godelmann, *op. cit.*, pp. 25–7.

11 Weyer, *Histoires*, pp. 152–3.

12 *Ibid.*, p. 113.

13 On Masius (1514–73), see Max Lossen, *Brief von Andreas Masius und seinen Freunden, 1538 bis 1573* (Bonn, 1886), pp. xvi–xx. For Masius's correspondence with Weyer, see Lossen, pp. 341–2, 370–2, 510–12.

14 It is interesting to note that the most recent investigations into English witchcraft

have tended to stress this explanation which Scot offers as a simple, common-sense observation. See Alan Macfarlane, *Witchcraft in Tudor and Stuart England* (London, 1970); K. V. Thomas, *Religion and the Decline of Magic* (London, 1971).

15 Cf. Jean Bodin, *De la Démonomanie des Sorciers* (Paris, 1580), fols 165–72.

16 Leonardus Fuchsius (Leonhard Fuchs), *De curandi ratione libri octo* (Lyons, 1548), Lib. I, cap. 31, pp. 74–5. This chapter, 'De incubone', follows chapters on epilepsy and convulsions, and precedes those on mania, melancholia, and trembling.

17 Bodin is certainly guilty of using the stories of Medea and of Circe as historical evidence. See, for example, the *Démonomanie*, fol. 119. On the vanity of poetic fictions, cf. Cicero *De div.*, II. lv.

18 See Giovanni Pico della Mirandola, *Oration on the Dignity of Man*, trans. Elizabeth Livermore Forbes, in *The Renaissance Philosophy of Man*, ed. E. Cassirer, P. O. Kristeller, and J. H. Randall (Chicago, 1948), p. 226. See, in the same volume, Pietro Pomponazzi, *On the Immortality of the Soul*, trans. W. H. Hay, p. 282. Cf. Pomponazzi, *De naturalium effectuum causis sive de incantationibus* (Basle, 1556), pp. 290–1. For Weyer's opinions concerning lycanthropy, see *Histoires*, III, 10; IV, 23.

19 See Jean Calvin, *A Harmonie upon the three Evangelists* (London, 1584), pp. 130–1, where Matthew IV and Luke IV are discussed. See also Calvin, *Sermons of Master John Calvin upon the Booke of Job*, trans. A. Golding (London, 1574), Sermon VIII, pp. 36–41.

20 Bodin, *Démonomanie*, fols 220–1.

21 See Charles Wriothesley, *A Chronicle of England*, ed. W. D. Hamilton (Camden Society, London, 1875–7), I, pp. 75–6; Gilbert Burnet, *The History of the Reformation of the Church of England*, ed. Nicholas Pocock (Oxford, 1865), VI, pp. 194–5; *Letters and Papers, foreign and domestic, of the Reign of Henry VIII* (London, 1862–1910), XIII, i, No. 231. On the ambiguity of oracles, cf. Cicero *De div.*, II. lvi–lvii.

22 On Giovanni Battista Porta's popular and influential *Magiae naturalis sive de miraculis rerum naturalium* (first ed., Naples, 1558), see Lynn Thorndike, *A History of Magic and Experimental Science* (Columbia University Press, 1923–58), VI, pp. 418–23; John Ferguson, *Bibliotheca Chemica* (Glasgow, 1906), II, pp. 215–17.

23 Henricus Cornelius Agrippa, *De incertitudine & vanitate scientiarum declamatio* (Cologne?, 1531), sig. h. viii. Cf. James Sanford's trans., *Henrie Cornelius Agrippa, of the Vanitie and uncertaintie of Artes and Sciences* (London, 1569), fol. 61v: 'all this is nothing else but a certaine sporte of allegories, the whiche idle men busied in letters, pointes, and numbers, which this tongue and manner of writinge dothe easily suffer, accordinge to theire pleasure doo forge and reforge.'

24 Weyer, too, had stressed the importance of protecting oneself with the armour of God. See *Histoires*, p. 459.

25 G. L. Kittredge, *Witchcraft in Old and New England* (Harvard University Press,

1929, repr. New York, 1956), pp. 86–7, cites the story of Brandon, but, by omitting Scot's explanation of the feat, misses the point both of what Scot is trying to do and of how he does it.

26 The first published version of the *Pseudomonarchia Daemonum* was that included with the *De Praestigiis Daemonum* in the ed. published by the heirs of Johann Oporinus at Basle in 1577.

27 On the *Clavicula Salomonis*, see Lynn Thorndike, *op. cit.*, II, pp. 279–89.

28 See especially Kittredge, *op. cit.*, pp. 341–2. And cf. below, n. 33.

29 *The Discoverie of Witchcraft*, ed. Montague Summers (London, 1930); ed. Hugh Ross Williamson (London, 1964). Neither editor explains his omission of the *Discourse upon divels and spirits*.

30 Psellus is singled out for especial ridicule because of his tendency to regard spirits and devils as corporeal beings; and his suggestion, that devils are so physically weak that the stones they hurl down at men do no harm, is crushed with the retort: 'if a babe of two yeeres old throwe stones from Powles steeple, they will doo hurt' (p. 495). Scot would know the work of Michael Psellus (*c.* 1019–*c.* 1078) either in the Latin version, *Dialogus de energia seu operatione daemonum* (Paris, 1577), or in the French version, *Traicté par dialogue de l'energie des diables* (Paris, 1573).

31 Weyer, *Histoires*, pp. 218–19, 441.

32 *Ibid.*, pp. 18–19.

33 It is true that Scot, p. 505, says that he thinks, with Calvin, that angels are 'creatures of God'; and again, at p. 541, that the devil is a 'creature made by God'. But to accept these terms literally when Scot himself has interpreted them metaphorically, and when he deliberately reduces their power to nothing, is to ignore the whole purport of the *Discourse upon divels and spirits*. Amongst those who thus misinterpret Scot are Kittredge, *op. cit.*, p. 342; Christina Hole, *Witchcraft in England* (London, 1945), p. 139; Montague Summers, *Witchcraft and Black Magic* (London, 1945), p. 145; Barbara Rosen, *Witchcraft* (London, 1970), p. 171.

34 The most bitter modern critic of Scot has been Montague Summers, who concludes the introduction to his version of the *Discoverie* (London, 1930), with an extremely hostile assessment of Scot, who is described as a 'myopic squireen'; as 'utterly without imagination, a very dull, narrow, and ineffective little soul'; and as one who, had he dared, 'would have openly denied the supernatural'. All this is solemnly quoted from some anonymous 'cautious and circumstantial investigator'. However, upon examination we find that this investigator is none other than Montague Summers himself, fulminating against Scot in his *Geography of Witchcraft* (London, 1927), pp. 128–9.

35 Cicero's attack on dreams, *De div.*, II, lviii. Cf. Scot, p. 180.

36 St Hippolytus, *Philosophoumena* or *Refutation of all Heresies* was discovered in 1842 and first published in 1851.

37 On Oresme: see Lynn Thorndike, *op. cit.*, III, pp. 424–39, 466–71.

38 Erasmus Alberus, *Alcoranus Franciscanorum* (Frankfurt, 1543). I cite the English

version, *The Alcaron of the Barefote Friers* (London, 1550), Preface, sig. ã. ii–iii.
39 James Pilkington, *The Burning of St Paul's Church: The Addition and Confutation of the Addition*, ed. J. Scholefield (Parker Society, 1842), p. 587.
40 Thomas Becon, *An humble supplication unto God, for the restoring of his holy word unto the Church of England* (1533), repr. in *Prayers and other Pieces of Thomas Becon*, ed. John Ayre (Parker Society, Cambridge, 1844), p. 234.
41 See the *De incertitudine & vanitate scientiarum declamatio*, Caps 30, 31, 47, 48, 90. For a general study of Agrippa, see Charles G. Nauert, Jr, *Agrippa and the Crisis of Renaissance Thought* (Urbana, 1965). See also Walker, *Spiritual and Demonic Magic*, pp. 90–6; Frances A. Yates, *Giordano Bruno and the Hermetic Tradition* (London, 1964), pp. 130–43.
42 Ludwig Lavater, *De spectris, lemuribus et magis* (Geneva, 1570); French trans., *Trois livres des apparitions des esprits, fantosmes, prodiges et accidens merveilleux* (n.p., 1571); English trans. by Robert Harrison, *Of ghostes and spirites walking by nyght* (London, 1572).
43 Jean Calvin, *Institutio*, Lib. I, cap. xiv, n. 19.
44 R. Trevor Davies, *Four Centuries of Witch Beliefs* (London, 1947), pp. 5–12. For a less hostile view, see E. W. Monter, 'Witchcraft in Geneva, 1537–1662', *Journal of Modern History*, XLIII (1971), pp. 179–204.
45 Pietro Pomponazzi, *De incantationibus* (Basle, 1556), p. 363. Cf. Scot, *Discoverie*, p. 220; and his Epistle to the Readers, sig. B. iii.
46 *De incantationibus*, p. 123.
47 *Ibid.*, pp. 249–50. This is cited by Weyer, *Histoires*, p. 527.
48 *De incantationibus*, pp. 216–17, 327.
49 *Ibid.*, pp. 290–1.
50 Walker, *Spiritual and Demonic Magic*, p. 111.
51 See especially, *De Civitate Dei*, X. viii, xviii; XI. iii.
52 The oft-repeated story that James I caused Scot's book to be burned by the common hangman seems to derive from Gisbert Voetius, *Selectarum Disputationum Theologicarum, Pars Tertia* (Utrecht, 1659), p. 564. Neither Brinsley Nicholson nor Montague Summers was able to adduce contemporary evidence for such a burning; but the idea is not inherently impossible.
53 The attack on astrology has, of course, a long and ancient history. But, in particular, Scot would know Agrippa's famous attack in the *De vanitate*. Nevertheless, though Agrippa rejected the possibility of foreknowledge, he did accept heavenly influences upon human activity; and Scot even rejects these.
54 See above, n. 33. In some ways the most striking parallel for Scot's independent, anti-professional approach to magic is Michel de Montaigne, especially in his essay, *Des Boyteux*. See Alan M. Boase, 'Montaigne et la sorcellerie', *Humanisme et Renaissance*, II (1935), p. 418.

A TUDOR ANTHROPOLOGIST: GEORGE GIFFORD'S *DISCOURSE* AND *DIALOGUE*

Alan Macfarlane

In the county of Essex between 1560 and 1680 there are 496 surviving Assize Court prosecutions against supposed 'black' witches.[1] A further 230 men and women from Essex are known to have been presented at ecclesiastical courts for offences related to witchcraft. Some 229 out of 426 Essex villages are connected in some way with witchcraft prosecutions. This is merely the surface, visible to us through court records. Behind it lie the thousands of suspicions and half-formulated accusations which never reached the courts. The majority of the prosecutions occurred in the period 1570–1600, and one of the first areas to be troubled was a belt of central Essex at the level of Chelmsford and spreading eastwards to Maldon. It is therefore a great stroke of good fortune that there should have lived at the very centre of this witch-craft-conscious area, during the crucial period 1580–1600, a man who in his sensitive ability to understand and portray popular mentality anticipates the work of modern anthropologists. George Gifford in *A Discourse of the Subtill Practises of Devilles by Witches and Sorcerers* (1587) and *A Dialogue Concerning Witches and Witchcraftes* (1593) provides us with the best account we now have of many aspects of witchcraft beliefs.

We may wonder how Gifford's upbringing and career fitted him to write the second work in English on witchcraft, and the first in that language based mainly on English evidence.[2] Gifford was probably born in about 1548, at Dry Drayton in Cambridgeshire.[3] According to Wood he was a student of Hart Hall, Oxford 'several years before 1568', the college which Reginald Scot, author of the *Discoverie of Witchcraft*, had attended. Yet it is strange that Gifford should then have graduated BA and MA from Christ's College, Cambridge (1569–73). As the *DNB* puts it, 'It is probable that he is the George Gifford who, aged 30, was ordained by the Bishop of London both deacon and priest in December 1578'.[4] The publication of his first work[5] may have helped him to the living of All Saints with St Peter's at Maldon, Essex, to which he was presented in 1582.[6] In the next few years he published several books and won a reputation as a great preacher. Strype says of him that:

> This man was a great and diligent preacher, and much esteemed by many, and of good rank in the town, and had brought that place to some sobriety and knowledge of true religion . . . he was valued much . . . for the good reformation he had made in that market-town by his preaching, where very notorious sins reigned before his coming, and others had been, by his diligence, nourished and strengthened in grace and virtue, as the inhabitants in a petition to the bishop on his behalf had set forth at large; and that in his life he was modest, discreet, and unproveable; that he never used conventicles, but ever preached and catechised in the church.[7]

But in 1584 he was suspended from his ministry because he refused to subscribe to the articles of the established church, and was tried before the High Commission. Despite a petition on his behalf by fifty-two of his parishioners, and an intercession by Burghley and Sir Francis Knowles, he was deprived of his living, being considered 'a ringleader of the nonconformists'. He was allowed to hold the office of lecturer and continued to preach in his old church and the market place. Two years later his successor, Mark Wyersdale, desired to resign in his favour, but the request was refused. Meanwhile he had attended several synods of ministers, and was active in the local classis. Yet he was not an extreme Puritan and attacked those further to the left, the 'Brownists', in a series of pamphlets which defended read prayer, and to which Barrow and Greenwood replied.[8]

The ecclesiastical and doctrinal struggles in which he was involved were intricately intertwined with political issues, both at the national and local level. Within Maldon there appears to have been a power struggle in which various factions in the town contended for supremacy. Gifford, possibly unwillingly, became identified with 'The Company', the stronger element in the town's local government. The members of this group tended to be younger and more recently settled Maldon inhabitants who were opposed by a group of older inhabitants both within and outside the town corporation. This second group supported Robert Palmer, who was placed in Gifford's old living in 1589. Much abuse was hurled back and forth: for instance,

'The Company' were called 'schismaticks, young men, greenheads, intemperate and factitious'. Palmer several times attempted to prevent Gifford from preaching in Maldon, despite the latter's licence to do so. The details of the controversy are too complicated to describe here, and are recounted elsewhere.[9] One point about Gifford's character emerges from this faction-fighting: 'one man alone comes out well of all that was said and done. . . . Mr George Gifford held his peace'.[10]

Maldon was a small port and market-town with approximately 1,000 inhabitants during the later sixteenth century.[11] It was less noted for its witchcraft accusations than other nearby villages such as Hatfield Peverel and St Osyth, yet it shared in the series of trials that swept the county at the time. Some of these trials indicate the widespread magical activities forming a background to witchcraft accusations. Thus in 1580, about the same time as Gifford's arrival in the town, Humfrey Poles of Maldon was ordered by the Privy Council to be apprehended for conjuring.[12] A few years earlier some Maldon inhabitants had been involved in the escape of a conjuror and treasure-seeker, Robert Mantell.[13] In 1591 Edmund Hunt of Maldon was examined concerning his attempt to search for lost treasure at Beiligh Abbey. It emerged that he had used a magical parchment during the proceedings and had thought of approaching Doctor Dee, the famous magician, to enlist his help.[14] One of the earliest witchcraft presentments in the county also occurred at Maldon, when the 'wife of Nethersall' was summoned to the archdeacon's court in 1566, where she denied the charge that she was 'suspected to be a witche'. She was ordered to bring forward eight people who would swear to her innocence, and was noted as a pauper. But we learn nothing more of the case.[15] There were three major trials for witchcraft concerning inhabitants of Maldon, and a description of these will give some idea of the beliefs circulating when Gifford wrote.

The first two cases occurred in the 1570s before Gifford arrived, but they indicate the tensions then present. In 1572 Alice Chaundler of Maldon was accused in the Maldon borough court, and two years later exactly the same charge was brought against her at the Assizes, as well as two further indictments. She was accused of bewitching Mary Cowper of Maldon, aged eight years, and her father Francis, a fletcher, to death; of bewitching to death Robert Briscoe (aged 30 years), his son aged two years, and daughter aged five years. All were found true bills, and the defendant found guilty and hanged.[16] Five years later her daughter Ellen Smythe of Maldon was accused at the Assizes of bewitching Susan Webbe, aged four years, who languished and then died. Again the accused was found guilty, and presumably executed.[17] Fortunately for us, an eye-witness account of the trial was written and survives in a pamphlet. It gives a rare glimpse of the hostilities which lay behind formal accusations, which makes a full quotation necessary.

> There was one Jhon Chaundeler dwellyng in Maldon, whose wife named Alice Chaundeler, was mother unto this Elleine Smithe, and for Witchcrafte was executed long before, after whose execution he went unto his daughter in lawe Ellein Smithe, and demaunded certaine money of her, whiche she had received of her mother his wife, by meanes of whiche money thei fell out, and in fallyng out the saied Elleine in greate rage saied unto hym, that it had been better for hym, he had never fallen out with her, and so it came to passe, for the same Jhon Chaundeler confessed before his death, that after the same hower that she had saied so unto hym, he never eate any meate that digested in hym, but ever it came up againe as soone as it was done, by which meanes he consumed, and wasted awaie to his death.
> 2. The sonne of the foresaide Ellen Smithe, of the age of thirteene yeres, or thereaboutes, came to the house of one Jhon Estwood of Malden, for to begge an almose, who chid the boye awaie from his doore, whereuppon he wente home and tolde his mother, and within a while after the said Estwood was taken with very greate paine in his bodie, and the same night follovvying, as he satte by the fire with one of his neighbours, to their thinkyng thei did see a Ratte runne by the Chimney, and presently it did fall doune again in the likeness of a Tode, and takying it up with the tonges, thei thruste it into the fire, and so helde it in forcesibly, it made the fire burne as blewe as Azure, and the fire was almoste out, and at the burnying thereof the saied Ellen Smithe was in greate paine and out of quiete, whereuppon dissemblyngly she came to the house of the foresaied Jhon Estwood, and asked how all that were there did, and he saied well I thanke God, and she said, I thought you had not been well, and therefore I came to see how you did, and so went her waie.
> 3. Also it was avouched, and by this prisoner confessed, that where as her daughter, and the daughter of one Widdowe Webbe of Maldon aforesaid, did fall out and fight, the same Ellein Smithe offended thereat, meetyng good wife Webbes daughter the next daie, gave her a blowe on the face, whereupon so soone as the childe came home she sickened, and languishying two daies, cried continually, awaie with the Witche, awaie with the Witch, and so died. And in the mornyng immediately after the death of the same childe, the saied good wife Webbe espied (as she thought) a thyng like to a black Dogge goe out at

her doore, and presently at the sight thereof, she fell distraught of her wittes.

4. Besides the sonne of this Mother Smith, confessed that his mother did keepe three Spirites, whereof the one called by her great Dicke, was enclosed in a wicker Bottle: The seconde named Little Dicke, was putte into a Leather Bottle; And the third termed Willet, she kepte in a Wolle Packe. And thereupon the house was commaunded to be searched. The Bottles and packe were found but the Spirites were vanished awaie.[18]

There are no recorded trials of Maldon inhabitants in the 1580s, but this is the decade when many prosecutions occurred in nearby villages, particularly in 1582 and 1584 when some 53 indictments from villages in Essex have survived. Gifford's first written reference to witchcraft occurred in 1583, when he wrote: 'Some seeke helpe of Witches & Conjurours, when theyr bodyes, their Children, and cattel are hurt: which is to seek at the devil.'[19] The first of his major works on the subject in 1587 was probably a delayed reaction to the 1582 and 1584 holocausts.[20] On the other hand the *Dialogue* of 1593 was possibly, at least partly, inspired by local events in Maldon.

In April 1591 Elizabeth Maun and her daughter Margaret Wiseman of West Mersea were presented at the ecclesiastical court for witchcraft. The latter was also stated to be of Bradwell-juxta-mare near Maldon and is almost certainly the same person as the Margaret Wiseman who the following May was cleared on the oath of six Maldon inhabitants of 'all occation of suspicion of Witchcrafte',[21] but again accused in July and ordered to bring further witnesses. The second of these accusations occurred at a court held at Maldon and it seems very possible that Gifford would be present. He would also have been aware that in the same year Margaret Wiseman was being tried in the borough court of Maldon. On 10 January 1592 fourteen people, and two others whose names are crossed out, were put on a recognisance to witness against Margaret Wiseman, and five days later John Wiseman, brewer (Margaret's husband), and three others of Maldon were bound over for the sum of ten pounds for Margaret's good behaviour. On 17 April a note was made that 'where there hadd bene heretofore divers speches geven foorthe of the suspicioun that Margaret Wyseman was a wytche' and that John, her husband, 'reported that he had seene a broome in his house to swype the house without any hands', John was brought before the bailiffs and denied that he had ever said such a thing or believed it to be true.

Unfortunately, we do not know the outcome of either borough or ecclesiastical prosecution, and there is no record that the case went to the Assizes.

Nor is there any reference in Gifford's *Dialogue* to the type of witchcraft described above. Yet it is likely to be more than a coincidence that the following year he published his powerful attack on the credulity of those who believed in witches. It was from direct experience in Maldon and neighbouring villages that he was able to write of a situation so serious that, as one of the characters in the *Dialogue* put it, 'there is scarce any towne or village in all this shire, but there is one or two witches at the least in it.'[22]

One of the most important aspects of contemporary beliefs shown us by Gifford's work is the way in which suspicions of witchcraft built up and finally exploded in country villages. He lays bare the interweaving of gossip, fear and tension which lay behind the formal court presentments for witchcraft. The *Dialogue* is full of material on this, but the best single sustained description occurs in a brilliant passage in the *Discourse* beginning 'Some woman doth fal out bitterly with her neighbour....'[23] The type of evidence brought to the courts and upon which suspects were convicted is also well illustrated.[24] The description of the popularity, faith-healing basis, and magical methods of 'cunning folk' who were believed to cure people of the effects of witchcraft is excellent. It is of considerable interest that in all but one of the nine cases in which Gifford described counter-action against suspected witches in his *Dialogue* the victims or near friend went to a cunning man or woman.[25] Indeed, Gifford was very concerned with the need to destroy the power of such magical practitioners, men and women who were not only pivots of the witchcraft mentality, but were also a threat to the clergy. Finally, Gifford's works show clearly that the oft-repeated generalisation which links witch-hunting with Puritan fanaticism is too simple. Gifford was a 'Puritan' by most definitions, yet his work is one of the most humane and rational attacks on current beliefs about the evil power of witches.[26]

Yet even Gifford had to admit the reality of witchcraft. In his two witchcraft works we are watching a mind trying to rise above the limitations and assumptions of its time, to argue its way out of a closed and circular system. The fascination and importance of watching this process is given a tragic greatness when we remember the huge background of suffering against which it occurred. As Gifford wrote, hundreds of people, mostly old women, were being executed or imprisoned throughout England for an offence which we now know they could not have committed. The theme was a great one, and it is not too much to say that the treatment also entitles Gifford to the position of one of the great minor writers in English history.

The inhabitants of sixteenth-century Essex suffered the endless misfortunes and irritations endemic in all societies, but particularly painful in those lacking modern medical facilities and insurance agencies: animals died, uninsured houses burned down, children died of painful and lingering diseases, butter and beer would not process properly. There are a number of ways in which human societies have explained such misfortunes: some, like the Nupe, accept that events may happen by random accident; others, among whom the Azande are the classic case, seek for an explanation in terms of a living agent.[27] Gifford's works and contemporary literature show that in everyday life people made a choice between the following explanations: God (trying his servants), oneself (angering God or breaking a taboo), another person (a witch), the stars (astrology), 'natural causation', or chance. The problem for us is why people tended to select certain causes of misfortune in certain situations and why, during the sixteenth and seventeenth centuries, witchcraft became a favoured explanation, only to die away towards the end of this period. In discussing this problem it is of crucial importance to realise that England, even in the sixteenth century, had developed from the Azande-type situation where it is believed that 'Death has always a cause, and no man dies without a reason'[28] to a more complex set of beliefs where 'natural' illness and death were accepted. In other words, not every death needed an explanation in personal terms: some people, for instance the very old or infants, might die or be ill from causes unrelated to divine or human will. This acceptance is indicated by Gifford, who argued that 'we must consider that there bee naturall causes in the bodies of men and beastes of grievous tormentes and diseases, yea even causes of death', and later, that though God sometimes allows the Devil 'to strike some in their bodies for their haynous sinnes, yet the most which the witches thinke their spirits doe kill at their request, doe die of naturall diseases'.[29] That astrological beliefs were widespread, and misfortune and success ascribed to the stars, was also obvious to Gifford: 'If men did prosper, it was ascribed unto that lucky planet under which they were borne. In adversity they blamed the Starres.'[30]

Yet the central issue in Gifford's discussion is whether, as many of his congregation and neighbours believed, witches were to blame for a large proportion of the pain and misfortune in the environment, or whether the suffering individual himself was to blame. His position was made more difficult by the fact that, like the vast majority of his contemporaries, both intellectuals and villagers, he was aware that the Bible said 'thou shalt not suffer a witch to live', and he accepted that the world was alive with warring spiritual forces of good and evil. At first sight, therefore, he seems to share the basic belief in witchcraft of those for whom he wrote. Thus he stated that 'For my part, I go not about to defend witches. I denie not but that the devill worketh by them. And that they ought to be put to death . . .' and 'A witch by the word of God ought to die the death not because she killeth men, for that she cannot ... but because she dealeth with devils.'[31] Yet here, in the phrase 'not because she killeth men, for that she cannot' we see the gulf between Gifford and his opponents. The popular view was that the witch *could* kill men; their malice was the cause of evil. Eliminate witches and much of the suffering in the world would disappear, it was argued. People seized old women 'as if they were the very plagues of the world, and as if all would be well, and safe from such harmes, if they were rooted ... for it is thought that the witch which has her spirits, is even lyke a man which hath curst dogges, which he may sett upon other mens cattell'.[32] To hang witches would decrease suffering; 'the country being rid of the witches and their spirits, mens bodies and their cattell should be safe'.[33] The law of the land, in making it a felony to injure or kill people or animals by witchcraft was likewise based on the assumption that such acts were possible. This view may be illustrated as follows:

Witch → *Familiar*[34] → *Victim*
(motive: anger)   (power, from Devil)

Thus the witch provided the original evil intention; the familiar, pretending to act as her servant, provided the power. The reason for the anger was almost always an unneighbourly action on the part of her future victim. The sequence of events is excellently illustrated in many of Gifford's accounts of the type of evidence upon which people were convicted. For instance, 'One woman came in and testified ... that her husband upon his death bed, tooke it upon his death, that he was bewitched, for he pined a long time. And he sayde further, he was sure that woman had bewitched him. He tooke her to be naught, and thought she was angry with him, because she would have borrowed five shillinges of him, and he denyed to lend it her.'[35] This set of connections had many functions and supports and some of these will be discussed later. How did Gifford, who still shared many premises with his audience, attempt to break out of the system?

The first thing he did was to change the definition of 'witchcraft'. Instead of concentrating on the physical effects, and distinguishing between 'black' witches, who harmed people, and 'white' witches or cunning folk, who countered witchcraft and helped people find lost goods, a distinction made by his audience, he concentrated on means. Was the mystical power sought through the conventional Christian channels of prayer and humility, or were the sources elsewhere, in the dark realms of magic and the Devil? Thus he defined a witch as 'one that woorketh by the Devill, or by some devilish or curious art, either hurting or healing, revealing thinges secret, or foretelling thinges to come . . . the Conjurer, the enchaunter, the sorcerer, the deviner . . . are indeede compased within this circle'.[36] His motives for this broad definition were probably mixed. He realised that the whole witchcraft belief-system was given coherence and support by the many hundreds of witch-doctors then flourishing in England. If they could be prosecuted as 'witches' the whole system might collapse. At the same time, a profession which threatened the spiritual monopoly of the Church would be eliminated; he knew that 'there be thousands in the land deceived. The woman at R.H. by report hath some weeke fourtie come unto her, and many of them not of the meaner sort', and that many of these would agree with the character in his *Dialogue* who said of this woman 'she doeth more good in one yeare than all these scripture men will doe so long as they live'.[37]

The cunning folk were, in fact, a symptom of what Gifford really feared— a form of Manichaean heresy in which evil powers had somehow become autonomous. For the common conception of witches had revived the idea, probably always present throughout the Middle Ages, that pain and suffering are the result of forces outside the Christian God. This dualism was all the more worrying for Gifford since his brand of Christianity was especially unable to compete with magical and effective alternative remedies to the cunning folk. He was asking people simultaneously to abandon their magical counter-actions against misfortune and not to feel threatened. His constant argument was that 'men do so little consider the high soveraignety and providence of God over all things; they ascribe so much to the power of the devils and to the anger of witches, and are in such feare of them' that they entirely neglect Christian remedies.[38] What was the Christian attitude which he proposed?

His basic tenet was that God was all-powerful; nothing could occur without His permission. Although people fear the Devil, he can, in fact, 'doe no violence to the bodie of a poore swine, naie he can not at his pleasure kill so much as a seelie flie',[39] for as one character argued when told that a hen had been bewitched by the devil's power, 'Christ saith, a Sparrow can not fall without the will of your heavenly Father: and is not a henne as good as a Sparrow?'[40] Instead of the witch being the origin of pain, and controlling the devils (familiars), Gifford pointed out that all power and decision flowed from God. It was He who permitted the Devil to act; and the Devil, while pretending to be the witch's slave, was really her master. 'The witch is the vassall of the devill and not he her servant.'[41] Why did people refuse to see this, Gifford asked. Because the consequence of such an explanation of suffering was to take the blame off the witch and place it either on the victim's own shoulders or on those of God. The common people 'can by no means see, that God is provoked by their sinnes to give the devill such instruments to work withall, but rages against the witch, even as if she could do all'.[42] Pain then, was mainly the result of people's sins against the Lord: 'I say that God in justice giveth power unto Satan to delude, because men refuse to love his trueth: but that maketh not that the devill obtaineth any power to hurt, because the witch sendeth, but the fault is in men, the sinnes of the people give power to the devill: for God is offended.'[43] The chain of causal links which Gifford hoped to substitute for the popular one described above is as follows:

  God → Devil → Witch → Victim
 (motive and power)

Thus responsibility was transferred to God, and hence back to the victim who had angered God, rather than on to another human being (the witch).

 Basically God had two motives for sending misfortunes, according to Gifford. He might, on the one hand, be toughening his followers, trying their faith as He did with Job. 'For touching the godly, the Lord doth use Satan to afflict them in their bodies and in their goodes, for to trie their faith and patience.'[44] Or, as a loving but just father, He might be punishing His erring children with 'the roddes & scourges of his wrath'.[45] Although this allowed suffering Christians to feel that at least some of their misfortunes were not the direct result of their own offences, in practice the response to suffering advocated by Gifford was always the same. 'If thou feare God, and Satan afflict thee, stand fast in faith and patience, and waite upon God for thy deliverance. If thou endure temptation, thou art blessed, and shalt be crowned Jam. I. ver. 12. If thy sinnes have provoked God . . . fall downe and humble thy selfe with fasting and prayer . . . looke not upon the witch, lay not the cause where it is not.'[46] If only people would accept this argument, both intellectually and emotionally, then the hunt for witches would disappear.

 The problem, as Gifford realised, was that people did not just want a theologically sound explanation; they wanted something that really held out some chance of healing present pain and minimising the recurrence of misfortune in the future. This the anti-magical Puritan version of Christianity advocated by Gifford could not promise to do. He only had to look round him to see that many godly folk were as wracked by pain as were the ungodly. His audience also noted this. 'For many nowe doe even quake and tremble, and their faith doth stagger. Hath hee [i.e. the Devil] power (thinke they) over such as be cunning in the scriptures, then what are they the better for their profession? the witch is on their bones as well as upon others. By this it might seeme, and so they take it, that other helpes and remedies are to be sought than by the scriptures.'[47] Although a fund of spiritual power was available to the staunch Christian, this was provided against generalised evil forces, the Devil who might be overcome 'by faith in the Gospell of Jesus Christ', combined with 'sincere integritie of heart, and with a godly life, with zeale, with patience, and with all other heavenly vertues'.[48] But as for specific evil people, thought to be witches, 'it were a straunge thing for the holy Scriptures to appoynt a medicine for such a disease as it never mentioneth. The word of the Lord doth never mention that Witches can hurt the bodie at all: & therefore it doth no where prescribe any remedie for that which is not.'[49] This was a logical, theologically sound position, but it was hardly likely to satisfy a man whose child was dying a lingering death; such a man would want to be shown a specific course of action against a specific evil agent.

Both Gifford and his opponents shared the assumption that social and physical worlds were interlinked, bad thoughts and bad actions would set off a chain of mystical power which would lead to suffering. They differed, however, in their view of whom it would harm. Gifford was arguing that a man's sins would bounce back onto him from the Great Reflector above. This was an argument for responsibility: a man himself is to blame for his misfortunes, he stands alone with God and cannot, childlike, plead that it was someone else's fault. His opponents argued that the witch's malice was bounced off the satellite-like familiar and struck elsewhere. In the latter theory the enormous weight of explaining pain in a pre-industrial society need not be borne either by God, or by the suffering individual. The great division is between accepting pain as justified, to be suffered with patience, or to see it as a hostile attack by outside agents, to be repulsed and fought. In the former case there will be soul-searching; what did I do wrong that I should suffer so, why was God angry? This will result in a considerable measure of guilt and bewilderment. It will probably appeal to a person already feeling worthless and guilt-ridden. It will lead to an increased attempt to prune away all personal behaviour that might offend the All-Seeing One. The witchcraft explanation, on the contrary, will fit a mood of righteous indignation and feelings of aggression. It will also offer relief to a person who has a generalised feeling of anxiety, and who is relieved to be able to ascribe this to a specific factor which may justifiably be assumed to have caused such anxiety. Gifford's theory appears to be much more demanding, involving a much greater degree of responsibility. It entails what might be thought to be an almost intolerable load of guilt when it forces people to believe that their own faults are causing great suffering to those they love. We might therefore expect that in the years after the publication of his works the majority of the population would continue to choose a witchcraft explanation. This would also be encouraged by the fact that, as we have seen, such an explanation busied the person concerned in a whole set of consultations and rituals which made him feel that he had control of the situation. Christian faith alone left a man an importunate pleader, to be rewarded at the end perhaps, but liable to suffer every time he relaxed his godly standards or whenever God decided to test his faith.

Another reason why we might have predicted, had we visited Maldon in 1593, that the witchcraft explanation would, in the next century, destroy Gifford's appeal, lies in the contrasted effects the two patterns of explanation have on social relationships and individual norms. A brief analysis of the expanding population, new industrial enterprises, increasing gap between prosperous villagers and their less fortunate neighbours who were beginning to show signs of becoming a landless labouring force, would have indicated to an anthropologist that what was needed was a philosophy which would justify an increasing flexibility in social relations. People needed to find some rationalisation as to why they felt uneasy when they refused traditional obligations and Christian precepts which stressed that charity to those slightly worse off than oneself was a cardinal virtue. To find that the shunned neighbour, instead of righteously invoking the power of God through a widow's curse, was an evil old witch was a considerable relief. Anthropologists have tended to stress the way in which witchcraft accusations have a conservative effect, forcing people to adhere to their traditional ideas. But, depending on the flow of accusations, the effects of witchcraft prosecutions may also be disruptive. The two approaches are illustrated by the respective punishments in the ecclesiastical and secular courts in England at this period. The church courts were based on the assumption that the purpose of justice was to purge the community and then to re-integrate the ritually cleansed offender into the village again. If this had been successful in Essex we might have had the Azande-type situation where 'some of one's best friends' might be witches. But in Essex the major recourse was to the secular courts where the guilty were imprisoned or executed; the aim was to eliminate witches, not to restore social harmony.

Witchcraft accusations were a method of splitting apart, of distancing people. On the personal level they justified disruptive feelings of anger and hostility which ran contrary to the traditional pressures towards harmony and charity instilled by Christianity. Furthermore, witchcraft beliefs did not force people to examine their own conduct to see in what way they had deviated from traditional ideals of behaviour. If suffering had been accepted as the consequence of personal sin, then people would have had to admit that they had failed in charity, that the old woman was justified in laying a curse. The whole organic, distributive rather than acquisitive, communal rather than individual, 'thou art thy brother's keeper', traditional Christian ethic would have had to be adhered to. As it was, the enormity of the witch's reciprocal retaliation, and her association with foul behaviour and hidden power, so overshadowed the situation that the victim's original offence was forgotten. In a subtle way the whole traditional morality could be altered without appearing to change. Charity and love were fine, but could not, of course, be expected to include those beast-like witches—just as today we are to love all our brethren, except for those foul and scarcely human protagonists of 'enemy' states we fear.

The approach advocated by Gifford and his fellows, if strictly adhered to, would have meant that in the context of sixteenth-century villages traditional values were re-affirmed. The gap between communal ideals and individual practices would either have had to be eliminated by modifying powerful economic forces, or else the anxiety which arises from this acute clash would have grown even greater. Given the presence of a great deal of suffering, to explain it in terms of a communal God meant that the community must constantly come together and join in sacrifice and prayer to eliminate such suffering. Such ritual would tend to strengthen the traditional morality and draw villagers closer together. Furthermore the individual would try not to deviate from traditional norms, for, as Hallowell has shown for the Saulteaux who connect sin, sex, and sickness, such deviation is foolhardy, for it leads to disease.[50] God the Schoolmaster was ready with his rod and a vigilant eye; the outward conformity which this enforced under Catholicism was made even more strict when Puritans developed the sense of God being 'nearer than the skin'. Yet it is one of the most puzzling historical problems why such Puritans, appealing to traditional morality and ever-vigilant in their attempt to cut away any sinful, deviant, behaviour which might bring down God's wrath, should have been, in literature, politics, and science, among the most important architects of the modern secularised world. The way in which their ultra-sensitivity to the connection between sin and suffering led finally to a complete rejection of any connection (in the case of the Quakers and several extremist sects); the process by which their insistence on traditional charity led to the emergence of the phenomenon which has been termed the 'theory of possessive individualism': these and other extraordinary developments could hardly have been predicted by an observer standing in Gifford's shoes. Nor could such an observer have predicted the vogue for Gifford's type of explanation of suffering, shown in so many seventeenth-century diaries.[51] For within a century Gifford's opponents were in disarray.

It would be pleasant to think that Gifford's books helped in this process, but there is no evidence that this is so. His *Discourse* is not known to have been republished, and the *Dialogue* was only republished once, in 1603. He is scarcely referred to by later writers on the subject. Yet these two works, largely ignored in the century after their publication, and frequently misunderstood in our own, are among the most important sources in any language for the study of popular witchcraft beliefs.

Notes

1. The sources for these statistics, and discussion of the various definitions of witchcraft, may be found in Alan Macfarlane, *Witchcraft in Tudor and Stuart England* (London, 1970). Basically a 'black' witch was a person believed to do physical harm, a 'white' witch, someone who did physical good.
2. Reginald Scot, *Discoverie of Witchcraft* (London, 1584), based his work mainly on Continental demonologists.
3. Dry Drayton is given as his birthplace in the Maldon Borough records. Unfortunately, the Dry Drayton parish register does not go back far enough to confirm this, though Mr A. H. Lloyd Dunn of Fenstanton, Hunts, kindly informs me that there were many Gifford/Giffards in the parish.
4. This brief biographical account is based on the much fuller details in the *DNB*, *s.n.*; T. W. Davids, *Annals of Evangelical Nonconformity in the County of Essex* (London, 1863), pp. 117-18; and Jay P. Anglin, 'The Court of the Archdeacon of Essex, 1571-1609: An Institutional and Social Study' (University of California PhD thesis, 1965), pp. 362, 436. James Hitchcock, 'George Gifford and Puritan Witch Beliefs', *Archiv für Reformationsgeschichte*, 58 (1967), no. 1, pp. 90-9, is a very useful discussion of Gifford's views on witchcraft.
5. *A briefe discourse of certaine points of the religion which is among the commo(n) sort of christians* (London, 1581).
6. For other biographical details concerning Gifford, and especially his relations with other Maldon inhabitants, I am indebted to Dr W. Petchey's Leicester University PhD thesis entitled 'The Borough of Maldon, 1500-1688' (1972).
7. Strype, *Annals of the Reformation*, quoted in Davids, *Annals*, p. 117.
8. The polemical works in this controversy may be found under the names of Barrow, Gifford and Greenwood in A. W. Pollard and G. R. Redgrave, *A Short-title Catalogue of Books ... 1475-1640* (reprinted, 1963), which also lists all Gifford's other works.
9. The thesis by Dr Petchey, referred to above, contains, in chapter 5, a full account of the controversy.
10. The judgment of Dr Petchey in the above-mentioned thesis.
11. Patrick Collinson, *The Elizabethan Puritan Movement* (London, 1967), p. 376,

describes religious life in the town and the whole of Collinson's book provides a useful background account of the ecclesiastical situation in Essex at this time.

12 *Acts of the Privy Council*, n.s. xii, p. 34.
13 *Ibid.*, pp. 29, 353–4; *State Papers*, 12/186, fols 221–5. Other details concerning Mantell are given by K. V. Thomas, *Religion and the Decline of Magic* (London, 1971), p. 420. The whole background to witchcraft and magical beliefs is excellently portrayed in Mr Thomas's book, and the interpretation of Gifford's work in the following pages, though written before his work was published, overlaps in many ways with his central arguments.
14 ERO (Essex Record Office, County Hall, Chelmsford), D/B 3/1/8, fols 23, 23^v, 87^v. I am grateful to the County Archivist for permission to quote from the documents, and to all at the Record Office for their assistance.
15 ERO D/AEA/3, fol. 85^v.
16 ERO D/B 3/1/6, fol. 149^v and cases 67–9 in C. L'Estrange Ewen, *Witch Hunting and Witch Trials* (London, 1929).
17 Case 119 in Ewen, *op. cit.*
18 *A Detection of damnable driftes, practized by three Witches arraigned at Chelmisforde in Essex, at the late Assises there holden, which were executed in Aprill 1579* (1579; a copy in the British Museum, and extracts reprinted in C. L'Estrange Ewen *Witchcraft and Demonianism* (London, 1933), pp. 149–51), sigs Av^v–Avi^v.
19 *A Catechisme* (London, 1583), sig. E6^v.
20 Gifford's *A Discourse of the Subtill Practises of Devilles by Witches and Sorcerers* (1587), does not tell us the immediate cause which prompted him to write. He said in the preface that he wrote it to counter two contrary beliefs: that witches were all-powerful, or that they did not exist at all.
21 ERO D/ACA/19, fol. 157^v and D/AEA/16, fols 64, 94. Dr Petchey has provided some indirect evidence of Gifford's involvement in the Wiseman case, and of the way in which witchcraft accusations and local faction-struggles may have been connected. Of the compurgators who appeared on behalf of Margaret Wiseman, at least three (Agnes Fludd, Elizabeth Pratt, Susan Ionions) are known to have been supporters and friends of Gifford, whereas none of those who gave evidence against her are known to have had any connection with Gifford.
22 *Dialogue*, sig. A4^v.
23 *Discourse*, sigs G4–G4^v.
24 For example, *Dialogue*, sig. L3.
25 The cases are in *Dialogue*, sigs B, B, B^v, B2^v, C, D4^v, E3^v, E3^v, I^v.
26 There is further discussion of the supposed link between Puritanism and witchcraft in Macfarlane, *Witchcraft*, ch. 14.
27 S. F. Nadel, *Nupe Religion* (London, 1954), p. 37; E. E. Evans-Pritchard, *Witchcraft, Oracles, and Magic among the Azande* (Oxford, 1937), *passim*. The latter book is a classic account of witchcraft beliefs; a basic text for understanding seventeenth-century witchcraft.
28 Evans-Pritchard, *op. cit.*, p. 111.

29 *Dialogue*, sigs D3, E3ᵛ.
30 *Discourse*, sig. B4ᵛ. An excellent description of the widespread belief in the power of stars is given in Thomas, *op. cit.*, chs 10–12.
31 *Dialogue*, sigs B2ᵛ, K3.
32 *Dialogue*, sig. D.
33 *Dialogue*, sig. H2ᵛ.
34 A 'familiar' is a small demon, often in the shape of a toad or cat, which carried out the witch's orders.
35 *Dialogue*, sig. L3.
36 *Discourse*, sig. B2.
37 *Dialogue*, sigs H, M3ᵛ.
38 *Dialogue*, sig. M2ᵛ.
39 *Discourse*, sig. D2ᵛ.
40 *Dialogue*, sig. Mᵛ.
41 *Dialogue*, sig. C4.
42 *Dialogue*, sig. D3ᵛ.
43 *Dialogue*, sig. Kᵛ.
44 *Dialogue*, sig. D2ᵛ.
45 *Discourse*, sig. B4ᵛ.
46 *Dialogue*, sig. H3ᵛ.
47 *Dialogue*, sig. D4.
48 *Discourse*, sig. I3ᵛ.
49 *Discourse*, sig. I3.
50 A. I. Hallowell, 'Sin, sex and sickness in Saulteaux belief', *British Jnl Medical Psychology*, XVIII (1939), pp. 191–8.
51 A classic case, which makes an interesting comparison with Gifford, is described in Alan Macfarlane, *The Family Life of Ralph Josselin* (Cambridge, 1970), part 4.

7

KING JAMES'S *DAEMONOLOGIE*: WITCHCRAFT AND KINGSHIP

Stuart Clark

It is the glory of God to conceal a thing: but the honour of kings is to search out a matter. (Proverbs XXV. 2)

And hereunto I might add the disposition of King James, who was ever apt to search into secrets, to try conclusions, as I did know some who saw him run to see one in a fit whom they said was bewitched. (Godfrey Goodman, *The Court of King James the First*, J. S. Brewer, ed., 2 vols (London, 1839), I, 3)

James VI and I published his *Daemonologie* in Edinburgh in 1597, a slim quarto of eighty pages which went through two London editions in 1603 and was later translated into Latin, French and Dutch. Since it is neither original nor profound, its significance, in anonymity, would lie only in being one of the first defences of Continental beliefs about witchcraft in English. But as the work of James I it possesses quite unusual additional meaning and interest in the literature of demonology. It was the only book of its kind written by a monarch, naturally someone with enormous potential influence over the incidence and severity of prosecution. In fact, there is a good deal of evidence of James's personal involvement; and the origins of the *Daemonologie* can be traced to his part in bringing the witches of North Berwick to trial in Edinburgh in 1590–1. In addition, although its ostensible purpose was simply to refute the two major sceptics, Reginald Scot and Johann Weyer, the treatise was also intended, together with other theological and political writings, to demonstrate James's intellectual and religious *bona fides* as a ruler. Both in genesis and in content the *Daemonologie* may be read as a statement about ideal monarchy. Finally, there is a sense in which demonism was, logically speaking, one of the presuppositions of the metaphysic of order on which James's political ideas ultimately rested. There is a temptation to view his concern for witchcraft as an isolated, even aberrant interest. He, on the contrary, thought of the *Daemonologie* as one of his most important works. This essay will argue that it was integral, indeed necessary, to his political career and mental world, and that only in this wider context can its various layers of meaning be fully understood.

I

It now seems clear that James showed no interest in witchcraft until the summer and autumn of 1590.[1] The idea that his affectionless childhood and violent political apprenticeship made him sensitive to the macabre and so receptive to the subject from an early age has been canvassed without becoming convincing.[2] He was certainly neurotic and easily terrified, and the fact that until 1587 Scottish politics centred on possession of his person did not help. Fontenay wrote that he was 'nurtured in fear' and Robert Johnston that his troubles 'molested his inward quiet'.[3] But his experiences were by no means unique in rulers of the period, and there is no actual evidence to support the psychological speculation that they inclined him to study witchcraft. His early work on the Book of Revelation, used to illustrate his supposedly abnormal preoccupations, could not have been *more* normal, given his education in the Protestant tradition that the Pope was Antichrist. The whole theory rests on the assumption that an interest in witchcraft and demonology needs some sort of special explanation, a misconception arising from the failure to see it in its appropriate context. What *is* significant in the case of James is that his belief in witchcraft was based on the demonic pact and the sabbat, and that he was almost certainly responsible for introducing these specifically continental notions into Scotland. Drawing on all the available evidence, Christina Larner has recently argued that he acquired them in the winter of 1589 during a six months' nuptial stay at the Danish court which included a meeting with Niels Hemmingsen, an authority cited in the *Daemonologie*. Until his return domestic cases were based on the primitive doctrine of *maleficium* or they were essentially political in character. Despite an act of 1563 against witchcraft, sorcery and necromancy, there was no really significant indigenous concern for persecuting witches at all.[4] It was James's personal diligence in the affair of North Berwick that dramatically changed the situation. In October 1591, after a year of unprecedented revelations, a commission for the examining of witches was issued and the first period of intensive persecution in Scotland was given official recognition.

Although the principal North Berwick defendants were charged with a number of individual crimes, running the whole gamut of traditional witch activities, the central feature of their trials was communal devil-worship. On Halloween 1590 over a hundred local witches had supposedly sailed into the town in an armada of sieves and danced into the kirk to the sound of a trumpet. The Devil, a small black monster in gown and hat, addressed the assembly; 'his faice was terrible, his noise lyk the bek of ane egle, gret bournyng eyn; his handis and legis wer herry, with clawes upon his handis and feit lyk the griffon, and spak with a how voice'. Presenting his buttocks for the customary greeting he told them, 'Spair nocht to do ewill, and to eit, drink and be blyth, taking rest and eise, ffor he sould raise thame up at the latter day gloriouslie.' The proceedings reached their finale with the desecration of graves; 'thay opnit up the graves, twa within and ane without the kirk, and tuik of the jountis of thair fingaris, tais and neise, and partit thame amangis thame; ... The Devill commandit thame to keip the jountis upoun thame, quhill thay wer dry, and thane to mak ane powder of thame, to do ewill withall.'[5] There was worse to come. To his horror James soon 'discovered' that a good deal of this diabolical energy had been expended on his own behalf. The accused were alleged to have convened another meeting with the Devil at Newhaven, also near Edinburgh, and been given the recipe for a mixture of venom of roasted toad, stale urine and adder skin with which to infect the royal linen. They had also asked the Devil to activate a wax image of the king which would then be destroyed by fire. Most amazing of all were the supposed plans for drowning James and his bride on their voyages to and from Denmark. Adopting a traditional procedure for raising tempests, covens of witches in Leith and Prestonpans had each taken cats, 'christened' them, tied to them 'the chiefest parts of a dead man' and, on a signal, cast them simultaneously into the seas off Edinburgh. There was even a report that Danish witches were involved in trying to destroy James's flotilla, of which one vessel was in fact lost.[6] Even this was not the end of the business. What had begun as a matter solely of witchcraft, albeit treasonable, was transposed into a political and dynastic key by the allegation that the toad poison and wax image had been specially commissioned by Francis Stewart, Earl of Bothwell, James's volatile cousin and figurehead of the ultra-Protestant opposition party. Each of the witches at Newhaven had apparently 'blessed' the wax effigy with the words, 'This is King James the Sext, ordonit to be consumed at the instance of a noble man Francis Erle Bodowell.' Bothwell protested his innocence but was committed to custody in May 1591. After his escape a proclamation spoke of his having 'gevin himself ower altogidder in the handis of Sathan' and consulted 'nygromanceris, witcheis, and utheris wickit and ungodlie personis'. The charges were never substantiated, but they certainly served to compound James's fears.[7]

The complex tangle of interests involved makes it difficult to see what reality, if any, lay behind these alleged crimes or to apportion exact responsibility for the confessions extorted from defendants.[8] But it is clear that James himself, his conversations with Hemmingsen fresh in mind, had a good deal of influence, and the supposition must be that the presence for the first time of Continental beliefs in Scottish indictments ('dittays') was his own work. It is evident from the pamphlet *Newes from Scotland* (1591), which reads very much like an official version of the trials, that he took a prominent part in interrogating the principals, and he claimed publicly that 'whatsoever hath bene gotten from them hath bene done by me my selfe'. Agnes Sampson, for instance, was said to have been persuaded to confess 'by his owne especiall travell', though this seems merely to have meant extreme torture and the search for *stigmata sagorum*. Typical of the pedantic curiosity that never left him was his desire to confront the trappings and sometimes the very fact of magic. On Christmas Eve 1590 a demoniac was summoned to the royal chamber where 'suddenly he gave a great screach, and fell into a madness . . . to the great admiration of his Majesty and others then present'. Sampson spoke of the procession into North Berwick kirk and the music and singing of the witches' congregation: 'These confessions made the King in a wonderful admiration, and he sent for the said Geillis Duncane, who upon the like trump did play the said dance before the King's Majesty; who, in respect of the strangeness of these matters, took great delight to be present at their examinations.'[9]

Remarkable evidence of James's active and vicious personal campaign can also be found in a letter to Chancellor Maitland in April 1591:

> Trye by the medicinairis aithis gif Barbara Nepair be uith bairne or not. Tak na delaying ansour. Gif ye finde sho be not, to the fyre uith her presesentlie, and cause bouell her publicclie. Lett Effie Makkaillen see the stoup tua or three dayes, and upon the suddain staye her in hope of confession. Gif that servis, adverteis; gif not dispatche her the next oulke anis, bot not according to the rigoure of the dome. The rest of the inferioure uitchis, of at the naill uith thaim.[10]

When eventually brought to trial on 8 May Barbara Napier was found guilty of consulting with witches but unexpectedly acquitted of treason. On 10

May James wrote demanding the death penalty; but at the end of the month he had decided to reverse the verdict by an assize of error, making doubly sure of the outcome by a prior 'consultation' with the assizors and by himself taking the chair. Both the assize and the royal presence were unprecedented. But Robert Bowes, the English ambassador, wrote, 'the King is earnest about it; it may open the way to other matters, and he would be present at the hearing'.[11] The dittay against the original jurors in the king's name was the fullest account of the North Berwick and other sabbats yet offered in court. The accused chose to yield to the royal will, whereupon James lectured them:

> For witchcraft, which is a thing growen very common amongst us, I know it to be a most abhominable synne, and I have bene occupied these three quarters of this yeere for the siftyng out of them that are guylty heerein. We are taught by the lawes both of God and men that this synne is most odious, and by Godes law punishable by death: by man's lawe it is called *maleficium* or *venificium*, an ill deede or a poysonable deede, and punishable likewise by death.[12]

He had clearly grasped some demonological commonplaces and learnt to make capital of the famous text in Exodus. Whether or not he had already read Weyer or Scot, he anticipated their position: 'As for them who thinke these witchcraftes to be but fantacyes, I remmyt them to be catechised and instructed in these most evident poyntes.' Finally, in some closing remarks he foreshadowed the argument of Book III of the *Daemonologie* that, as in cases of treason, so in witchcraft trials 'infamous persones' might be admitted as witnesses, since 'none honest man can know these matters'. There was no need to worry about false accusation; as in the *Daemonologie*, James assured the assizors that only evil-doers were ever charged with witchcraft.[13] The speech shows that the kernel of his later arguments, and some of their logic, had already formed in his mind; he was convinced 'that such a vice did reigne and ought to be repressed'. Confirmation of these twin beliefs was the end-product of his extraordinarily close contact with the North Berwick witches and the starting point for his academic research in demonology.

Scotland's first witch craze lasted until 1597, but of James's actual presence at further investigations we have only glimpses. At the trial of Christian Stewart in November 1596 it was revealed that the accused had testified 'in presence of his Majesty' at a hearing at Linlithgow. On 16 September 1597 James wrote to the authorities at Stirling to ask them to bring a witch to Linlithgow 'that scho may be reddy thair that nycht at evin attending our cuming for hir tryell in that depositioun scho hes maid'.[14] More important, he was also involved in a series of cases at St Andrews in 1597 which were strikingly reminiscent of the North Berwick episode. On 13 July Bowes reported that James had already spent more than a week examining charges against the university 'and for the trial and punishment of witches'. A great many had been condemned and executed for covenanting with the Devil, receiving his mark and renouncing their baptism. As in 1591 'sundry fantastical feats' had been brought to light and were to be set down for publication. The affair dragged on. A month later Bowes wrote that the king had been 'pestered and many ways troubled in the examination of witches', of which there were now 'many thousands'. Again, his life was in danger; the accused were alleged to have 'practised to have drowned the King in his passage over the water at Dundee at the late General Assembly of the Church there, and the life of the prince has been likewise sought by the witches'. On 5 September it was still being said that James had his mind 'only bent upon the examination and trial of sorcerers',[15] but these were the last recorded personal contacts with witches in Scotland, and there is nothing comparable in his dealings with them in England. Why was this so? In order to appreciate why his active involvement with witch-hunting and demonology was, in the end, short-lived we have to look beyond 1603 to the style and ideals of his English monarchy.

II

The notion that King James descended as a persecutor from the north, enacted a savage new witchcraft statute, and was responsible for many hundreds of executions in England was comfortably disposed of some years ago. The actual rate of prosecutions after 1603, at least in the strongly affected counties of the Home Circuit, was shown to have dropped from the Elizabethan level, while analysis of the legislation of 1604 revealed that it was only marginally more severe than the previous English act of 1563 and a natural reflection of informed opinion at the time. It is now agreed that although the new law codified aspects of the English attitude, bringing it more into line with Continental doctrines on the diabolical compact, the actual practice of the courts did not change very rapidly or, indeed, very much. The point at issue after 1604, as it had been before, was simply the power of witches to do harm.[16] In fact, not only does it appear that James's impact was much less than expected; in the end, there is little to suggest that he had any interest in propagating witchcraft beliefs in England at all. In explanation of this, it has become usual to suppose that he grew sceptical about the very reality of witchcraft as a result of cases like those in Lancashire in 1612 and in Staffordshire in 1620, where accusations of bewitching were found to be fraudulent. In 1616 he was himself responsible for exposing a trickster at Leicester who had secured the execution of nine women and the imprisonment of six more by simulating possession. Certainly these cases affected the bench. There is no direct evidence of their effect on the king, but Thomas Fuller's verdict has often been quoted: 'The frequency of such forged Possessions wrought such an alteration upon the judgment of King JAMES, that he receding from what he had written in his Demonologie, grew first diffident of, and then flatly to deny the workings of Witches and Devils, as but Falshoods and Delusions.'[17]

The difficulty with this view is that a sceptical disposition and a reputation for probing impostures did not come to James late in life. He had scarcely arrived in London when he interested himself in the case of Mary Glover, a teenage girl suspected of counterfeiting possession.[18] In 1605 Sir Roger Wilbraham noted that the king had already solved two mysteries involving 'a phisicion that made latyne & lerned sermons in the slepe' and a woman who vomited pins and needles. The doctor was Richard Haydock of New College, Oxford. James heard him 'preach' one night, instructed the Earl of Worcester to examine him, and then frightened him into dropping his pretence by running at him with a sword and threatening to cut off his head. The case of the woman was very similar to that of Ann Gunter, whom James treated with a kindness so far removed from his behaviour in 1591 that she readily confessed her deceit and even secured a royal dowry.[19] Early in 1605 he investigated a prophet who spoke of imminent calamities, and had two bewitched women sent to Cambridge where university doctors certified that they were suffering from natural disorders. His pronouncements on the subject of marvels were equally indicative of a constant frame of mind. To Prince Henry he wrote that 'most miracles nou-a-dayes proves but illusions' and to an unknown correspondent that 'pretended wonders' and miracles 'should be all ways and diligently tested'. He was quite as blunt about the efficacy of the royal touch itself.[20]

Not so often recognised, but surely of more significance, is the caution which James showed in witchcraft affairs even before he left Scotland. In 1597 it was revealed that a Fifeshire witch Margaret Aiken had falsely accused a number of innocent women who were burnt. James felt obliged to revoke all commissions for the apprehension and punishment of witches on the grounds that honest citizens were not properly safeguarded against malicious or faulty charges.[21] On three occasions in 1597–8 the Scottish Privy Council upheld complaints from individuals accused of witchcraft and dismissed proceedings against them. Twice James intervened, once to mitigate punishment and, in the case of the trials at Aberdeen in 1596-7, to order the authorities to drop all charges against two defendants who had been wrongfully accused by their enemies.[22] Even during the North Berwick affair, he was supposed to have shown a persistent incredulity. The writer of *Newes from Scotland* claimed that on hearing the confessions of Agnes Sampson 'his Majesty said they were all extreme liars'. Only her ability to repeat verbatim his pleasantries to Queen Ann on their wedding night was said to have convinced him that there was substance in her extraordinary dittay.[23] His determination to attend so many examinations, to scrutinise the evidence and even test the charms was itself, in part, an aspect of that 'fortunate judgment in clearing and solving of obscure riddles and doubtful mysteries' of which he always boasted. It seems quite compatible then for James to have always accepted the principles of witchcraft and yet, in each individual attribution that came to his notice, to have felt the need to be convinced, if possible by personal investigation.[24] In 1590-1 the evidence seemed overwhelming; on other occasions the same sceptical frame of mind uncovered fraud and trickery. Nor must we forget the very important point that James's famous detections were mostly concerned with child possession, a matter not essential to witch belief as it is set down in the *Daemonologie*. There is no evidence or suggestion that he ever changed his mind about the central canons of demonological theory, notably the possibility of the demonic pact.

However, if the King was not significantly more shrewd in the 1610s than in the 1590s and did not experience what R. Trevor Davies called 'a radical change of his views', we still have to explain his comparative lack of concern for English witchcraft. Partly, the answer lies in the far less virulent temper which surrounded it. The full force of the Continental persecution was not felt in England, where the courts were more sensitive, the use of extreme torture quite rare, and the charges often restricted to simple *maleficium* involving animal familiars rather than attendance at sabbats and other sensational matters. The Church of England did not wage a holy war against witches but against exorcists; and an exposé of exorcism by one of its most redoubtable scourges Samuel Harsnett was reported to have been presented to James soon after his accession.[25] Some English demonologists were also noticeably open-minded. Quite apart from Reginald Scot's comprehensive scepticism, reservations about aspects of witchcraft and witchcraft trials were expressed by George Gifford, John Cotta and even William Perkins. In this atmosphere the obsessive fear of witchcraft and magic never assumed the proportions it did elsewhere. In Ben Jonson's *Masque of Queens*, presented before James in 1609, a coven of hags is vanquished easily by Virtue and led bound before Fame's chariot. In *The Devil Is an Ass* (1616) Jonson's character Pug, a junior demon allowed a day's mischief on earth, is repeatedly outwitted and has to be rescued from Newgate by Satan.[26] When the king earnestly inquired the answer to the well-known demonological teaser about the preponderance in witchcraft of old women over young, Sir James Harrington replied with a 'scurvey jeste' to the effect that 'the devil walketh in dry places'. Even James himself became flippant about the powers of darkness. In 1605 he informed Cecil that he was busy 'with hunting of witches, prophets, puritans, dead cats, and hares', but that Lord Montgomery had 'conjured all the devils here with his Welsh tongue, for the devil himself I trow dare not speak Welsh'.[27] One circumstance which undoubtedly eased his fears was the simple fact that English witchcraft and magic were rarely directed against his person. In this respect, it was the Jesuits who became the principal objects of his lively apprehensions. In his controversy with Bellarmine he waged a war of words against deposition and regicide by papal command. Since English priests proclaimed treason and were convicted of it, it was natural that he should regard them with a horror previously reserved for witches and speak of them as emissaries of the Devil. On the other hand, only one case of attempted bewitching of the king came to light, involving a schoolmaster called Peacock. Significantly James forgot his scepticism on the subject and reverted to former practices. Peacock was promptly committed to the Tower and tortured.[28]

Once again, however, the effect of the less compelling nature of English witchcraft and demonological opinion cannot in itself have been decisive. Before 1590 Scotland too was uninfluenced by Continental notions regarding witch practices, yet within a few years James's personal concern for the subject had contributed largely to a craze of the Continental type. The phenomenon of witchcraft was no doubt related to social conditions in the pre-industrial world, but the pattern of persecution could be influenced dramatically from above. Thus, to speak of James being mollified by the tenor of English witchcraft may be to put the cart before the horse. And while fear for his own life must have been a powerful motive for participation in the trials of 1590-1 it will not explain the writing of the *Daemonologie*. How then are we to account for the apparent change which took place in his attitudes after 1603? The answer must surely be that James became a witch-hunter and demonologist in order to satisfy political and religious pretensions at a time when they could be expressed in few other ways. In fact, he found in the theory and practice of witch persecution a perfect vehicle for his nascent ideals of kingship. In England these ideals did not change; they simply found alternative fulfilment.

It is patently clear, for instance, both from *Newes from Scotland* and from his speech to the jurors of Barbara Napier, that James wished to play the part of the people's teacher and patriarch. But this desire existed independently of the fact that witchcraft was the matter in hand. It was integral to his view of monarchy as expressed in the *Basilikon Doron* and the *Trew law of free monarchies* and it led to his famous self-identification with King Solomon as the paradigm ruler. According to orthodox literature on the subject, the perfect prince was a model of virtue to his people, devoted to their welfare and education, sensitive in the care of religion and unity, respectful of rights, laws and advice, and above all wise and just in all his proceedings. For James too the images of monarchy were those of divine lieutenancy, fatherhood and headship of the body politic. Brought up on a diet of treatises *de regimine principum* but continually thwarted in his ambitions as a ruler, it was natural that he should seize this early opportunity to unravel publicly, in court and in print, the mysterious vice of witchcraft, especially by drawing on the 'latest' Continental theories. Now the occasions for indulging in the *ex cathedra* were vastly multiplied after 1603, and James's passion for public debates and speeches need scarcely be emphasised. The point, however, is that his behaviour at Hampton Court, his harangues to Parliament and interference with its proceedings, his attempts to influence judicial opinion, even his brand of foreign policy, were only more elevated examples of the same obsession with the image of the philosopher-king which had involved him in the North Berwick affair. Another parallel and quite transparent piece of pedagogy was his public claim that he 'did upon the instant interpret and apprehend some darke phrases . . . contrary to the ordinary Grammer construction of them' in the famous Monteagle letter during the Powder Plot, a feat which was later magnified in a published account of the treason in just the way that *Newes from Scotland* had capitalised on James's witch-hunting.[29] The disputations at the universities, the mealtime seminars, the judgments in private cases all helped to divert the royal attention from any further investigation into the diabolical while satisfying the same instincts. The expression of his opinions in print was another extension of the desire to settle controversies and instruct his subjects. The *Daemonologie* was in this sense only one of the earliest of a long line of royal textbooks. At the other end of the scale, his intellectual appetite was whetted in less respectable and more trivial matters. One wonders to what extent his fascination with the details of the North Berwick conventions and with the Devil's 'mark' in particular was transmuted into the prurient interest he later showed in the sexual habits of his relations and courtiers.

But the most important ingredient of James's monarchy was surely his highly developed public religiosity. Nor in this instance was North Berwick merely an occasion for indulging a certain style of government; demonology was in fact intrinsically related to the presuppositions of godly rule. The recurring theme of both the dittays of 1590-1 and *Newes from Scotland* was that the king's Christian rectitude made him the Devil's principal target, and yet at the same time protected him from all his machinations. This was an issue which naturally arose whenever the role of authority in the war against witchcraft was discussed. Demonologists like Bodin and Nicolas Rémy, for instance, argued that the actual efficacy of magic and witchcraft waned to the point of non-existence in proportion to the determination of the public official in rooting them out; quite simply, the witch was disarmed of her occult powers if brought face to face with the godly magistrate. James discovered this argument at precisely the time when he was elaborating his belief that the ruler was a divine lieutenant on earth, and incorporated it into the *Daemonologie*:

> If they be but apprehended and deteined by anie private person, upon other private respectes, their power no doubt either in escaping, or in doing hurte, is no lesse nor ever it was before. But if on the other parte, their apprehending and detention be by the lawfull Magistrate, upon the iust respectes of their guiltinesse in that craft, their power is then no greater then before that ever they medled with their master. For where God beginnes iustlie to strike by his lawfull Lieutennentes, it is not in the Devilles power to defraude or bereave him of the office, or effect of his powerfull and revenging Scepter.[30]

This fundamental principle of the politics of demonism is of crucial significance. It transformed the very impotence of the North Berwick witches into an affirmation of the truly divine nature (or the more powerful magic) of James's early, and hitherto very hesitant magistracy. According to Agnes Sampson's confession, which he personally extorted, they had wondered why 'all ther devellerie culd do na harm to the King, as it did till others dyvers', to which the Devil had answered, 'Il est un home de Dieu'.[31] James could not have provided himself with a better statement of legitimacy, nor, in the circumstances, from a more impeccable authority. Secondly, it meant that the *Daemonologie* was not tangential to, let alone aberrant from, his other early political writings. Its arguments complemented the Biblical, historico-legal and patriarchal defences of monarchy attempted in the *Trew law of free monarchies* and it dealt with one aspect of a kingship idealised in the *Basilikon Doron*. Finally, it helps us to explain why James took his religious duties with a seriousness which has recently been described as millenarian in nature and content. In 1616 his editor Bishop Montagu claimed that the paraphrase on the Book of Revelation composed around 1588 was the key to all the other royal works. W. M. Lamont has recently re-emphasised this point and argued that much of James's behaviour was inspired by a confidence derived from the Apocalypse. Millenarian kingship in its turn justified the persecution of witches; they were agents of Satan and swarmed more thickly as the end of Antichrist approached. James wrote in the *Daemonologie*, 'the consummation of the Worlde, and our deliverance drawing neare, makes Sathan to rage the more in his instruments, knowing his Kingdome to be so neare an ende'.[32]

If witch-hunting and the exegesis of Revelation were all that a Christian Prince could achieve in Scotland, the opportunities in England were once again so much more important. The caution enforced by the international diplomacy of the 1580s and 1590s was no longer necessary. From the position of subordination to which the Kirk had sought to depress him, James was suddenly given charge of a church which, in origin and ideology, was inseparably linked with the concept of the godly ruler. He could now take full advantage of what Lamont calls the 'centripetal millenarianism' of Foxe and Jewel, and associate himself with the Christian Emperor who would secure the final victories. The new role immediately occupied his attention, as Hampton Court again demonstrates. In 1609, his defence of the oath of allegiance gave him the chance to return to Revelation in order to demonstrate that the Pope was Antichrist. More generally, his close association with eminent scholars and divines, his insatiable appetite for sermons, his attempts to enforce conformity and his harrying of recalcitrants like Vorstius all reflected a scrupulous concern for the public obligations of godly rule that it had been simply impossible to satisfy fully before. Here too, then, we can see how James's essentially uniform ideals responded to the change in his circumstances after 1603, and how demonology was superseded as their most effective expression.

III

But what of the *Daemonologie* itself? What contribution did James make to the international debate on witchcraft and how successfully did he dispose of the sceptics? The treatise is a conversation between the demonologist Epistemon and the doubter Philomathes. Though one could scarcely speak of him as devil's advocate in this context, Philomathes is made to put the principal contemporary objections to orthodox opinions on magic and witchcraft. His role is thus that of a surrogate Weyer or Scot and identical to that of Mysodaemon in Henry Holland's *Treatise against Witchcraft* (1590). Are the Biblical references to witchcraft decisive? Is magic really either harmful or unlawful? Do witches only imagine what they confess? How is it that God permits such evil? Epistemon is prompt to reassure his friend of the reality and power of the enemy. Magic and witchcraft, he says, are practices consistent with Christian belief and everyday experience; they are mentioned unambiguously in Scripture and confirmed by daily confessions. By permitting them God tests the patience of the elect, strengthens the faith of waverers, and punishes the wicked and reprobate. The Devil is given limited powers to entice the curious, revengeful and grasping into his service. His subtle and airy quality, his ageless experience of things and his profound knowledge enable him to perpetrate magical phenomena and acts of *maleficium* by which men are deceived and finally damned.

In magic and necromancy (Book I), the Devil permits himself to appear to be commanded in the performance of trivial feats by teaching magicians and spell-makers how to conjure him with charms. These have no intrinsic power and only work because the Devil co-operates with the charmer. Similarly, the effects of magic are not true in substance, for only God's miracles are real; they are in fact counterfeit, appearing to be true 'onelie to mennes outward senses'. In witchcraft (Book II) the Devil himself is commander and the witches his instruments, contracted into allegiance by a formal pact and marked as a sign of service. Again, there are agreed ceremonies and formulae, in this case for injuring men and beasts, but the means employed (excepting actual poison) are only the external forms for inward effects wrought by the Devil; just as the sacraments are outward means for God's inner workings. A twofold delusion is involved in that witches, like magicians, think themselves responsible for what is effected and, more important, believe themselves capable of doing things which are in fact 'against all Theologie divine, and Philosophie humaine'. Thus, while there are witches who hold actual sabbats, Philomathes is right to doubt some of their confessions. The world of spirits (Book III) is also filled with fabulous as well as real phenomena. Epistemon explains that there are spirits which haunt places, pursue and possess men and women and act as incubi and succubi. On the other hand, wraiths and werewolves are delusions. Nor can monsters be generated naturally, these, together with fairies, being products of the Devil's trickery. Against both magic and witchcraft the magistrate must fight unceasingly, the punishment in each case being death; the private man must amend his life and pray against the assaults of Satan.

These arguments were the stock-in-trade of orthodox European demonology. The absence of citations and case histories reduces James's book to a fraction of the customary bulk, but it has all the other features of the typical Renaissance witchcraft treatise. The idea that demonology was best conducted in the catechetic form had been pioneered in the scholastic *Malleus Maleficarum* (?1486) and adopted by most major writers. Two dialogues which could have been actual models for the *Daemonologie* had recently appeared in England, Lambert Daneau's *Les sorciers* translated as *A dialogue of witches* (1575), and Holland's *Treatise against Witchcraft*. Discussions of magic as well as witchcraft, of spirits and possession and of examinations and punishments were usual. Most writers in the field would have agreed with Epistemon's views—his definitions of magic and witchcraft, his theological and philosophical explanations of demonic activity, his Biblical exegesis, his lists of possible acts of *maleficium*, his account of the Devil, his description of remedies and penalties. Even when he appears to be sceptical, Epistemon follows a well-worn path. A popular but wrongly ascribed early Canon Episcopi which questioned the reality of night flight and sabbats was often quoted and had to be explained away by the authors of the *Malleus*.[33] Several sixteenth-century demonologists argued that spiritual transportation to sabbats, generation of children and monsters by incubus devils and metamorphosis of humans into wolves and other shapes violated natural and theological laws, and it therefore became traditionally permissible to cast doubt on these particular witch activities. The explanations why these things nevertheless appeared in confessions are often quite baffling and fall oddly upon the modern ear. What, for instance, are we to make of Nicolas Rémy's point that, absurd as it was to believe that anyone could really be changed into a wolf, so well were the witches endowed with the natural qualities of the animal that they differed 'but little' from the actuality? Or the generally held view that the Devil could totally disrupt human perception with sensory delusions and *glamours*, 'that thinges are beleved to be sene, harde, and perceyved, which notwithstandinge are no such maner of thinges'.[34]

James's own mixture of religious and naturalistic arguments and his confusion of the real with the illusory seem no less astonishing but are in fact quite typical. While allowing that witches can be bodily transvected through the air, Epistemon insists that they cannot pass through keyholes in the shapes of small animals. The Devil might create this impression by 'his woorkemanshippe upon the aire', but it is in fact a physical impossibility. Similarly, the idea that witches can, as they confess, attend meetings in spirit only is against all theology; but the Devil creates the necessary dream in their minds, simultaneously illudes third parties into believing they have met them, and even commits the murders and injuries claimed by the witches while in the spiritual state. Henri Boguet used these same arguments when he 'explained' the phenomenon of lycanthropy, and they are in fact a perfect example of the tortuous dialectic employed by all demonologists.[35] Some, it is true, felt reluctant to admit any exceptions to the power of witchcraft and to the reality of what was confessed; Bodin and Rémy (the latter not consistently) both argued that supernatural phenomena could not be subjected to the ordinary criteria of nature and physical causation but should be accepted on trust. James felt otherwise. By showing scepticism in the officially approved areas he hoped to 'saill surelie, betwixt Charybdis and Scylla', between doubting all and believing all. Although he condemned Scot as a Sadducee and suggested that Weyer was a wizard posing as an intellectual, he also criticised Bodin's *De la Démonomanie des Sorciers* (1580) as a product more of diligence than judgment.

In fact, Weyer's denouncement of witchcraft was in part only the logical *reductio* of James's own position. In the *De Praestigiis Daemonum* (1563) he argued that 'witches' were either innocent victims of ignorant physicians and superstitious clergy, or deceived into accepting their own culpability by the Devil, who took advantage of the hallucinations accompanying natural conditions like melancholy and nightmare. Whichever the case, the supposed pact on which conventional witch-theory was ultimately based, together with all the various witchcraft ceremonies, were illusions of the impossible. 'Witches' were harmless old women needing medical and religious guidance, not accusation and execution. Witchcraft was in fact a demonic imposture with no warrant in Scripture, a hideous lie perpetrated by the Devil in order to disrupt society. Now although there are strongly empirical and humanitarian elements in Weyer's argument it differs from normal demonological theory in degree only. All writers in the tradition, including James, agreed that though the Devil had superhuman endowments which enabled him to produce true effects, there were areas where God had made him impotent and where he was forced to deceive men's perception by *glamours*. All writers, including James, also admitted that in witchcraft the real agent of *maleficium*, true or illusory, was the Devil. And, as we have seen, orthodox demonologists had to allow for some deception of the witches themselves, some even admitting the similarities between witch phenomena and hallucinatory illnesses. Weyer simply extended these arguments until the witch became totally redundant in the effecting of *maleficium*, and the area of illusion wide enough to cover all rather than part of her confession. Otherwise he remained quite traditional and his discussions of devils, magic, possession and other matters were in essence as commonplace as those of Epistemon. Weyer even allowed the magician precisely that actual collusion with the Devil which he denied the witch.

James cannot have seen that theories of sensory delusion and mental illness were double-edged, for he comes perilously close to conceding Weyer's position. Lycanthropy is, he admits, a disease resulting from 'a naturall super-abundance of Melancholie'. Nightmare leads to physical sensations of constriction by 'some unnaturall burden or spirite'. Tales of fairies are produced by the Devil illuding 'the senses of sundry simple creatures, in making them beleeve that they saw and harde such thinges as were nothing so indeed'. In fact, 'all our senses, as we are so weake, and even by ordinarie sicknesses will be often times deluded'. These admissions are hardly compensated for by his actual refutation of the *De Praestigiis Daemonum*. Epistemon bluntly denies Philomathes's suggestion (following Weyer) that the scriptural *loci* refer only to magicians and poisoners, and claims that Weyer's medical diagnosis is in any case the wrong one since witches, contrary to the symptoms of the melancholic disposition, are 'rich and wordly-wise, some of them fatte or corpulent in their bodies, and most part of them altogether given over to the pleasures of the flesh, continual haunting of companie, and all kind of merries'.[36] Quite apart from the fact that neither argument deals satisfactorily with the difficulties raised by Weyer, both had been deployed previously with much Biblical exegesis and etymological and quasi-medical reasoning by Bodin. In his anxiety to be rational about some aspects of witchcraft James clearly failed to grasp the full significance of Weyer's adaptation of the theory of illusion. Nor did he appreciate the fact, ably demonstrated by Bodin, that Weyer's dismissal of witchcraft was fundamentally incompatible with his orthodox acceptance of magic.

Like Bodin, Reginald Scot also wished to avoid the inconsistencies involved in rejecting some aspects of demonism while accepting others. But while Bodin opted for total credulity, Scot's *Discoverie of Witchcraft* (1584) attempted to demolish its very foundations. In an important appendix, Scot developed the view that the Devil and his demons were not to be conceived of as having corporeal existence or tangible qualities but rather as spiritual powers of evil, and that scriptural texts which spoke of them carnally were to be interpreted not literally but metaphorically and 'significativelie'. This, as Gabriel Harvey remarked at the time, 'hitteth the nayle on the head with a witnesse', for it destroyed at one blow the very essence of witchcraft and magic as physical collusions with spirits. Scot removed the Devil altogether from the world of material concepts and actions and reduced the belief in the demonic agency of physical events to a species of idolatry practised by 'children, fools, melancholic persons [and] papists'. Since the age of real miracles had passed with Christ, the only explanation left for the confessions of witches and the claims of magicians was that they were either purely imaginary or produced by 'prestigious juggling' and 'nimble conveiance of the hand'. Thus, Scot adopted the suggestion that witches were often either sane and innocent or deluded by illness and 'dotage', but added a further dimension to the theory of deception to account for all phenomena attributed by Weyer to devils. This extra ingredient was 'meere cousenage' or legerdemain and it covered not only modern instances but Biblical episodes like that of the witch of Endor. Indeed, the main purpose of the *Discoverie of Witchcraft* was, following a proposal of Weyer's, to reinterpret the many different Old Testament Hebrew words uniformly translated as 'witch' or 'magician' but in fact referring either to poisoners or to a variety of fraudulent practices ranging from augury and alchemy through to necromancy and ventriloquism. In short, witchcraft was an impossibility, 'a cousening art, wherin the name of God is abused, prophaned and blasphemed, and his power attributed to a vile creature'.[37]

To this wholesale scepticism James replies simply that it is Sadducism to doubt the existence of spirits and likely to lead to a questioning of God himself. This is not strictly fair. Scot did not deny that the Devil had been created as a living being but only insisted that he was 'ordeined to a spirituall proportion', the exact essence of which was hidden from man's understanding. James, on the contrary, makes specific provision for the physical appearance of devils and spirits but admits rather weakly that the visible proof of corporeality which Scot demanded is 'reserved to the secreete knowledge of God, whom he wil permit to see such thinges, and whome not'. And although he too questions some of the physical attributes of devils, his general insistence on the physical reality of the witches' pacts and subsequent *maleficium* makes it impossible for him to concede Scot's principal point. Since Christ the 'appearances of Angels or good spirits' *has* ceased, but not those of 'abusing spirites'. Epistemon explains that whereas it is more difficult for Satan himself to have visible dealings with men and move 'familiarlie amongst them' since the era of Gentildom and the overthrow of Catholicism in England, nevertheless he compensates by the more frequent use of the medium of witchcraft and the other unlawful arts. It was to this passage that James later referred Archbishop Abbott, who had expressed doubts about the grounds for nullity *propter maleficium versus hanc* in the Essex divorce case. And he added, 'that the Devil's power is not so universal against us, that I freely confess; but that it is utterly restrained *quoad nos*, how was then a minister of Geneva bewitched to death, and were the witches daily punished by our law?'[38] The simple fact that witchcraft existed and was punished was sufficient refutation of Scot's arguments. James could not see it the other way round.

There is, then, little that is original in the *Daemonologie*, perhaps only the curious theory that witches can be carried bodily through the air like Habakkuk but only for the duration of one intake of breath. Nor are the objections of the two sceptics against whom the treatise is directed effectively met and overcome. Thomas Ady was later to complain with some justice that, 'blinded by some Scotish Mist', James had only 'written again the same Tenents that Bodinus and others had before written, and were by Scot confuted'.[39] It is true that James only intended to reason, as he said, 'upon *genus* leaving *species*, and *differentia* to be comprehended therein'. But it is doubtful whether it was possible any longer to write successful primers in orthodox demonology. Now that the interpretation of so many scriptural *exempla* was disputed, demonologists needed to be equipped to counter the intricate etymology on which sceptics like Scot, and later Ady and Filmer, were increasingly coming to rely. In this respect, neither the *Daemonologie* nor the new translation of the Bible made any headway. After Weyer, believers in witchcraft also had to argue the pathology of the subject. Here James seems to have been in a dilemma. His recognition of the effects of melancholy and nightmare and his readiness to submit bewitched women and children to clinical examination suggests an empirical open-mindedness. Indeed, he may even have learned something from Weyer's chapters on feigned possession. On the other hand, the argument *a posteriori* that witches are fun-loving hedonists because they attend spectacular orgies shows that he could not see beyond the myth to the real character of the majority of those accused.[40] Most important of all, after Weyer and Scot it was essential to find more satisfactory criteria for distinguishing the actual from the illusory. Hitherto the canons of theology had served this purpose. But so much had had to be attributed to the imagination and the corruption of the senses that the definition of what was real became less and less meaningful. In a sense, the diametrically opposed approaches of Bodin and Scot were the only logical solutions to this problem. By attempting to be reasonable about witchcraft without giving up his belief in its fundamental features James tried to find a compromise between common sense and faith. Like Weyer's it involved too many inconsistencies to be really successful.

IV

As we have seen, the interest of the *Daemonologie* lies elsewhere, in the circumstances of its genesis and as an early expression of an ideal kingship. In addition, there is an important sense in which, original or not, it was necessary to the world-view of order on which James's political philosophy rested, just as demonology in general has been seen as the logical extension of a whole cosmology.[41] In the sixteenth and seventeenth centuries political order was defended in terms of 'arguments by correspondence' in which analogies were drawn between parallel features of the various planes of the hierarchy of being. James's own use of this language involved the classic 'similitudes' between monarchy, divine power, patriarchal authority and the role of the head of the human body.[42] However, the cogency of the arguments for order also depended on the elaboration of a world of disorder. Recourse might be had to the idea of the decay of nature or to historical cases of dislocation, but the language often used was that of 'contrariety' in which the antitheses of orderly relationships were described. Especially persuasive was the image of the upside-down world, in which the normal patterns of authority were inverted by, for instance, the rule of the body over the head or of sons over fathers and subjects over princes.[43] The primary polarity in this way of thinking was of course God-Satan, the very prototype of what might be called the 'argument by antithesis'. Contrariety was thus a presupposition of Christian philosophy of history and political thought; Augustine's antithetical two cities and the contrasts drawn between monarchy and tyranny in medieval writings on the prince are paradigm examples. The Reformation concepts of election and reprobation, and the increasingly literal interpretation of the millennium and the activities of Antichrist encouraged still further the tendency to polarise experience. But antithesis was not confined to religious language. Its formal role in traditional logic and rhetoric guaranteed its use in a wide range of contexts. 'Contraries laid together', it was typically said, 'doe much set forth each other in their lively colours.'[44] The *mundus inversus* too was invoked in a number of ways, as a literary and artistic device, as the basis of fooling, comic drama and other entertainments, and as both a part of the mentality of popular revolt and a way of condemning it.[45]

James himself acknowledged the usefulness of the argument by antithesis in distinguishing monarchy from tyranny, 'for *contraria iuxta se posita magis elucescunt*'.[46] He also used the language of inversion to describe the disorder that would follow disobedience to kings. In 1609 it was Antichrist in the shape of papal supremacy which seemed the major threat; 'the world it selfe must be turned upside downe, and the order of Nature inverted (making the left hand to have the place before the Right, and the last named to bee the first in honour) that this primacie may bee maintained'.[47] But the most elaborate attempt to characterise disorder by inversion was surely to be found in Renaissance treatises on witchcraft. In describing its antithesis, orthodox demonologists presupposed an orderly world and so sustained it.[48] James summarised perfectly the purpose and the method when he wrote in his own *Daemonologie*, 'since the Devill is the very contrarie opposite to God, there can be no better way to know God, than by the contrarie'.[49] Conventional accounts of the nature of Satan, the character of Hell and the activities of witches owed much of their inspiration and cogency to this basic premise. The particular version of the upside-down world they offered, on which both the North Berwick dittays and the *Daemonologie* were based, must have confirmed many of James's political values.

The Devil, of course, *was* disorder, the first rebellious subject who tried to bring chaos to Heaven and succeeded in bringing it to man. Yet Hell itself was not simply a confusion. Although he disliked giving devils titles of honour or military ranks, James conceded that they 'could not subsist without some order', and theological justification for distinguishing between them on grounds of natural inequality could be found in Aquinas.[50] Renaissance demonologists and pneumatologists therefore drew freely on the language of political and military organisation. The vital point was that the order they discerned in the Devil's government was a spurious version of the legitimate order of divine politics; Weyer's demography of Hell, for instance, was entitled *Pseudomonarchia daemonum*. Demons co-operated only out of a common hate for mankind, not from the mutual love and respect for magistracy that cemented all properly constituted human societies. Moreover, 'that the inferior are subject to the superior is not for the benefit of the superior, but rather to their detriment; because since to do evil belongs in a preeminent degree to unhappiness, it follows that to preside in evil is to be more unhappy'.[51] To complete these inversions, the Devil's style of government was universally acknowledged to be tyranny, the antithesis of true kingship: 'the prince is a kind of likeness of divinity; and the tyrant, on the contrary, a likeness of the boldness of the Adversary'.[52]

In describing witchcraft itself, demonologists again concentrated on the systematic reversal of traditional priorities, symbolised by the contrariness which made witches do things back-to-front or left-to-right, 'in a ridiculous and unseemly manner . . . opposite to that of other men'.[53] The point was often made, as it was in the Scottish dittays of 1590–1, in connection with the dance, a widely used image of political harmony and considered to have in itself the power to teach participants and spectators the principles of order. In contrast, the grotesque gyrations of the sabbat were 'festes de desordre' and the dancers were not humanised but dehumanised by the experience.[54] Similarly, the Devil's liturgy was portrayed, as in the *Daemonologie*, as deliberately *un*ceremonious. It was a hideous parody or 'aping' of true worship and therefore offensive to the sacramentalism in which state churches expressed their commitment to the orderly world. The sexual exploits of witches also negated order, dethroning reason from a sovereign position on which not only individual well-being but social relations and political obligation were thought to depend. The surrender to passion was disorderly in more than the physical sense; kissing the Devil's arse, like the Quaker refusal to meet authority bare-headed, was a highly-charged symbolic act of political defiance. A further inversion of good government lay in the anti-familial aspects of witchcraft. It was notorious that witches were able to prevent the consummation of marriages by ligature. Pierre de Lancre thought that they also disordered the family by subverting patriarchal authority and destroying filial love, and the dramatists Broome and Heywood made the upside-down family a theme of their comedy of 1634, *The Late Lancashire Witches*. If familial and political duties were analogous, if the state was based ultimately on the actions of heads of households, then *maleficium* of this sort was especially damaging. Above all, the condition of a society dominated by women must have been seen as one of fundamental contrariety. 'I demand,' wrote Bacon of the Amazons, 'is not such a preposterous government (against the first order of nature, for women to rule over men) in itself void, and to be suppressed?'[55] Finally, there was the fact that witchcraft was defined technically in terms of re-baptism and a formal compact. The full force of this voluntary rejection of the conventional world only becomes apparent if we recall the non-sacramental implications of infant-baptism, but the main point is clear. The activity of witchcraft was founded in the sin of disobedience, the primary cause of disorder. Witches, like rebels and social climbers, were motivated by pride and ambition; rebels, like witches, abused the sabbath and tried to turn society and the state upside-down. Theorists of order and demonologists alike demonstrated the essential identity of these 'unnatural' treasons by glossing the text from 1 Samuel XV. 23, 'For rebellion is as the sin of witchcraft.' William Perkins, for instance, wrote:

> It is a principle of the Law of nature, holden for a grounded truth in all Countries and Kingdoms, among all people in every age; that the traytor who is an enemie to the State, and rebelleth against his lawfull Prince, should be put to death; now the most notorious traytor and rebell that can be, is the Witch. For she renounceth God himselfe, the King of Kings, she leaves the societie of his Church and people, she bindeth herself in league with the devil.

The political implications of witchcraft could not have been stated more bluntly.[56]

V

Locating classic demonology in this way within the wider linguistic context of Renaissance political thought surely helps us to discern its essential rationality and intellectual appeal. Norman Cohn has recently said that the study of the mental world of late sixteenth- and early seventeenth-century magistrates may enable us to understand 'why so many of the educated and privileged *needed* to believe' in witches. The answer lies partly in the transposition into a specifically political mode of the principle of inversion, to which Cohn himself attributes the rise of the traditional medieval stereotype of the Devil-worshipper.[57] The conceptual world of men like Bodin, Rémy and James I was dominated by the principle of order, but the meaning of order could only be grasped by exploring its antithesis or 'contrary'. The existence of one was a necessary condition for the understanding of the other, and a single vocabulary was sufficient for the description of both. Hence their portrayal, in what seems to us morbid or absurd detail, of the deliberately disorderly aspects of witchcraft, notably the horrendous sabbat. With his fondness for the analogies which could be drawn between the government of the body, the family and the state, James must have been particularly sensitive to the unruliness which allegedly characterised demonism. But, like the Book of Revelation, both the confessions forced from the witches of North Berwick and his studies in demonology were also a source of comfort. At a vital stage in his early career they helped him to establish a view of monarchy and his own fitness for implementing it; but at a deeper level they reinforced his entire political philosophy. For the *Daemonologie* was not, as it were, a fresh statement about the world, but a re-statement of the need for order and its goodness, seen from a different perspective. Our understanding of James VI and I would not be complete without some attempt to come to terms with it.

Notes

1 The earliest evidence of direct contact is in R. Pitcairn, *Ancient Criminal Trials in Scotland*, Maitland Club, 3 vols (Edinburgh, 1829–33), I, p. 203 (case of Hector Munro); and *Calendar of State Papers relating to Scotland* (*C.S.P.S.*), X, pp. 348, 365 (case of Dutch prophetess of Leith).
2 See for example D. H. Willson, *King James VI and I* (London, 1956), pp. 26, 64–5, 81–2.

3 R. Ashton, *James I by his Contemporaries* (London, 1969), p. 2; Robert Johnston, *The Historie of Scotland*, trans. T. Middleton (London, 1646), in R. Buchanan, ed., *Scotia Rediviva* (Edinburgh, 1826), pp. 370-1.
4 Christina Larner, 'James VI and I and Witchcraft', in A. G. R. Smith, ed., *The Reign of James VI and I* (London, 1973), pp. 74-90. I am grateful to Mrs Larner for her advice on an early draft of this essay, and for permission to consult her PhD thesis: Christina Larner, 'Scottish Demonology in the Sixteenth and Seventeenth Centuries and its Theological Background' (Edinburgh University, 1962). On Scottish witchcraft in the period, see C. K. Sharpe, *A Historical Account of the Belief in Witchcraft in Scotland* (London, 1884); F. Legge, 'Witchcraft in Scotland', *Scottish Review*, XVIII (1891), pp. 257-88; and the records of individual cases in Pitcairn and G. F. Black, *A Calendar of Cases of Witchcraft in Scotland 1510-1727* (New York, 1938).
5 Sir James Melville, *Memoirs 1549-93*, Bannatyne Club (Edinburgh, 1827), p. 395; Pitcairn, I, pp. 211, 239.
6 *Newes from Scotland* (1591), repr. *Gentleman's Magazine*, XLIX (1779), p. 449; Pitcairn, I, pp. 211, 236-7, 245, 254; C.S.P.S., X, p. 365.
7 C.S.P.S., X, 501-2, 504-5, 530-1; Melville, p. 395; *Register of the Privy Council of Scotland* (R.P.C.S.), IV, pp. 643-4.
8 M. A. Murray, 'The "Devil" of North Berwick', *Scottish Review*, XV (1917-18), pp. 310-21, suggests that Bothwell was in fact the 'devil' who preached at North Berwick, a theory shared by Montague Summers, *The History of Witchcraft and Demonology* (London, 1926, repr. 1965), p. 8. Helen Stafford, 'Notes on Scottish Witchcraft Cases, 1590-91', in Norton Downs, ed., *Essays in Honour of Conyers Read* (Chicago, 1953), pp. 96-118, is much more sceptical. Her account and that of William Roughead, 'The Witches of North Berwick', in *The Riddle of the Ruthvens and other Essays* (Edinburgh, 1936), pp. 144-66, are the best of the North Berwick trials. The full indictments are in Pitcairn, but there is important additional material in *Newes from Scotland*.
9 C.S.P.S., X, pp. 524, 430; *Newes from Scotland*, pp. 450, 394-5.
10 C.S.P.S., X, p. 510.
11 C.S.P.S., X, pp. 514-15, 519-20; Pitcairn, I, pp. 242-4.
12 C.S.P.S., X, p. 524.
13 C.S.P.S., X, p. 525; *Daemonologie, in forme of a dialogue* (Edinburgh, 1597), pp. 79-80 (all references are to the original edition reprinted in facsimile in the series *The English Experience* by Theatrum Orbis Terrarum, Amsterdam, 1969).
14 Pitcairn, I, p. 400; Black, p. 29.
15 C.S.P.S., XIII, pp. 56, 73, 78.
16 C. L'Estrange Ewen, *Witch Hunting and Witch Trials* (London, 1929), pp. 98-113; Alan Macfarlane, *Witchcraft in Tudor and Stuart England* (London, 1970), pp. 28-9, 200; G. L. Kittredge, *Witchcraft in Old and New England* (Cambridge, Mass., 1929, repr. New York, 1958), pp. 276-328; Barbara Rosen, ed., *Witchcraft* (London, 1969), pp. 19-29, 331-2; K. V. Thomas,

Religion and the Decline of Magic (Penguin edn, Harmondsworth, 1973), pp. 517–51. Wallace Notestein, *History of Witchcraft in England, 1558–1718* (Washington, 1911; repr. 1965), pp. 93–109, gives the least extreme version of the old view.

17 Quoted by Kittredge, p. 326. Classic expositions of James's supposed change of heart can be found in R. Trevor Davies, *Four Centuries of Witch Beliefs* (London, 1947), pp. 58–63, 76–84, and H. N. Paul, *The Royal Play of Macbeth* (New York, 1950), pp. 75–130.

18 Paul, pp. 103–12.

19 H. S. Scott, ed., *The Journal of Sir Roger Wilbraham, 1593–1616*, Camden Miscellany, X (London, 1902), p. 70; Edmund Lodge, *Illustrations of British History*, 3 vols (London, 1791), III, pp. 283–5, 287–8; Willson, p. 310; Kittredge, pp. 321–2.

20 *Historical Manuscripts Commission Records*, IX, Salisbury XVII (London, 1938), pp. 19–20, 22, 33, 36–7, 65, 222–3; J. Nichols, *The Progresses of King James the First*, 4 vols (London, 1828), I, p. 304; Kittredge, pp. 316, 319.

21 Andrew Brown, *History of Glasgow and of Paisley, Greenock, and Port-Glasgow*, 2 vols (Glasgow, 1795), I, pp. 39–40; *R.P.C.S.*, V, pp. 409–10.

22 *R.P.C.S.*, V, pp. 405–6, 448, 495; Black, p. 29 (case of Bessie Aitken); *Spalding Club Miscellany*, I (Aberdeen, 1841), pp. 163–4.

23 *Newes from Scotland*, p. 449; the fact that James was personally responsible for Sampson's confession supports Mrs Larner's view (*op. cit.*, pp. 84–5) that this report of his scepticism was, however, inserted in hindsight to enhance his reputation with English readers of the pamphlet.

24 Possibly a common attitude; see Alan Macfarlane, *The Family Life of Ralph Josselin* (Cambridge, 1970), pp. 191–2.

25 Notestein, pp. 73–92; Rosen, p. 313; Paul, pp. 107–8.

26 G. L. Kittredge, 'King James I and "The Devil Is an Ass"', *Modern Philology*, IX (1911–12), pp. 195–209, argues that Jonson was being openly contemptuous towards beliefs in witchcraft, particularly the idea of demonic possession.

27 Nichols, I, p. 492; *Historical Manuscripts Commission Records*, IX, Salisbury XVII, p. 121.

28 *Calendar of State Papers Domestic 1619–1625*, CXII/104, p. 125; Notestein, p. 399.

29 *A Discourse of the maner of the discoverie of the powder-treason*, in *Workes* (London, 1616), pp. 227–8, and *A speache in the Parliament House, ibid.*, p. 502.

30 *Daemonologie*, pp. 50–1; cf. Jean Bodin, *De la Démonomanie des Sorciers* (Paris, 1580), pp. 139–44, and Nicolas Rémy, *Demonolatry*, Montague Summers, ed. (London, 1948), pp. 4–5.

31 Melville, p. 395.

32 'To the Reader', *Workes*, D3^v; W. M. Lamont, *Godly Rule: Politics and Religion 1603–1660* (London, 1969), pp. 28–52; *Daemonologie*, p. 81.

33 H. C. Lea, *Materials Toward a History of Witchcraft*, 3 vols (Philadelphia,

1939, repr. New York, 1957), I, pp. 178–80; *Malleus Maleficarum*, Montague Summers, ed. (London, 1928), pp. 3ff.

34 Rémy, *Demonolatry*, p. 113; Andreas Hyperius, 'Whether that the Devils Have Bene the Shewers of Magicall artes' in *Two Common Places taken out of Andreas Hyperius*, trans. R. V. (London, 1581), p. 47. On 'glamours' see Johann Weyer, *De Praestigiis Daemonum*, trans. as *Les illusions et tromperies des diables*, 2 vols (Paris, 1885), I, pp. 51ff; and Francesco Guazzo, *Compendium maleficarum*, Montague Summers, ed. (London, 1929), pp. 7–9.

35 *Daemonologie*, pp. 38–42; cf. Henri Boguet, *Examen of Witches*, Montague Summers, ed. (London, 1929), chapter 47. On types of demonological argument in the period, see J. L. Teall, 'Witchcraft and Calvinism in Elizabethan England: Divine power and human agency', *Journal of the History of Ideas*, XXIII (1962), pp. 21–36; Wayne Shumaker, *The Occult Sciences in the Renaissance: A Study in Intellectual Patterns* (Berkeley and Los Angeles, 1972), pp. 70–107, especially pp. 91–9; and H. C. Erik Midelfort, *Witch Hunting in Southwestern Germany 1562–1684: The Social and Intellectual Foundations* (Stanford, 1972), pp. 10–66, who stresses the flexible and varied character of witchcraft theory.

36 *Daemonologie*, pp. 61, 69, 74, 52, 28–30. James seems to have had specific individuals in mind; in a manuscript of the *Daemonologie* which contains corrections in his own hand, the initials EM, RG and BN appear in the margin opposite the phrases 'rich and wordly-wise', 'fatte or corpulent', and 'given over to the pleasures of the flesh' respectively. Rhodes Dunlap, 'King James and some witches; the date and text of the "Daemonologie" ', *Philological Quarterly*, LIV (1975–6), pp. 40–6, suggests that these refer to three of the North Berwick defendants: Ewfame Makcalzane, the heiress of Lord Liftounhall, a Senator of the College of Justice; Richard Graham, client of Bothwell's; and Barbara Napier, wife of Archibald Douglas, burgess of Edinburgh.

37 Reginald Scot, *Discoverie of Witchcraft* (London, 1584), p. 472.

38 *State Trials*, T. B. Howell, ed., II (London, 1816), p. 801.

39 Thomas Ady, *A Candle in the Dark* (London, 1656), pp. 140–1.

40 James's socio-psychological appraisal of witchcraft was, however, influenced by the fact that some of the principal North Berwick defendants were of considerable social status; *Daemonologie*, pp. 28–30 and note 36 above.

41 H. R. Trevor-Roper, *Religion, the Reformation and Social Change* (2nd ed., London, 1972), pp. 177–83, 185, 192.

42 W. H. Greenleaf, *Order, Empiricism and Politics: Two Traditions of English Political Thought 1500–1700* (London, 1964), pp. 21–6, 58–67.

43 For examples of other analogous inversions in the world of disorder, see John Christopherson, *An exhortation to all menne to take hede of rebellion* (London, 1554), sigs T1^r–T2^r, T6^v–T7^v.

44 William Gouge, *Of domesticall duties* (London, 1622), 'Epistle Dedicatory'.

45 E. R. Curtius, *European Literature and the Latin Middle Ages*, trans. from the German by W. R. Trask (London, 1953), pp. 94–8; Enid Welsford, *The Fool:*

His Social and Literary History (London, 1935), pp. 197–217; Ian Donaldson, *The World Upside-Down: Comedy from Jonson to Fielding* (Oxford, 1970), *passim*; E. Le Roy Ladurie, *Les paysans de Languedoc*, 2 vols (Paris, 1966), I, pp. 405–14; Christopher Hill, *The World Turned Upside Down: Radical Ideas of the English Revolution* (London, 1972), *passim*.

46 *Basilikon Doron, Workes*, p. 155.
47 *A premonition to all most mightie monarches, Workes*, p. 307.
48 The same way of thinking is said by some theorists to underlie the labelling of deviance in modern societies; see, for instance, J. D. Douglas, 'Deviance and Respectability in the Social Construction of Moral Meanings', in *Deviance and Respectability: The Social Construction of Moral Meanings* (New York, 1970), pp. 3–30.
49 *Daemonologie*, p. 55.
50 *A premonition to all most mightie monarches, Workes*, p. 305; Aquinas, *Summa Theologica*, Part I, Q. 109, 'The Ordering of the Bad Angels', in A. C. Pegis, ed., *Basic Writings of Saint Thomas Aquinas*, 2 vols (New York, 1945), I, pp. 1012–16.
51 Aquinas, *loc. cit.*, p. 1014.
52 John Dickinson, trans. and ed., *The Statesman's Book of John of Salisbury* (London, 1927, repr. New York, 1963), pp. 335–6, 339; cf. Erasmus, *The Education of a Christian Prince*, L. K. Born, ed. (New York, 1936, repr. 1965), pp. 157, 174.
53 Rémy, *Demonolatry*, p. 61.
54 Compare Pierre de Lancre, *Tableau de l'inconstance des mauvais anges et demons* (Paris, 1612), pp. 199–212, with Sir Thomas Elyot, *The boke named the governour* (London, 1531), sigs K1^r–M4^v.
55 *Works*, J. Spedding, R. L. Ellis and D. D. Heath, eds, 14 vols (London, 1857–74), VII, 33.
56 William Perkins, *Discourse of the Damned Art of Witchcraft*, in *Works*, 3 vols (London, 1616–18), III, pp. 651, 639; cf. Isaac Bargrave, *A sermon preached before king Charles* (London, 1627), based on 1 Samuel, XV. 23.
57 N. Cohn, 'Europe's inner demons', *Times Literary Supplement* (14 March 1975), p. 278, and *Europe's Inner Demons* (London, 1975), *passim*; cf. the plea that demonology be seen in a wider intellectual context made by Teall, *op. cit.*, p. 36. I hope to explore the points made in the last section of this essay more fully on another occasion.

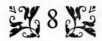

PIERRE DE LANCRE'S
TABLEAU DE L'INCONSTANCE DES MAUVAIS ANGES ET DEMONS:
THE SABBAT SENSATIONALISED

Margaret M. McGowan

On the evening of 15 November 1609 Henri IV, king of France, having dined with his friend and banker Zamet, retired to his chamber in order to converse in private with one of the leading astrologers of his time: the sieur de Thomassin 'qu'on dit même avoir un diable'. This devil's inspiration apparently worked wonders, for Thomassin was able to warn the king of dire attacks to be perpetrated upon his person in the month of May 1610. As is well known, his warning went unheeded and the king was duly assassinated in that very month. Whether this story, recounted by Pierre de Lestoile, is literally true or not, based on hindsight or foretold through skill or chance, does not really signify. It is truthful in the sense that in France, at the beginning of the seventeenth century, even the most judicious prince, the most learned magistrate, and the most enlightened priest believed in the Devil and his power to disturb the affairs of men in multiple ways.[1]

Some ten months before the incident just described, Henri IV had ordered an investigation into the unusual events which had been disturbing the country around Bayonne, called the Labourd, a place which had suffered from the persecutions of witches for more than a century.[2] It was reported to the King's Council that renewed strange happenings had occurred and that witches roamed the gardens of this land more numerous than caterpillars, destroying the fruit and inflicting dread diseases upon the cattle. Letters Patent, dated 17 January 1609, gave instruction to two judges from the Parlement of Bordeaux—Jean d'Espagnet and Pierre de Lancre—'pour aller au pays de Labourt faire le procès aux sourciers et sourcières et les juger souverainement'.³ Four weeks later, further royal letters were sent, more imperious in tone, urging the judges to begin their investigations at once. The two judges set out on their journey, but before their commission was under way D'Espagnet, President of the Council at Bordeaux and Councillor of State, was recalled to Bordeaux on business.⁴ Pierre de Lancre continued his investigation of the 30,000 inhabitants alone. He heard the evidence of over 500 witnesses; and, in the space of four months, he burned and had tortured some 600 souls.⁵ As a recompense for such efficiency Lancre was made a Councillor of State.

The account of his activities—his investigations, trials, and condemnations—is recorded in *Le Tableau de l'Inconstance des Mauvais Anges et Demons*. Originally written in 1610, the book was published in Paris in 1612, and it was immediately followed by two issues of an augmented version in 1613. The 1612 and 1613 editions are, in substance, the same work: though the later edition allows a greater expansiveness in argument, and provides more explicitness in detail. In addition, it carries the engraving of the Sabbat by the Polish artist Jan Ziarnko, famous by reason of its rarity.⁶ This augmented version quickly became authoritative, based as it was on Lancre's personal experience, carefully measured against the evidence accumulated by earlier French demonologists, notably Bodin, Del Rio, Boguet and Rémy.⁷

Councillor Pierre de Lancre (c. 1550–1630) had a facile pen. The Jesuits at the Collège de Clermont had trained him well, and his travels in Italy in 1575 and later in 1600 provided him with a valuable background for his work. He was a cultured man, a knowledgeable lawyer, a moralist, and an accomplished writer. In 1607 he had published a vast moral work *Tableau de l'Inconstance et Instabilité des choses*, which copied the detail but not the spirit or the critical acumen of Montaigne's *Essais*;⁸ like his first work on demons (1612) and his *Livre des Princes* (1617),⁹ this compilation attempted to draw men's minds away from the impermanence of worldly and devilish things.

It was, however, the success of the *Tableau ... des Demons* which shaped his future writing career. Henceforth, Lancre became positively obsessed with demons. Often consulted as an expert, he boasted that he could detect a devil's mark anywhere, even when it was hidden in the eye of a victim.¹⁰ Furthermore, infuriated by the many enlightened men who had begun not only to question the activities of magistrates who tortured and burned human beings as witches, but also actively to condemn them, Lancre composed *L'Incrédulité et Mescreance du Sortilege plainement convaincue* (1622). Dedicating his work to Louis XIII he maintained: 'si ces esprits legers et incredules veulent prendre la peine de lire exactement cet ouvrage, qu'ils changeront d'avis'.¹¹ This long defence frequently engages in difficult and technical problems: whether sorcery is real or illusory; on fascination; on the powers of doing evil through touch; methods of divination; those features which distinguish good apparitions from bad; and the validity or otherwise of the Canon Episcopi which had declared sorcery a mere illusion. This exhaustive volume aroused the indignation of Gabriel Naudé, who, in his *Apologie pour tous les grands personnages qui ont esté faussement soupçonnés de magie*, exposed it as 'ce grand Colosse de Rhodes, qui ne fut ruiné que par sa hauteur vaste et prodigieuse'.[12] Naudé argued that Lancre's *Incrédulité* and Bodin's *Démonomanie* confused great learning and enquiring minds with magical practices; buttressed an already prejudiced view with a barrage of sources of doubtful authority; and sought merely to assemble indiscriminately examples mingling truth and fiction. By 1625, Lancre had retired and had time to contemplate his reply. While he supervised, with his wife, the establishment of a house of Jesuitine nuns at Bordeaux—an order founded some fifteen years earlier by Montaigne's own niece, Jeanne de Lestonnac[13]—he wrote *Du Sortilège* (1627) which contains a quite impressive set of arguments for the publication of works on witchcraft, with a further 250 pages on the different methods of divination arranged alphabetically, and on remedies which might be used effectively against the power of witches.[14] Three years after the publication of this work Lancre died.

Naudé had attacked Lancre's credulity, while the latter countered with arguments such as, 'en ces matières il n'y a moings de vice de ne rien croire que de tout croire'.[15] Such was, in fact, the common view; and when D'Espagnet praised Lancre's skill in discovering witches, he was voicing an opinion shared by many contemporaries who expressed amazement at the numbers of witches Lancre uncovered, and admiration for his efficiency and conscientiousness.

Lancre intended the *Tableau . . . des Demons* to have both a specialist and a general appeal: explicitly stated on the title page of the 1613 edition as 'Livre tres utile et necessaire, non seulement aux Iuges, mais à tous ceux qui vivent soubs les loix Chrestiennes'. Primarily, however, Lancre is writing for his colleagues, to awaken them out of their laxity, and to convince them of the need to exercise control. They are, he maintains, faced with a serious social problem which threatened to disturb the political order. It was, therefore, their duty to seek out and punish the criminal, thereby upholding the supremacy of the Law, which he considered the eye of the world 'au dessus du roi'.[16] Significantly, Lancre dedicated his work to Chancellor Sillery, chief of all the institutions which set in motion the banishment of magicians, devils and sorcerers. For Lancre, crimes of witchcraft made justice synonymous with punishment. Since a witch is a voluntary accomplice of the

Devil, the crimes she commits are odious, extreme, and extraordinary, and they require that magistrates deal rigorously in exacting punishments of suitable size.[17] No punishment is too cruel. In this view Lancre follows the way charted by Sprenger and Kramer, who set out in print justifications for tortures, cripplings, stranglings and burnings;[18] while other contemporary demonologists supported Lancre in his conviction that 'on ne scauroit estre trop hardy'.[19] He cites Bodin, Del Rio, Rémy, and especially Boguet who, in the case of children, advised the death penalty, not burning to death but 'some gentler means such as hanging'.[20] These lawyers worked according to the adage: 'nourrissez un loup, apprivoisez-le, il sera tousjours un loup'.[21]

To justify this notion of 'justice', Lancre (as many before him) claimed to be performing a duty which redounds to the greater glory of God. He saw himself as the servant of the Lord, enlightening the ignorant, confounding the guilty, and protecting the innocent. He defended his speed of punishment on the grounds of the extraordinary range of people affected: 'le nombre des Sorciers y estant si grand, que Satan est demeuré maistre absolu'.[22] Of the 30,000 inhabitants of the Labourd, 3,000 had the Devil's mark; and those accused of witchcraft were by no means confined to the poor and ignorant as was usually the case: men of quality, judges, and even priests were afflicted.[23] In his *advertissemens* Lancre withholds the names of these august personages, in order to avoid the scandal (and in the hope that they might recover their senses), but the names of those priests actually brought to trial are given. The fact that educated, socially acceptable people were involved only served to convince Lancre further of the reality of witchcraft, and strengthened his will to exterminate the disease.

While the two-fold aim of divine mission and just retribution might suffice to explain his investigation, how did Lancre justify the vast publication of his findings? His reasons follow on naturally from his belief in the Devil and from his fear of the disorders witches could bring about. He had a duty to instruct the public; to provide the means of discovering yet more witches; and to convince both the ignorant and atheists.[24] He felt bound to reveal the size of the temptations which might beset the faithful, and the weight of the cross God had given them to bear.[25] By the time he came to refute the accusations advanced by Naudé, Lancre had thought up more sophisticated reasons. Publication encouraged the search for cures; and, furthermore, his own work should be considered as a parallel to the Fathers of the Church who had exposed the fictions of the poets. In addition, Lancre claimed to have made manifest the close links between magic and heresy; the same sins of pride and curiosity were at work in both, and secrecy could only help such devil's work.[26]

Le Tableau . . . des Demons is Lancre's first work on demons, and it is his most influential. It is divided into six books, which deal with the more important problems which confronted him during his investigation. First he establishes the inconstant nature of demons, their number, and their special appeal to women. Books II and III enlarge on the Sabbat; Lancre then returns to themes already suggested at the beginning: the ability of demons to change their shape, either in fact or through illusion, a problem discussed by means of specific case histories. Book V enumerates the cures a man might adopt to counteract the wiles of the Devil, giving special attention to the 'lave-main', a persistent hand-washing technique, peculiar to the Labourd, which was held to be most effective against the power of charms. Lancre concludes his work with an important discourse on priests and witchcraft, and a learned rebuttal of the Canon Episcopi which leads him to stress the need to exact the severest punishment for crimes of witchcraft.

In layout and mode of argument, in the discovery and handling of evidence, Lancre's work is hardly to be distinguished from that of his illustrious predecessors: Bodin, Del Rio, or Le Loyer. He faithfully imitated their standards of erudition; and, thus, his compendious volume is decorated with an impressive array of authorities from classical literature and the Church Fathers; and often this glittering display of knowledge seems either gratuitous or misplaced. While one might conceivably accept the need for ten pages of names of witches (with accompanying quotations from 34 poets and 52 historians) in order to prove that there are more witches among women than men,[27] to devote almost 20 pages and 30 authorities to a discussion of the cock and its attributes seems somewhat excessive.[28] Equally irrelevant and extraordinary are the extended comments on lycanthropy (covering some 90 pages),[29] only of marginal interest to the main purpose of the commission. Indeed, as one reads the same specious arguments, found here as in earlier demonologists, about why witches meet at midday or midnight, or on the subject of how to distinguish good angels from bad, one begins to wonder just how far the worst features of Scholasticism extended into what is normally termed the Modern Period, or how peculiar such argumentation is to the lawyers of the time or to their subject. Poets and their fables are quoted in the same breath as historians and their partial facts, or as child witnesses and their fevered imaginings. Lancre claims to be discriminating and criticises those (among them, the judicious Alciatus) who play around with their texts, and quote out of context:

> Ils tronquent lesdicts passages, s'arrestent quand il leur plaist et font valoir la seule objection par la resolution et decision qui suit apres,

laquelle ils suppriment, par ce qu'elle dict tout le contraire de ce qu'ils veulent prouver.[30]

But his own sins and lack of judgment are equally great. Though Lancre had many times written that he would not treat of certain problems because they had been sufficiently dealt with by experts, he was unable to control the impulse to let everyone see the huge extent of his knowledge.

Among the vast numbers of names he cites there are some authorities on whom he regularly relies: Grillandus and Bodin for elucidating technical points;[31] Rémy and Boguet because they both had had experiences and tasks similar to Lancre's own; Vair, whose work he praises as equal to all those found earlier put together;[32] and that prodigy of learning, Martin Antoine Del Rio, who, at the age of 19, had produced a three-volume commentary on Seneca, citing some 1,300 authorities. In 1613, Lancre refers to Del Rio as 'celuy de tous qui en a escrit le plus sainement, et le plus iudicieusement';[33] and, in 1622, he extols the *Disquisitionum Magicarum* (1599) as 'le plus grand, le plus rare et le mieux censé qui ait jamais esté sur ce subiet'.[34] This praise hides a relationship with Del Rio which Lancre does not mention, and a common source of inspiration. Born within a year of each other, Lancre and Del Rio had both studied at the same time at the Jesuit College; and, in the winter season 1571–2, they had most probably heard Father Maldonat pronounce his public lectures on witchcraft. The sense of his arguments has been preserved for us by a co-pupil François de la Borie in *Traité des anges et demons* (Paris, 1605), a work based on the lecture notes he took in the 1570s.[35] In the circumstances, it is not surprising that Lancre should draw attention to the similarities between his discussion on these subjects and that of Del Rio.

Lancre's handling of evidence from live witnesses seems as credulous and as capacious as his use of erudite sources. He had no knowledge of Basque and was, thus, forced to use an interpreter; he was persuaded in advance that all suspects were guilty; and the majority of his witnesses were a few witches who had recanted,[36] or children and adolescents with ages ranging from ten years (Bertrand de Hauduch) to nineteen years (Marie d'Aspilecute), who went to the Sabbat daily so that they might regale Lancre with their news. He anticipates adverse criticism and counters it by stressing the number of witnesses he used (500 in all) and the conformity of the children's testimony. Lancre inspires little confidence when he describes one child witness of fourteen years—Catherine d'Arreioúgue d'Ascain—as 'un merveilleux esprit . . . un de nos meilleurs tesmoins et qui parloit le plus asseurément'— precisely because she provided him with so much information.[37] Lancre openly supported indiscriminate acceptance of evidence: since the crime is extraordinary, the evidence of any witness goes;

> on voit clairement que le sortilege est un crime si privilégié, que non seulement la deposition des tesmoins singuliers est receüe, mais bien des enfans . . . et non seulement des enfans communs, mais bien des enfans contre leurs propres pères.[38]

As a lawyer, Lancre had been trained to produce evidence, and evidence had come forth in abundance. As a man, he could not measure the extent of the impact of received thinking upon his judgment, nor could his imaginative and passionate nature give him the objectivity required to place fabulous tales in their true perspective. His love of the extraordinary, and his need for miracles, were, and still are, a common human weakness.[39]

This critical and rather negative account of Lancre's modes of argument and his use of evidence, although justified, does not give an altogether fair view of his achievement in the *Tableau . . . des Demons*, nor does it explain the size and extent of his impact on the critics as well as on the supporters of witch-hunts. Many aspects of his work—the Devil's transforming powers and the discourse on cures, for instance—do no more than accumulate received learning, as Lancre himself acknowledges. There are other elements, however, which stimulated keen interest and which deserve to be discussed in some detail. First, the theme of inconstancy which sets Lancre's work within a general moral context; then, his sensational account of the Sabbat which earned for him both recognition and influence; and finally—perhaps his greatest claim (now) to remembrance—his literary merit.

In his dedication to Chancellor Sillery, Lancre explained:

> I'ay cy devant representé à la France l'inconstance des hommes et ay mis en comparaison toutes les nations, pour sçavoir qu'elle estoit plus ou moins inconstante. Mais maintenant ie vous represente des choses de plus haute levee et consideration, qui est l'inconstance des mauvais Anges et Demons.[40]

In this way, Lancre very deliberately sets his work on demonology within the philosophical framework of his earlier study on inconstancy. To draw attention to the inconstancy of man and his world was, of course, by no means new. Religious tradition had long stressed the frailty of man, the insecurity of his fortune, and the topsy-turvy nature of his world. This vision of man in his universe had been taken over and recorded in the compendious volume of Louis le Roy, *De la varieté et vicissitude des choses humaines*;[41] and, more particularly, it had been sharpened by the personal appropriation of the theme in the *Essais* of Montaigne. In the accounts of Le Roy and Montaigne, a fairly complex view emerges, intermingling notions of fundamental weakness with a sense of great variety. In Lancre's extension of the theme to include the emissaries of Satan, the view (potentially rich) seems more one-sided.

Lancre develops his theme in a very determined and often confusing way. 'Inconstancy' is a blanket term used to cover any sense of weakness or impermanence; it embodies mutability, mobility, mental restlessness or fluctuation, moral fickleness, temperamental capriciousness, and even ambiguous expression. After establishing that 'le monde est un theatre où le Diable ioue une infinité de divers et dissemblables personnages',[42] Lancre goes on to state that while constancy is the property of God alone, inconstancy is the natural element of lesser spirits. This antithesis runs throughout the discussion. Happiness belongs to the good spirits; dissatisfaction and inability to quench their desires to torment men, beset the mind of devils. Of the Devil's form, Lancre comments:

> Il n'a point de forme constante, toutes ses actions n'estans que mouvemens inconstans pleins d'incertitude, d'illusion, de deception et d'imposture.[43]

To stress the moral waywardness of demons, Lancre resorts to a great show of erudition which confuses inconstancy with plurality. One example will illustrate the kind of confusion that frequently occurs. Lancre has embarked on a series of contrasts: the total lack of reliability of the demons on the one hand, and the moral constancy of the Romans on the other. As he writes, Lancre remembers that this stability is severely undermined by the Roman belief in a bewildering array of gods; and, forgetful of his original demonstration, Lancre is already on the way to proving that plurality of gods means false gods, and that these are created through the agency of evil spirits who utter false messages or ambiguous words wrongly interpreted.[44] As leaves of similar hue fall in the autumn, so Lancre chases any term which suggests some form of inconstancy—in this case, ambiguity. Ambiguity is inherently part of a devil's make-up, and serves to mislead and influence weak mortals who, bereft of God, pine after worldly satisfactions which are naturally impermanent.

The inconstant mortals most subject to devilish influence are women: their minds are flighty, their bodies are weak, their feelings are changeable, and their desires incontinent.[45] In the country of the Labourd, with its 27 parishes and three languages, women are particularly susceptible to the Devil for social, psychological, geographical, and climatic reasons. It is an arid, mountainous land which runs down to the sea; a land swept by rains and fierce winds, themselves symbols of inconstancy. Because the country is infertile, the men have to seek their fortunes on the uncertain waters of the sea 'un chemin sans chemin'.[46] Unstable by nature, environment, and work, made arrogant by the infiltration of Spanish blood, and frequently involved in clashes between French and Spanish vessels, they leave their wives for long periods without aid, provisions, or companionship. The women, whose very manner of dress and dancing symbolises their Spanish influence and their shifting nature—'la legereté du corps passe iusques dans l'ame'[47]—seek satisfactions elsewhere, with devils, creatures as vacillating as themselves. Lancre expands over 40 pages these explanations of the susceptibility of the people of the Labourd. The reasons taken from the geography of a place and the psychology of the people are relatively new and anticipate much modern discussion of these problems. Lancre's main originality lies, however, not so much in the direction of his thought, but rather in the detail and the extent of his explorations. Del Rio had already suggested the significance of place and climate, just as Nider had done much earlier in his *Formicarius*, but neither writer seems to have responded as enthusiastically and as antagon/ istically as the Gascon Lancre to first-hand experience of the Basque country.[48]

If contemporaries and subsequent writers were impressed by Lancre's repressive view of the Law and by his investigations into the causes of the witch disease, they were more stirred up, overwhelmed even, by his passionate descriptions of the activities at the Sabbat. Indeed, so addicted is Lancre to this particular manifestation of sorcery that the Sabbat became the main focus of the *Tableau . . . des Demons*.

Although the Sabbat is not mentioned in the *Malleus Maleficarum*, the nightly activities of witches were known from about the twelfth century.[49] Lancre's investigations served to extend and diversify previous knowledge, while confirming the findings of many of his predecessors, particularly Grillandus, Boguet, and Elich.[50] Lancre's work subsequently became the major source of information on the Sabbat: F. Delacroix, for instance, sees the Sabbat as the centrepiece of sorcery and quotes extensively from Lancre; while Chapter VI of Jules Baissac's study is devoted to the Sabbat, and is lifted almost verbatim from the *Tableau . . . des Demons*.[51]

Convinced of the reality of the Sabbat, Lancre devotes many pages to refuting those who claim that it is all illusion. The best means of persuasion which he finds is to examine the different methods of transport used by witches to arrive at the Sabbat, through the precise examples of his witnesses. In this way he can confound potential critics by demonstrating that the fact

THE SABBAT SENSATIONALISED

of transport is possible by proof of evidence to which he adds other reasons: the celerity of demons, and the inseparability of body and spirit. The Sabbat really exists, because not only do all his innumerable witnesses tell him so, but they also all agree on the detail of what happens there; their bodies still bear the marks of beatings from the Devil; and, furthermore, their meetings coincide with local disasters such as storms and boats lost at sea.[52] As for the authority of the Canon Episcopi, he demonstrates that it no longer applies to the new situation.[53] And if further evidence is needed to prove his point, he appeals to the testimony of the Holy Roman Catholic and Apostolic Church, which can never err.

The witches in the Labourd, it seemed, could meet at any time, day or night, although it was most common to start the proceedings at midnight and end at cock-crow. The place of meeting was usually at crossroads, in squares, or in wild desert parts; but, given the abundance of witches in the Bayonne area, they seemed to meet anywhere: in the church at Dordach, for instance, in private houses in the parish of St Pré, or even (Lancre allows himself to be persuaded) in his own hotel, and in his very room! The number of participants naturally varied according to the time and place. On festival days upwards of 12,000 might be present, or in the words of eighteen-year-old Marguerite, 'il y avoit autant de monde comme d'estoilles au ciel'.[54] The Devil furnished different images of himself for the different Sabbats happening simultaneously, and manifested himself differently to his flock: sometimes appearing as a goat growing out of a large, round pot; sometimes assuming the shape of a dark tree, without arms or feet, seated on a throne 'ayant quelque forme de visage d'homme, grand et affreux'.[55] At other times, his goatlike forehead was surmounted by three horns with a blue light flickering around the centre one; or he appeared as a huge, lazy bullock of bronze. For some, he presented himself as a serpent; but, whatever his bestial form, always the witnesses agreed on the great size and scaly nature of his sexual organs. The occasion was invariably splendid, in complete contrast to the tedium of everyday life, reminding some of a wedding, and others of a magnificent court with suitable accompanying festivities. The order of these events apparently varied. Most witnesses, however, agreed on the following: the proceedings started with each witch boasting of the evil she had perpetrated since their last meeting; for tasks not properly performed, after some discussion, a delay was allowed or a punishment exacted. The children they had stolen from neighbours, they now offered to the Devil, who accepted them as his servants, worthy of tending to his toads, after making a pact with them which involved their renunciation of God, the Virgin Mary, and the saints, of their baptism and Holy Communion, and of their priest, parents, and godparents. As a reward, the child was branded with the Devil's mark.[56] If a child did not make such a pact spontaneously, he did so willingly after being threatened with fire and the abyss. Then the witches after adoring the Devil as their lord (usually by kissing his hind parts), fell to making ointments and poisons out of black bread and rendered-down children's fat. There followed a banquet where some say tasteless food was consumed, while others fall into raptures over the limbs of children and toads they had eaten. Then came the lascivious dances, performed naked and back to back, before the ceremonies culminated in a frantic sexual orgy, broken only by the crowing of the cock.

Two hundred pages fill in the details of this picture, almost gloatingly presented by Lancre. There are many times when his fevered imagination gets the better of him, and one marvels at the ease with which an experienced lawyer, in his fifties, gives credence to the undisciplined imaginings of frustrated children and adolescents who solemnly recount, as in a fairy story, the baptismal ceremonies of toads 'habillez de veloux rouge, et parfois de veloux noir, une sonnette au col, et une autre aux pieds'.[57] One wonders, also, just how far the magistrate's own vision suggested the events to the untutored minds of his witnesses; or, indeed, one might even suspect Lancre of being more seriously involved, busily burning his victims to save his own skin, as Bordelon neatly commented: 'je ne crois pas qu'on en fut mieux instruit, si l'on y avoit été soi-même'.[58] On the other hand, since Lancre accepted wholeheartedly the authenticity of the Sabbat, and since the Devil's power was limited only by that of God, how could he not believe to be true the most outlandish perversions that the human mind could think of? The marvel is that the imaginings should be so poor and so repetitive.

One reason for this paucity might well be the long-established fact that the ceremonies of the Sabbat were a deliberate and perverse mimicking of the ceremonies of adoration dedicated to God. Tertullian had first called Satan 'Simia Dei' (Lancre's translation is 'ce ruzé singe de Dieu'[59]), and Grillandus had stressed early on that the Sabbat was a conscious turning upside down of the Church's ritual.[60] The new servant of the Devil acquires new godparents, and a new baptism, takes oaths and worships his new lord, turns the sacred kiss into an abomination, and transforms the sacred bread into the Devil's food. The Devil's mark merely copies the saintly stigmata. In the words of a gratified follower of Satan, the Sabbat constituted 'la meilleure religion', a remark made because 'elle y avoit veu souvent dire quelque forme de Messe avec plus de pompe que dans la vraye Eglise'.[61]

Although Ziarnko's engraving does not offer a Black Mass, it does nevertheless show a splendid scene of the religious and court reversals detailed by Lancre.⁶² At the top of the engraving the Devil-Goat is enthroned with a light (reminiscent of the sign of the Holy Ghost) hovering over his elongated horns. On his left sits a nun on a throne decorated with toads; while on his right the Queen Witch crowned and dressed in flowing robes imperiously receives the gift of a new-born child. Through the centre of the picture, in a pall of smoke which rises from a cauldron—fed with toads, serpents and lizards, and heated by human bones—fly winged devils, witches on broomsticks, fragments of human flesh, and stray bones. These shafts of rising smoke seem to cut through a scene which, on the surface, presents an harmonious look, as bejewelled spectators of high rank gaze on the spectacle which appears highly organised. For an instant one catches a glimpse of the magnificences at the late Valois Court; but that vision quickly fades as one realises that the apparently harmonious circular groups are actually mocking the concord usually conjured up on such court occasions. The two sets of dancers perform naked and perversely back to back; a pond of toads tended by children in one corner provides the source of food for a banquet of children's limbs in another. The music of lute, violin, harp and trumpet imitates in appearance the harmony of the Muses (the central figure of the musical group even looks like one), yet Lancre assures us that the sounds emitted were invariably cacophonic.

Lancre argues that such reversals of common practice, habitually found, have a special significance in the Labourd where priests were ignorant and stupid but were regarded as 'demy-dieux', and where 'pasteurs, Prestres et Curés sont establis par le Diable'. Ministers of Satan, 'ils disent la Messe de iour és vrayes Eglises, ils la disent de nuict és Sabbats . . . leurs croix sonnent et leurs Prestres dansent, et sont les premiers au bal'.⁶³ Their debased minds can be seen from the important role in the Church that priests here have given to women, who follow the deplorable practice of helping to prepare the Sacrifice of the Mass, take the offerings, and look after the holy vessels. What are their motives, Lancre asks? Who knows what goes on between these women and these priests when they are so frequently alone in the Church, 'le matin à l'obscur, et sur le midy, qui est l'heure du silence des Eglises, et sur le soir, lorsque l'Esprit tenebreux commence à tirer les rideaux pour faire esvanouir la clarté'? How can they be trusted 'puisque la plus grande partie des Prestres sont Sorciers, et que nous avons trouvé deux Eglises ou Chapelles où le Diable tient le Sabbat'.⁶⁴

Lancre's antagonism towards the priests in the Labourd may have had several causes: he certainly held prejudices against the country and against Spanish influence;⁶⁵ he was convinced that priests encouraged and took part in Sabbats, and quotes evidence of witnesses who saw so many priests at the Sabbat that they thought this place Heaven, and that Hell was non-existent;[66] and, more particularly, he failed to persuade the Bishop of Bayonne to degrade and hand over all the priests he suspected of sorcery. This failure clearly worried him, since it could be interpreted as a way of undermining his own authority: if bishops continued to allow priests to escape scot-free 'chaque sorcier ou sorciere a l'advenir, pourroit regratter nos iugements'.[67]

Indeed, as Lancre proceeds he tends to become more and more critical of priests and of ecclesiastical justice as it was practised by the Spanish inquisitors: 'leur forme de Iustice est toute autre que la nostre'.[68] To demonstrate their unfortunate leniency, he gives a circumstantial account of the elaborate ceremonial with which inquisitors delighted the crowd for two whole days at Logroigne in Castille (November 1610). He describes the procession as it made its way to the market place; details the garments of the penitents, variously coloured according to their crime; the porters and secretaries on their handsome horses; the chest of black velvet containing the sentences of the accused; and the musicians who play, as the inquisitors proceeded up the eleven levels of the grandstand erected for the occasion. The crowd of 1,000 was no ordinary crowd, made up as it was of knights and principal citizens, eager to witness the display of condemnations, penitence, prayers, music, whippings, and sentences of excommunication and banishment on the 53 accused. Lancre adds 'on usa de beaucoup de misericorde envers les susdictes personnes, considerant beaucoup plus leur repentance que l'énormité de leurs fautes'.[69] So writes an ardent Catholic who was persuaded that the civil courts were better equipped to exterminate the women and priests who took to the Sabbat all the attributes of Catholic worship: the cross, the rosary, incense; the words, gestures and offerings usually made to God; the sermons; and, worst of all, the Elevation of the Host—black in colour. To allow such crimes to go insufficiently punished was to ensure 'le venir de l'heresie [qui] en fin infecteroit tout'.[70]

In such a prolific work, stuffed out with erudition, it might seem strange to single out its literary qualities for special comment. Nonetheless, Lancre was acutely conscious of an audience to please and to move, and some of his remarks in his Preface apologising for his explicitness and his length are proof of this awareness. Referring to the attitude of a witness recounting her experiences at the Sabbat, Lancre noted that she had 'un merveilleux plaisir à le dire'.[71] It is precisely this impression that one has when reading Lancre's own prose; he is excited, aroused, and personally committed to what he writes, and he manages to convey this passion very effectively. Such power of communication was noted by Michelet, who declared:

> Quelle passion! D'abord une passion populaire, l'amour du merveilleux horrible, le plaisir d'avoir peur, et aussi, s'il faut le dire, l'amusement des choses indécentes. Ajoutez une affaire de vanité: plus ces femmes habiles montrent le diable terrible et furieux, plus le juge est flatté de dompter un tel adversaire. Il se drape dans sa victoire, trône dans sa sottise, triomphe de ce fou bavardage. . . . . Les sorcières entrevirent qu'avec un pareil homme il y avoit des moyens de salut.[72]

Michelet perhaps overdoes the effect on the witches, but he has underlined the enormously emotional effects that Lancre achieves: 'il écrit bien', he asserts.

Strange to relate, the fervour in Lancre's writing is confined almost exclusively to those moments when he stands back from the detail of an incident and describes a total effect. His general description of the Sabbat as a bustling market scene is extremely vigorous, full of excitement, and revealing both gullibility and enjoyment.

> Le Sabbat est comme une foire de marchands meslez, furieux et transportez, qu'arrivent de toutes parts. Une rencontre et meslange de cent mille subiects soudains et transitoires, nouveaux à la verité, mais d'une nouveauté effroyable qui offence l'oeil, et soubsleve le coeur.[73]

An offended eye and a heaving heart hardly seem to describe accurately the feelings of anticipation which Lancre had conveyed in his first sentence; they hardly account for the sense of noise, bustle, and confusion which he stirs. Nor do they seem a true reaction when one reads the transported descriptions of the wild dances of the witches, amid a profusion of a thousand false lights and festivities (p. 121).

There are a good many such passages and scenes worth evoking, but Lancre's excited eloquence is perhaps most aptly caught in his description of the transport of witches at the Sabbat:

> Elles arrivent ou partent (car chacune a quelque infauste et meschante commission) perchees sur un baston ou balay, ou portees sur un bouc ou autre animal, un pauvre enfant ou deux en croupe, ayant le Diable ores au devant pour guide, or en derriere et en queue comme un rude foueteur. Et lors que Sathan les veut transporter en l'air (ce qui n'est donné qu'aux plus suffisantes) il les efflore et eslance comme fusees buiantes, et en la descente elles se rendent audict lieu et fondent bas, cent fois plus viste qu'un aigle ou un Milan ne sçauroit fondre sur sa proye.[74]

The general effect suggests a glorious, exhilarating party, where the guests have reached the highest point of excitement as the fireworks race through the air. The extraordinary nature of the occasion comes over, almost approvingly. At other times, however, Lancre does manage to convey a high sense of horror through the adverbs and adjectives which carry the weight of his disgusted feeling against the celebrant of the Black Mass:

> Ce faux prestre a la teste en bas, et les pieds contre-mont, et le dos ignominieusement tourné vers l'autel. Enfin on y voit en chaque chose ou action des representations si formidables, tant d'abominables objects, et tant de forfaicts et crimes execrables, que l'air s'infecteroit si ie les vouloy exprimer au plus long. Et peut-on dire sans mentir, que Satan mesme a quelque horreur de les commettre.[75]

It is in this last, well-timed, rhetorical twist, that Lancre reaches the climax of his description of the Sabbat. Whereas one is often tempted to place the work of demonologists like Weyer[76] within the story-telling modes of Boccaccio or Bonaventure Des Periers, Lancre's book falls largely outside such a tradition. He had no particular skill in story-telling unless he himself was implicated in some way; and, for the most part, he argued vigorously against the idea that his work could be considered as a collection of tales, and he stressed consistently that the facts he recounts were real and unadorned.[77]

Nevertheless, as one reads his famous summary of devilish activities at the Sabbat, one cannot escape the thought that Lancre has very deliberately dressed up the facts to ensure that the reader shares to the full his own feelings of astonishment and abomination. The rhythm, largely dependent on the careful placing of long adverbs, vague and suggestive in meaning, is gradually built up, and the phrases grow longer, until even the lengthiest words are doubled:

> Dancer indecemment, festiner ordemment, s'acoupler diaboliquement, sodomiser execrablement, blasphemer scandaleusement, se venger insidieusement, courir apres tous desirs horribles, sales et desnaturez brutalement, tenir les crapaux, les viperes, les lezards, et toute sorte de poison precieusement: aymer un Bouc puant ordamment, le caresser amoureusement, s'acointer et s'acoupler avec luy horriblement et impudamment.[78]

His fertile imagination has conjured up a powerful world which gains authority from fevered accumulation of words and from the sheer weight of evidence produced. At the beginning of the seventeenth century few doubted the reality of the Sabbat. Guibelet, Naudé, and Von Spee are important exceptions[79] at a time when broadsheets continually published salacious details of such manifestations of the Devil, and when innumerable interrogations detailing the nightly happenings at the Sabbat were minuted and printed.[80] Yet, no account ever rivalled Lancre's in his prodigious joy of discovery and in his profound horror at what he revealed; though many (unfortunately) emulated the rigour of his executions.

A hundred years later, after sustained efforts by Colbert to check the witchcraft craze, an altogether different opinion of Lancre's notions prevailed.[81] It found its most detailed expression in Abbé Laurent Bordelon's satirical novel, *L'Histoire des Imaginations extravagantes de M. Oufle*, where Lancre's monstrous stories and specious arguments were deployed to expose the ease with which the study of visions makes a man a visionary.[82] For instance, he used Lancre's proofs and examples concerning both the Devil's power to transport men (p. 19), and apparitions (pp. 96, 127); and he quoted at length his ideas on the form of devils and their crimes, and on the cures one might use to undo the charms of witches (p. 240). Lancre is then taken to task because, like the idiot-hero of Bordelon's story, he believes (along with other demonologists)[83] that there is nothing which magic cannot achieve. The adventures of M. Oufle come to a rather lame conclusion, but Bordelon's novel ends on a fitting note, giving a straightforward account of the Sabbat, lifted almost textually from Lancre's *Tableau*. Nevertheless, Bordelon's act of demolition did little to erase Lancre's name from accounts of French intellectual history. The detail with which the Gascon lawyer had recorded the events he had witnessed, and the earnestness and erudition with which he had pleaded his own case against the criticism of the more enlightened, gave him an authority and an influence which commands continuing notice.[84]

Notes

1 Pierre de Lestoile, *Journal* (ed. Société de l'Histoire de France, Paris, 1875–96), X, p. 225.
2 See Francisque Habasque, *Episodes d'un procès en sorcellerie dans le Labourd au XVIIe siècle (1605–7)* (Biarritz, 1912); Robert Mandrou, *Magistrats et Sorciers en France au XVIIe siècle* (Paris, 1968), pp. 185ff; and Julio Caro Baroja, *The World of Witches* (London, 1964), ch. 11.
3 The Letters Patent are quoted fully in Mandrou (p. 134), and read as follows: 'Nos chers et Bien Aimés, les manans et habitants de nostre pays de Labour nous ont fait dire et remonstré que depuis quatre ans déjà il s'est trouvé dans ledict pays ung sy grand nombre de sorciers et sorcières qu'il en est quasy infecté en tous endroicts dont ils recoivent une telle affliction qu'ils seront contraincts

d'abandonner leurs maisons et le pays, s'il ne leur est pourveu promptement de moyens pour les préserver de tels et sy fréquents maléfices.'

4 Apart from the poem praising Lancre's ability and printed at the beginning of *Tableau... des Demons*, Jean d'Espagnet was more famous as an alchemist and a stubborn researcher of the philosopher's stone. His book on chemistry *Enchiridion physicae restitutae* (first Latin edition, 1633) was a classic. He seems to have taken little interest in the trials.

5 *Le Tableau de l'Inconstance des Mauvais Anges et Demons* (Paris, 1613), cited hereafter as *Tableau*, p. 560. There has been little analysis of this work: Baroja devotes an informative chapter to Lancre (ch. 12); Jean Bernou's *La chasse aux sorcières dans le Labourd (1609)* (Agen, 1897) is entirely uncritical.

6 Jan Ziarnko was working in Lemberg in 1596, and moved to Paris in 1605, where he stayed until 1629. He engraved the carrousel of 1612 and the States General of 1614, specialising in such crowd scenes, though he also engraved portraits. A. Potocki established a catalogue of his work in 1911, *Katalog dziel J. Ziarnki* (Cracow, 1911).

7 Jean Bodin, *De la Démonomanie des Sorciers* (Paris, 1580); Martin Del Rio, *Disquisitionum magicarum libri sex* (Lyons, 1608); Henri Boguet, *Discours exécrable des sorciers* (Paris, 1603); and Nicolas Rémy, *Demonolatriae* (Lyons, 1595).

8 For further details on these borrowings see the important article of Alan M. Boase, 'Montaigne et la Sorcellerie', *Humanisme et Renaissance* (1935), pp. 402ff.

9 Lancre added a further book to his *Tableau de l'Inconstance et Instabilité des choses* in 1610. His *Livre des Princes* was probably inspired by D'Espagnet's discourse on royal virtues—*Traité de l'Instruction du jeune Prince*—which he had appended to his *Rozier des Guerres* (Paris, 1616).

10 See *Tableau*, p. 192, where he writes of the times his legal colleagues consulted him: 'MM de la Grandchambre me faisoient appeler quelquefois, et encore MM de la Tournelle plus souvent, pour s'esclaircir avec moy de quelque point de sorcellerie.'

11 *L'Incrédulité*, p. 5; here, Lancre seems principally to have in mind Cardanus, Della Porta, and Weyer.

12 Published in Paris in 1625. I quote from pp. 612-13. *L'Incrédulité* was specifically singled out for criticism in Naudé's Preface.

13 For details of this establishment see Alan M. Boase, *The Fortunes of Montaigne* (London, 1935), p. 42.

14 Mandrou, p. 336, note 44 *bis*, thought that *Du Sortilège* was never published or was lost, though he knew from Naudé's correspondence (no. 271 of the *Lettres inédites écrites d'Italie à Peiresc*, Paris, 1887, pp. 64-5) that Lancre intended to reply. The Municipal Library at Bordeaux owns one of the rare copies and kindly furnished me with a microfilm.

15 *Tableau*, p. 270.

16 Thus Lancre defined the Law in his *Livre des Princes* (cited by F. Delacroix, *Les Procès de Sorcellerie au XVIIe siècle* (Paris, 1894), p. 55).

17 *Tableau*, p. 71.
18 Jakob Sprenger and Heinrich Kramer, *Malleus Maleficarum*, especially Book III.
19 *Tableau*, p. 104.
20 Henri Boguet, *Examen of Witches*, trans E. A. Ashwin, article 63, p. 234.
21 *Tableau*, p. 301.
22 *Ibid.*, sig. ã iij^v.
23 *Ibid.*, sig. ã iij reads: 'Anciennement on ne cognoissoit pour sorciers que des hommes vulgaires et idiots nourris dans les bruyeres et la fougiere des landes, mais maintenant les Sorciers qui confessent, deposent, qu'on y void une infinité de gens de qualité que Satan tient voilez et à couvert pour n'estre cognus'; and below Ziarnko's engraving: 'Ce sont les grands Seigneurs et Dames, et autres gens riches et puissans, qui traictent les grandes affaires du Sabbat, où ils paraissent voilez, et les femmes avec des masques, pour se tenir tousiours à couvert et incogneus.'
24 Lancre takes this idea from Peter Binsfeld, *Tractatus de confessionibus maleficorum* (Treves, 1589); see H. C. Lea, *Materials Toward a History of Witchcraft* (New York, 1957), II, pp. 576ff.
25 *Tableau*, sigs ĩ ĩ^r–ĩ iij.
26 *Du Sortilège*, pp. 6–26. It was, of course, traditional to link magic and heresy.
27 *Tableau*, pp. 45–54.
28 *Ibid.*, pp. 155–73.
29 *Ibid.*, pp. 237–328.
30 *Ibid.*, p. 79. It was primarily on the ground of indiscriminate and excessive use of useless knowledge that Naudé mounted his attack on Lancre, Bodin, Le Loyer, Del Rio, and others like them who aimed to 'ramasser et recueillir tout ce que l'on peut dire, et ce qu'on s'est jamais dit sur le sujet que l'on entreprend de traicter, n'étant plus question de viser à qui mettra dedans, mais à qui fera de plus belles courses, plus longues et mieux diversifiées' (*Apologie*, p. 607).
31 Paul Grillandus, *De Sortilegiis* was composed about 1525, and published in Lyons in 1536.
32 *Tableau*, sig. ã iij. The French edition of Leonard Vair's *Trois Livres des charmes, sorcelages, ou enchantemens*, was published in Paris in 1583.
33 *Tableau*, p. 485. Del Rio was born in Antwerp in 1551; he became a Jesuit at the age of 30, and died in 1608.
34 *L'Incrédulité*, p. 527.
35 Three further editions were published in 1616, 1617, and 1619. Boase, *art. cit.*, should be consulted for the unravelling of these relationships, especially pp. 416–17.
36 *Tableau*, pp. 410ff.
37 *Ibid.*, p. 92.
38 *Ibid.*, p. 548.
39 Lancre condemned astrology as 'ce sont propositions temeraires et pleines de superstition et de vanité, d'assujectir les ames des Mortels à la vertu des Estoiles'

(*Du Sortilège*, p. 107); and one would have thought that such a man of culture might have judged the opinions of Cardanus or Montaigne, for example, more critically.

40 *Tableau*, sig. ã ij.
41 First published in Paris in 1579.
42 *Tableau*, p. 12.
43 *Ibid.*, p. 64.
44 This idea is developed more fully in *L'Incrédulité*, pp. 300ff, and in *Du Sortilège*, pp. 269ff, where Lancre explains how lying is most common to devils, but adds that they do tell the truth 'pour tromper et decevoir le monde par la verité mesme'.
45 There is an erudite development of this theme, to which Lancre gives an entire section of his book, *Tableau*, pp. 45ff.
46 *Tableau*, p. 31.
47 *Ibid.*, p. 44.
48 For references to these discussions see Lea, *Materials*, I, pp. 245ff for Del Rio, and I, pp. 260ff for Johannes Nider's *Formicarius*, of which Book V is devoted to witchcraft (written in 1435–7 and published in 1475).
49 For details, see Lea, *Materials*, I, pp. 170–98, 201–5. Despite recent controversy concerning the authenticity of the Toulouse trials of 1335, the early history of the elements which went into the making of the Sabbat idea seem clearly established.
50 See Lea, *Materials*, I, pp. 395ff, where a summary of Grillandus's views can be found; Boguet, Caps XIV–XXI; Philipp Ludwig Elich, *De daemonomagia* (Frankfurt, 1607), pp. 27, 41, 52–60, 86, 121, 131–9.
51 Delacroix, pp. 52–5, 221ff; Jules Baissac, *Les grands jours de la Sorcellerie* (Paris, 1890), pp. 398ff.
52 Lancre recounts, for example, 'de faict on y feit perdre le navire de Marticot, de Miguel Choverra de Siboro, lequel estant sorcier ayda lui-mesme à le perdre'; *Tableau*, p. 91.
53 He refers to 'Les Parlemens qui en ont maintenant plus de cognoissance et certitude et plus d'experience que du temps du canon Episcopi'; *Tableau*, p. 99; this is copied from the arguments advanced by Del Rio. In *L'Incrédulité* he discusses the problem in greater detail, relying heavily on *the* authority in these matters: the Dominican inquisitor, Nicolas Jacquier, whose main contribution in *Flagellum Haereticorum Fascinariorum* (composed 1458) was to establish witchcraft as a new heresy. See Lea's discussion, *Materials*, I, pp. 98, 276.
54 *Tableau*, pp. 64, 134.
55 *Ibid.*, p. 67.
56 According to Lancre more than 2,000 children were thus presented in the Labourd; *Tableau*, p. 92.
57 The account of Jeannette d'Abadie, aged 16, *Tableau*, pp. 130–1.
58 Laurent Bordelon, *L'Histoire des Imaginations extravagantes de Monsieur Oufle causées par la lecture des livres de magie* (Amsterdam, 1710), p. 12.

59 *Tableau*, sig. ã iij.
60 See Lea, *Materials*, I, p. 395.
61 *Tableau*, p. 124.
62 Ziarnko's engraving is printed opposite p. 118 of the *Tableau*.
63 *Tableau*, p. 37.
64 *Ibid.*, pp. 56–7.
65 *Ibid.*, pp. 31ff.
66 *Ibid.*, p. 126.
67 *Ibid.*, p. 453.
68 *Ibid.*, p. 391.
69 *Ibid.*, p. 395.
70 It was customary to link heresy and sorcery in this way. Lancre gave a fuller discussion in *Du Sortilège*, pp. 16ff; the main source seems to be the Jesuits, Del Rio and Maldonat. See *ibid.*, pp. 17, 26, 30.
71 *Tableau*, p. 132.
72 *La Sorcière* (Paris, 1862), pp. 33ff.
73 *Tableau*, p. 119.
74 *Ibid.*, p. 120.
75 *Ibid.*, p. 122.
76 See the augmented French ed. of Weyer's work, *Histoires, disputes, et discours, des illusions et impostures des diables, des magiciens infâmes, sorcières et empoisonneurs* (Geneva, 1579).
77 See *L'Incrédulité*, p. 7.
78 *Tableau*, sig. ũ i.
79 All three writers doubted the reality of the Sabbat and attributed the illusion to a diseased imagination or saw it as a consequence of melancholia. Jourdain Guibelet, *Trois discours philosophiques* (Evreux, 1603); Naudé, *Apologie*; and Friedrich von Spee, *Cautio criminalis* (Rinteln, 1631).
80 See J. P. Seguin, *L'Information en France avant le Périodique* (Paris, 1964), pp. 38–45, 'Manifestations du Diable'.
81 A full account of Colbert's efforts can be found in Mandrou, *op, cit.*, pp. 425ff.
82 See above, note 58. Bordelon's work was immediately successful and was quickly translated into English and Italian.
83 Others include Bodin, Le Loyer, Del Rio, Sprenger, Weyer, and *Le Comte de Gabalis ou entretiens sur les sciences secrètes* (Paris, 1670), by the Abbé de Montfaucon de Villars.
84 In addition to the works already cited—of Michelet, Habasque, Mandrou and Baroja—Lancre's name inevitably appears in other general histories of witchcraft such as H. Pensa, *Sorcellerie et Religion* (Paris, 1933); it also occurs in most editions of Continental witch-trials.

COTTON MATHER'S *WONDERS OF THE INVISIBLE WORLD*: SOME METAMORPHOSES OF SALEM WITCHCRAFT

M. Wynn Thomas

I

Ezra Pound, speculating that William Carlos Williams's freedom from conventional American prejudices was the result of a mixed European ancestry still so potent in him as to make him seem more of a lifelong visitor to the United States than a native American, went on to say: 'At any rate he has not in his ancestral endocrines the arid curse of our nation. None of his immediate forebears burnt witches in Salem, or attended assemblies for producing prohibitions.' T. S. Eliot, when he edited *The Literary Essays of Ezra Pound*, added a footnote at this point: 'Note: we didn't burn them, we hanged them. T.S.E.'[1] In both the remark and the footnote, and in particular in the relation between them, can be sensed something of the ways in which modern Americans have been seriously interested in the Salem witch trials.

In his essay on Williams, Pound is growling about American provincialism in particular as it is unimaginative and intolerant; and the 'burning' of witches is paralleled with prohibition to suggest that there is an inherited mean, and potentially sinister, Puritan streak in the American character. It is a response to Salem, and through it to Puritanism and modern America, that is typical not only of Pound but of his period. That Eliot, like Pound, felt there was a blood-relationship between Americans of his own time and the Puritans of the late seventeenth century is clear from his striking use of the word 'we' in his footnote. By the rather grim dry humour of its correction of Pound's extravagance Eliot manages to suggest that under such circumstances as these there is between burning and hanging only the difference that there is between a louse and a flea. But there is also perhaps something of the tone of a rebuke in Eliot's footnote. It succinctly makes the point that in getting his facts wrong Pound may also be getting the wrong idea altogether about what happened in Salem. It hints that Pound is blameworthy because by preferring legend to history he is also encouraging prejudice and ignorance. Eliot's footnote is disapproving, in a half-amused kind of way, of Pound's intemperance and unfairness. Salem, after all, mattered differently to Eliot than it did to Pound: he was more than an American, he was himself a New Englander, whereas Pound was not.

The 'disagreement' between Pound and Eliot is, in particular in so far as it is a disagreement between two writers about the terms in which it is appropriate to speak of the relationships between past and present, an interesting one. Pound is really using a language of metaphor and simile, bringing events together so as to reveal a coherence which suggests not a causal connection but an underlying consistency of character. It is also William Carlos Williams's way, to suggest that the past is in the present in the same way as a man's past is present in him. That is why the Mather of Salem matters so much to him:

> Against his [Valery Larbaud's] view I continually protested. I cannot separate myself, I said, from this ghostly miasm. It grips me. I cannot merely talk of books, just of Mather as if he were some pearl—I began to be impatient of my friend's cultured tolerance, the beauties he saw. . . .
> Very well, he assented, you are from that place. You are caught by a smell. It is good that you struggle to appreciate it. Proceed. Mather. *What* a force, still to interest you; it is admirable. . . .
> [Williams replies] This fiery breath, as of a dragon, is to us a living thing. Our resistance to the wilderness has been too strong. It has turned us anti-American, anti-literature. As a violent 'puritanism' it breathes still. In these books is its seed. I cannot discuss Mather with you like that! I must grow angry. I must be disturbed. . . . Cotton Mather's books, to you an enchanting diversion, a curious study, to me they are a vessel that vomits up a thing that obsesses my quiet, that allows me no tranquillity, a broken, a maimed, a foul thing—that they tell me is sweet, PURE.[2]

II

Cotton Mather's name has always been associated with Salem. He is perhaps best known as the author of a notorious contemporary account of the trials, *The Wonders of the Invisible World*. The tone and contents of that book seemed obnoxious even to some contemporaries who, in their own writing, insinuated that Mather had zealously incited others to hunt and prosecute manifestly innocent people. They sought to demonstrate that he had acted from political ambition, personal vanity, spiritual pride, malice and revenge, and that he was feverishly excited by the drama in which he was a principal actor. It was even suggested, most effectively by Robert Calef, that Mather obtained vicarious sexual satisfaction of a kind best suited to his febrile hysterical temperament from his highly-charged emotional relationships with the adolescent girls that he believed to be 'possessed'.

Some nineteenth- and early-twentieth-century historians, convinced, as much as anything by the violent extremes of emotion in Mather's writing, that he was indeed a deeply disturbed and dangerous man who compulsively acted out in his political, social and religious life the drama of his inner tension, sought to elaborate and consolidate their understanding of him. It was pointed out that in him the names and ambitions of two of the greatest Puritan families, the Cottons and the Mathers, were united, and that from childhood there was instilled in him a belief, almost visionary in its intensity, that he was the chosen of the Lord in His great purpose of salvation towards His chosen people in New England. Therefore the Puritan process of rigorous and constant self-examination to search out the workings of sin and of grace in the soul became in Mather, who was already by nature nervous and excitable, so intense as to damage his imagination and judgment permanently, and condemn him to exhausting extremes of mood. The historians pointed out that Mather was encouraged to find in all persecution of himself and his powerful family evidence of his own spiritual destiny and of the Devil's anger and jealousy. The more disliked and disregarded his family became as the social, political and theological atmosphere in New England changed the more convinced was Mather of his own role in the great cosmic drama and the more intensely did he concentrate his energies upon the struggle.[3]

Historians hostile to Mather argued that his earlier work, *Memorable Providences*, published in 1689, created an atmosphere of expectancy and witch-hysteria. They pointed to the credulity of Mather as evidenced in that book and to the indecisiveness of his opposition to spectral evidence being used as conclusive proof of guilt in the trials of 1692. Some also saw him as an influential and sinister political figure manipulating the Government and the judges: 'every member of the Council owed his seat to the Mathers, and, politically, was their creature.'[4] Even his offers of help were ascribed to base ulterior motives. His failure to show any signs of an anguished conscience over the affairs of Salem, even in retrospect, disturbed historians deeply, and in the decline of his popularity among his people after 1693 they read the popular condemnation of Mather for his part in the trials.

The Wonders of the Invisible World, considered as a book not only recording but also seeking to explain what went on in the trials of 1692, clearly compared unfavourably with other contemporary discussions. A vigorous dialogue between S and B (Salem and Boston), in an anonymous pamphlet probably written by the Reverend Samuel Willard, debated crucial issues. What evidence should be considered adequate not only for the conviction of witches but also for arrest on suspicion of witchcraft? It basically argued that the following alone should be allowed to be convincing evidence: full and free confession without pressure, and testimony of two independent witnesses to one and the same fact; both kinds of evidence had to be present, neither alone was to be judged adequate. The testimony must be human, must have come via the human senses: spectral testimony should be disallowed; and this ruled out the evidence of the bewitched or afflicted (Or are they possessed? he queried); a witch's confession should not be allowed as evidence of another's guilt. Finally he urged great caution since 'the more horrid the Crime is, the more Cautious we ought to be in making any guilty of it'.[5]

A decisive intervention was that of Thomas Brattle, a merchant who was known even in England as an astronomer and mathematician. During October he circulated, in manuscript form, a letter dated 8 October purporting to be addressed to a gentleman in England. In this letter, which was never sent, and not published until after Brattle's death, he made his objections succinctly and rationally. He objected to the methods used in the Salem court, particularly the use of the afflicted as witnesses and as a test. He warned against easy belief in confessions when obviously the confessors were confused, self-contradictory and deluded. Moreover, he pointed out that if the original indictment had been properly referred to most of the evidence would have been seen to be irrelevant to it. Finally, Brattle asked awkward questions about why certain influential people, though under close arrest, had been allowed to escape. He put his plea in few words: 'I am very sensible, that it is irksome and disagreeable to go back, when a man's doing so is an implication that he has been walking in a wrong path: however, nothing is more honourable than, upon due conviction, to retreat and undo (so far as may be), what has been amiss and irregular.'[6] It was a sensible, humane letter, but would have been a braver one had it been written and made public two months earlier. It was significant, above all, as Perry Miller pointed out, because it adopted a new tone and language, free of the old biblical metaphors.

Significantly, Brattle ends his letter by lamenting the stain on 'our Land' and not 'God's land'.[7]

That same October Cotton Mather wrote his exercise in the old language, *The Wonders of the Invisible World*. On 3 October his father read a paper to a conference of ministers reaffirming, in stronger language, the doubts about the trials that the ministers had already stated a month previously. The earlier statement had been disregarded by the authorities, but by October circumstances had changed and moreover the new statement by the ministers was more clear, unequivocal and weighty. Governor Phips took notice and the court proceedings were suspended indefinitely.

But the book that did the most damage to Mather's reputation did not appear until 1700 in London. It was Robert Calef's *More Wonders of the Invisible World*, written around 1697 but published in 1700 in London because no New England printer dared touch it.[8] Written by a totally unknown Boston merchant, the book was probably inspired by Thomas Brattle, who was by then the sworn political enemy of the Mathers. It was an important book because Calef appealed to Scripture to disprove the whole of the witchcraft belief of the past centuries; and it was a moving book because there for the first time were published accounts of the trials of such people as Rebecca Nurse and the petitions of Mary Esty and John Proctor. But it was particularly memorable because of its comedy. In it Calef painted a vivid picture of two men, one ageing, the other still young, both pillars of the religious community, solemnly and earnestly stroking a young girl's stomach while her breast was not covered by the bedclothes. The two men seen solemnly and innocently playing their role in the sexual fantasies of a nubile and near-nude adolescent girl while earnestly praying for her deliverance from evil were the Mathers, father and son. The comedy came in Calef's report of what he saw in September 1693 when he went to see how Cotton and father handled (literally) the case of a young 'possessed' girl, Margaret Rule. Without permission he printed from manuscript Mather's own excited version of what happened during the months that he treated her. The account was called 'Another Brand Pluck't from the Burning'. He also printed his own version of what he saw, which he had sent to Cotton Mather in order to see his reaction. He then printed the whole of the correspondence that followed, in which Mather, outraged by the innuendos, strove to prove an innocence that Calef never directly challenged, and Calef simply refused to admit that any such innuendo had ever been intended. The whole incident seemed farcical, but it had its sinister element. Calef clearly wished to suggest that Mather had encouraged the girl to name the spectres that afflicted her; Mather denied that vehemently. It is probable that his method of treating Margaret Rule was identical with that he used in dealing with another possessed girl, Mercy Short, late in 1692. In his account of that case, 'A Brand Pluck't from the Burning', he made it perfectly clear that he was deeply concerned that no new scare should be allowed to start, and that prayer and fasting were the only treatment to be used.[9]

The Wonders of the Invisible World read by anyone innocent of the precise circumstances of its writing cannot fail to give an unfortunate impression of the author. It is clearly so very badly constructed as to be virtually incoherent in places, and it endlessly postpones the fulfilling of its avowed purpose of printing extracts from the trials themselves, apparently because Mather keeps breaking out into uncontrollable exclamations, exhortations, lamentations and prophecies. The book's structure, or rather its lack of a rational or logical or polemical or even rhetorical structure, has clearly been influential in the forming of people's impressions of the character of Cotton Mather. It has seemed to some to suggest a naivety in the man that blurted things out just as they came, and a credulousness which half appals and half fascinates a modern reader with its open-mouthed wonder and panic-stricken denunciations. But then it has also seemed to suggest an unbalanced personality, incapable of sustained rational thought and swept by gusts of emotion; or it has been supposed to reveal a person so egotistically intent on what he knows and feels that he cannot see beyond that to measure its effect upon a reader. Finally, some have seen *The Wonders of the Invisible World* as the work of a man intent upon cunningly evading the difficulties and objections while simultaneously, and partly through his indirectness, creating an atmosphere of drama and tension conducive to a belief in witchcraft.

The Wonders of the Invisible World was, in fact, a book composed 'to order', or at least 'by request', as Cotton Mather never tired of pointing out in his own defence. Governor Phips was in considerable political difficulty over the Salem trials. By October doubt had grown, and grown vocal. Phips, returning from fighting the French and the Indians, sensed trouble, and wanted an official account made of what had happened. He had already suspended the court, pending further investigations, but he also knew that his own Lieutenant-Governor, William Stoughton, chief of the judges at Salem, still believed that spectral evidence in itself was certain proof of guilt. Cotton Mather wrote to the clerk of the court at Salem, Stephen Sewall, on 20 September, reminding him of the objections being made to court procedure and asking him for 'a narrative of the evidence given' at some of the trials. He pledged himself to do his utmost in defence of his friends, but asked that Sewall 'should imagine me as obstinate a Sadducee and witch-advocate, as any among us: address me as one that believed nothing reasonable; and when you have so knocked me down, in a spectre so unlike me, you will enable me to box it about, among my neighbours, till it come, I know not where at last.'[10] The reference to 'a spectre so unlike me' is perhaps a grimly ironic reference to the argument about spectral evidence then raging.

Two days later, on 22 September, he met with a group of his friends, the judges, to discuss what evidence should be made public, and how. His own association with the judiciary was therefore close: no wonder that he found it necessary to state in *The Wonders* that 'I report matters not as an Advocate, but as an Historian.'[11] The court could not immediately supply the material needed; nevertheless Mather began his writing. Unfortunately, the material still didn't arrive, and Mather continued writing. As a result, the book is a series of anticlimaxes and unfulfilled promises. The report of the trials is as confidently expected and as long delayed as the end of the world that Cotton Mather equally confidently expected.

T. J. Holmes has plotted Cotton Mather's progress.[12] Having written his 'Enchantments Encountered', he unearthed a sermon delivered on 4 August, and included it under the title of 'A Discourse on the Wonders of the Invisible World'. This he also probably expanded by adding the corollaries, etc. He ended this section by saying, 'But so much for our *Corollaries*. I hasten to the main thing designed for your entertainment. And that is,' but the promise ends abruptly with the comma and instead Mather proceeds to 'An Hortatory and Necessary Address'. But before he actually wrote this address Mather probably sent the manuscript as completed up to that point to Stoughton: in reply he received the letter which he published in his 'Authors Defence' which he next composed. Returning to his comma, he inserted the 'Address', promising at the end to supply next 'the chief Entertainment which my Readers do expect, and shall receive . . . a true History of what has occurred'. However, since he could not supply what he didn't have, he instead moved on to 'A Narrative Of An Apparition'. At the end he made a determined effort to will the reports into being: 'But I shall no longer detain my Reader from his expected Entertainment, in a brief account of the Tryals.' Faith may move mountains, but the court remained unmoved, so Mather had to move on to his account of the famous Bury St Edmunds trial under Sir Matthew Hale. At last the report from Salem arrived, and Mather could pretend that all had worked out as he had planned, as he introduced the trial of the Reverend George Burroughs in a businesslike manner.

Holmes suggests that Mather may well have sent each section off to the printer as he completed it. He points out that 'a further evidence of haste is seen in the typography of the book. There is no clear, logical arrangement of the text, no adequate typographical design, no grouping of the contents.'[13] The book was probably available to the public shortly after the date, 11 October, on which Stoughton and Sewall signed their letter of endorsement. Certainly, the Governor drew heavily on the book for information when writing his letter, later that month, to the government in London.[14] Book and letter probably left Boston in the same boat. The book was published in London on 29 December 1692, but given the date 1693.

In appointing Mather as official court reporter Phips knew that he was appointing a man who had publicly expressed doubt on the adequacy of spectral evidence. In writing to the clerk of the court, Mather had declared himself friend and advocate, 'an inquisitive person that entirely loves you and Salem', and the court had declared itself convinced by spectral evidence.[15] It was an impossible position. For once in his life Cotton Mather found himself not wanting to make enemies. He made the worst of it: he equivocated. His own doubts he could not, and did not wish to deny, but the exact implications of those doubts he could, and did, conceal, even from himself. Mather could not bring himself to admit that the innocent had died at Salem. It is a strange performance. Mather defends the justice of the court, yet can actually argue that New England ought not to be considered the den of witches since many of those witches were innocent victims of the Devil who used their shapes for his evil purpose. He doubts the judgments of the court, but blurs the issue by defending the integrity of the judges. What is wrong is not that he should respect the motives of the judges in acting as they did, but that he should refuse to see what those actions amounted to.

But it is only fair to say that Mather did not see clearly into this issue partly because his attention was caught elsewhere. He saw in what was going on a great opportunity to bring home to people his belief that each and every human life was to be considered as the battleground of spiritual forces. In speaking thus he was probably, unconsciously, speaking to and for that in the ordinary people's sense of their situation which had otherwise found expression in the witchcraft accusations. Larzer Ziff has convincingly argued that rural New Englanders, sensing a profound shift from a religious to a secular social and political order in their society, recognising the consequent emergence of a deep division between ministers and men of affairs of a very different kind from before, and feeling their own insignificance in the new order of things, made their presence felt in the only way they instinctively knew how: by dramatising in the most extreme but traditionally acceptable terms the spiritual consequence of their lives. What they made use of, as Ziff shows, was the great belief, central to Puritanism, that each man had direct access to the spiritual world: ordinarily there were checks on the potential anarchy of such a belief, not least being the establishing of an agreed character of true spiritual experience and also therefore of spurious spiritual experience; but by 1692 such was the state of religious life, as seen by ministers such as Mather, deprived of their traditional power in the society, that any opportunity of recalling people to an immediate and dramatic experience of the struggle for salvation going on in their lives was eagerly to be taken. It was not the time for faint-heartedness and nice scruples.[16]

The very relation in which Mather stood to the court and the judges, and which so complicated his writing of *The Wonders*, was the result of the removing of the ministers and church from the centre of affairs, without so changing the beliefs and practices of the society that affairs had a new, natural and predominantly secular centre. Consequently the court struggled with crucial theological distinctions the importance of which it could not find reason enough to dispute, but about which it could not allow the clergy to decide. Had the ministers been a part of the judiciary, which could only have been possible had the social and religious atmosphere of the period in New England been different and more favourably disposed towards the old order than it was, then it is likely that their concern about spectral evidence in particular would have weighed with them and with the court rather more than in the event it did. As it was, and excluded from the proceeding as he was, Cotton Mather naturally felt that there was the greatest danger in encouraging the court to doubt, because there were doubters enough already, and Cotton Mather had his own domino-theory about the way things could all too easily go: 'We shall come to have no Christ but a light within, and no Heaven but a frame of mind.'[17] That was the world of the Sadducee, the materialist, the person who did not believe in the invisible world and the angels and demons of that world. Had not the great Joseph Glanvil himself entitled his famous book on witchcraft *Sadducismus Triumphatus*, Sadducism defeated?

Moreover, the condemning to death as witches of several respectable members of the church and the local community because the Devil had, in their shape, afflicted several people was a late, perverse triumph of the Puritan belief in the difference between grace and good works. In a society more confidently settled in its Puritanism there would have been far less need to make so dramatically and disastrously clear how unreliable and even misleading a guide to his inner spiritual state a man's outer life, however full of good works, could be. But there was to some ministers an undoubted attractiveness to events that made it so clear, to a society increasingly intent on blurring the distinction, how little social status had to do with spiritual status.

But, however complicated his feelings on the subject, Mather in *The Wonders* continued to voice his doubts about spectral evidence. The doctrine of spectral evidence was old and respectable. It stated that once the witch had signed the covenant with the Devil, Satan assigned to him a devil who, taking on the witch's shape, could, at his command, persecute his enemies and the godly. The crucial question was whether the Devil could also impersonate the innocent and persecute others in their shape. Mather had consistently expressed doubts about the validity of spectral evidence when unsupported by other kinds of evidence of a criminal compact between an individual and Satan. It had been an important theme in a letter he had written at the very height of the trouble to Richards, one of the judges presiding at Salem: 'And yet I must most humbly beg you that in the management of the affair in your most worthy hands, you do not lay more stress upon pure spectre testimony than it will bear. . . . If mankind have thus far once consented unto the credit of diabolical representations, the door is opened!'[18] Two days before the execution of Burroughs and Proctor, he wrote a letter in the same vein to a prominent member of the Council, John Foster: 'That the Divels have a natural power which makes them capable of exhibiting what shape they please I suppose nobody doubts, and I have no absolute promise of God that they shall not exhibit mine.'[19] He did, however, add that such evidence could be used as strong supporting evidence, and that in any case the judges of Salem had rarely or never (he is ambiguous) taken spectral evidence as proof of guilt. He advocated transportation in cases of doubt and finally added: 'You see ye Incoherency of my Thoughts, but I hope you will also see some Reasonableness in those Thoughts.' His remarks on spectral evidence in *The Wonders* are consistent with his earlier views, a point he brings out by quoting from the *Return of the Ministers*, which he had himself written in June. Also, he quietly and indirectly criticises Stoughton himself by saying that 'A wise and just Magistrate, may so far give way to a common Stream of Dissatisfaction, as to forbear acting up to the heighth of his own Perswasion, about what may be judged convictive of a crime.'[20] But still, as previously, he insists that the court condemned to death only those against whom the evidence independent of spectral evidence was overwhelming. And still, as previously, he settles the whole matter by making it a different issue: a matter of respecting the integrity and the authority of the judges so that social order and stability is maintained. Not for the last time in American politics law and order becomes an important issue.

He is particularly concerned to prove that both he and the judges knew the best authorities' opinions of what should be taken as grounds for investigation of a man on a charge of witchcraft, and what constituted adequate legal proof of guilt. This demonstration of his expert knowledge of the subject was partly for the benefit of those in New England who argued against the court's findings, and partly for the benefit of those in England who, he feared, doubted the competence of the judges and might want to find an excuse for interfering in the legal, political, economic and religious life of the colony. Mather, in writing *The Wonders*, had more than half an eye on the English.[21]

The trial reports, although slow to appear, seem to be essentially accurate. Mather's main concern was to group the material so that he could stress the various kinds of evidence given, and stress the cumulative weight of evidence in all cases. What he added, of course, was the unique flavour of his own descriptions and commentary. He it is who calls Martha Carrier a 'rampant Hag', and Susannah Martin 'one of the most impudent, scurrilous, wicked Creatures in the World'.[22] What he omitted, or what the court chose he omit, were all the most poignant and memorable trials where innocence was abused. Rebecca Nurse, John Proctor, Mary Esty and many others are never mentioned.[23] As it was he could not conceal absurdities—the absurdity that made a vice out of George Burroughs's physical strength, and Susannah Martin's cleanliness and neatness. Neither could he hide how many of the accusations came from mere gossip, fantasy, irrational fears, petty vengeances, quarrels, misunderstandings, hysteria.

The reports, in fact, although ostensibly the purpose of the work, are not really central to Mather's purpose in *The Wonders*. That purpose informs the language of the whole work and gives it a direction almost in spite of itself. Mather proclaims it when he says in the first few pages that he means here to minister to his people by bringing them to a full spiritual understanding of what is happening and what in turn they should do. New England is presented as being so godly a community that the Devil is exasperated by it into fierce action. He has long resented this incursion of the elect into these his territories, the uttermost ends of the earth, allotted to him until Christ returns in all His glory, but he has been powerless to revenge himself on the New England community until it fell away from grace through sin. The fathers were firm in purity, the present generation is deteriorating into worldliness and ungodliness. Incurring God's wrath, the people also become vulnerable to the Devil's wrath: God lengthens the Devil's chain so that he can reach, tempt and torment the sinful community. But the Devil, as always, is really God's instrument in chastising and recalling His people to Him. They should repent, be humbled, be vigilant, and mend their ways. They should be encouraged by the very severity of God's judgment of the sinners among them and understand that although there are witches in all countries, only in New England does God cause them to be revealed so suddenly and thoroughly and punished so justly. Even the Devil's wrath is a tribute to the spiritual temper of his New England opponents: he scorns to waste time corrupting Europeans, who are corrupt enough to go to the Devil anyway. Moreover it seems likely that this is the Devil's last fling, that these are the last days, that the kingdom of God is at hand.

The Wonders of the Invisible World was the last important work to use the old language of the chosen people, of God's special providence. Some contemporaries must have found it comforting, not least because in warning of God's wrath it also assured men of God's particular attention and suggested the traditional ways back to grace. It was a great Jeremiad, that powerful mixture of lament, rebuke, and exhortation so characteristic of the preaching of the second and third generations of Puritan settlers.[24] But it leaves an impression of rhetoric that is strained, that is tall by walking on tip-toe. The emotion in the metaphors is moving but unfocused, and when we finally glimpse the figures of George Burroughs, Bridget Bishop, Susannah Martin and others in the middle of it all there seems to be a monstrous disproportion between them and the Apocalypse of which they are supposed to be the signs.[25] There is in the same way something grotesque about Mather's attempt to metamorphose the political bargainings of his father with the English crown into something new and strange and prefiguring the new earth: 'It may be fear'd, that in the Horrible Tempest which is now upon ourselves, the design of the Devil is to sink that Happy Settlement of Government, wherewith Almighty God has graciously enclined Their Majesties to favour us.'[26] It is no wonder that Mather, so aware of the considerable opposition that there was to the New Charter arranged by his father, made so much of the need, in face of this assault by the Devil, for men to close ranks. His theme in *The Wonders* is the sinfulness of being quarrelsome, of the Devil's being in the wrathfulness of men; and Mather works particularly hard on this theme, often using little stories to illustrate the argument:

> I have heard it affirmed, That in the late great Flood upon Connecticut, those Creatures which could not but have quarrelled at another time, yet now being driven together, very agreeably stood by one another. I am sure we shall be worse than *Brutes* if we fly upon one another at a time when the Floods of Belial make us afraid.[27]

The Wonders seems a work less intimately expressive of its author's personal concerns when it is realised how many books Cotton Mather wrote:

> On each of the following themes he wrote 1, 2, or on some subjects 3 books: pirates, captives, criminals, thieves, imposters, evil customs,

murder, drinking, taverns, dancing, cursing, anger, idolatry, hypocrisy, slothfulness, slanders, the ark, the tabernacle, sacrifices, adversity, prosperity, fifth of November, new year, winter, summer, heat, change, time, heavenly world, terrors of hell, natural science, Sabbath-keeping, antinomianism, arianism, quakerism, rules for right living, civil affairs, society to suppress disorders, commerce and trading, debtor and creditor, fidelity in engagements, masters, servants, parents, children, widows, orphans, youth, catechisms, oaths, calamitous fires, earthquakes, storms, rainbow, aurora borealis.[28]

The list shows the variety of Mather's interests, and suggests that the minister, prevented by the change in New England society from playing, as did his fathers, an important part in contemporary social and political life, improved his time by trying to improve society. Traditionally considered to be a man the intense, concentrated, introverted and therefore morbid energy of whose life darkened towards 1692 and Salem, Mather now appears to be prodigal, if not profligate, of energy and interests. The list should perhaps be allowed to suggest that there was, within the relatively narrow limits imposed upon it, a reasonable breadth to Mather's life sufficient to include an interest that made him a member of the Royal Society, and a courage and foresight that led him to pioneer, in 1721, smallpox inoculation.[29]

If more should be made of some things in Mather's life, less should clearly be made of others. What must be admitted is that, in spite of the writings, little is known of important periods in Mather's life. Much therefore tends to be made of the tone of the writing; but the more that is understood of Puritanism in general the less peculiarly revealing of the emotional state of a particular man do Mather's works, including the diary, seem to be. The old tone of familiarity which people used when writing about Mather, as though unwittingly he gave himself completely away in his writing, seems as ill-judged as the confidence with which they traced in his every word and action, from gossip about his childhood onwards, a perfect character of bigotry, intolerance, self-satisfaction, vengefulness, hypocrisy and meddlesomeness. That Mather's writing still moves people to speculation, but that the speculation is now more often friendly to Mather than hostile to him, is shown by a recent suggestion that the high, even florid rhetoric of the *Magnalia*, previously supposed by some to be the style most revealing of the empty grandiloquence of the man, may rather be a style of exaggerated fluency developed by a stammerer (for Mather was afflicted with a stammer) out of his need, when speaking, to form sentences with impetus enough to sweep him through all hesitations and impending stutter. Whether this is true matters less than that such an explanation could be offered, born of a sympathetic rather than an unsympathetic attention to the possible relations between the different things that are known about Cotton Mather.

III

When Sir Walter Scott read his friend James Hogg's story *The Brownie of Bodsbeck* he was incensed because of the unpleasant picture Hogg painted there of the powerful hunter-down of Covenanters, Claverhouse. He rebuked Hogg for perpetuating old legends instead of looking to the known historical facts, and in his own novel *Old Mortality* he did Claverhouse the justice of representing him according to his (Scott's) historical lights. Moreover, as an act of defiance to legend and as an act of homage to history, he hung the portrait of the previously hated Claverhouse in his study at Abbotsford. Writers dealing with the past have at least since the late eighteenth century had to reckon with history. Some found that it came naturally to their art to deal with the past historically, others found that there was something in the very body of their work that rejected such a historical past as being foreign to itself; but not for them, any more than for the former, could there be a simple return to the prehistoric.

American writers from before Whittier until after Arthur Miller have been interested in Salem witchcraft, and have made sense of it in ways that sometimes were related to a historian's sense of what happened and sometimes were not.[30]

Many historical novels, some of them interesting, most of them rubbish, have been written about what happened in 1692; but writers have traditionally found in Salem something very different from an interesting historical subject. H. P. Lovecraft's story 'The Dreams in the Witch-House' is a case in point:

> 'He was in the changeless, legend-haunted city of Arkham, with its clustering gambrel roofs that sway and sag over attics where witches hid from the King's men in the dark, olden days of the Province. Nor was any spot in that city more steeped in macabre memory than the gable room which harbored him—for it was this house and this room which had likewise harbored old Keziah Mason, whose flight from Salem Gaol at the last no one was ever able to explain. That was in 1692— the gaoler had gone mad and babbled of a small white-fanged furry thing which scuttled out of Keziah's cell, and not even Cotton Mather

could explain the curves and angles smeared on the gray stone walls with some red, sticky fluid.'[31]

Lovecraft is writing modern Gothic fiction. When Gothic writing was most popular in the early nineteenth century the New England of Salem was one of the few native settings available to an American writer wherein he might hope to create something of the sense of a dark, barbaric and cruel past. It offered the less imaginative of writers an easy way of translating into American terms the shuddering fascination, part fashion, part obsession, of Europeans for their own medieval past.

But the Gothic movement itself was quite complicated. Not only did it involve the more or less deliberate fashioning of stories which played in a sophisticated way upon the feelings in a manner which was directly related to the sentimental psychology of the time and was meant to reveal the mechanics of the emotional life of a man; it also included many another bias of interest which made American writers incline towards Salem. The writer in whose work all these different kinds of interest in Salem is most profoundly revealed is, of course, Nathaniel Hawthorne.[32]

The Gothic, in at least some of its forms, was an aspect of the late-eighteenth-century interest in popular legends, traditions, stories and ballads, which manifested the character and colour of a particular locality. At its best this was more than a taste for antiquarianism or an eye for local colour; it was an instinct for the ways in which a community continuously created itself by working and weaving a fabric of social meanings and memories. Whittier's interest in New England legends, many of them relating to Salem in 1692, was half fanciful half imaginative. Hawthorne's interest in them was deeply serious and part and parcel of his own kind of historical imagination.

Hawthorne's genius as a writer is inseparable from the kind of genius that he has for New England history, and that, as he points out in *Mosses from an Old Manse*, is inseparable from his being a New Englander. In the introduction he brings out the difference between different kinds of history. He was told that the river Concord was the scene of a fierce battle during the American War of Independence; but Hawthorne, recording the fact, can make little of it. On the other hand the poet Lowell told him a story about a young boy's killing of a wounded soldier, and that story has life enough to spare so that Hawthorne finds himself continuing it in his own mind: 'the story comes home to me like truth.'[33] And the story, as he briefly develops it, becomes an insight, an inroad, into the past. Contrasted with this are the merely picturesque thoughts that come his way and as fruitlessly depart when he picks up an arrowhead dropped centuries ago and so 'received directly from the hand of the red hunter'.³⁴ The fault is not in the object, which has a genuine enough history: the trouble is that it can never be Hawthorne's history because it has no claim upon him and therefore he can have no grasp of it. Yet the smallest apple in the orchard of the Old Manse can reveal in him a response to life which is wrinkled deep in time: 'an orchard has a relation to mankind and readily connects itself with matters of the heart.'³⁵ History is for Hawthorne an affair of the heart.

That Salem in 1692 is for Hawthorne a matter of the heart is evident from his story 'Alice Doane's Appeal'. The structure of the piece is really that of the tale within the tale. Hawthorne takes a group of lively, carefree young people on an outing to that grim embankment overlooking Salem known as Gallows Hill. A name evocative enough in itself, one would think; but familiarity has robbed it of its significance and the young people know nothing of its history. While on the hill, Hawthorne tells them a macabre Gothic story of his own invention, compounded of incest and murder, but so melodramatic is it that they merely laugh at its crudities. Humiliated, he turns from fiction to the past and tells them the story of the Salem witch-trials. As he speaks they fall silent, the chill of the past enters their bones, and they draw closer together for human warmth and comfort. The tale is composed of a confession of failure and a triumphant demonstration of success. It is an effective parable of one view that Hawthorne took of the relation of art to life, and it is also a parable of the relationship between past and present.³⁶ Robert Frost can speak of his experience of writing his poetry as 'remembering what I didn't know I knew'. This also is the nature of the recognition experienced by the young people on Gallows Hill. For them it is part of that process of self-knowledge that we call growing up; and to many an artist and historian Salem has an important place in the maturing consciousness of the American people.

Hawthorne himself was fascinated by the problem of understanding what his own relation was to what had happened in Salem in 1692. Measuring his distance from those events while admitting his kinship (literal and metaphoric) to those involved was an important part of the process of taking his own measure as a New Englander. Only in fiction could he work out all and at once the implications of his relationship to his Puritan forefathers. His short story 'Young Goodman Brown' is the concentrate of his understanding of his inheritance. Young Goodman Brown is drawn irresistibly to leave his young wife Faith, in spite of her pleadings, and to journey into the forest. There he meets the black man and discovers to his horror that all the most pious and respected members of the town are secret followers of Satan and members of a witch coven. His final heartbreaking discovery is that

Faith his wife is also there. In the different meanings of the story stand discovered the different implications of Puritanism in Hawthorne's experience.
Young Goodman Brown may be seen as a romantic hero who dares all for
truth, having the courage to sacrifice peace of mind and all home comforts
for one shattering glimpse of the evil in all human nature. That is to assume
that what he sees is true and is not dependent upon the spirit in which his
journey is originally undertaken. Even then it is questionable whether he
correctly interprets what he sees, whether he is right to assume that the
presence of evil is incompatible with the presence of good, and whether his
may not be a disastrously naive and dangerously simple moral imagination.
Beyond even that there is the serious possibility that the whole journey is
misconceived, that an act of true moral perception is just not like that, that
Young Goodman Brown's metaphor for the process of spiritual understanding is wrong. He heads in the wrong direction, away from the com-
plexities of real moral judgments with all their uncertainties and ambivalences
and towards the simplicity of the one, secret, conclusive test of a man's true
worth. Like Macbeth he heads into the realm of equivocation and confusion;
like the judges of Salem in 1692 he forgets that the Devil is a great deceiver,
and puts his trust in mere spectral evidence.[37]

'Young Goodman Brown' is the story which enables Hawthorne to hold
several aspects of man's moral nature in focus all at once. It is therefore also
Hawthorne's profoundest investigation of the spiritual meaning of the Salem
witchcraft trials for his own place and time. To his Puritan ancestors he
owed his imagination for the evil that was in man not by accident but by
nature.[38] In admitting his blood-relationship to Hathorne, one of the hanging judges of Salem in 1692, Hawthorne was at once bringing his own nature
into a revealing and damning relation with evil and at the same time sharply
distinguishing between his own sense of where evil might be and that of the
Puritans: Judge Hathorne was after all accounted in his own time a just and
godly man. The witch trials served in part to show Hawthorne how evil
could be bred from men's obsession or infatuation with evil, and so moved
him to explore all the more profoundly the mystery of goodness in human
nature. Hawthorne was led to see salvation not in terms of one man's solitary
struggle, but as an aspect of a man's involvement in the human community.
But he could also still make sense in his own way of the Puritan distinction
between conventional social morality and true spiritual worth: his fiction
revealed to him and to his readers so disturbing and unconventional an
assessment of the powers and gods that possessed people that he could only
speak, in a half-amused, half-appalled way, of the similarity between the
powers of a witch and the powers of an author.[39]

Apart from Arthur Miller, whose play *The Crucible* has received more than enough attention as a reading of the events of 1692, two other eminent modern American writers, William Carlos Williams and Katherine Anne Porter, have been interested in Salem, and particularly in Mather of Salem.[40] Their Mather is not a legitimate historical portrait; it is illegitimate, the child of passion, the product of a historically irresponsible exercise of the imagination, and judged by some to be a gross self-indulgence. But what their work does show is how, in the minds of some important American writers, the events of Salem arrange themselves in such a way as to describe or reveal some lasting aspects of American character. Their picture of Mather is not a child of chance, a wayward fancy; Salem is for them pregnant with meaning for modern America—is indeed made pregnant with such meaning when modern Americans pay proper intimate personal attention to what happened.

William Carlos Williams wrote a deliberately anti-historical book, *In the American Grain*, in order to recover the truths that he believed history had obscured. In it he declared his 'wish to draw from every source one thing, the strange phosphorous of the life, nameless under an old misappelation'.[41] What he most wanted to expose was the Puritanism ingrained in the American character; and history he saw as encouraging too objective and neutrally descriptive a view of the past. He believed it prevented the present from recognising and understanding the dynamic of the past at work in and upon it. The past, he argued, should be felt as a force and presented so that in its drama the present could experience the form and pressure of its own time.

The chapters on the Puritans in *In the American Grain* cannot be understood on their own, only in context. In a cluster of chapters Williams works out his sense of the difference between the various adventurers, explorers and settlers who came early to America. Of only a few could it be said that theirs was a 'discovery' and that their imagination was equal to their new-found land. Of others it could be said that they 'came upon' America—descended rapaciously upon it, narrowing its generous possibilities down to the scope of their own greed for wealth and power. And then there were those, like Raleigh, who nearly came to America but not quite, and who suggest what might have been, what different eyes might have seen, what different hands might have made of the land. Hands are important to Williams because a man's touch is expressive of the man. America felt the grasp and press of many hands but felt the delicate, inquisitive, sympathetic and responsive touch of but a few: modern America was born of rape. The Puritans were not rapacious but frigid, afraid to touch and of the touch, sullen and afraid before the body of the new world: 'The emptiness about them was sufficient terror for them not to look further. The jargon of God, which they used, was their dialect by which they kept themselves surrounded as with a palisade.'[42] They were ideally suited to survive and finally to prevail through 'their tough littleness and weight of many to carry through the cold'.[43] No wonder, therefore, that in Salem in 1692 the Devil, or the strange gods of this strange country, came upon them in a riot of touching, of pressing and buffeting and pinching, leading to a general hitting-out.

But Williams, all compact of strong and mixed feelings about the Puritans, needed to find some way of conveying them fully and forcefully. Hence the chapter in which he argues with a Frenchman, where the passion of his argument is justified by the context and where his own metaphors for understanding the Puritans are at once challenged and complemented by those of Valery Larbaud. Together they swell the subject into its full significance. For Larbaud the works of the Puritans have a charm, and he respects them for the great impressive structure of their theology which encompassed life and brought it into steady focus. For Williams the Puritans, retreating into and upon themselves, called their own barrenness a plenitude of spirit. The two cross metaphors as accomplished duellists cross swords, and always Mather's name is to be found at the very point where the metaphors cross.

Larbaud is surely right when he notices that Williams himself is part Puritan as well as part everything the Puritans ignored or destroyed in America. Williams in turn is convincing when he argues that the American past may be an interesting spectacle to a European, but must be an urgently personal matter for any American:

> I said, It is an extraordinary phenomenon that Americans have lost the sense, being made up as we are, that what we are has its origin in what *the nation* in the past has been; that there is a source in America for everything we think or do; that morals affect the food and food the bone, and that, in fine, we have no conception at all of what is meant by moral, since we recognize no ground our own—and that this rudeness rests all upon the unstudied character of our beginnings.[44]

That is why Americans should, in Williams's view, read some of the old books of the discoverers and early settlers: 'aesthetically, morally we are deformed unless we read'.[45] Unlike the Frenchman who reads American books carefully, attentively, Williams can only read Mather's *Wonders* and *Magnalia* impatiently and fitfully, since he immediately recognises the accent and bristles.

In the American Grain is a book very much of its time. Whitman's view of America, the 1920s arguments about the Puritans of the seventeenth and nineteenth centuries, a romantic nostalgia for wide open spaces and untamed wilderness, a romantic preference for turbulent passions and living life dangerously: they all colour Williams's sense of the past. The book was contemporary with two works, Lawrence's *Studies in Classic American Literature* and Hart Crane's poem *The Bridge*, which it greatly resembles, and with one work, Eliot's *The Waste Land*, to which it deliberately sought to provide an alternative view of an American's past. Williams was also in a way attacking the whole spirit of empire and of colonialism. But what is interesting here is how important those sections from *The Wonders of the Invisible World* which he included in his book were to William Carlos Williams. They enabled him to proclaim the ground on which he stood.

It surprises people who particularly admire her superb short stories that Katherine Anne Porter should have spent so much of her time over the last thirty years working on a biography of Cotton Mather; but it was her way of otherwise exploring a theme important in her fiction, the theme of personal, family or national history softened into flattering myth. The feelings about the Puritans that found a focus in the life of Mather are revealed in her review of a book about Puritanism: 'As a nation we are in danger of becoming myth-ridden to a point where our true story will be lost. . . . Nothing could be less true than that they [the Puritans] were looking for religious freedom in this country. This is a myth of later times.'[46] There is urgency in her criticism of the myth that the love of and care for freedom is natural to an American because it is part of the spirit in which America was founded. She ends her review by saying that the writer of the book

> has not been able to make his Pilgrims attractive, either as saints or sinners. But if God Himself could not do this, or at least did not choose to do so, our historian may well be content with his achievement and his readers with him. For myself, they are no forefathers of mine . . . and I wish I might never have to hear again that they brought the idea of political and religious freedom to this country. It got in in spite of them; and has had rough going ever since, which is the fault of all of us.[47]

She is, as always, writing partly as a Southerner to Northerners, and partly as an American from the South to Americans from the North. Part of her purpose in writing the biography was not only to score a point against the North by showing them what some of their Puritan fathers were like, but also, by persuading them that they had no monopoly of the American virtues, to persuade them to a more catholic view of the American tradition, a view which recognised the significance of what other regions had contributed. The efforts of all were needed to sustain values that were held precariously but in common.

Miss Porter's biography of Mather is unremarkable as history, and her interpretation of his character is, in the light of more recent research into Puritanism in general and the Mathers in particular, rather questionable; but her work has considerable presence.[48] The secret of its power lies in the style of the writing, in an integrated prose where each fact and insight is allowed its full independent force and makes its mark, but is at the same time gathered into the complete design of a life. It is as though the writer stands at the very centre of gravity of Cotton Mather's life. Inexorably this central and centripetal force pulls all the details of that life into shape around itself: experiencing it from the outside, as we do when we read, it seems as though everything presented to us were already moving down and away on an errand of destiny, and at the same time Mather himself was growing towards us, being formed in the image of this dark destiny which seemed to him so bright with spiritual promise. He seems a doomed figure and yet ridiculous because he seems so pleased with that very figure he cuts. Even worse is the sense we have that right at the centre of Mather's life are the lives of those people that (in Miss Porter's terms) he killed: it is as if they were there from the very beginning and every moment of Mather's growth into self-importance were felt as an increasing pressure being exerted upon their very lives. The fact that Miss Porter has not finished, or has not yet published, the chapters dealing with the witchcraft trials themselves is a lucky artistic accident. The horror of those events, instead of being dramatically dwelt upon and thereby made central, is differently and more effectively evoked by the loud silence at that point in the narrative. The sense of inevitability is heightened by our being led to see how clearly the shape of those events is defined by the mass of Mather's life that is present in the biography. It is like making a woodcut, or seeing a film in negative.

In trying to show how Cotton Mather became Mather of Salem, Miss Porter is also trying to make clear what the Salem trials mean for the American experience. She works to persuade events to reveal their inevitability in order to reveal the character of that inevitability: it lies not in the inexorable working of a fate external to man but in the character of a society as events reveal and fulfil it and people enact it. Mather enacted the Puritan idea of being chosen, set apart, an idea that Miss Porter believes to be still instinctive to Americans. His male egotism was flattered by the idea; and Miss Porter in a sense repeats the attempts made by the girls that he treated for possession to ridicule his self-importance. Their subversive intentions were foiled by the sheer flawless and invulnerable perfection of his egotism—he was not to be seduced out of his monstrous folly—but Miss Porter in laying bare the spiritual pride of the man hopes also to lay it low. The biography is written not out of hostility but out of an irreverence: it is a deliberate act of impiety which Miss Porter thinks is the greatest service she can do her country.

The work of Hawthorne, Williams and Porter is an imaginative enterprise different from but surely equal to the work of those historians who have dealt with Salem. In what they each make of Salem they differ almost as much as they all together do from the historians; but what they have in common is a particular kind of authority which they have not by virtue of any professional expertise or social status, but by virtue of the convincing force and quality of their vision. Their work is proof of how the experience of Salem, when it enters into an American writer's head that he might write about it, goes very deep in him, as deep as the sources of creative imagination in him and as deep as his darkest understanding of himself as an American. Through their work, what happened in Salem in 1692 is once again brought urgently to the attention of Americans in ways which make clear not only that it still matters but also how it still matters. What they offer is not history but images made from history, which can in turn become images from which history may be made. If there is any truth in W. B. Yeats's remark that 'nations, races, or individual men are unified by an image or bundle of related images', then the interest of historians and artists in Salem is partly the cause and partly the result of its force as an image of aspects of a national character; and, judging by the figure he cuts in the minds and stories of even fairly recent American writers, Cotton Mather is still a force to be reckoned with in modern America.

Notes

1 *The Literary Essays of Ezra Pound*, ed. T. S. Eliot, 1954, p. 391.
2 William Carlos Williams, *In the American Grain*, New Directions Paperbook, New York, 1956, pp. 115–16.
3 Those hostile to Mather include Robert Calef, Francis Hutchinson, Thomas Hutchinson, C. W. Upham, V. L. Parrington, as well as many others; more favourably disposed towards Mather are S. G. Drake, W. F. Poole, A. P. Marvin, B. Wendell, K. B. Murdock, T. J. Holmes and, recently, Chadwick Hansen. The best recent study of Salem, Paul Boyer and Stephen Nissenbaum, *Salem Possessed: the social origins of witchcraft*, Cambridge, Mass., 1974, starting from premises different from those usual to histories of Salem witchcraft, finds it unnecessary to mention Cotton Mather at all.

4 C. W. Upham, *Salem Witchcraft and Cotton Mather*, New York, 1869, p. 12. He argues the same thesis in his *Salem Witchcraft*, Boston, 1867. Even at the time he was attacked for his views; see W. F. Poole, *Cotton Mather and Salem Witchcraft*, Boston, 1869. See also *Cotton Mather and Witchcraft, Two Notices of Mr. Upham his Reply* (Notices from the *Watchman and Reflector* and from the *Christian Era*), 1870.
5 Samuel Willard, *Some Miscellany Observations on our present debates respecting Witchcrafts*, Philadelphia, 1692; reprinted Boston, 1869, p. 8.
6 Thomas Brattle, Letter, 1692, in *Narratives of the Witchcraft Cases, 1648–1706*, ed. G. L. Burr, New York, 1959, p. 169.
7 For a further discussion of the significance of the 'highly literate and satirical tone' of the letter see Perry Miller, *From Colony to Province*, Cambridge, Mass., 1967, pp. 196–7.
8 Burr in his *Narratives* reprints a substantial part of the book, but not all of it.
9 Reprinted in Burr's *Narratives*.
10 Quoted in Upham, *Salem Witchcraft and Cotton Mather*, p. 44.
11 Cotton Mather, *The Wonders of the Invisible World*, 1862 reprint, p. 110.
12 T. J. Holmes, *Cotton Mather. A Bibliography of his Works*, Cambridge, Mass., 1940, III, pp. 1255–7.
13 *Ibid.*, p. 1257.
14 The Governor's letter of October, 1692 and his letter of 1693 are both in Burr's *Narratives*.
15 Quoted in Upham, *Salem Witchcraft and Cotton Mather*, p. 44.
16 Larzer Ziff, *Puritanism in America*, 1973, chapter 10.
17 Quoted in Chadwick Hansen, *Witchcraft at Salem*, 1970, p. 27.
18 Quoted in Upham, *Salem Witchcraft and Cotton Mather*, p. 39.
19 Quoted in A. P. Marvin, *The Life and Times of Cotton Mather*, Boston, 1892, p. 133.
20 *Wonders*, p. 29.
21 The classic, and courteous, debate on the place of Salem in the history of witchcraft was that between Kittredge and Burr. G. L. Kittredge, *Witchcraft in Old and New England*, Cambridge, Mass., 1929, especially chapter XVIII. G. L. Burr, 'New England's place in the history of witchcraft', now most easily found in *George Lincoln Burr, His Life*, by R. H. Bainton, *Selections from his Writings*, ed. L. O. Gibbons, New York, 1943. There is a good summary of the important seventeenth-century English works on witchcraft, including those mentioned by Mather, in Wallace Notestein, *History of Witchcraft in England, 1558–1718*, Washington, 1911, repr. New York, 1965, especially chapters X and XII.
22 *Wonders*, pp. 159, 148.
23 An account of these trials can be found in Burr's *Narratives*; and the whole story of what happened in Salem in 1692 is well told by Marion E. Starkey in *The Devil in Massachusetts*, 1950.
24 Very interesting and contrasting accounts of the Jeremiad are offered by Perry Miller in *From Colony to Province* and Larzer Ziff in *Puritanism in America*.

25 Scholars have recently been paying particular attention to 'the Puritans' expectation of the imminent Eschaton'; see Michael McGiffert, 'American Puritan Studies in the Sixties', *William and Mary Quarterly*, 3rd series, XXVIII (1970), p. 54. That millennialism played a part in American Puritan theology from its very beginnings is shown by Joseph Rosenmeier in 'The Teacher and the Witness: John Cotton and Roger Williams', *W & M Q*, 3rd series, XXV (1968), pp. 411ff.
26 *Wonders*, p. 21.
27 *Wonders*, p. 23.
28 T. J. Holmes, *Cotton Mather. A Bibliography of his Works*, I, ix.
29 For a full account of the smallpox scare and a valuable discussion of Cotton Mather as a medical man see O. T. Beall, Jr and R. H. Shryock, 'Cotton Mather: first significant figure in American medicine', *Proceedings of the American Antiquarian Society*, 63, pt 1, 1953.
30 See G. Harrison Orians, 'New England Witchcraft in Fiction', *American Literature*, 2 (1930–1), pp. 54–71.
31 H. P. Lovecraft, 'The Dreams in the Witch-House', from *At the Mountains of Madness and other novels of terror*, ed. August Derleth, Panther, 1973, p. 113.
32 There is a good study of Hawthorne's use of Salem in his fiction in Tremaine McDowell's 'Nathaniel Hawthorne and the Witches of Colonial Salem', *Notes and Queries*, CLXVI (1934). Hawthorne drew a sympathetic picture of Mather in his 'Grandfather's Chair'.
33 *The Centenary Edition of the Works of Nathaniel Hawthorne*, Ohio, 1974, X, *Mosses from an Old Manse*, p. 10.
34 *Ibid.*, p. 11.
35 *Ibid.*, p. 12.
36 There is a very different and most challenging reading of this story and its meaning for Hawthorne's view of historical fiction in Harry B. Henderson III, *Versions of the Past*, 1974, p. 92.
37 It had been persuasively argued that Hawthorne had the Salem witchcraft trials and the use of spectral evidence in mind when writing 'Young Goodman Brown': see David Levin, *In Defense of Historical Literature*, New York, 1967, chapter 5.
38 The best discussion of Hawthorne's relation to his Puritan forefathers is that by Larzer Ziff, 'The Artist and Puritanism', in *Hawthorne Centenary Essays*, ed. Roy Harvey Pearce, Ohio, 1964.
39 Melville understood what he meant, as he showed in his marvellous and now famous review of *Mosses from an Old Manse*. That review, 'Hawthorne and His Mosses' is now to be conveniently found in *Hawthorne, The Critical Heritage*, ed. J. D. Crowley, 1970. D. H. Lawrence developed the theme in his own inimitable way in *Studies in Classic American Literature*.
40 Levin argues, I think convincingly, that *The Crucible* fails because Miller has insufficient respect for the complexity of the historical events with which he is

dealing. The relation of Miller's play to the witchcraft trials is discussed in chapter 4 of Levin's *In Defense of Historical Literature*.
41 *In the American Grain*, Preface.
42 *Ibid.*, p. 63.
43 *Ibid.*, p. 65.
44 *Ibid.*, p. 109.
45 *Ibid.*, p. 109.
46 *The Collected Essays of Katherine Anne Porter*, New York, 1973, pp. 141-2.
47 *Ibid.*, p. 144.
48 The chapters from her biography of Mather, dated 1934, are printed in her *Collected Essays*, pp. 313-51. David Levin has criticised these chapters very interestingly in chapter 2 of his *In Defense of Historical Literature*.

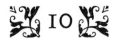

TWO LATE SCOTTISH WITCHCRAFT TRACTS:
WITCH-CRAFT PROVEN and *THE TRYAL OF WITCHCRAFT*

Christina Larner

Scotland has a thin witchcraft literature, considering the importance of that crime throughout the seventeenth century. In England the rich pamphlet literature was fed by exotic stories of spirits, necromancy, and witchcraft, exported from Scotland; but in Scotland itself the production of horror tales for entertainment was an industry very much in its infancy. Such pamphlets as there were tended to be improving, exhortational, and controversial, and the two discussed here belong to this type. They defend and expound the belief in witchcraft.

The tracts are *Witch-Craft Proven* published in 1697,[1] and *The Tryal of Witchcraft* published in 1705.[2] They came right at the end of the period of witchcraft persecution, at a time, that is to say, when the elite (magistrates, gentry, and clergy) were losing their convictions about the reality of the crime of witchcraft. These pamphlets are therefore interesting for the history of ideas in two ways: first, they show the rearguard action against developing scepticism; and second, in their unconscious and anachronistic use of concepts developed by fifteenth-century canon lawyers they show the tenacity of these ideas in the generation before Hume.

There is a considerable problem in the ascription of these two pamphlets. Both have been attributed to one man, John Bell of Gladsmuir, but it seems improbable from internal evidence that they came from the same pen. The ascriptions to John Bell are made by nineteenth-century historians and bibliographers who based them on evidence much of which cannot be re-examined, as it has disappeared. Bell cannot have written both pamphlets, and it is just possible that he did not write either of them; but the probability that he wrote the later one seems strong enough to warrant a brief account of his character and other writings, before moving on to the problems of ascription, and discussion of the context and content of the pamphlets themselves.

Information on the life of John Bell derives from his own manuscript autobiography[3] and the brief entries on him in Hew Scott's *Fasti Ecclesiae Scoticanae*.[4] He was born in Glasgow, the son of a merchant, on 2 February 1676, and held a bursary at the university there from 5 November 1694. He was licensed to preach by the Presbytery on 13 May 1697, called to the charge of Broughton in Lanarkshire in July, and ordained on the 24 September. He remained at Broughton until August 1701, when he transferred to Gladsmuir in East Lothian. He married Janet Learmond on an unknown date, and 'died of a violent fever' on 30 October 1707 at the age of thirty-two. He was survived by his wife and unspecified issue.

This bare outline is filled in by the autobiography only in some aspects. From it we learn most of what is known about his life and character, but unfortunately it is very selective, and there is nothing in it at all to indicate an interest in witchcraft or demonology. It consists mainly of a detailed account of his intrigues, his conversations, and his trips to Edinburgh, over the election of a Presbyterian rather than an Episcopalian minister to a vacant parish near by; and of the part he played in the negotiations over the establishment of Presbyterianism as the legal form of church government in Scotland in the proposed Act of Union.

The account reveals him as a man of some energy, and as a lover of power and intrigue. He was ordained at Broughton in 1697 when he was twenty-one, and spent a tranquil period there. But when in 1701 he was translated to Gladsmuir he found himself 'aparently in hard Circumstances having exchanged 200 obedient and submissive people at Broughtone, for 1200 obstinate people in Gladsmure, and a Loving Presbytry in Biggar to Be Collegiate with a set of Brethren to most of whom I was inwardly a Stranger many of them Lookt on by Superior indications as men of Cold Spirits, and who were Jealous of my Strictness'.[5] He went on to relate how he tamed his congregation within ten or twelve weeks, and how, in his relations with the Presbytery, 'after a year of conflict all Came to be notably Reformed, and the whole fraternity were in good Terms with me and we lived amicably together'.[6] By this time he was already, at the age of twenty-six, Moderator of Presbytery.

His personality combined self-righteousness, arrogance, and humourlessness. These characteristics, rightly or wrongly, tend to be associated with Presbyterian ministers of his period, and are certainly apparent here in his opening words:

I was born at Glasgou 2 February 1676 of Religious parents who devoted me to the Ministry from the womb, and aducated [sic] me agreeably. I should Sin against Gods goodness to me in my nonage if I did not remark Two Things. 1mo. That from the Cradle I was preserved from being tainted with the vices incident to Children, 2nd That so far Back as I can draw my life I loved prayer, and would be now and then preaching to the neighbour children Like myself.[7]

Further, in his philosophical studies, he wrote: 'I used a more than ordinary application Here; and all the time I was Learning my Logicks I can say, that Day never past wherein I was not Master of my Lesson, and I never opened my Book to Read without prefacing my Studies, with a short ejaculation to God.'[8] It is clear that it would have been quite in character for John Bell to have been a harrier of witches, but he makes no mention of this as an interest, nor indeed does he refer to any other works, published or manuscript. Despite this no less than six works, in addition to the autobiography, have been attributed to him.

There are the two witch tracts under discussion:

(1) *Witch-Craft Proven*, 1697.
(2) *The Tryal of Witchcraft*, 1705.

and, in addition,

(3) 'Discourse of Witchcraft': a fifty-page manuscript of 1705.
(4) *An Ingenious and Scientific Discourse of Witchcraft*, Anon, 1705.
(5) *Abridgement and Alphabetical Index of the Acts of the General Assemblies of the Church of Scotland from 1638 to 1706 by a Minister of the Gospel*, Edinburgh, 1706.
(6) *The Toleration Gazette*, August 1703 to March 1704. This survives as a single folio sheet.[9] It was part of a paper war against the proposed Toleration Act which, it was feared, might involve the reinstatement of episcopacy.

This was, even if we must throw some doubt on the authorship of some of these works, a fair literary output for a man who died at the age of thirty-two after having lived a life deeply involved in ecclesiastical politics.

Of the four witchcraft works only the first two survive. The lost manuscript 'Discourse of Witchcraft' is referred to and cited in Charles Kirkpatrick Sharpe's *Historical Account of the Belief in Witchcraft in Scotland*,[10] which had originally appeared as an introduction to Robert Law's *Memorialls* published in Edinburgh in 1818. The manuscript seems to have been last seen in Edinburgh in 1828, when it was noted as number 2908 in David Constable's *Sale Catalogue*, where it was bound up with two unrelated manuscripts and sold for £1. 4s. The last of the four witchcraft works attributed to Bell, the *Ingenious and Scientific Discourse of Witchcraft*, which may or may not be the published version of the manuscript 'Discourse of Witchcraft', is mentioned by Hew Scott in the *Fasti Ecclesiae Scoticanae* along with the *Abridgement and Alphabetical Index* as Bell's only publications,[11] and is also attributed to him in W. T. Morgan's *Bibliography of British History, 1700–1715*.[12] Morgan is said to have personally examined all the materials listed, but does not say where he saw them. No copy of this work is known.

To confuse matters further, there was another minister called John Bell, who, in the absence of handwriting evidence identifying the author of one or other of these tracts with the author of 'The Life and Times of Mr J.B.', is a possible candidate. Unfortunately this John Bell does not feature in the *Fasti Ecclesiae Scoticanae*, but he is known and identified as one of the witnesses at the trial of Philip Standsfield for patricide in 1688,[13] and is wrongly assumed by Laing[14] to be the same John Bell as the minister of Gladsmuir. This older Bell, a minister near Haddington, was about forty at the time of this trial. This would have made him only fifty-seven in 1705, so there is no reason why he should not have written either tract. He is an appealing candidate since at Standsfield's trial he spent some time describing his fear of evil spirits and the way in which he mistook the sounds of murder for the activity of demons. References to 'Bell', however, in the remainder of the article, will be to Bell of Gladsmuir, unless otherwise specified.

The ascription of *Witch-Craft Proven*, the earlier of the two pamphlets, to John Bell of Gladsmuir is made by John Ferguson in his *Bibliographical Notes on the Witchcraft Literature of Scotland*, published in 1899.[15] Despite the fact that Ferguson usually had good reasons for his ascriptions,[16] the reasons are not given, and it seems, in fact, extremely improbable that John Bell of Gladsmuir was the author of the 1697 *Witch-Craft Proven*. He was only twenty-one in 1697; he was occupied with the completion of his studies in Glasgow, his licence to preach, and his ordination to Broughton. And, as already noted, he makes no mention in his autobiography of having published a book at this time—or indeed at any time. He probably did have sufficient talent and energy to publish his first book in the middle of such an active year, but it seems unlikely that he did. In addition, there is some internal evidence. The author of *Witch-Craft Proven* frequently introduces and explains Hebrew words and terms.[17] It is not very clear from the way in which he does this whether he knew a good deal of Hebrew, or only a few useful words; but it seems most likely that he knew a fair amount. In his autobiography Bell gives a clear account of his studies, including his progress and prowess in Greek, but makes no mention at all of ever having studied Hebrew. Such an omission would have been out of character had he in fact become a Hebrew scholar before the age of twenty-one.

A further reason why it is unlikely that Bell wrote *Witch-Craft Proven* is that he probably did write the later tract, *The Tryal of Witchcraft*; and internal evidence again makes it most improbable that these two works were written by the same person. There are marked differences, both in subject matter and in general approach. The earlier work is far more credulous than *The Tryal of Witchcraft*. Its author includes among the different marks of witchcraft, in addition to those known to demonologists throughout Europe, two or three particularly absurd local superstitions. The author of *The Tryal of Witchcraft* on the other hand is a good deal more circumspect. He takes pains to emphasise that most of those signs commonly thought of as sure marks of witchcraft are in fact only 'pregnant and shrewd assumptions', and asserts that the death penalty ought never to be enforced unless it is satisfactorily established, within his terms, that there has been a pact with the devil.

The two tracts also have a totally different set of references apart from a few obvious biblical ones in common. There are only two non-biblical allusions in *Witch-Craft Proven*, but a fairly wide selection in *The Tryal of Witchcraft*. Further, the author of *The Tryal of Witchcraft* knew, or at least used, no Hebrew.

Perhaps the strongest reason for assuming that these two tracts were by different hands is that *The Tryal of Witchcraft* was almost certainly written by the author of the lost manuscript 'Discourse of Witchcraft', attributed to John Bell by Charles Kirkpatrick Sharpe. The manuscript of *The Tryal of Witchcraft* was sold for 2s. 6d. and numbered in the lot with the 'Discourse of Witchcraft' in Constable's sale of 1828 already mentioned. Both were said in this catalogue to be by the Rev. John Bell, minister of Gladsmuir, and it seems almost certain that a disparity in the handwriting of the two works would have been observed then. The discovery of these lost manuscripts, and a comparison of the handwriting with that of the autobiographical manuscript, would finally settle the matter; but in their absence we have no certain evidence to corroborate the entries in the catalogue to the effect that Bell of Gladsmuir, and not another John Bell, was their author.

Even without that, however, it becomes clear that the same man could not have written *Witch-Craft Proven*. *Witch-Craft Proven* is a highly credulous work, and it was published in Glasgow the same year that seven witches were executed in Paisley. Bell refers to this occasion in the first of the three extracts given by Sharpe, and is extremely scornful of the credulity of the clergy and professoriate of Glasgow during this episode. Those against whom his scorn was directed probably included the anonymous 'Lover of the Truth' who wrote *Witch-Craft Proven*.

> I own there has been much harm done to worthy and innocent persons in the common way of finding out witches, and in the means made use of for promoting the discovery of such wretches, and bringing them to justice; that oftentimes old age, poverty, features, and ill fame, with such like grounds, not worthy to be represented to a magistrate, have yet moved many to suspect and defame their neighbours, to the unspeakable prejudice of Christian charity; a late instance whereof we had in the west, in the business of the sorceries exercised upon the Laird of Bargarran's daughter, anno 1697, a time when persons of more goodness and esteem than most of their calumniators were defamed for witches, and which was occasioned mostly by the forwardness and absurd credulity of diverse otherwise worthy ministers of the gospel, and some topping professors in and about the city of Glasgow.[18]

The ascription of *The Tryal of Witchcraft* to John Bell of Gladsmuir, however, is made by Robert Wodrow, an earlier, and to that extent certainly more reliable identification than that for *Witch-Craft Proven*. In addition, the Gladsmuir district had for long been a notable area for cases of witchcraft,[19] and Bell must have been very conscious of the problem during his ministry there. The later ascription by Ferguson of *Witch-Craft Proven* to the same man may have been because of the phrase 'witchcraft arreign'd and condemn'd' which occurs in the long version of both titles. Ferguson did not have a copy of the later book in his collection, but may have seen a reference to it somewhere, and confused it. In the absence of more positive evidence the most that can be said is that *The Tryal of Witchcraft* was probably written by Bell of Gladsmuir, and that *Witch-Craft Proven* remains anonymous.

Witch-Craft Proven is an extremely rare tract. Only two copies, both in the Ferguson Collection in Glasgow University Library, appear to be known. It is catalogued as number 3719 in Aldis's List.[20] It is a small sixteen-page volume and the place and date of its publication suggest, as mentioned earlier, that its appearance was connected with the Paisley witchcraft trial of that year. There is no actual reference to the case in the text, and unfortunately there is no means of knowing whether it appeared before or after the trial. The convicted witches were executed in June, and certainly the whole subject of witchcraft was much discussed in the west of Scotland at this time.[21] Witchcraft trials were by this time sufficiently rare to excite comment, speculation, and discussion of general principles. The Paisley trial resulted in the last mass execution for witchcraft, and apart from one or two isolated cases in the eighteenth century, it was the last altogether.

The centre of the case was the victim, Christian Shaw, the eleven-year-old daughter of the laird of Bargarron. She had spoken rudely to two women, the first a young servant whom she had seen stealing a drink of milk, and the other an old woman who was already of 'ill fame'. Both cursed her roundly. The night after her scene with the older woman, Christian Shaw was seized with the first of a series of fits during which she vomited up many curious objects: pins, eggshells, lumps of candle grease, gravel stones (all of which she herself could easily have obtained). She cried out accusations, first against those two women, and then against various other people. She frequently claimed that her tormentors were present, and urged them to repent of their sins. The onlookers could see no-one, but on one occasion the child exclaimed that she had got hold of a warlock's jerkin. The tearing of material was heard, and she exhibited two pieces of red cloth in her hands. These fits continued into the following year, when the authorities took notice and began examining (i.e. torturing) more than twenty people accused by the girl. Some of them confessed. In April seven of the accused were convicted of witchcraft and were hanged and burnt the following June. The girl herself was presumably an hysteric or an epileptic (one of the examining doctors suggested 'hypochondriac melancholy' until he was persuaded otherwise[22]), but she never had another fit after the case was over, and survived her experiences to achieve fame in another way by importing machines from Holland and initiating Paisley's thread-spinning industry.[23] *Witch-Craft Proven*, it can be assumed, reflected and expressed much of the discussion about witchcraft which was stirred up by this case.

The first four pages are devoted to proofs of the existence of the spirit world. Without spirits, according to the author, there would be no eternal death, no local place of punishment for the damned, nor 'any Heavenly Joy and Solace to be expected by the truly Godly'. In fact these opening pages show clearly why it was so firmly held that disbelief in witchcraft amounted to disbelief in God, and particularly disbelief in the God who adjusted the unfairness of life upon earth with appropriate rewards and punishments. The author argued that so many people could not be wrong on this point, and cited random historical examples of witchcraft to emphasise his point. He then went on to describe the witches' sabbat, combining in his account the fantasies of popular belief and theological speculation. He described the witches using 'the veryie Churches themselves' to meet in, the black candles burning about the pulpit, the devil himself handing out praise for the most 'horrible villanie'. When they are met, the author states that 'they be often richly feasted (tho' but in show) with meat, drink, and musick of the best, or with whatever else may ravish & captivat the senses'. Also 'by anointing themselves with certain oyntment, compounded at the command of the Devil, they are carried in Spirit through the Air, hither or thither, by one mean or another'.

These are interesting passages, for they show the author expounding a traditional view of witchcraft, but very worried about the physical possibility of many aspects of it. In a later passage Satan 'unmasks himself' 'as to present to the tormented (by a sort of corporeal representation) the persons of their tormentors in their various habits'. The author nevertheless felt able to give a classic account of the demonic pact:

> and when any to be entred, they be recommended, and presented by the Society, whereupon giving their right hand to Satan, and renouncing the Christian Faith and Sacraments, and upon transferring the Dominion of themselves, Soul and Bodie to him for ever, with a promise to worship Him as their Lord, they are sworn and solemnly admitted, and they have given to them one Hellish imp or moe, for their Titular and Gardian (by way of Spirit Familiar) to direct and guide them throughout all the passages of their time, whereby they perform afterwards all their lewd and wicked deeds.

But late medieval Scholasticism, in which context these formulations were first made,[24] was by the late seventeenth century beginning to lie very uneasily with current perceptions of the physical world; and this anxiety about the physical world is partly resolved by the author by an identification of witchcraft with physical pleasures. It is interesting, too, to speculate on the kind of effect which the picture of an elaborate ritual with the fascinating and ubiquitous black candles and their blue flames, might have had on a people denied almost all forms of visual aids to worship.

The author moves on to a description of the different kinds of witchcraft (mostly, in fact, of different kinds of fortune-telling), with frequent biblical references and recourse to Hebrew words. The writer then goes on to describe 'the several Parts and Species of Witchcraft', and to discuss why witchcraft is not worthwhile. Here again the worldly pleasures of witchcraft are admitted; but 'the momentary pleasure here, is [n]ever able to counter-balance the loss hereafter, the Devil seldom gratified the man but with the destruction of the Soul, hence it is that the truly Godly never trace these stops, for that they be ranked among the works of the flesh and all such be severely threatned by God, that he will judge them'.

Seven marks of witchcraft are then given. Four of these are more or less standard: the insensible mark, the inability to drown when thrown bound into water, the inability to shed tears, and the inability to repeat 'the heads of the Christian religion as they be summarily comprehended in the Decalogue, Lords Prayer, and Belief'. The second of these, however, the inability to drown, was an unusual ordeal for witchcraft in Scotland, and was more likely to have been gathered from the author's general reading than from experience. The other three marks of witchcraft, the fourth, sixth, and seventh in his list, are more curious and local. The writer describes 'the Basilisk, or Serpentine sight' (which is found, though infrequently, in Continental witch manuals), through which witches 'be endued to kill pyson, and destroy, what and whensoever they please, were it not that a Divine overruling providence doth often restrain and curb them'. The visible sign of the Basilisk sight was that the image of a person in the eyes of those possessing it is seen to be upside down. His sixth mark is a tendency to urinate on seeing salt being burnt because, the author thinks, it reminds the witch of brimstone and therefore of the 'horrible noise and Sulphurious burning that is abiding them in Hell'. His last mark is an idiosyncratic witch's smell. This smell 'neither flows from the nestiness of Cloaths, Vermine, or the like, but a contradistinct smell from any such thing, which may seem the more probable for that the five Senses being the Doors of the Soul whereby what is within is ordinarily disclosed, and the Devil being in Full Possession of their Souls, must needs emitte his own sent even that of the Pit'. The work ends with an injunction to put on all Spiritual Armour 'whereby we shall be enable to quench all the fiery Darts of the Devil'.

In general, the author reveals himself as one anxious to prove the existence of witchcraft by mentioning more or less everything he has ever heard about it, without much distinction between the possible and the absurd. The main points—the demonic pact, the witches' sabbat, the proofs of witchcraft—are transmitted more or less intact through two centuries. But the author makes more use than an earlier generation would have done of the distinction between body and soul as a means of explaining some of the more improbable activities of witches; and he reflects his Calvinist background in his vivid mythology of Heaven and Hell, his constant Biblical references, and his efforts to maintain the ultimate supremacy of God over all the activities of the devil. The devil and the witches are able to do many remarkable things, but it is always 'by permission'. A further touch which may be peculiar to Scottish writers and which also occurs in *The Tryal of Witchcraft* is the fairly frequent use of the words 'league' and 'covenant' for the demonic pact. Such words would have emotional overtones in a Scotland where the Solemn League and Covenant was a fairly recent memory that they could not be expected to have elsewhere.

The author of *Witch-Craft Proven* can be assumed to have an educational and intellectual equipment fairly typical of a Presbyterian minister of his time. He may have been slightly more learned than average—the very fact of his writing a book suggests this; he may have been one of the 'topping professors' of whom John Bell of the manuscript 'Discourse of Witchcraft' speaks so scathingly. But so far as direct sources go, there are very few references in *Witch-Craft Proven* to any authorities other than the Bible. The author does say tantalisingly that he, 'will give some vive and shrewd Marks, and some unquestionable tokens, as they be recorded in the most approven Authors, how and by what means a Witch (in League, and Covenant with the Devil) may be decerned to be so', but he gives no further indication who these 'approven Authors' might be.

He gives some historical as well as Biblical examples as proof of the existence of witchcraft, but the only non-biblical scholastic references he makes are to a Latin oracle, and, somewhat surprisingly, to the twelfth-century Spanish Rabbi, Moses Maimonides. The Latin oracle he cites when discussing the powers of the devil: 'Satan either suggested to them, that which was desired to be known, or otherwayes by crafty and ambiguous answeres concealed his ignorance of that he could not reveal as by these following Oracles appear,

> Aio te Æacide, Romanos vincere posse,
> Craesus Chalim penetrans magnum pervertet opum vim.'

The passage is in fact a misquotation from Cicero's *De Divinatione*.[25] He clearly did not have the work to hand, and may well have borrowed it from some other treatise.

A work by Maimonides (1131–1204), was *Witch-Craft Proven*'s other non-biblical reference. Maimonides was a prolific author on all branches of knowledge, and was the compiler and commentator on a complete code of Jewish law. His *De Idolatria Liber* was cited here in a discussion of the meaning of some Biblical words. There may have been an English edition current in the seventeenth century, since the author refers to the work in English, but I have not been able to trace one. It seems more likely, in fact, that his Latin, or possibly even his Hebrew, were up to extracting this information from the Hebrew and Latin edition of *De Idolatria* published in Amsterdam in 1641.[26] Copies of this and of the 1668 edition were available in Scotland at the time. Even more persuasively the reference to Saul is to be found not in Maimonides's text, but in the Latin commentary by Dionysius Vossius found in this edition.[27]

Witch-Craft Proven is not in fact over-laden with learning. The author's most frequent references are to the Bible—and therefore available for supportive checking to the majority of his readers. But his short treatise owes very much less to the Bible and Biblical ideas than do the surviving witchcraft sermons of the 1697 witch hunt.[28] The 'Lover of the Truth' dwells with evident pleasure on traditional and spectacular forms of witchcraft, and hints at the obscene. More than the rest of the Bargarron witch literature, *Witch-Craft Proven* reveals the fascination which witchcraft had for the godly as well as for the ungodly, and suggests the excitement which the Paisley trial injected into the drab and monotonous lives of the local inhabitants.

The second tract, *The Tryal of Witchcraft*, appears to be the last work of serious demonology (as opposed to chapbook horror stories, which were beginning to increase in number) to be produced in Scotland before the death penalty for witchcraft was abolished in 1736. It was published anonymously, probably in Glasgow, in 1705, and the copy in the National Library of Scotland appears to be the only one known.

The Tryal of Witchcraft opens with a 'Letter from a Friend', asking for illumination on three points: how you can be certain that a particular disease has been inflicted by witchcraft, how to cure the bewitched, and how in general witchcraft can be proved. John Bell thought this a hard task. His work lacks the confidence found in the 1697 tract.

He divides his twenty-three-page book into three sections. In the first he discusses how one can know that one is bewitched, and warns against attributing to witchcraft what may have had some natural cause. He pointed out that a great many very strange diseases, which the unenlightened might wish to attribute to witchcraft, did in fact have natural explanations, and cites some examples. In order to be quite certain that the disease has been inflicted by witchcraft it must be shown to be one which can have no natural explanation. Examples of these are diseases for which renowned physicians can find no ordinary cause, such as sudden swellings, fits, vomitings of strange objects, and paralysis.

His attitude, then, was an empirical one. He accepted the findings of scientists so far as he knew them, which seems to have been only up to about fifty years before his own birth. Part of the difficulty, certainly, was that neither he nor his contemporaries in Scotland knew much about the physical manifestations of the phenomenon we now call hysteria. Also Bell gives a little less weight than seems reasonable to the possibility of deception in the supposed victim of witchcraft.

The second section is devoted to the problem of how the bewitched can be helped out of their bewitched state. This was always an acute problem in Scotland, especially for the clergy, since the old remedy of exorcism was not allowed. As is suggested by an earlier Scottish writer, Sir George Mackenzie, in his defence of an accused witch,[29] the original spell-binder was often appealed to to remove the spell. This, it was conceded, was legitimate provided that a new application to the devil was not involved. John Bell, as a convinced Calvinist, rejects all these traditional devices out of hand, and goes to some length to explain the futility of using the touch of the witch as a cure. In much the same terms as the pre-Scholastic theologians he says that, 'The best means is fasting and prayer, for God only can best free us from Divels, and in the use of his means alone it is, that we are to expect a blessing; So that if we would prevent Witches, and whatever else the Devil can do, let us always rely on God, who hath promised to such, that he will cover them under his wings.'

In the third and longest section of his tract, Bell deals with the real proofs and presumptions of witchcraft. This part he begins dramatically, with his habitually curious syntax: 'Great is the Mystery of iniquity, and its hard to discover the Members of that Kingdom and darkness, where the king is Satan, the fiery Dragon, the Roaring Lyon, and deceiver of the Nations; and where the subjects are faggots of hell, Deceivers and deceived. . . .'

The following, he wrote, are not proofs, but only presumptions of witchcraft: cursing and maledictions with misfortune following those who were cursed, unsolicited visitations on the bewitched by a suspected person, and the naming of the witch by the bewitched. Such things may be mere coincidences, and 'the devil may lie'. When he calls these but presumptions, 'in so doing,' he says, 'I say no other than what pious and learned Writers on this head have spoken, who withal are of opinion (as I also am) that such pregnant and shrewd presumptions sufficiently witnessed are just cause of imprisonment, and are worthy (after tryal) of most severe and condign punishment, but ere the life can be taken away from them, it will perhaps be found needful, that a league with the Devil be once proven.'

On the diabolic pact, which he thus established as the central feature of witchcraft, he made some comments. In the first place, the devil only seeks out for his followers those whom he finds 'some way prepar'd either by impenitency and obduredness, distemperedness of passion, prophaneness, and the like: for he will not willingly ataque and surprize, where he thinks not to gain ground'. In the second place, he appears to his intended victims in a guise which will impress them according to their station in life. And in the third place, Satan promises great things to his witches, and then deserts them when they need help; and fourthly, the covenant once made, 'he proceeds to confirm it, which (some say) must be done by blood: therefore, some offer him a Sacrifice; perhaps of a cat, dog, &c.' The sucking of blood is followed by the bestowal of the devil's mark and the acquisition of a familiar spirit.

The methods of actually proving the demonic pact are the discovery of the devil's mark; the witches' own boasting and confessions, 'as also, their speaking of transportation from home to forraign places'; witches' deeds: 'as their feeding creatures secretly, which some say they send on their errands; their making of pictures [i.e. wax images]; giving anything to any Man which causes pains or death'; and also the confession of fellow witches 'especially if appearing penitent'.

The confession of a 'white witch' will also count against them. The white witches are known as 'healers' or 'blessers', but are themselves witches and in league with the devil. A further proof of witchcraft is what Bell calls a 'Divine witness'; this occurs when the accused witches 'pray for a token from God of displeasure against them if they be guilty, and it accordingly falls out'. This is a rather uncommon variant on the trial by ordeal. The last and most important proof of witchcraft is the confession of the witch herself.

Bell ends with a plea that there be not bestowed on him the dangerous stigma of originality: 'but now Sir, after all that is said, I desire not to be so understood, as if hereby I design'd to force any to a complyance with the Conclusions already laid down, further than the reasons brought by grave Authors already hinted will perswade.'

In fact, John Bell is assiduous in his references to authorities, and gives a wider range of sources than was normal for a clerical writer. There are the usual Biblical allusions, and the Faust story, the only non-biblical allusion in common with *Witch-Craft Proven*, is referred to; but the other references are nearly all to various Scottish and English divines (mostly English). It is significant, however, that none of these English works are contemporary, or even near contemporary, except for a back number of the *Athenian Mercury* for 1690. Apart from this, they range from an English witch tract of 1593 to Richard Bernard's *Guide to Grand Jury Men* of 1627. And it would have been hard to find an intelligent man in England in 1705 to accept the substance of any of these works. The English had hanged their last witch when Bell was six years old.

Nearly all demonologists made routine complaints about the prevalence of scepticism, but Bell seems less worried about this than most. He is, or appears to be, totally unaware of the intellectual isolation of his position, and does not seem to realise that his authorities, though many of them were non-Scottish, would no longer be regarded as authorities anywhere outside Scotland, except possibly in some non-conformist groups in England. Bell was still convinced that examples and references from any period of history would prove his points in 1705. He asks us to consider especially 'how much light may be borrowed from the writings of learned men both of old and of late, [and] the direful experience of former ages, as well as of this'.

His first references are given when he is discussing the list of diseases which, though curious, cannot be said to have been caused by witchcraft:

> . . . famous writers instancing in their books many strange and wonderful diseases, yet no work of witchcraft, as are the Apoplexy, Carum, Catelepis, Cramp, with many more mentioned by Dr. Cotta in his Empericks and Dr. Mason in his practice of philosophy and R. Bernard in his Guide to Grand Jury Men. All which authors do yet still affirm these to proceed from natural causes, and yet to be curable by natural remedies; tho' scarce would a common person look on the party thus distempered, without concluding witchcraft to be there.

Dr John Cotta (1575?–1650) was the author of *A True Discovery of the Empiricks with the Fugitive Physition and Quicksalver, who Display their banner upon Posts; whereby His Majestie's Subjects are not only deceived, but greatly endangered in the Health of their Bodies*. This was published in London in 1617, but was in fact simply the remaindered copies (with a new title-page) of an unsuccessful work of 1612.[30] Cotta also published a year earlier, in 1616, *The Triall of Witchcraft, showing the true Methode of the Discovery with a Confutation of Erroneous Ways*, which ran to a second edition in 1625 under the title of *The Infallible True, and Assured Witch*. It seems unlikely that Bell did not know of the existence of this work, which was certainly that by which Cotta made his name in England. It is just conceivable that he did not mention it in order to avoid drawing attention to the fact that the title of his own work was not original; but this is not very likely, as Bell laid no claims to originality, and in fact took pains to disclaim it.

Dr Mason and his *Practice of Philosophy* are untraced at the time of writing. Richard Bernard's *Guide to Grand Jury Men*[31] is, however, one of the English witchcraft classics. Bernard, who lived from 1568 to 1641, was a Puritan who conformed. There was a pamphlet warfare between him and the Separatists over this, but in fact he remained Puritan in his doctrine, and in his parish of Barcome he was indulged by his diocese in his objection to 'ceremonies' in public worship. He was involved from time to time in various cases of attempted exorcism. Bell cites him four times in *The Tryal of Witchcraft*. The first is that just quoted; the second occasion is in his consideration of the question whether a witch can take off a spell by her own touch:

> Their touching is an uncertain thing, because (as writers on this head have sufficiently instructed) by Touching they even sometimes bewitch the afflicted party. Thus Daneaus in Dialogis suis de Sortiariis, witnesseth, that a Witch touched but the breasts of a woman that gave suck, and her milk dried up: and the forcited Rector of Barcomb, R. Bernard reports of one Mary Suton a Bedfordshire Witch, that having but touched the neck of one Mr. Engers servants with her finger, he was presently after her departure miserably vexed, how then can their touch cure the diseased?

What Bernard wrote was

> A witch touched but the brests of a woman that gave sucke, and dryed up her milke; this Daneus witnesseth. Mary Sutton, a Bedfordshire Witch did but touche the necke of one Mr. Engars servants only with her finger, and he was presently after her departure miserable vexed.[32]

In view of the relative position of the reference to Daneus in these passages, and since this is the only mention Bell makes of Daneus, it seems probable that he had not actually read Daneus's tract.[33] In fact Daneus, a French Protestant demonologist, seems to have been curiously unread in Scotland, considering that he was a fellow Calvinist.

Bell also refers to the *Guide to Grand Jury Men* in a description of the 'Grand Witch Lewis Guasfridus', a rich and learn'd Priest, as Bernard calls him,[34] and again in giving examples of the way in which the devil maltreats his followers: '... the Devil ... designs violence unto them, upon their refusing to do as he bids them, as Bernard reports he did to old Dembdike, whom he pusht into a Ditch, because she would not go help Chattox, another witch, (whom she could not abide) to make Pictures. The same authors says, the Devil came sometimes to Witch Chattox gaping upon her in the Form of a Beare, with open mouth as if he could have worried her.'[35]

Bell's next reference is to the 'holy and learn'd Mr Durham', who is said to have observed that 'the Devil cannot create any inward species of representation, this being a work of omnipotence'. 'Despite this', wrote Bell, 'God permitting him; he working upon what is already within the person may misrepresent objects, by disturbing inwardlie the faculties.' 'Mr Durham', who is also quoted on the title-page, was James Durham (1622–58), a Covenanting preacher famous for his piety and preaching. His many volumes of sermons were mostly published posthumously, and he seems to have had a considerable vogue.[36]

Bell also gives one reference to William Perkins, whose works he claimed to have studied at university.[37] Bell wrote that, 'Mr Perkins, in his discourse of Witchcraft, chap 2 Explains this while he says that when a person desires in heart to have such or such a thing effected by superstitious forms, &c And the Devil consents thereunto, if he then do the business, there is a Secret compact'.[38]

An earlier English witch tract of the popular type—as opposed to the more formal demonological treatise—also provided Bell with material. As an example of 'Divine witness', he refers to one 'Mother Samual the Warboys Witch that tormented Mr Throgmortons children, who by bitter curses on herself if she were guilty: presently her Chin did bleed, the place (as afterwards she confest) where the Spirits did Suck Blood'.[39]

The most recent work to which Bell referred was *The Athenian Mercury*,[40] a periodical which consisted mainly of miscellaneous information and discussion of assorted topics. Bell enlisted its support: 'Some define a witch to be such as do act beyond the ordinary power of Nature, by the help of wicked Spirits. Athen. Merc. V.I. N.3. Q.6.' This 'Question 6' was 'Whether there be witches, and what good books have been written on that Subject?' The answer: 'I answer there are Witches, unless we can suppose both God and Man would conspire to deceive us; the Good Books written on that Subject, are the Holy Bible, and the Histories of all Nations. To be more explicit: by witches we mean such as act beyond the ordinary Power of Nature, by the Help of wicked Spirits: the Proof whereof being matter of fact must rely wholly on the Credibility of the Evidence: Gods authority is unquestionable: Thou shalt not suffer a Witch to live.'

This then is the 'scholarship' which went into *The Tryal of Witchcraft*. The majority of the references are to English Puritan writers. The interesting fact is that although Bell seldom swerves from his allegiance to writers of his own theological party, he ends up by producing a doctrine of witchcraft which, in its essentials, is that formulated by the pre-Reformation theologians. According to Bell, 'three things concur to the bewitching of a Person: viz, a Divine permission, a Devilish operation, or the evil Spirits working; and lastly, the Witches consent'. And according to the *Malleus Maleficarum*, 'The three necessary concomitants of witchcraft ... are the Devil, a witch, and the permission of Almighty God'.[41]

It is not clear just how Bell came by his formulation, but it is unmistakable: here in the eighteenth century, at the birth of the age of reason, we find a clear echo of fifteenth-century Scholasticism.

Notes

1. *Witch-Craft Proven, Arreign'd and Condemn'd in its Professors, Professions, and Marks, by diverse pungent, and convincing Arguments, excerpted forth of the most Authentick Authors, Divine and humane, Ancient and Modern,* by a Lover of the Truth, Glasgow, 1697.
2. *The Tryal of Witchcraft; or, Witchcraft Arraign'd and Condemn'd in Some Answeres to a few Questions anent Witches and Witchcraft, Wherein is shewed, how to know if one be a Witch, as also when one is bewitched; with some Observation upon the Witches Mark, their compact with the Devil, the White Witches, &c.* Anon., n.p., n.d., but probably John Bell, Glasgow, 1705.
3. 'The Most Memorable passages of the Life and Times of Mr J.B. written by Himself, 1706.' (71 pages 4to) Wodrow MSS. LXXXII, National Library of Scotland.
4. Edinburgh, 1866; Vol. I, Part I, pp. 212, 335.
5. Wodrow MSS, LXXXII, p. 34.
6. *Ibid.*, p. 35.
7. *Ibid.*, p. 30.
8. *Ibid.*, p.31.
9. In a collection of tracts in the National Library of Scotland, *Miscellaneous*, vol. 4, no. 64.
10. Glasgow and London, 1884.
11. *Op. cit.*, p. 335.
12. 5 vols, Bloomington, 1934, vol. I, p. 374: H.46 [John Bell] *An Ingenious and Scientific discourse of Witchcraft,* 1705.
13. William Cobbett, *State Trials,* London, 1811, vol. XI, p. 1400.
14. David Laing, MS notes in Edinburgh University Library.
15. Edinburgh, 1899, p. 61.
16. According to the late Mr Clifford Dobb, the Keeper of the Special Collections in Glasgow University Library, who until his death had been working on the Ferguson MSS. It is still possible that further work on these MSS may produce more definite information about this tract.
17. E.g. 'The word *Mecashepha* mentioned before is of the feominine gender, either for that the woman was by Satan first deceived, or for that Sex is more readily circumvented.' *Witch-Craft Proven,* p. 12.
18. C. K. Sharpe, *A Historical Account of the Belief in Witchcraft in Scotland,* London, 1884, p. 173.
19. William Wiseman, *Third Statistical Account of Scotland,* East Lothian volume, Edinburgh, 1953, p. 229.
20. *Witch-Craft Proven,* 1697, Glasgow University Library, Al. c. 25. See H. G. Aldis, *List of Books Printed in Scotland before 1700,* Edinburgh, 1904.
21. See *A History of the Witches of Renfrewshire burnt on the Gallow-green of Paisley,*

ed. John Millar, Paisley, 1809, *passim*. There was also much interest outside the area, as is indicated in the publication of *Relation of the Diabolical Practice of above Twenty Wizards and Witches of the Sheriffdom of Renfrew*, London, 1697.
22 *A History of the Witches of Renfrewshire*, p. 118.
23 *Scottish Historical Review*, vol. 7, 1910, pp. 390–1.
24 See H. R. Trevor-Roper, *The European Witch-Craze of the 16th and 17th Centuries*, Harmondsworth, 1969, chapter 3; and Norman Cohn, *Europe's Inner Demons*, 1975, for accounts of the development of the witch theory.
25 *De Divinatione*, II, 56:

> Aio te Aecida, Romanos vincere posse,
> Croaesus Halym penetrans magnam pervertet opum vim.

26 *R. Moses Maemonidae de Idololatria Liber, cum interpretatione Latin & Notis Dionysii Vossii*, Amsterdam, 1641.
27 *Ed. cit.*, p. 75.
28 See Christina Larner, 'Scottish Demonology in the Sixteenth and Seventeenth Centuries' (unpublished PhD thesis in Edinburgh University Library), 1962, pp. 177–206.
29 *Pleadings in Some Remarkable Cases*, Edinburgh 1672, p. 185.
30 This was *A Short Discoverie of the Unobserved Dangers of Severall Sorts of Ignorant and Unconsiderate Practisers of Physicke in England, profitable not only for the Deceivd Multitude and Easie for their Meane Capacities, but raising Reformed and More Advised Thoughts in the Best Understandings: with Directions for the Safest Election of a Physition in necessitie*, London, 1612.
31 *A Guide to Grand Jury Men, divided into two books. In the First, is the Authors best advice to them what to doe, before they bring in a Billa vera in cases of Witchcraft, with a Christian Direction to such as are too much given up on every crosse to think themselves bewitched. In the Second, is a Treatise touching Witches good and bad, how they may bee knowne, evicted and condemned with many particulars tending thereunto*, London, 1627. The second edition, from which the quotations below are given, was published London, 1630. This first reference by John Bell was to Book I, chap. II: 'That strange diseases may happen from onely naturall causes and neither be wroght by Divels nor Witches, and how to be discerned' (p. 11).
32 *A Guide to Grand Jury Men*, Book II, chap. XIII, pp. 174–5.
33 *De Veneficis quos olim Sortilegos, nunc autem vulgo Sortiarios Dialogus*, Geneva, 1574.

> *Antonius:* Earum vero rerum exempla mihi alique proferit, Theophile.
> *Theophilus:* Faciam. Ac primum eos in homines quasdam certo certius est. Id enim quotidie fieri cernimus. Quosdam enim venenis auis interficiunt: alios lauquentes & tabidos reddunt. Vidi quo nutricium mammas veneo & solo manus attactu lacte exhausissent & exsicca sunt. (Caput III, p. 51).

34 'To Gaufredy, a Priest, one of some learning and wealth, hee appeareth in some human shape.' *Guide to Grand Jury Men*, Book II, chap. IV, p. 104.

35 'He will threaten the Witch, and offer some violence unto her, if she will not doe what he could have her, as the spirit did old Dembdike, who shoved and pushed her into a ditch, because she would not goe and help Chattox the witch (whom Dembdike could not abide) to make pictures. So Chattox spirit thred her down, because when he appeared, shee would not speake unto him.' *Guide to Grand Jury Men*, Book II, chap. VI, p. 161.
36 *Dictionary of National Biography.*
37 Wodrow MSS, LXXXII.
38 William Perkins, *Discourse of the Damned Art of Witchcraft*, Cambridge, 1608. In chapter II, Perkins deals in detail with the question of 'compact', explicit and implicit.
39 *The most strange and admirable discoverie of the three Witches of Warboys arraigned, convicted and executed at the last Assises at Huntingdon for the bewitching of the five daughters of Robert Throckmorton Esquier, and divers other persons, with sundrie Divelish and grivous torments And also for the bewitching to death of the Lady Crumwell, the like hath not bene heard of in this age*, London, 1593. The references in *The Tryal of Witchcraft* are to f. C.II and J.I.
40 *The Athenian Mercury: Resolving WEEKLY all the most Nice and Curious Questions Propose'd by the INGENIUS*, no. 3, Tuesday, 31 March 1680.
41 Jakob Sprenger *Malleus Maleficarum*, trans. Montague Summers, London, 1928, p. 1.

EPILOGUE:

THE DESIDERATA OF DISBELIEF

Sydney Anglo

Scholars concerned with the witch persecution of the Middle Ages and the Renaissance have pondered the reasons both for its evolution and decay. Deep-rooted psychological pressures; seismic disturbances of the 'social structure'; ideological tensions; the growth of technology; the development of scientific rationalism; and a changing 'world-view': all these have been postulated. And they all have some validity, though, in themselves, they do not constitute a sufficient answer to the question raised implicitly and explicitly throughout this volume. Since all those who were agreed on the reality of witchcraft and the need for persecution rested their case—in the last resort—upon hallowed authority, how was it possible to subvert that authority? What were the desiderata of disbelief? The Scriptures, patristics, classical mythology, medieval science, and the evidence of confessions, had all to lose their cogency in debate. The mere accumulation of such material had, somehow, to lose respectability as a dialectical procedure. How this came about—how thinking men moved from the authoritative to the analytical and experimental mode of argument—is a problem which would require several volumes of elucidation; and it is certainly beyond the scope of this collection of independent essays in the literature of witchcraft. One thing, however, is clear. For such a revolution to take place, thinkers had no longer to be overawed by the massive authorities of the past. They had to recognise that the ambiguities, inconsistencies, and intrinsic illogicalities of these bastions of belief could no longer support the edifice of persecution. And they had, above all, to accept the force of these words written by Reginald Scot in 1584:

> Howbeit, how ancient so ever this barbarous conceipt of witches omnipotencie is, truth must not be measured by time: for everie old

opinion is not sound. Veritie is not impaired, how long so ever it be suppressed; but is to be searched out, in how darke a corner so ever it lie hidden: for it is not like a cup of ale, that may be broched too rathe. Finallie, time bewraieth old errors, & disovereth new matters of truth.

INDEX

Aaron, 111, 123
Abbott, archbishop, 172
Aberdeen witch trials, 163
Abraham, 98
Adam, 89
Ady, Thomas, 173
Aeromancy, 43
Agrippa, Henry Cornelius, 13–14, 59, 65, 71–2, 73 n16, 74 n17, n22, 75 n35, 87, 121, 125, 131–2, 139 n53
Aiken, Margaret, 162
Albertus Magnus, 12, 65
Albigensians, 39
Alchemy, 11, 13, 124, 131
Alciato, Andrea, 40, 41, 69, 186
Alcoranus Franciscanorum, 130–1
Amazons, 176
America, witchcraft in, 97, 202–26
Anania, Lorenzo, 108, 126
Angel, guardian, 86
Angels, 4–6, 12–13, 40, 57, 81, 83–8, 94, 106, 109, 119, 124, 126–7, 129, 131, 133, 172, 186, 210
Ann, Queen, 163
Apollo, 86; oracle of, 119
Apollonius Rhodius, 37
Apostasy, 23–4, 82, 86
Apparitions, 184, 197
Apuleius, 37–8, 129
Aquinas, St Thomas, 18, 63, 91, 98, 175
Archers, magicians, 92
Aristotelianism, 91, 92

Aristotle, 10, 18, 19, 40, 42, 43, 84
Arreioúgue d'Ascain, Catherine d', 187
Asclepius, 11, 104 n47
Aspilecute, Marie d', 187
Astrology, 4, 5, 11, 12, 13, 15, 43, 84, 88, 95, 121, 130, 131, 134, 139 n53, 146, 199 n39
Atheism, 8, 84, 133
Athenian Mercury, 239, 242
Augury, 120–1; *see also* Prophecy
Augustine, St, 8, 11, 18, 55, 62, 69, 98, 133, 134, 174
Autistic behaviour, 68
Aventon, Monsieur d', 78
Azande, 33, 146, 151

Bacon, Francis, 176
Baissac, Jules, 190
Balaam, 7
Balak, 7
Baptism, 61, 161, 191
Barbarelli, Domenica, 45
Barrow, Henry, 141
Basle, 53
Bayonne, 182, 191; Bishop of, 194
Becon, Thomas, 131
Behemoth, 6, 95
Beiligh Abbey, 142
Belial, 213
Bell, John, of Gladsmuir, 227f
Bell, John, of Haddington, 230
Bellano, 47
Bellarmine, 164

INDEX

Bells, baptism of, 55, 65
Benandanti, 48–9
Benvegnuda, 46–7
Berge, Peter van den, 73 n6
Bernard, Richard, 239–41
Bexley, 119
Bishop, Bridget, 213
Black Mass, 192, 196
Boccaccio, 196
Bodin, Jean, 2, 10, 13, 14, 28, 30 n30, 31 n41, 53, 71, 72 n6, 73 n17, 74 n23, n24, 75 n33, 76–105, 108, 113, 116, 118, 119, 122, 166, 170, 171, 173, 177, 183, 185, 186, 187, 199 n30; *Démonomanie*, 2, 10, 53, 71, 76–105, 170, 184; *Heptaplomeres*, 83, 87, 89, 90, 93, 98, 102, 104 n61; *Methodus*, 79, 81, 82, 86, 89, 91, 93; *Oratio*, 82; *Paradoxon*, 93; *Réponse*, 79–80, 93, 101; *République*, 71, 79–82, 89, 93, 101–2; *Theatrum naturae*, 88–9, 91, 93
Boguet, Henri, 1, 3, 5, 6, 13, 28, 169, 183, 185, 187, 190
Boiastuau, 95, 104 n49
Bordelon, Laurent, 192, 197
Borie, François de la, 187
Bosch, Hieronymous, 38
Bowes, Robert, 160, 161
Brain function, 16
Brandon, juggler, 123
Brattle, Thomas, 205–6
Breno, 44, 46
Briscoe, Robert, 142
Broome, Richard, 176
Broughton (Lanarkshire), 228
Brownists, 141
Bruno, Giordano, 33
Bungay, mother, 128
Burckhardt, Jacob, 32–4, 39, 48
Burghley, Lord, 141
Burroughs, George, 208, 211–13
Bury St Edmund's trial, 208
Butterfield, Sir Herbert, 32

Cabbala, 13, 59, 84, 87, 88, 89, 90, 91, 121, 131
Caesarius of Heisterbach, 12
Calef, Robert, 204, 206–7
Calfhill, James, 9
Calvin, 117, 130, 131, 133
Campani, Guglielmo, 46
Canon Episcopi, 41, 91, 115, 169, 184, 186, 191
Canonical purgation, 28
Cardano, Girolamo, 33, 41, 45, 47, 48, 68, 74 n17, 198 n11, 200 n39
Carrier, Martha, 212
Cascini, Samuele da, 40, 41
Catholic Church, magic of, 8–9, 54, 55, 59, 65, 109, 110, 119, 122, 125, 128, 131, 132
Catholic saints, 55, 57, 87, 119, 128, 131, 191
Cato, 18
Cecil, Robert, 164
Chaldea, 10
Charity, 79, 80–1, 114, 151–2
Chasaph, 118
Chaucer, 116
Chaundler, Alice, 142, 143
Chaundler, John, 143
Chelmsford, 140
Chiromancy, 43
Christ, 7, 9, 10, 36, 54, 56, 57, 59, 63, 66, 83, 87, 110, 117, 120, 125, 129, 131, 171, 212
Christ's College, Cambridge, 140
Chrysostom, 18
Cicero, 18, 120–30, 236
Circe, 10, 37, 42, 43, 117, 137 n17
Claverhouse, 215
Clavicula Salomonis, 125
Clermont, Collège de, 183
Cohn, Norman, 177
Colbert, 197
Como, Bernardo da, 39, 44
Confessions, 1, 13, 24f, 44–6, 47, 68,

250

INDEX

98, 109, 114–15, 130, 159, 168, 169, 171, 177, 205, 239, 246
Confirmation, 131
Conjurations, 109, 125, 168
Correggio, 38
Cotta, John, 163, 240
Cotton family, 204
Counter-maleficia, 79, 93, 94, 96
Cowper, Francis, 142
Cowper, Mary, 142
Crane, Hart, 221
Cunning folk, 4, 46, 145, 147, 148
Cyrano de Bergerac, 61

Daemon, 38, 83
Dancing, 45, 192, 195
Daneau, Lambert, 90, 108, 169, 241
D'Aubigné, 95
David, 11, 128
Davies, R. Trevor, 163
Death penalty, 24, 33, 67, 70, 99, 147, 185, 210, 231
Dee, John, 142
Delacroix, F., 190
Delphos, 120
Delrio, Martin, 28, 183, 185, 186, 187, 190, 199 n30
Delusion, *see* Fantasy
Demoniac, *see* Possession
Demons, 4–6, 8, 12–14, 17, 19, 38, 40, 56–7, 81, 83–91, 93–4, 106, 109–11, 116, 124, 126–7, 131–4, 144, 169, 171–2, 186f, 210–11; *see also* Gods of the Gentiles
Des Cars, Charles (Bishop of Langres), 95
Descartes, 73 n10
Des Periers, Bonaventure, 196
Devil, the, 5–8, 38, 49, 56, 61, 63, 106, 110–12, 117, 129, 158, 175, 189, 191–2, 209, 212, 233–4; deceits of, 54f, 86, 91, 94, 96; powers of, 9, 15–16, 20–2, 36, 54f, 70, 126, 132, 146, 148–9, 168, 172,

182; *see also* Pact with the Devil; Witch mark
Devil-worship, 38–9, 43, 47–9, 53–5, 158, 177
Diana, 38, 41, 45, 48, 49
Dionysius, the Pseudo-Areopagite, 18
Disease, 15, 16, 26, 116, 129, 131, 237, 240
Disorder, *see* Perversity
Dittays, 159, 160, 163, 166, 175
Divination, *see* Prophecy
Dodo, Vincenzo, 39
Dominicans, 27, 39
Dordach, 191
Dossi, Dosso, 37–8
Double truth, 133–5
Dreams, 43, 48, 120, 130, 169
Dry Drayton, 140
Du Bartas, 95
Duncan, Gillis, 159
Dundee, 161
Durham, James, 241–2

Eastwood, John, 143
Egypt, Egyptians, 10, 11, 57, 58, 60
Elich, Phillip, 190
Eliot, T. S., 202–3, 221
Elymas, 53
Enchantment, 121–2
Endor, witch of, 7, 8, 39, 56, 110, 111, 118–19, 132, 136 n9, 172
England, witch trials in, 107–8
Erasmus, 43, 69, 72, 73 n6, 75 n35
Erastus, 54, 71, 74 n24, 75 n33, 78, 108
Ergotism, 68
Espagnet, Jean d', 182–3, 184, 198 n4
Essex, witchcraft in, 140f
Essex divorce case, 172
Esty, Mary, 206, 212
Eugenius IV, 33
Eustathius of Antioch, 8
Eve, 16, 54
Evil, 20, 22, 150

INDEX

Evil eye, 23, 34, 235
Exorcism, 24, 55f, 64f, 67, 86, 93, 96, 97, 99, 121, 163, 238

Fairies, 168, 171
Fantasy and imagination, 16, 36, 41, 42–3, 56, 58, 61–2, 71, 111, 127–8, 130, 132, 168, 169, 170, 171, 173, 186
Fascination, 58
Fathers of the Church, see Patristics
Faust, 239
Faye, Barthélémy, 81
Ferguson, John, 230
Ferrara, 37, 38, 51 n35
Ficino, Marsilio, 11, 13, 32, 65
Filmer, Sir Robert, 173
Fincelius, 91
Florence, 49
Folk medicine, 47, 145, 239
Fontenay, 157
Fortune-telling, see Prophecy
Foster, John, 211
Foxe, John, 167
France, witchcraft in, 95, 97
Fraticelli, 40, 45
Free will, 15, 21–2
Friuli, 48
Frost, Robert, 217
Fuchsius, Leonardus, 116
Fuller, Thomas, 162

Garin, Eugenio, 32–3
Gaufridi, Louis, 241
Geneva, 131
Geographical influence, 190
Geomancy, 43
German law, 67
Germany, witch trials in, 78
Gerson, Jean, 9
Gifford, George, 140–53, 163
Gladsmuir (East Lothian), 228
Glamours, see Fantasy
Glanvil, Joseph, 210

Glover, Mary, 162
God: law of, 90, 93, 95, 98, 99f; permission of, 15, 20–2, 64, 67, 70, 91, 146, 148, 149, 192, 212, 235, 242
Gods of the Gentiles, 7, 11, 38, 43, 49, 55, 95, 128, 189
Goodfellow, Robin, 48, 119
Goodman, Godfrey, 156
Gothic movement, 216
Greece, 58
Greenwood, John, 141
Gregory of Nyssa, 8
Gregory the Great, 18
Grillandi, Paolo de, 47, 69, 90, 187, 190, 192
Guibelet, Jourdain, 196
Gunpowder Plot, 165
Gunter, Ann, 162

Habar, 121–2
Habbakuk, 62, 173
Haguenone, 78
Hale, Sir Matthew, 208
Hallowell, A. I., 152
Hallucinations, 120, 133
Ham, 55
Hamelin, Pied Piper of, 56
Hampton Court Conference, 165, 167
Harrington, Sir James, 164
Harsnett, Samuel, 163
Hart Hall, Oxford, 106, 140
Hartumim, 122–4
Harvey, Gabriel, 171
Harvillier, Jeanne, 76f
Hatfield Peveral, 142
Hathorne, judge, 218
Hauduch, Bertrand de, 187
Hawthorne, Nathaniel, 216–18, 223
Haydock, Richard, 162
Hecate, 37
Hemmingsen, Niels, 108, 157, 159
Henri IV, 182
Henry, Prince, 162

INDEX

Henry VIII, 119
Heresy, heretics, 13, 15, 24–7, 39–41, 49, 68–9, 81–2, 100, 185, 201 n70
Hermes Trismegistus, 11, 33, 58
Hermeticism, 57–9, 65, 74 n24, 83, 84, 87, 91, 95, 104 n47
Heywood, Thomas, 176
Hippolytus, 130
Hobgoblin, 119
Hogg, James, 215
Holland, Henry, 9, 168–9
Holmes, T. J., 208
Holy Communion, 191
Holy Water, 56, 65, 96, 121, 125
Homer, 10, 36–7, 121
Hooper, John, 30 n12
Horace, 122
Howard, Henry, 109
Hugh of St Victor, 34
Humanists, humanism, 32f
Hume, David, 227
Hunt, Edmund, 142
Hussites, 49
Hydromancy, 43, 46
Hysteria, 64, 104 n62, 233, 237

Iamblicus, 33
Iconoclasm, 130–1
Idolatry, 86, 96, 99; *see also* Gods of the Gentiles
Iidoni, 124–5
Illusion, *see* Fantasy
Incantations, 38
Inconstancy, 188f
Incubi, *see* Demons
Innocent VIII, 14, 33, 50
Innsbruck, 19
Inquisition, 47, 49–50, 109, 194
Insanity, 13, 15–16, 117, 119, 127, 129–31, 171; *see also* Melancholia
Invocation, 89
Isaac, 98
Isidore of Seville, 18
Italy, witchcraft in, 32–52

Jacob, 7
Jacquier, Nicolas, 200 n53
Jacquot, Jean, vii
James I, 2, 156–77
Jason, 37
Jerome, St, 18
Jerusalem, 36
Jesuits, 164, 183
Jewel, John, bishop, 167
Jews, 39, 81–2, 121
Job, 117
Johnston, Robert, 157
Jones, Ernest, 3
Jonson, Ben, 163–4
Joseph, 7
Judaism, 80, 82–7, 89, 91, 93, 96, 102
Judges in witch trials, 19, 23f, 70, 78, 81, 98f, 107, 108f, 166, 177, 185f, 209f, 211
Juggling tricks, 118, 123–4, 131, 172
Julius II, 33
Justin Martyr, 8, 44

Kasam, 120
Knowles, Sir Francis, 141
Kramer, Heinrich, 14–29, 39, 185

Laban, 7
Labourd, 182f
Lactantius, 11, 18, 55, 90
Lamont, W. M., 167
Lancashire witch trials, 161–2
Lancre, Pierre de, 2, 28, 92, 176, 182–197, 199 n30
Lange, Ursula, 92
Laon, 76f, 97
Larbaud, Valéry, 203, 220
Larner, Christina, 157, 178 n4
La Rossa, Orsolina, 45
Lavater, Ludwig, 131, 132
'Lave-maine', 186
Law, Robert, 229
Lawrence, D. H., 221
Lazarus, 119

INDEX

Learmond, Janet, 228
Leicester, 162
Leith, 158
Le Loyer, Pierre, 186, 199 n30
Leo Ebreo, 89
Leo X, 33, 50
Le Roy, Louis, 188–9
Lestoile, Pierre de, 182
Lestonnac, Jeanne de, 184
Leviathan, 95
Levites, 99
Ligature, 176
Linlithgow, 160
Logroigne, 194
Lollards, 49
Lombardy, 47
Louis XIII, 183
Lovecraft, H. P., 215–16
Lowell, Robert, 216
Lucan, 122
Lucian, 130
Lucifer, 126
Ludus, 35–8, 39, 40–1, 44–5, 49
Luther, 9, 49, 54
Lycanthropy, 62, 68, 90, 116–17, 168–71, 186; *see also* Metamorphosis
Lycurgus, 80

Macfarlane, Alan, 79
Mackenzie, Sir George, 238
Macrocosm and microcosm, 4
Magic: black, 55, 66, 70–1, 131; Christian, 71–2, 106, 131; definition of, 88–9, 92; demonic, 49, 106, 109, 118, 126, 128, 132; image, 12, 47, 88, 158, 239; natural, 5, 106, 109, 112, 122–3, 124; spiritual, 49, 106, 109; sympathetic, 7; talismanic, 5, 12, 65, 90, 96; verbal, 59, 65, 67, 88, 90, 121–2; white, 55, 66, 70; *see also* Catholic Church; Hermeticism
Magician, 4–5, 13, 53, 61–2, 84, 125; burning of, 59, 70; definition of, 30 n30, 34, 74 n24, 83, 101; status of, 33
Magistrates, *see* Judges in witch trials
Maitland, Sir John, 159
Maldon, 140f
Maldonat, Father, 187
Maleficium, 34–5, 40, 47, 49, 157, 160, 163, 168–70, 172, 176
Malleus Maleficarum, 2–3, 14–31, 39, 44, 46, 61, 65, 71, 78, 82, 113, 116, 169, 190, 242
Malnutrition, 68, 75 n29, 78
Manichaean heresy, 148
Mantell, Robert, 142
Mantua, 46
Marian persecutions, 114–15
Martin, Susannah, 212–13
Masius, Andreas, 112–13, 117
Mason, Dr (*Practice of Philosophy*), 240
Mass, 9, 35, 45, 110
Mather, Cotton, 202–23
Mather family, 204
Maun, Elizabeth, 144
Medea, 37, 137 n17
Medical science, 26, 41, 68, 114, 116, 123, 129, 171
Melancholia, 16, 41, 54, 61–2, 68, 73 n17, 91, 108, 111, 170–1, 173, 233; *see also* Insanity
Mesnard, Pierre, 101
Metamorphosis, 9, 37–8, 116, 132–3, 169, 186, 211; *see also* Lycanthropy
Michelet, Jules, 194–5
Milan, Duke of, 47
Millenarianism, 166–7, 174, 225 n25
Miller, Arthur, 215, 219
Miller, Perry, 205
Miracles, 8–9, 12, 40, 57, 59, 92, 109–10, 112–14, 119, 123, 125–8, 130–5, 168, 171
Mirandola, 35, 45, 51 n35
Misogyny, 16–17, 39
Misraim, 55
Modena, 45–7

INDEX

Momus, 107
Monarchy, 156f, 173–7
Montagu, Bishop, 166–7
Montaigne, 41, 75 n34, 91, 139 n54, 183, 189, 200 n39
Monteagle letter, 165
Monter, William, 78
Montgomery, Lord, 164
Moon, powers of, 88
Moors, 82
Morgan, W. T., 230
Moses, 7, 10–11, 57, 60, 69–70, 80, 92, 99, 111, 120, 123; Law of, 53, 67, 70
Moses Maimonides, 87, 89–90, 104 n47, 236–7
Mother Samual the Warboys Witch, 242
Murray, Margaret, 92

Nahas, 120–1
Napier, Barbara, 159, 165
Naudé, Gabriel, 184–5, 196, 199 n30
Nebuchadnezzar, 117, 126, 132–3
Neoplatonism, 10, 83, 87–8, 91
Newes from Scotland, 159, 163–6
Newhaven (near Edinburgh), 158
Nicholas V, 33, 50
Nider, Johannes, 19, 190
Nightmare, 170–1, 173
Noah, 55
North Berwick witch trials, 156f
Numerology, 4
Nupe, 146
Nurse, Rebecca, 206
Nyakyusa of Tanzania, 48

Ob, 118–19, 124
Odysseus, 37
Ointments, 18, 35, 37–8, 120, 192, 234
Ojibwa Indians, 48
Onen, 120
Ordeal, 235, 239

Oresme, Nicholas, 130
Orgies, 49
Origen, 8, 18
Orpheus, 43
Orpheus the Theologian, 11
Orphic hymns, 87
Oufle, Monsieur, 197
Ovid, 10, 37, 41, 117, 122

Pact with the devil, 5, 18, 23, 43, 61, 89–90, 99–101, 113, 115, 118, 125, 157, 161, 163, 168, 172, 176, 192, 211, 231, 234, 235, 238–9, 242
Paisley witchcraft trial, 232, 237
Palma Vecchio, 38
Palmer, Robert, 141–2
Pascal, 73 n10
Pasquier, Etienne, 75 n34
Patristics, 8, 10–11, 18, 36, 69, 109–110, 185–6, 246
Peacock, schoolmaster, 164
Pentateuch, 67, 80–2, 84
Perkins, William, 10, 163, 176, 242
Perversity, 35, 39–40, 45, 91, 174–7, 192, 194
Petchey, W., 153 n6, n9, n10, 154 n21
Pharaoh, magicians of, 7–8, 12, 57, 59–60, 74 n24, 92, 110–12, 122–3, 132, 136 n10
Philo, 89, 94
Phips, Governor, 206, 207, 209
Pico, Gianfrancesco, 32–50, 51 n35
Pico, Giovanni, 33–4, 87–8, 117
Piedmont, witches of, 69
Pimander, 49
Plato, 10–11, 38, 66, 80, 86, 122, 126
Plotinus, 126
Pneumatomachi, 128
Poetry as evidence, 10, 36, 113, 117, 122, 186
Poison, poisoners, 58, 62, 66–7, 118, 168, 172, 192
Poitiers, 78, 86, 95
Poles, Humfrey, 142

INDEX

Pomponazzi, Pietro, 5, 8, 40, 92, 111–12, 117, 122, 132–4
Ponzinibio, Gianfrancesco, 40–1, 69
Porlezza, 47
Porphyry, 33, 126
Porta, G. B. Della, 33, 120, 198 n11
Porter, Katharine Ann, 219, 221–3
Possession, 7–8, 54, 63–4, 90, 93, 97, 159, 163, 173, 179 n26, 206, 222
Pound, Ezra, 202–3
Presbyterianism, 228
Prestonpans, 158
Prierio, Silvestro de, 39, 49
Priests and witchcraft, 46, 193–4
Prisci Theologi, 10
Proclus, 126
Proctor, John, 206, 211–12
Prodigies, 84, 91
Prophecy, 12, 40, 43, 55–6, 84, 86–8, 95, 114, 120, 125, 129–30, 162, 184, 207, 234; *see also* Augury
Protestants, credulity of, 125, 128
Proteus, 38, 43
Psellus, 126, 138 n30
Purgatory, 85
Puritanism, 145, 149, 152, 202f, 209f, 219f
Pyromancy, 43
Pythonicus spiritus, 118

Quakers, 152, 176

Rahab, 98
Raleigh, Sir Walter, 219
Relics, *see* Catholic Church, magic of
Rémy, Nicolas, 28, 166, 169–70, 177, 183, 185, 187
Richards, judge, 211
Roman Empire, 10
Roman law, 99f
Rome, 58; appeals to, 28
Ronsard, 95
Rood of Grace, 119, 128
Royal Society, 214

Royal Touch, 162
Rule, Margaret, 206–7

Sabbat, 2, 39, 45, 48, 62, 90, 92, 109, 157, 160, 163, 168–9, 175–6, 177, 183, 186, 190–7, 233, 235
Sacrifices, 120
Sadducees and Sadduceeism, 126f, 128–9, 133–4, 170, 172, 207, 210
Sadism, 27
St Andrews, 160–1
St Antony, 36
St Brigitta, 9
St Julian, 47
St Osyth witches, 108, 142
St Pré, 191
Salem, 202f
Sampson, Agnes, 159, 163, 166
Samuel, 7–8, 56, 111, 119
Sanudo, Marino, 52 n36
Saracens, 81
Sarah, 98
Satan, meaning of, 84; *see also* Devil
Saul, 7–8, 39, 96, 111, 119
Saulteaux, 152
Savanarola, 43
Scarpategio, Bartolomeo, 45
Scepticism, 3, 13, 35–6, 43–4, 106–35, 162–3, 173, 227, 239
Scholasticism, 234, 242
Scholastic method, 19f
Schook, Martin, 73 n7
Science, medieval and Renaissance, 12
Scot, Reginald, 2, 6, 10, 31 n41, 61, 70, 101, 106–35, 140, 156, 160, 163, 167, 170–3, 246–7
Scot, Sir Thomas, 106
Scotland, witchcraft in, 157f, 227–42
Scott, Hew, 228, 230
Scott, Sir Walter, 215
Scriptures: as evidence, 1, 6–7, 8, 18, 36, 70, 87, 89, 98, 109–10, 125, 130, 168, 206, 235, 237, 246; interpretation of, 112, 127, 131, 133,

INDEX

172; texts, Deuteronomy, 7, 36, 80, 86, Exodus, 7, 24, 99, 118, 146, 160, 242, Isaiah, 36, 60, 126, James (Epistle), 149, Jeremiah, 36, 99, Job, 6, 85, 95, John (Apocalypse), 7, Kings I, 39, Leviticus, 7, 36, 89, Luke, 57, Matthew, 36, 87, Paul (Ephesians), 122, Proverbs, 156, Psalms, 47, 85-6, 93-4, Samuel I, 176, Samuel II, 118, Zacharia, 88

Scriverius, Petrus, 136 n3
Seneca, 18, 187
Sewall, Stephen, 207, 209
Sextus Empiricus, 43, 130
Sexual activities, 17, 39, 90, 109, 115–116, 165, 176
Sharpe, Charles Kirkpatrick, 229, 231
Shaw, Christian, 233
Short, Mercy, 207
Sibyls, 55-6, 90, 104 n47
Silléry, Chancellor, 184
Simon, 53
Simon Magus, 57
Sirens, 10
Smallpox inoculation, 214
Smythe, Ellen, 142-3
Socrates, daemon of, 85
Sodomy, 17
Solemn League and Covenant, 236
Solomon, 10, 84, 86
Sondrio, 44-5
Sorbonne, *Determinatio* of, 83
Sovereignty, concept of, 82, 102
Spee, Friedrich Von, 196
Spectral evidence, 99, 204f, 207f
Spina, Bartolomeo de, 39, 44, 49, 51 n35
Spirit, definition of, 129; *see also* Angels; Demons
Sprenger, Jacob, 14-29, 39, 90, 93, 96, 126, 185
Staffordshire witch trials, 162
Stewart, Christian, 160

Stewart, Francis, Earl of Bothwell, 158-9
Stirling, 160
Stoughton, William, 207, 209, 211
Strype, John, 141
Succubi, *see* Demons
Summers, Montague, 14, 29 n11, 31 n34, 138 n34
Sun-worship, 86, 103 n32
Sutton, Mary, 241

Taboo, 146
Taillepied, Noel, 7
Talion, penalty of, 25
Templars, 81
Terence, 18
Tertullian, 8, 55, 192
Tetragrammaton, 89
Theophrastus, 18
Thomas, Keith, 3
Thomassin, sieur de, 182
Tobias, 74 n23
Torah, 82
Torquemada, 91, 104 n49
Torture, 6, 13, 23, 27, 45-7, 65, 98, 115, 119, 130, 159, 164, 185, 233
Transvection and transportation, 35-6, 40, 43, 47-8, 62, 90, 109, 117, 120, 169, 173, 191, 195, 197, 234, 239
Trevor-Roper, H., 53, 58, 78, 91
Trois Echelles, magician, 81
Trojan War, 10
Turks, 55, 115

Vair, Leonard, 108-9, 187
Valerius Maximus, 18
Valla, Lorenzo, 43
Valois Court, 193
Vampirism, 37, 40, 49
Ventriloquism, 118-19
Verdena, Giuliano, 46
Vignate, Ambrogio da, 42
Virgil, 10, 41, 121-2
Virgin Mary, 16, 47, 87, 191

INDEX

Vorstius, 167
Vossius, Dionysius, 237

Waldensians, 81
Walker, D. P., 32–3, 74 n24, 134
Warburg, Aby, 32
Webbe, Susan, 142–3
Weyer, Johann, 2, 6, 31 n41, 41, 53–75, 77, 84, 92–5, 101, 104 n62, 108, 110–13, 117, 118, 122, 124–5, 128, 131, 156, 160, 167, 170–3, 175, 196, 198 n11; *De Lamiis*, 71, 75 n33, 77, 108; *De Praestigiis*, 53–75, 78, 108, 112, 132, 170–1; *Pseudomonarchia*, 124–5, 175
Whitman, Walt, 220–1
Whittier, John, 215–16
Wilbraham, Sir Roger, 162
Willard, Samuel, 205
William III, Duke of Cleves, 53, 69, 71
Williams, William Carlos, 202–3, 219, 223
Wiseman, John, 144
Wiseman, Margaret, 144
Wise women, *see* Cunning folk
Witch(es): activities, 4–5, 15, 53, 71, 93–5, 102, 113f; craze, 3, 14, 33, 50, 58, 72, 81, 91, 97, 131–2, 246; definition of, 34, 58, 83, 101, 112, 117, 147–8, 176; mark, 159, 161, 165, 168, 183, 185, 192, 235, 239; punishment of, 3, 23f, 33, 54, 66–71, 77, 81, 97f, 100–1, 145, 151, 184f, *see also* Death penalty; smell of, 235; stereotype of, 90; trials, 13, 15, 23–29, 34, 44f, 78, 114–15, 142f, 160, 187f, 205, *see also* Aberdeen, Bury St Edmunds, Lancashire, North Berwick, Paisley, Staffordshire
Witchcraft: accusations, 151–2; conspiracy, 15, 17–18, 50; definition of, 110, 125, 147–8, 172; legislation, 157, 161; proofs of, 238–9
Wodrow, Robert, 232
Women, 16–17, 39, 41, 46, 61, 69, 73 n17, 176, 186, 189–90, 193; *see also* Misogyny
Worcester, Earl of, 162
Word of God, 67, 118, 133–4, 135, 150
Wyersdale, Mark, 141

Yates, Frances, 11, 32–3, 74 n20
Yeats, W. B., 223

Zamet, banker, 182
Zauberer, 58, 113
Ziarnko, Jan, 183, 192, 198 n6, 199 n23
Ziff, Larzer, 209
Zohar, 90
Zoroaster, 11